DREAMS OF THE FUTURE

DREAMS
OF THE
FUTURE

A preview of the futures that lie before us

Chet B. Snow

Featuring hypnotic future-life progressions by
Helen Wambach

THE AQUARIAN PRESS

First published as *Mass Dreams of the Future* by McGraw-Hill
Publishing Company, New York, USA, 1989

This edition 1991

British Library Cataloguing in Publication Data

Snow, Chet B.
Dreams of the future: a preview of the futures that lie
before us.
1. Future life
I. Title   II. Wambach, Helen *1925-1985*   III. Mass dreams
of the future
133.9013

ISBN 1-85538-027-7

*The Aquarian Press is part of the Thorsons Publishing Group,
Wellingborough, Northants, NN8 2RQ, England*

Printed in Great Britain by Hartnolls Limited, Bodmin, Cornwall

1 3 5 7 9 10 8 6 4 2

To my parents, who gave me this opportunity,
and
to Helen Stewart Wambach, Ph.D., (1925–85),
mentor, colleague and friend, whose vision
and pioneering spirit were matched only by
her warm humor and love for humanity.

Helen, I look forward to joining you at
that "Great Bar in the Sky" to lift a glass
and watch the next act unfold.

ACKNOWLEDGMENTS

Although the final responsibility for the words and ideas expressed in this book are mine, obviously they have not matured in a vacuum. While it is impossible to thank personally all who have helped me on this journey of self-discovery and spiritual awakening, I owe a special debt of gratitude to those individuals whose material assistance and moral support between 1985 and 1989 helped make *Dreams of the Future* a reality. Thus, in addition to those to whom this work is dedicated, my heartfelt thanks go to the following:

In the United States: I cannot thank Joanne Biggs enough for her friendship, hospitality and dedication to handling the material details that made my wandering life-style between Paris and the Napa Valley possible. More important has been her faith in my ability to complete this project, even when I was filled with self-doubt. It would not have happened without you, dear soul.

Special thanks go to my McGraw-Hill editor, Elisabeth Jakab, whose strong support and gentle guidance helped make the manuscript what it is. My agent, Helen McGrath, spared no effort to get this book's message before the widest possible audience. Helen Wambach's daughter, Julie Rubenstein, and her secretary, Starlyn Smith, helped me collect her research data and interview transcripts.

My aunt and uncle, Lee and Ron Crisman, opened their Los Angeles home to me for several important visits and helped me select a printer I could take to Paris. Dr. Walter Snow provided valuable technical help from his computer analysis and physics background, as well as hospitality and brotherly advice.

Without Pat and Dave Cook's nurturing help and computer advice, I might have never mastered word processing sufficiently. Friends from the Association for Past Life Research and Therapy, including Hazel Denning, Winafred Lucas, George Schwimmer and Bill Baldwin, introduced me to several new books and concepts, while Leo Sprinkle helped me get in touch with Ida K. and other UFO contactees, as well as providing data from his future-life workshops. I am also grateful to Dr. Charles Musès and Martye Kent for special assistance along my path. Longtime friends "Mack" McLane and Bob Sacher provided hospitality during several New York editorial visits. Lillian Bennett and the Napa A.R.E. group added prayers and fellowship. Thanks go also to Ruth Montgomery, Raymond Moody and Cathy Lake who gave me helpful advice.

In Paris, France: Words cannot express my deep gratitude to Patricia Kozlowski, who read the chapters as they were produced and helped ensure their safe arrival in New York despite French mail strikes and other hazards of international living. She and other Paris A.R.E. study-group members provided me much-needed weekly spiritual support. Elke Pion, Gilles Guattari and Frédéric Baudry opened their metaphysical libraries to me, while Ralph and Chris Rizzuto used their American contacts to help me secure American-size computer paper and printer ribbons. Finally, special thanks go to Joseph Doucé for a place to live and write and to all those, both in Europe and in the United States, who helped organize Helen Wambach's and my research workshops.

CONTENTS

future. Based on conversations held prior to her death in 1985, this chapter reports Dr. Wambach's theories of time travel via hypnosis, her thoughts on the material presented in Chapter 1, and what other subjects, sent ahead to the same time period as Dr. Snow, have reported that correlates with his vision. It also discusses evidence that our culture is currently haunted by dreams of the Apocalypse as we head into the last decade of this millennium.

* 3 *
Hunting for the Future,
an Ancient Tradition
PAGE 54

Dr. Snow looks at how humanity's age-old tradition of prophecy relates to different concepts of Time. Is Time strictly linear or does it also have recurring, circular qualities? Using the zodiac as a natural model of cyclical Time, he introduces the concepts of the Great Tropical Year and succeeding World Ages and describes why our forthcoming entry into the "Age of Aquarius" may be related in humanity's collective unconscious to the Great Flood of Noah, thereby creating disaster consciousness among many of today's predictions of the future. Included are discussions of Hopi Indian prophecies, an analysis of predictions associated with the Great Pyramid and recent research into the ancient Sumerian civilization, which reveals that the Biblical Deluge may be nearly 13,000 years old.

* 4 *
"Channeling" the Future Today:
The "Ageless Wisdom" and Edgar Cayce
PAGE 83

The phenomenon of "trance channeling," or seeking guidance from discarnate spiritual sources speaking through someone in an altered state of consciousness, is becoming increasingly popular today. In this chapter Dr. Snow explores the "Ageless Wisdom" philosophy behind this concept, a philosophy that teaches the immortality of the soul, human reincarnation and the doctrine of karma. He goes on to discuss the future predictions of Edgar Cayce, the twentieth century's best-known psychic, and how what he has said about a possible shifting of the Earth's poles around 2000 A.D. has contributed to today's "Apocalyptic spirit."

* 5 *

Mass Dreams of 2100–2200 A.D., Part I:
Life in Space and a Budding New Age
PAGE 105

Between 1981 and 1984, Drs. Wambach and Snow, along with Dr. R. Leo Sprinkle of the University of Wyoming, offered over 2,500 Americans an opportunity to "progress" hypnotically to a future lifetime, in about either 2100 or 2300 A.D. The results of these group workshop experiences are discussed in Chapters 5 through 8. In this chapter Dr. Snow tells how the data from 2100 A.D. indicates a steep population drop from today and can be divided into just four basic social environments. He then describes the first two of these groups in which subjects found themselves either living on space stations or in small New Age-style communities. Vivid personal accounts by progressed subjects about their future lives are included.

* 6 *

Mass Dreams of 2100–2200 A.D., Part II:
Hi-Tech Cities and Primitive Survivors
PAGE 131

In the concluding half of his analysis of how future-life workshop participants view life in the twenty-second and twenty-third centuries, Dr. Snow presents cases where subjects found themselves either in ultramodern, artificial environments underground or living simple, rural lives in isolated villages. He also reports on his own 1985–88 future-life workshops in the U.S.A. and France, where participants were given an identical opportunity to progress to 2100 A.D. and how their experiences match the data collected earlier. He concludes with a discussion of how such visions reflect today's "Apocalyptic spirit."

* 7 *

Mass Dreams of 2300 A.D. and Beyond, Part I:
The Outward Wave
PAGE 156

This chapter continues the discussion of Drs. Wambach and Snow's group future-life progressions. Here Dr. Snow analyzes the reports of those who experienced a future life in the 2300 to 2500 A.D. time period and who found themselves living either in an artificial space environment or on an alien planet somewhere else in the galaxy. He again divides their experiences according to home environment and compares their stories with those 2100 A.D. subjects who experienced lives on orbiting space stations.

* 8 *

Mass Dreams of 2300 A.D. and Beyond, Part II:
Operation Terra
PAGE 183

Dr. Snow concludes his analysis of the future-life progressions with a look at what subjects who found themselves returning to the Earth some three to five centuries from now discovered about the future of this planet. The data sheets again reveal the same few basic types of future civilizations as in 2100 A.D. These are growing spiritual communities living in harmony with their surroundings; an artificial Hi-Tech culture living inside domed cities and people in a rural, rather technically backward, environment. He compares the subjects' stories with each other and with similar reports from the 2100 A.D. era and concludes that what was a fractured world of disaster survivors in 2100 is slowly rebuilding a more natural, harmonious civilization several centuries later.

* 9 *

Is the "Future" Already Past?
"New Age" Physics and the Holographic Universe
PAGE 219

A presentation of some of the recent controversial findings of today's quantum mechanics theory regarding Time, Space and human consciousness. How does the increasingly popular view of the created universe as a hologram affect our viewpoint regarding precognition, future predictions and prophecy? If it is possible that all Time is a projection of a single reality, what is the meaning of such experiences as visions of past and future lifetimes? Dr. Snow looks at the works of physicists Fred Wolf, Paul Davies, David Boehm and biologist Rupert Sheldrake's intriguing "morphogenetic fields" theory along with Nobel chemist Ilya Prigogine's dynamic model of progressive evolution to help answer these and other thought-provoking questions.

* 10 *

Spaceship Earth:
UFOs, "Star People," "Walk-ins" and the Future
PAGE 253

Is the Earth today being watched over by a gathering of "Space Brothers," alien entities interested in how humanity copes with upcoming changes? If so, who are these beings? Are their intentions friendly? What's behind their apparent concern, as reported by many people who report bizarre "contacts"? In this chapter Dr. Snow includes discussions of people who feel they have been physically taken aboard space vessels, those who have had psychic contacts and others who feel their ancestors were Starmen. He also compares the UFO phenomenon with that of "out-of-body experiences" and the stories of individuals who feel their current personality has "walked in" to their body as an adult in order to help humanity prepare for the predicted shift of the poles and other hardships.

* 11 *

"In His Presence"
PAGE 286

This chapter begins with Dr. Snow's last future-life progression by Helen Wambach ahead to a new lifetime in the twenty-first century, where he finds himself continuing the work they began in the 1980s in a most unusual setting. It is a time when a universal Being of love and light, experienced by Dr. Snow as a Christ-like figure, fills the lives of those who accept His presence. Dr. Snow then concludes the book by comparing the two archetypical models of future change discovered during this study. In his view humanity today faces a choice between a violent Apocalypse of conflict and destruction or, if we are willing to evolve spiritually, we may awaken to our true multidimensional identity as immortal spirits and learn to cooperate in humanity's age-old dream of initiation and rebirth. He finishes this look at our "mass dreams of the future" by offering some personal suggestions for individual action to favor the latter alternative.

PROLOGUE

I first met Berkeley, California, psychologist Dr. Helen Wambach in early 1983. At that time writing a book about foretelling the future was perhaps the farthest thing from my mind. A resident of the nearby Napa Valley, I was working as a civilian employee for the United States Air Force, keeping archives and writing military history. A series of circumstances, including mysterious, recurring back pain from an earlier work-related injury, the emergence of some inexplicable psychic phenomena in my heretofore "normal" life and a persistent writing block that was interfering with my job performance, all combined to lead me to seek Dr. Wambach's professional help. Having heard of her success in helping others find the causes of current problems in events and attitudes inherited from earlier lifetimes, "past lives" as she put it, I hoped she could help me find out what was happening to me so I could solve my personal problems.

In just a few past-life regression sessions with Dr. Wambach, I made significant progress and was very satisfied. Moreover, from our first meeting we had established an unusually close and warm personal relationship as well. At first, naturally, our conversation centered around the difficulties I was experiencing and what the hypnosis sessions into my past were revealing. Apparently I proved a very good subject who was able to relax and "let go" of the conscious mind's control, thereby allowing hidden memories to surface quickly and easily.

In addition, from my very first past-life regression, at Helen Wambach's suggestion, I had made it my practice to write a summary of what I had experienced and bring it to our next meeting. This not only helped me recall what had happened more vividly but also was excellent therapy for the writing block that then plagued me. I came to look forward to our weekly appointments.

As we came to know each other better, Helen began to discuss her study of the future with me as well. Recognizing that I was a good subject and impressed with my weekly written reports, she asked me if I would be willing to volunteer to make a personal trip "ahead" in time. After some discussion of just what such a venture entailed, I consented. We chose the week of my birthday in July 1983 for the session as we both agreed that meaningful personal dates usually stand out better at all levels of the mind. We decided to advance approximately fifteen years ahead, time enough to note any important changes in my life but, as I was just turning thirty-eight, unlikely to overshoot my current physical lifespan. The story of that first personal "progression" into the future forms the narrative of Chapter 1 of this book.

For some time before I met her, Helen Wambach had decided to complement her earlier research into the process of past-life and prenatal recall via hypnosis with a study of how contemporary Americans viewed their potential future lifetimes. Her pioneering past-life and prenatal work had been discussed in her two published books, *Recalling Past Lives* (Harper & Row, 1978) and *Life Before Life* (Bantam Books, 1979). Each of these books compared the reports of several hundred subjects who, while in a light "waking trance" state induced during group workshops, had remembered incidents from earlier lives or prenatal events before being reborn into their current bodies and personalities.

Having demonstrated to her satisfaction that her group process successfully enabled most people to recall the past, she wondered how it would work when applied to the future. Therefore, she began giving similar workshops, offering participants a chance to look ahead at their possible future lives in 1980. Her longtime friend Mrs. Beverly Lundell and Dr. R. Leo Sprinkle, a licensed counseling psychologist and professor at the University of Wyoming, agreed to help her. They also gave several identical future-life workshops in which participants were mentally "progressed" ahead in Time to potential future lifetimes in the periods between 2100 and 2200 A.D. and 2300 to 2500 A.D. using her methods.

Helen Wambach was thus already collecting written data from these workshops when I met her in 1983. As our friendship developed I became more and more interested in the study. Impressed with my demonstrated research and writing skills and faced with increasingly failing health, eventually in 1984 Helen enlisted me to help her complete the research, analysis and writing of the future-lives project she had begun. It thus became our joint venture. The results of these group "future-life progressions" are discussed in Chapters 5 through 8.

As I became more closely associated with her work, Helen Wambach and I spent many hours discussing the process of hypnotically induced progressions to the future and her ideas on how to interpret the data thus received. She provided me with details of how she had become interested in the topic and why she felt it was important to publish our findings. Furthermore, we also discussed her individual progressions of a few select volunteers into the near future, i.e., ahead in their current lifetime, to see how their stories would match mine, which she felt intuitively to be pretty accurate. I have used my recordings of these conversations and Helen's personal research session notes to provide a background to this unique method of "inner Time travel." This material appears in Chapter 2.

Nonetheless, despite the progress made in obtaining research data and starting preliminary analysis in late 1984, two events of 1985 have led to a rather lengthy delay in the final writing and publication of this manuscript. First, Helen Wambach's physical health deteriorated much more rapidly than either of us had anticipated. She was soon physically unable to gather additional data or write up the results of what we had discovered. Second, my own interest in past-life therapy and continuing job dissatisfaction had led me to quit my civil service job, obtain hypnotheraphy certification and set up a private practice in regression therapy.

I was also developing a cross-cultural past-lives study of my own, which involved spending time abroad, specifically in Paris, France. Interestingly, this move had been foreseen during one of my personal future progressions of 1983! Consequently, I was overseas when I learned of Helen's untimely passing as the result of a sudden heart attack in August 1985. Although I returned for her memorial tribute at the Association for Past Life Research and Therapy's annual conference, I simply couldn't face continuing with our joint future-lives project at once. Thus it remained "on hold" for nearly three years.

Now, however, it is time to present this important study to the world as so many of the trends foreseen by myself and other progressed subjects begin to unfold with greater clarity. With the recent upswing in worldwide earthquake activity and the discovery of deeply hidden fault lines under areas heretofore considered as "safe," the scenario projected in Chapter 1 is no longer as unlikely as it seemed several years ago. Only the timing of the "great California quake" remains in doubt.

Further, global wind and weather patterns, instead of calming down, as widely predicted in the mid-1980s, are becoming more and more extreme. We seem to be oscillating between the threat of a new ice age and the much-discussed "greenhouse effect," which could melt the polar ice caps and cause widespread flooding. Nor are current economic and political developments reassuring. Despite the West's seeming ability to rebound from the largest stock market crash in recorded history (October 1987), a worldwide monetary crisis and international trade war seem closer than ever, while new droughts continue to push food prices higher. Finally, the AIDS epidemic, virtually unknown when Dr. Helen Wambach began collecting her future-lives data a decade ago, today poses a very real threat to future generations, one which could help produce the significant population drop over the next 150 years that our "future lives" data suggests.

These current factors combine with the predictions of humanity's most venerable religious and prophetic traditions, nearly all of which agree that our species is posed on the brink of a major life-cycle change. Whether or not one believes in the message of the Great Pyramid, astrology, Biblical warnings about Armageddon or the channelings of contemporary seers such as psychic Edgar Cayce, their pronouncements of impending drastic change form part of today's "Apocalyptic spirit."

This spirit is certain to intensify as we head toward the end of this fateful millennium. The year 2000 A.D. looms barely a decade away, and although our rational conscious mind may reject "gloom and doom" predictions as mere superstition, Apocalyptic images reinforced over several thousand years of joint human culture lurk beneath the conscious mind's surface, affecting us in ways we only vaguely realize and recognize. These archetypes of our "collective unconscious," as the famed Swiss psychologist Carl Jung termed it, form the parameters within which our daily decisions are made. It is time *now* to look at some of the images we hold of the ties ahead and their potential impact on our individual and collective future.

Still, for reasons that will be discussed in Chapters 10 and 11, despite today's ominous trends and portents, I remain personally optimistic about humanity's future. Further, I would be the first to agree that the exact timing of individual future events is by far the least reliable aspect of all precognition, prediction and prophecy. Finally, as someone who believes in the reality of human "free will" and our ability to change personal future conditions at least, I feel that those now alive hold the collective power to shape our planetary destiny.

However, this power of choice is liberated only when people are intelligently informed. Thus in no way would either Dr. Wambach or I present the following previews of the future, as seen personally or by our subjects, as incontrovertible or irreversible. They are, nonetheless, part of the "mass dream" of the future that we here on Earth are projecting, through our subconscious minds, today. As such they are important harbingers of what we may consciously be living through tomorrow.

* 1 *
The Day the Bottom Dropped Out

The cold, clammy wind stung my face and chilled my bones. Shivering despite the thick navy peacoat and ski cap I found myself wearing, I strode briskly up a small rise overlooking a bleak desert landscape which stretched out before me.

"What am I doing here, anyway?" I thought to myself. "Today's my birthday and it ought to be July."

Even before these words formed in my mind, however, I knew the answer. Yes, it was my birthday. And it was July. Only it was July in 1998 and the world had turned upside down—"the day the bottom dropped out."

As my body continued to stride up the slope before me, I "remembered" that I was out here to check on the horses and to make sure the old wooden corral we'd built was still holding together. So far, so good; the horses were still there and I could see no visible breaks in the rough stockade we'd fashioned. A steady, chilly drizzle linked the nearly black sky with the mountains at the horizon. A few lonely saguaro cacti still dotted the scrubby Arizona landscape, but even now, at midday, only their spare silhouettes were visible under the lowering clouds. I was cold and hungry. My job done, I wasted little time as I turned to head back to the ranch house and a warm fire.

"All right, now you've returned to the house and you are about to eat your evening meal. Where are you?"

1

The gentle, yet demanding voice of my friend and colleague, Dr. Helen Wambach, broke in on my cold, lonely reverie. For an instant I experienced the warmth of California's summer sunshine again and the reassuring closeness of her presence. I knew at that moment that my physical body was stretched out comfortably on the bed in her hypnotherapy office. Yet my mind remained far distant in Time and Space, propelled ahead into that bleak Arizona landscape of 1998.

Responding to Dr. Wambach's question, I once again found myself in Arizona, this time in a spacious wood-paneled kitchen, warming my hands by an old-fashioned potbellied stove. Nearby about a dozen others were settling in around a rough wooden table on long benches. A chair at one end of the table waited for me. My wet, chilled hands warmed at last, I joined them. Someone poured me a mug of a hot beverage. There was a pitcher of fresh milk, but I noticed to my surprise no meat or green vegetables on the table. Everyone was dipping into a large steaming bowl of oatmeal or porridge. It looked nourishing. A warm, spicy smell made it irresistible.

"Hunger is the best sauce," I thought as I dug in with the rest.

"Now the meal is finished and you are looking around the ranch house that is your home. What draws your attention? Is there anything that may look different now or that leads you to some special thoughts?"

Helen Wambach's gentle yet insistent voice helped me focus again on my Arizona surroundings. As a couple of the others cleared the table and began washing the dishes, I let my gaze wander over the scene. Almost automatically it shifted toward the room's southwest corner. I realized now that it was partially damaged and the roof sloped oddly down there. Somehow I knew this had happened earlier that year in one of the violent earth tremors that had struck the area. We'd made a makeshift repair to keep out the wind. A strange feeling of sadness swept over me momentarily as I remembered how one of our group, Jimmy, I think his name was, had been killed, either in that cave-in or in some other incident during the earthquake.

Recalling Jimmy's accident made me aware that I'd not paid much attention to my friends at the dinner table earlier. I commented on this. Responding to my remark, Helen suggested that I go to a recent moment when I was talking about my earlier life in California with one of my current companions. Even as she spoke I realized that I hadn't known any of these people then. I got the distinct impression that we'd gotten together only in the last few years prior to July 1998. In general we avoided talking about earlier events in our lives. They didn't seem important somehow. In fact, it seemed funny, and although I knew it was my birthday, and Helen's initial suggestion had been to go to that day, I couldn't remember any celebration or particular attention being paid to that either. It was as if only the immediate moment and necessary activities mattered for us.

Oddly enough, the thought of being so wrapped up in sheer survival that I'd nearly forgotten my own birthday deepened the overall desolation of this strange future scene. I wanted to shout or cry or do something just to affirm my personal identity. My breathing grew harsh and stifled. My throat became parched and rasping. My body, now tense and defensive, twisted uncomfortably on the bed. I wanted out of this weird, unfamiliar place.

Before I could speak, however, Helen sensed my distress. Reacting in her usual warm and caring manner, she at once began to draw me back from where my subconscious awareness had taken me. Her words soon absorbed my attention and I quieted as I listened to her voice.

"Now it's after nightfall on the same day, your birthday in 1998, and you're ready to go to sleep. Let yourself stretch out comfortably in the place you normally sleep. Allow your mind and body to relax as you drift gently off. And as you drift off to sleep now, your relaxation deepens. . . . All body tensions and emotional discomfort fade as you go deeper and deeper within. . . . You can even return to your warm, safe, and comfortable cloud now. It's an old friend and traveling companion. . . . But no matter how deeply you drift, how relaxed you become, you will remember vividly, vividly all the scenes and events you experienced on this trip. . . ."

Helen's throaty hypnotic voice lulled me into that pleasant and relaxed state I'd experienced with her so many times before. My earlier anxiety lightened. As I mentally sank back into the familiar softness of my puffy white cloud, the strange events and recollections of that cold, dark day I'd identified as 1998 faded from my mind. I knew that soon Helen would lead me back to the "here and now" of her California apartment and the warm sunshine of July 1983. I sighed as I leaned back into my cloud pillow and began the trip back into "ordinary waking reality" once again.

*   *   *

Thus ended my first experience with what has come to be known as Progression Therapy, where, instead of attempting to regress someone to the past, a therapist uses an altered state of consciousness, often via hypnosis, to project an individual into what one ordinarily perceives as the future. Indeed such terms as "past" and "future" seem to have little objective meaning in areas of the mind that fall outside conscious awareness of the everyday material world where most of us work and play. I know that both my many fascinating, instructive journeys into the past, via past-life regression, and this almost overwhelming thrust into what my mind told me was a very real future had punctured my heretofore rather blasé attitude about objective "reality" and Time and Space.

Although by July 1983 I had been working with Dr. Helen Wambach for several months, making weekly forays into a number of my "past lives," this first trip into the future, and especially to such a realistic near future, left me a good deal more troubled than I cared to admit that afternoon. I don't remember much of the rest of the session, except I'm sure that Helen gave me her usual inspiring suggestions of renewed energy and feelings of personal well-being. I also know that we discussed for a while what I'd experienced during the progression. Probably until she was satisfied that I was indeed totally back in the "here and now," as she put it, and able to drive home safely.

It was all too soon time to depart. As I struggled with the evening rush-hour traffic clogging the freeways between her office and my Napa, California, home, I realized that I'd seen no automobiles at that Arizona ranch, seemingly just a few years away.

"Will traffic jams go the way of the passenger pigeon and the dodo?" I mused. At that moment it was almost a comforting thought.

It had become my practice, since our first past-life session together, to make detailed notes of what I had experienced during the regressions, which Helen induced using her "Wambach method" of light hypnosis. I usually typed up my notes and comments several days after a session. I would then take them with me to her office the following week for discussion. I had begun this procedure at Helen's suggestion to improve my memory of what I'd experienced while regressed. I also realized that it was excellent practice in helping break down the subjective "writing blocks" that, along with persistent back pain following an injury at work, had helped send me to Helen in the first place.

However, so powerful and startling were the images I'd received that July day that I broke this habit. I sat down almost as soon as I returned home to commit to paper all the details I could remember of that dark, bleak Arizona scene.

I was both intrigued and a bit frightened by what that "future" vision seemed to imply. Especially as this was not some surrealist science-fiction fantasy with exotic rockets or faraway planets with strange alien creatures. The kind of thing I'd read about for years. No, it was just a short "hop" of about fifteen years ahead, filled with things that, at that point in my life, I certainly never would have imagined for the late 1990s! Staring into that dark, chilling wind sweeping across the desert was far scarier than the appearance of any monster from 2500 A.D. or alien from outer space.

Thinking about the session later, I asked myself, "Why this strong reaction, so untypical for me?"

Perhaps it is because the late 1990s are so close in time, as measured by ordinary, rational reckoning. Therefore they are much more dangerous territory for the conscious mind to enter than a far-distant future. Our conscious mind and its logical, analytical thinking, which is apparently filtered through the left hemisphere of the brain's cerebral cortex, naturally resists the intrusion of nonlinear time or timelessness into our mental awareness. Yet such concepts, easily accepted as "real," seem to be a normal operating condition for other levels of our mind—those which are accessible through the brain's right hemisphere when we experience so-called altered states of consciousness.

This is true for the regression experience to past lifetimes as well as future progressions. Yet perhaps our conscious minds can more easily accept the idea of reviewing the past because we believe that it has "already happened." Thus it seems to be less disconcerting to review a series of past-life events, even if painful or dramatic, than to scan something from the near future. Not to mention the possibilities of alternate planes of reality or probable dimensions and their relationship to human consciousness. The perspectives are endless.

But to return to this fascinating glimpse of the late 1990s . . . What else had I experienced there as Helen deftly moved me through that wintry July day in 1998? One thing I remembered clearly was the feeling that the sudden and drastic changes in the area's climate had not resulted from some nuclear holocaust or nuclear power accident. Although the symptoms were perhaps a bit similar, the black skies and frigid windstorm didn't seem to be the much-touted "nuclear winter" projected by Carl Sagan and other scientists in the 1980s. I had no memory of being worried about radiation sickness or anything like that at the Arizona ranch.

Most of the concerns I recognized during the progression session were more basic and related to immediate survival. We spent a great deal of time arranging for simple things like having enough food, and especially enough different vitamins to ensure healthy nutrition. We also worried about keeping basic power and heating systems operating. Protecting our small herd of livestock, and particularly the horses, was also vital. We depended on the few cows for milk and on the horses for local transportation. I didn't get the impression that we traveled very far from the ranch in any case.

The other, perhaps more frightening, thought that gnawed at the edges of my consciousness during much of that first future trip was, frankly, an underlying fear of discovery by other human beings! Even though I felt both rather isolated and protected at the ranch, inside I knew that if outsiders became aware of our relatively secure existence there, we would have to defend it or flee. It wasn't a pretty idea, and perhaps it was a bit selfish of me, but I couldn't deny that the thought of self-preservation was definitely there!

Above all these day-to-day concerns and fears, however, came the realization that this group had been drawn together for a specific purpose. That in some way we had been given this situation as an opportunity, not just to survive, but to learn and to help those who needed such assistance and who would and could receive it. The natural leader of our group was a woman. I remember calling her "Patsy," though I am not sure if this was an actual name or rather my subconscious mind's way of identifying her character traits with those of a 1980s friend of mine nick-named Patsy. I knew that they were not the same person but quite similar in personality.

Highly intuitive, the woman I "knew" in 1998 had chosen the location I experienced well ahead of the various events which had caused so much apparent destruction and change. Although I had never visited that spot before the July 1983 progression (and still haven't as of June 1989), I somehow realized that it was located north of Phoenix, Arizona.

Apparently, Patsy had had some kind of precognitive knowledge of the coming climatic and Earth changes and had decided that this area would be spared. It would provide our group with shelter and security, even from what apparently had become our most dangerous enemy—the roving bands of half-crazed marauders spawned by the major cities. I also knew that our group had come together to develop our psychic and/or ESP faculties at this desert spot. At that point, after only the first progression session, I wasn't sure just why or how this had come about, but it felt okay and I accepted it as necessary.

What I've just described represents the sum total of what I could extract from that first progression to the future as I reviewed it at home afterwards. The feeling of acceptance and purpose I had received stayed with me after I had completed my notes, which were mailed to Helen the next day.

Despite my vivid curiosity about what this all meant, both Helen and I agreed to postpone another future trip until we had completed the series of past-life regressions concerning my current career. We both felt that understanding the issues I was apparently working through just then would be crucial to interpreting the 1990s data. This feeling, combined with vacation and business trips, led us to allow several months to go by before we discussed making a second journey ahead in Time.

When the issue did eventually arise, we decided to concentrate on the period leading up to whatever had caused such dramatic climatic and cultural changes as I had experienced in the first progression. As fate would have it, the second session actually fell on October 31, 1983. Yes, on Halloween!

"Your eyes are closed and it feels good to close your eyes. . . . All your facial muscles relax now and your breathing is easy and regular. . . ."

Once again my mind tuned in to Helen's familiar gravelly hypnotic tone. Eyes closed, body stretched out on her slightly sagging office bed, I concentrated on her voice and let the outside world slip away gradually.

This time, however, unlike previous past-life regressions, I found my conscious mind actively resisting the now-familiar procedure of letting go. It kept chattering away inside my skull, reminding me of current projects and concerns even as I continued to listen to Helen's relaxation instructions. It was almost as if part of me knew that somehow I wasn't going to enjoy this experience. Maybe I really didn't want to know what lay ahead of me in the late 1990s! After all, part of me reasoned, that future hadn't happened yet, or at least it wasn't yet actualized in three-dimensional terms. My conscious, reasoning self, speaking through my half-awake left brain, was definitely interfering in my attempt to center myself and leave the present behind for a while.

As mentioned above, I feel that the conscious mind finds it much easier to deal with information from regressions to the past than from future progressions because it accepts the idea that the past is somehow already "fixed" whereas the future ought to remain "open" and changeable. This bias can overflow from one's conscious-mind "observer" into the subconscious during the initial moments of transition from ordinary linear-time awareness to the timelessness of the inner world. If, as Jane Robert's channeled "Seth" entity claims, we do in fact create our own reality, then this is probably a healthy ego defense mechanism under ordinary circumstances.

Nevertheless, once having opened the Pandora's box of future progression, I felt determined to explore this new territory further. I used my desire to forge ahead and gradually wean myself again from conscious prejudices.

"Now, as you drift and float along, totally and peacefully relaxed, you can pass swiftly through the vastness of what we call Time and Space. . . . And you can move forward now going beyond 1983 into the future. . . . More and more swiftly as you let yourself be propelled faster and faster forward through Time. . . . And as you move forward you find yourself becoming increasingly aware of that time period around Christmas of 1996. . . . You've moved through the 1980s now and past 1990 and it is Christmas of the year 1996 and you are there, *NOW*! . . . Where are you?"

Finally "tuned in" to Helen's voice and positive, insistent suggestions, I sighed and allowed my inner "observer" to relax. As I did I felt a slight tugging on my awareness and began to move ahead mentally. Fleeting, ghostlike images flowed across my mind's eye. I caught momentary glimpses of them as they flashed by. It was something like watching the flickers and flashes of a video cassette recorder set on "fast forward."

One image stuck in my conscious memory, however. As I lay there on Helen Wambach's hypnotherapy office bed, on Halloween 1983, I vividly saw the Eiffel Tower. It was a familiar sight, as I had studied and lived in Paris previously. Then, before my very eyes, the tower transformed itself into a giant saguaro cactus such as is found in the Arizona desert. As this transformation occurred I knew that I was seeing two places where I would live between then and my target destination of December 1996.*

As this insight reached my awareness, my mind stilled and the images stopped flashing rapidly by. I found myself again at the Arizona ranch, already familiar from my first future trip to 1998. Only this time the colors all seemed much brighter and clearer. Had everything just been painted?

"Oh, of course," I exclaimed to myself after an instant's reflection. "The sun is shining today!" And so it was. Looking out the window of the room I found myself standing in, I could even see a bright blue sky. The tawny brown mountains appeared but a stone's throw away. What a

---

*As of December 1988, the first half of this precognitive glimpse of the future has come true. For reasons totally unrelated to this book, I moved from Napa, California, to Europe in 1985 and have written most of this manuscript in Paris!

contrast with the dark, cold haze I'd experienced for 1998! Seen like this, Arizona seemed positively beautiful.

At this point Helen interrupted my daydreaming to instruct me further. "Now it is Christmas of 1996. You will find yourself discussing the events of the past year with some others around you now or possibly watching a retrospective news program on television."

Despite Helen's words, I continued to experience myself in the ranch house all alone. Perhaps part of my consciousness was still resisting facing up to knowledge of what lay ahead. I "knew," however, that it was Christmas Eve afternoon and that the others were somewhere nearby. Eventually, as Helen repeated her gentle but insistent suggestions, I found myself going outside to the corral, where Patsy and a couple of the men were having a heated discussion.

"No, we simply cannot use plastic containers for food storage," I heard Patsy telling one of them. "Even though they seem perfectly all right, over time the plastic will contaminate the things inside. A subtle chemical reaction takes place and alters the food's vibrations and ultimately its effect on the body. This doesn't matter so much nowadays for most people since their bodies are usually so grossly out of tune with universal vibrations anyway. But you know that our students are extremely sensitive. And with what's coming we all will be depending more and more on their sensitivity—and on our own—as it all unfolds."

As I heard her speaking I had the insight that this matter of food storage was critical for our future survival. Somehow I knew that Patsy's keen intuitive awareness had led her to understand the upcoming shortages of essential foodstuffs and vitamins. A key purpose of our move to this central Arizona location was to establish a school for the development of psychic communication skills, or mental telepathy. In view of what seemed to lie just ahead, we wanted it to be accessible yet somewhat isolated. The children and young adults that Patsy knew would be attracted to this school as the world situation worsened and would in fact be harbingers of the New Age to follow.

Already, by late 1996, I felt that the staff and some students had been drawn to this location to prepare things. It was much more than a matter of mere physical survival, although that was important of course. What counted was the safekeeping of those who would assist in the transformation of humanity as the old order crumbled and new forms of thought, communications and a new interpersonal awareness emerged.

My attention drifted back to the conversation going on around me outside the ranch house. One of the men was speaking.

"Okay, but if we can't use plastic containers, how will we protect the foodstuffs over a long period of time? You know that glass bottles won't work, especially if the earthquakes and ground shifts you say are going to occur actually happen around here. The glass will just shatter. That will contaminate the food a heck of a lot worse than a little plastic if you ask me!"

"Yes," continued the other guy, "and besides, glass is so much more expensive already. It's going to be all we can manage to scrape up money for the kinds of dried fruits, beans, grains, and vitamins that you're talking about, let along buy enough big glass storage jars."

"Don't think I'm not aware of all the problems," Patsy replied, "but what good is it going to do to spend our resources on buying and storing food that won't be any good when we need it? There are alternatives and we still have time to find them. After all, that's why we came out here in the first place, isn't it?"

"Hey," I said, entering the discussion, "maybe we could try some kind of combination of materials. What about putting the dried foods into paper sacks or cardboard boxes first and then placing the paper containers inside plastic? That way they'd be sealed up against moisture or rodents and at the same time protected from possibly harmful chemicals. Do you think that'd work, Patsy?"

"Well, it just might. Of course we'll have to check the paper or cardboard to see what kind of chemicals are used to treat it first. But I know that using even commercial paper will be a lot safer than long-term direct contact between the food and plastic bins. The most important factor is keeping the things we do store intact and safely hidden underground. Even if there are tremors and some ground shifting around here, I don't think they will be severe enough to bury our stuff if we work carefully."

"Well, we'd better settle on a method pretty soon," the taller of the two men with Patsy concluded. "You know how high the price of food has gone already. I saw that the pinto beans you're counting on as a basic source of protein have just about doubled in price this past year alone. The inflation for foodstuffs has been terrible already these last several years, and with last summer's big drought in the Midwest, food will soon be even more expensive."

"I agree," Patsy replied. "Let's make this a priority project. We need to see what kind of containers we can develop as soon as possible."

The voices and outdoor scene faded then as Helen's voice again broke in on my outer awareness:

"Now you've moved back inside the ranch house and it's time for the evening TV news report. You and some of the others are watching the evening news together. Listen in for a moment and then tell me what the announcer is saying."

Following her suggestion, I let myself become aware of a fire and a group of eight to ten of us watching the TV news. The President was on briefly, saying something about his foolproof plan to revitalize the economy, restore confidence, and reduce inflation. It was someone much younger than Ronald Reagan and he had more prominent ears. The face seemed vaguely familiar but I didn't recognize it in the short TV clip shown. I got the feeling that this man had been a United States senator or prominent governor in the 1980s but not someone I'd have predicted as President a dozen years later.

Then the announcer switched to a story about the situation in the Middle East. I got the impression that a radical Jewish group in Israel was bent on kicking all the Arab inhabitants from the Israeli-occupied territories, and especially Jerusalem, in order to reestablish the biblical kingdom of David and Solomon. Their proposal to tear down the mosque of the Dome of the Rock and rebuild the Jewish temple there was causing widespread controversy. Angry denunciations from the Arab states had been followed by new threats of a jihad, or holy war, if such a plan were ever carried out.

The world's crazy weather continued to be a major news item as freak storms and conditions set new records of hot and cold, drought and rainfall in various places around the globe. I got the distinct impression that there had been ongoing widespread flooding of major coastal areas as the sea level rose and storm intensities increased. Even in Arizona the winter climate was cooler and wetter than a dozen years earlier.

The world's economy was also in a tailspin and nothing that the government had proposed so far seemed to be working. The price of food in particular had skyrocketed and credit was practically impossible to get. Trade wars and tariff barriers had gutted international cooperation efforts to end the crisis. It was hardly a pretty end-of-year picture!

As I watched this scenario of less than pleasant events flash across the screen, I "remembered" that here on the ranch Patsy had predicted most of what was now coming to pass. Under her leadership, which was natural and never imposed, we were developing our intuitive skills through meditation and other spiritual exercises as well as training to be a self-sufficient community. Everyone was learning to ride horses well instead of relying on automobiles or jeeps. We still had a truck for hauling heavy loads, and although gasoline wasn't rationed, it had gotten more expensive.

Our group had grown to a couple of dozen people. Some maintained vegetable gardens while others worked with livestock, including sheep, cattle and horses. Others made handicrafts for sale at local markets. I knew that we'd acquired a special pump to ensure our own water supply (from a well found by a dowser hired when we'd acquired the land). A couple of the men were working on a wind-powered electric generator for emergency use in case the power supply failed.

I need to note here that I had an exceptional amount of time to reflect and question myself concerning these future surroundings and potential activities during this second progression session on Halloween evening 1983. Unlike most of our hypnosis sessions, which were only an hour long and during which Helen kept moving me around in Time so as to obtain as much information as possible, this evening's session was frequently interrupted by a virtual army of "trick or treat" visitors. Helen had always loved children and so lived in an apartment complex that teemed with them. Since she often offered her neighbors' children little candy or cookie treats in exchange for small favors, and often just because she enjoyed their company, her apartment was undoubtedly the most popular Halloween stop in the neighborhood! Thus she was repeatedly forced to leave me "suspended" in some future scene while she went to the door to greet bands of ghosts and goblins and all sorts of other characters.

It was something of a novel experience to be at one and the same time viewing preparations for some kind of major catastrophe in the Arizona desert in the mid-1990s while also listening to Helen calmly and lovingly deal with the passel of neighborhood kids pounding on her California apartment door in 1983 asking for candy. Talk about a split personality!

Well, eventually Helen returned and suggested that I move ahead a year to the end of 1997. My impression was that life on the ranch was carrying on much as it had in the previous year except that now we had stocked what supplies we could afford and were living even more of an independent, self-sufficient existence. Crops had become more difficult to grow and the soil seemed very disappointing to me as I had tried hard to equal or surpass the preceding year's harvest. I think that increasingly bad and unpredictable weather was the major culprit. Patsy didn't seem to worry much about it at least. Our school was slowly developing. We had even begun small experiments in reaching out telepathically or psychically to other like-minded groups around North America. Apparently some kind of New Age network had sprung up across the country and our group had contacts with it. Still, our major focus was making internal preparations for the coming changes.

Reflecting about that Halloween session, I remain struck by my feeling of how familiar the events I was watching there on television in December 1997 seemed. They were awfully similar to world news headlines today. The economic problems starting to unfold now in the late 1980s remained an important factor affecting our lives in 1996–97, along with soaring food prices, which apparently will get worse. The weather situation had also deteriorated from 1983 as extreme conditions became more and more commonplace. The Middle East continued as a hotbed of tension and potential terrorism.

Nonetheless, for us Americans at least, most of life's ordinary business went on as usual. Things cost more and some items were hard to obtain; personal credit was tight and unemployment was high. But planes still flew overhead, cars still clogged the city highways at rush hour, and the telephone and television networks kept us in touch with the rest of the world.

If I insist on the normality that I felt at the end of 1997, perhaps it is because all that changed so rapidly when Helen took me ahead again, this time past my July 1998 birthday and on to the end of that fateful year. So unlike 1997, it now seemed as if the world had collapsed and everything that had been important before no longer mattered. In a way I felt depressed, as so much appeared to be lost. Still I realized that we had been aware that these changes were coming and so when they did hit we almost felt a sense of relief. Sort of like knowing that a killer hurricane is about to strike your home and then, after it does, being relieved just to remain alive at all.

This time, in December 1998, there were no TV news recaps because we no longer had a TV set. Radio broadcasts from Phoenix and Santa Fe were still on the air, however, and they kept us in touch with the rest of the country, what was left of it, that is. I immediately knew that large chunks of the former West Coast had quickly sunk into the Pacific Ocean as several earthquakes and volcanic eruptions had decimated the "Ring of Fire" borderlands surrounding the Pacific earth plate. It might be more accurate to say that the ocean had come rushing up into the California valleys as the bottom had literally fallen out at key coastal junctures, shaken by the seismic activity. Water stretched as far inland in some areas as parts of Nevada and Arizona.

Apparently something dramatic had occurred in 1998 that completed the disruptions already begun by rising ocean levels and minor earth collapses in the 1980s. Something had happened similar to what Edgar Cayce and many other psychics had predicted. At first I wasn't certain just when in 1998 this disaster had taken place, although I knew it had occurred before my July birth date and had happened in more than one jolt. Even now, in December, the ground still shook frequently. An aftershock had collapsed our already partially damaged ranch house, causing us to move a short distance away. When I "touched base" that December we were living in several tents made out of bright yellow plastic and set up at the side of some cliffs, like pyramids. They were apparently designed so that we could dig into the cliffs and make caves as well. Once again Patsy had had uncanny foreknowledge concerning the likelihood of such a calamity. Although I don't believe that anyone, including Patsy, had imagined the entire house caving in as it had, she had made sure we were prepared.

On the heels of these physical disasters, local government had been turned over to the National Guard. The President and Congress were still in charge of overall relief efforts, but in our area at least the National Guard, under the governor, provided effective law enforcement. Our group had made sure that two or three of our number were deputized by the county sheriff's office as a way of keeping our independence and getting accurate information. I wasn't sure if I was one of those deputies or not; it felt like I was. I did know I had been helping Patsy stabilize our group psychologically and also to move us out of the ruined ranch house into higher, more stable ground.

Even so, in that bleak December the Earth shook almost constantly and the climate was much colder and wetter than before. A cold, clammy wind was almost always blowing. The sky remained obscured, even in the daytime, by all the earth and ash thrown up by the earthquakes and volcanoes that had preceded the West Coast collapse. Although I could not see it from where we were living, I had the distinct impression that the Pacific Ocean now lay only a couple of hundred miles to the west. The sea was farther away in the east, but the United States had been all but cut in two. Most east–west transportation and communications links were severed.

"You will now go to a time in that week of December 1998 when you are listening to a news broadcast. . . . The announcer is telling some of the news in other parts of the United States and the world. . . ."

Helen's voice broke into my somewhat benumbed awareness. In response to her directions, I let myself focus on the radio. I knew that it remained our major link to the outside world. However, since our generator had collapsed in the recent upheavals, we were dependent on batteries for the time being. Consequently we limited our power consumption, as it was unlikely we'd have new ones any time soon.

Still, as I listened I heard repeated stories of disruption combined with individual heroism and courage. Apparently the entire Pacific area had been wracked with storms and various Earth changes: quakes, volcanoes or land sinks. On the opposite side of the continent there had also been some flooding and quakes, but in general the land had risen instead of falling into the sea.

Unfortunately, human greed and international politics had combined to worsen this scenario, as seen from the perspective of 1983. Instead of moving with immediate humanitarian relief, the Soviets had taken advantage of our temporary helplessness to take over West Berlin and most of West Germany. Yugoslavia was being undermined by a vicious civil war into which Soviet-led troops from Hungary and Czechoslovakia had intervened. Washington had protested vainly and had again cemented alliances with Great Britain, France and Italy but could do little else.

At this point Helen asked me about the Orient and especially Japan. I remember a numb feeling in the pit of my stomach as I replied simply:

"Japan as a country doesn't exist any longer. A lot of it's fallen into the sea."

It was the same when she asked about human casualties resulting from all these cataclysms.

"How many people have died as a result of these wars and natural disasters?" she asked.

"Millions," was my immediate and laconic reply.

Although my voice sounded so calm, that simple word, a mere number but with what implications, shocked my conscious mind, which was monitoring the experience as always. I thought, "I must be mistaken!" But sadly a feeling that this is a minimal figure remains with me long after that fateful October 1983 session and I must stand by that answer, hard as it is to accept rationally.

I also remember that when Helen kept asking me what the news was from other parts of the world such as Europe and Asia, places very meaningful to me now in the 1980s, my "future self" kept thinking, "How unimportant!"

Such places might as well have been the Moon for us in December 1998 when each day was a struggle just to survive. It seemed to take all our available energy just to keep on planning and working together to ensure our immediate future as a community. Moreover, I knew that our mission went beyond personal survival. We were also very concerned about contacting survivors, both individuals and groups, and bringing them in to add their talents to ours. For all intents and purposes our "world" consisted of the community and its efforts to reach congenial survivors. This included the work of the school of course. Patsy was convinced that those who could benefit from our help and training would be drawn to us. In addition we kept on working on perfecting the rudimentary psychic communications and healing network that had begun earlier. This network would grow in time but at the end of 1998 it was still being formed, mainly from people and groups we had already contacted before "the day the bottom dropped out."

"You can leave that scene now and I want you to let yourself drift forward in time. . . . You're moving forward in time now and the year 1999 has already gone by. . . . You are flowing forward and the year is 2000 A.D. . . . Keep going ahead and it is now near the end of the year 2000 and you are there, *NOW*. . . . Where are you? Do you hear voices? Who is with you and what are they saying?"

Helen deftly moved me forward in Time with her familiar tone. Even as she did it seemed as if I could feel the sky becoming lighter. It definitely seemed less obscured by the ash and dust at the end of the year 2000, although I still found myself living in the Arizona desert. Our group was larger now also. When I "beamed in" several of us were out riding on horseback, still looking for newcomers, for those who had been called to us by our psychically transmitted message of love and community.

That seemed to be our primary mission at this time, to offer warmth and shelter to refugees if they could "tune in" to our psychic wavelength. In this way I knew we had already added several dozen to our group. These included an engineer, who had repaired the generator so we once again had at least limited electric power for light and heat. Another newcomer had proven to be a ham radio operator. We thus gained additional two-way communication with other, like-minded groups in the Colorado Rockies and to the north, in what had been western Canada. Of course our telepathic communications net had become more sophisticated also. We now had enough trained operators to maintain around-the-clock reception.

Taking advantage of a short rest stop, I approached Patsy. "Tell me," I found myself saying, "what is it that the group near Cheyenne Mountain reported last night? I heard a rumor today at breakfast that there had been some kind of military coup."

"Well, I don't think anyone knows for sure, but it sounds as if the 'brass hats' decided they had to do something or they'd lose power as things get better. You know that the military center in Cheyenne Mountain [Colorado] has martial law authority over everything to the west of the central sea nowadays. Our friends in the center near Pikes Peak say that they can intercept military radio messages. They claim some kind of plot was uncovered and certain civilian leaders had called for an end to martial law, in the east anyway. So the guys in uniform simply eliminated a couple of them and that shut the others up pretty fast, at least for now. Of course there's not a word of all that in the official newscasts."

"Yeah, it's always the same story, seems like. Some types of people will never learn, I guess," I replied. "Any word about the situation up north?"

"Yes, good news. We've established contact on the third level with some pretty highly developed folks. Seems they still have real cities or least pretty large population centers up there. That area wasn't nearly as badly hit as down here. I'm hoping we can exchange some of our unskilled refugees for a couple of their teachers if we can establish a secure route across the mountains."

As Patsy spoke I knew that she was referring to western Canada and the inland areas of the Pacific Northwest. Apparently the area from Alberta to Saskatchewan and eastern Washington State to the Dakotas remained intact. It was still connected to our part of the continent by the Rocky Mountains and those parts of the Great Plains not inundated when the Gulf of Mexico had surged north as land under parts of the Caribbean rose and quakes collapsed the Mississippi Valley. Establishing contact with like-minded people whose civilization continued relatively unscathed would be a tremendous benefit for our work.

Before I could get any more information, however, once again the Halloween "trick or treaters" intervened and I was left riding alone in the chilly, damp wind. By this time I felt my hands and feet were positively numb! I cannot say whether it was from the prolonged mental suggestion of bone-chilling weather in the late 1990s or simply a physiological effect of lying still in a trance for so long on Helen's studio bed. I only knew that I was darned cold and uncomfortable.

As I debated with myself over whether or not I should simply break my concentration and pull myself back to 1983, I realized that although Helen remained outside, I was no longer alone in her bedroom office. I could feel the distinct presence of another entity next to the bed. Looking up, although my physical eyes remained closed, I perceived him as an elderly man, looking sort of like the Michelangelo statue of Moses: tall with a long, white beard and dressed in a flowing white robe. I instinctively knew he wasn't there in a physical body but more like a reassuring presence.

Without words he offered me the choice of breaking free from my uncomfortable situation and snapping back to the present moment or of continuing the "experiment," as he seemed to consider this experience. He indicated that the choice was up to me. He wasn't there to interfere, only to offer assistance if required. His presence and message somehow calmed and reassured me. I decided I would finish the progression session as planned. The "experiment" would continue.

In fact, perhaps Helen had also gotten a subconscious message that this situation had gone on long enough. For when she returned a few moments later, her suggestions began the deepening process that I knew would precede the end of this lengthy session. Skillfully she moved me through the process, reassuring my conscious mind that whatever I had experienced would not unduly disturb me, that it was actually like having a vivid dream. When I "woke up" I would feel rested and refreshed. Nonetheless, I would remember the events experienced in detail and be able to discuss them later. As by now I was well used to this procedure, I actually did feel better by the time she reached her ending phrase:

"One . . . Open your eyes, you're awake!"

Even though fully returned to October 1983, the images of that somber, cold and windy desert of the late 1990s remained with me. I felt chilled clear through to my heart.

*　　*　　*

Once again the pressures of outside events delayed further future progressions for several months. A number of factors contributed to this interruption. I had other commitments. Helen's physical health worsened. The holiday season arrived. Moreover, in the back of my conscious mind I knew I was resisting the idea of returning to such a desolate future environment again. I hate cold, windy weather! Escape from blizzards and snowdrifts had been an important reason for my moving to California from New York a few years earlier. The idea of moving to Arizona only to find it turned into a frigid wasteland was anything but appealing!

Nonetheless, it would be wrong to say that the intervening period was uneventful. I had received a strong feeling during the final moments of the Halloween '83 progression that somehow my voice, its pitch or resonance, would be important someday. That was one of the nonverbal messages conveyed by the presence, or guide, who had so mysteriously

appeared while Helen attended to her Halloween visitors. My earlier
sessions with Helen Wambach had already led me to a new, serious
interest in past-life research and therapy. Now I began to consider how
I might use my own abilities to help others benefit from this unique
therapeutic tool. I realized, of course, that voice tones are very important
in hypnotherapy. Helen Wambach's unique vocal quality, deep and gravelly
yet motherly, definitely contributed to her success in relaxing her clients.
Perhaps, if my guide was correct, I could learn to help others through
hypnotherapy as well. Further, learning more about how hypnosis works
seemed like an important first step toward developing my own intuitive
abilities, something that interested me more and more as these sessions
developed.

Helen supported my new ambition and gave me sound advice about
getting first-rate training. Thus by early December I found myself en-
rolled in a professional hypnotherapy program at the Hypnosis Clearing
House in Oakland, California, then under the direction of its founder,
licensed psychologist Dr. Freda Morris. The classes were held on eve-
nings and weekends so as not to interfere with students like myself who
had daytime jobs. For the first time since I had begun to see Dr. Wambach
I began to consider seriously the possibility of leaving the U.S. civil
service eventually and devoting full time to working with her.

The hypnotherapy training program took several months to complete. Combined with my regular employment and a physical disability
stemming from an earlier industrial accident, this led to postponement
of any more future progressions until well into 1984. Helen and I did
continue our past-life work together as we evolved through this transition
period, which would eventually unite us as professional associates.

Consequently, it was not until April 1984 that we again agreed it
was time for another trip forward into the closing years of this century
for a third glimpse of the world following "the day the bottom dropped
out." As usual the progression session took place at her spare bedroom
hypnotherapy office in Pinole, California.

"Your eyes are closed and it feels good to close your eyes. . . . A
state of profound relaxation moves now from your facial muscles to the
jaw muscles . . . and as your jaw muscles relax, your tongue falls gently
to the base of your mouth. . . ."

I sighed and sank deeper into the pillows on Helen's studio bed as
her hypnotic tones led me gently inward. It was by now a familiar journey,
even though I knew my conscious mind still felt a bit apprehensive about
facing that cold desert wind again.

". . . This time as you float and move forward in Time, you will let yourself experience what you see and hear or feel as if it were in a dream. . . . You will not become anxious or unduly concerned about what is happening around you. You will, in fact, be somewhat detached from the scenes. But you will remember it all clearly and vividly, just as if it were a very real dream. . . ."

Sensing my hesitation about returning to the late 1990s, Helen had agreed to suggesting that the experience be perceived like a dream this time. This way, we reasoned, the images might seem less personal. As I was no longer by any means an inexperienced hypnotic subject, we also wanted to test this approach to see whether my recall would be as sharp and exact. If so, perhaps we would be able to use it to project a couple of other volunteers to the same time periods to see what they would report.

As I relaxed and drifted along to the sound of Helen's voice, thoughts and images gradually formed in my mind. I was back in the ranch house this time, in the living room watching television, apparently before its collapse. Seen out the window, the sky looked crisp and clear blue. Rather like it can be in California after a winter storm has washed the haze and pollution away so that one can see for miles. It seemed like early spring.

"Very good," Helen's voice interrupted my spring day. "Now let yourself move forward to the middle of March 1998. . . . What is happening now that it is March 1998?"

"There have been some volcanoes erupting recently and terrible storms and land sinks that have caused major flooding along the West Coast. It's stirred up the atmosphere and caused quite a bit of damage in the whole Pacific Ocean region."

"Which volcanoes have erupted? Where did this begin?"

"Fuji."

"Where? Tell me the name of that volcano again? Your voice speaks clearly and distinctly as you let the entire scene come into your awareness, just like in a dream . . . now."

"It was Fujiyama, I think. A volcano in Japan at any rate. It erupted and triggered a chain of strong earthquakes and other eruptions around the Pacific up through Alaska. They're dubbing it the 'Lighting of the Ring of Fire' in the papers."

"When did this happen?"

"Around the beginning of March, it seems like. I don't get the exact date for there were some other minor quakes in the area before Fuji went off."

"What about California? Has anything happened there?"

"Yes, there have been violent storms, heavy tides . . . perhaps even what you'd call small tidal waves . . . and I think more earth tremors, possibly an important quake also. There's been heavy flooding. Some of the coast simply sank, letting a lot of seawater rush in toward the central valleys and lowlands. It's worst in Southern California, where a lot of the built-up areas have gone under."

After a moment I heard my voice continuing: "But I think that there must have been some warning or that all this didn't happen at once since I know there were massive evacuations to higher ground and the mountains. Now, toward the end of March, the television and radio are telling everyone that the worst is over. The water is receding slowly and we'll just have to adjust to the new situation. The federal government is already setting up temporary relocation centers farther inland and everyone is talking of rebuilding. A lot of cropland has been permanently lost, however, not to mention so much of the Southern California coastline. And Patsy is still telling us, despite what's being said, that it's not over yet."

"All right. Now you can move forward again in time. . . . You will advance several months, to the first day of June 1998. Now it's June 1, 1998. . . . Where are you? What's happening?"

Helen's voice moved me forward. At first everything appeared totally black around me. Then I realized that the sky was completely dark now. Soot and dirt particles filled the air, making it hard to breathe for a moment. As that feeling passed I realized that conditions were now basically the same as what I'd experienced on my July '98 birthday during that first future progression of July 1983.

"The other shoe has dropped," I replied. I then went on to recount how "it" had happened about a month earlier, in May. Precise dates seemed unimportant. I saw myself outside tending to the horses and the gardens that we had planted for our raw vegetable supply. I loved working with the animals and plants in addition to whatever teaching and research I was doing. There was a sudden rumble deep within the Earth and a quick rolling "lurch," which knocked me down for a moment. Part of the ranch house collapsed and people came pouring out, crying and yelling. We had had disaster drills so I knew to run to the big propane tank and turn the valve, shutting off the gas. Only then did I realize that I was trembling all over and very scared!

As Helen asked for more details about what had followed this crisis, I described how the immediate result had been mass confusion nearly everywhere. The overall impact of this disaster, a major earthquake in Southern California, apparently, was far more devastating than the earlier Pacific shakers and floods. This was the "Big One." It accelerated the sinking of major areas along the West Coast so that the coastline moved up to within a couple of hundred miles of Phoenix, Arizona, and only the mountain areas remained above water all the way up to Oregon.

Physical destruction was just part of the story, however. Reassured by numerous "experts," everyone had been conditioned to think that "the worst was over" and that the March calamities had marked the climax of the long-predicted California disasters. It was as if all the catastrophes that had been predicted had at last occurred so we could now sigh with relief at having survived after all. Now we could pick up the pieces and resume life as usual.

This time however, sometime in May, all that certainty had been shattered. No one felt they could be confident about the future anymore. Panic and then looting and lawlessness ensued on a large scale. State and local governments were unable to cope with the scope of devastation and collapse of commercial communications and transportation services. Periodic violent aftershocks disrupted relief efforts. I remembered thinking that even our compact community might have to move to a more secure area as the Earth continued to heave frequently.

Furthermore, this time the "ripple effects" of the jolting earth-plate movement spread far beyond California. Much of the desert southwest sustained significant damage, while simultaneous volcanic eruptions and earth shifts elsewhere around the planet compounded the problem. As the Gulf of Mexico surged inward over Texas, our part of Arizona was more or less cut off to both the east and west by water.

The weather had also worsened as tons of dust and volcanic ash were thrown into the atmosphere by this second series of eruptions. Although the worst occurred during the first few weeks of havoc, the Sun simply did not return through the thick black clouds that summer. Most green vegetation in a wide belt of the temperate zone withered and died, including my precious vegetable garden. Of course we had our buried pinto beans and other foodstuffs. But with the damage to the ranch house, the continuing aftershocks and near anarchy in town, even Patsy felt it might be safer to move closer to the mountains.

At this point Helen decided we had already explored that part of my future odyssey enough. She therefore suggested that I could let myself advance a few years.

"Go now to a time when you are experiencing something new or different, something connected with your contribution to the community," she suggested.

As she spoke I could sense the sky lighten up from that dull gray/black feeling of 1998. "Definitely things are better after the turn of the century," I thought to myself.

"Now, where are you? Do you know what time of year it is?" Helen's voice interrupted my train of thought as she asked me new questions.

"I seem to be traveling. I'm up in the mountains, going north. I'd guess it's summer since the air is just cool and brisk, not blowing or snowy."

I let my thoughts catch up with me for a moment as the new scene came more fully into my inner awareness.

"Yes, it's August or September of the year 2002. I'm going north to Canada. I've been called on a sort of exchange up there. Our group established telepathic contact with a number of well-developed groups several years ago. They sent us some of their teachers in exchange for some of our unskilled refugees after the big shift. Now they've asked me to come and join them, for a while at least. They want me to speak on the radio. I'm not clear just what it's all about but I think it has to do with my voice. I've been using it, yes, that's it. I've been using it as an instrument to help people to open up psychically. Somehow the pitch or tones behind the words I say brings them new awareness of themselves as total beings. It seems I can assist people to become more attuned to their natural telepathic or psychic abilities. Now this group in western Canada wants me to go on the radio and project my voice to help set up similar communications with other like-minded groups in different areas. It's their main project at this time. I'm excited about the idea and my possible contribution."

"There are six of us traveling together on horseback. I think we have to do it secretly since we seem to travel mostly around dusk. I get the impression that the American government doesn't exactly approve of freedom of movement outside of local areas, except for 'official' business. I don't know what they think of the Canadian communities. I guess they want people to concentrate on rebuilding locally where they are. It doesn't matter to us much; we stay out of their way mostly, there in Arizona."

"Very good," Helen broke in to ask me to go forward again. "Now you've arrived at your destination. It's your first week there. You're looking around the area. Can you describe what you see?"

"Yes, I'm somewhere in what used to be called Alberta, I think north of Edmonton, a new settlement. It's surprisingly warm here. I've been told that the climate has shifted significantly the past couple of years, making this region much more temperate now. Perhaps it's due to new ocean or wind patterns . . . something like that is affecting the weather. There are several thousand people living in this valley. It's not exactly what I'd call a city, but it's definitely quite populated. For one thing, there are only a few really permanent structures and these are of a geodesic dome design. Most everyone lives in lightweight collapsible buildings just one story tall. They're made of plastic or synthetic fabric stretched around aluminum or wooden poles, depending on how big they are. Sort of like Mongolian yurts, I'd say. The domes are covered with an aluminum-foil metallic skin. They're used mainly for supply depots, I've been told. I've not actually been inside one yet."

"They have preserved a pretty high level of technology here since most of the damage occurred farther south. I think some people go to the larger cities like Calgary and Edmonton and work to produce building materials and other things modern society counts as necessities. We avoided the big towns on our journey up here so perhaps they were also partially destroyed or have unfriendly governments. I've been told that there were quite serious earth movements here too for a while during 1998. Nothing like what we experienced in the Southwest, to be sure, but still enough so that most people feel better about living in these yurt-like collapsible structures, which can fall down without doing appreciable damage."

"They are preparing for a series of radio broadcasts in a few months. I've seen some of their communications equipment and it is spectacular, even though I can't claim to understand it, as I've no technical background. Someone has invested quite a bit of time and talent in adapting things to the new conditions. My hosts have told me that they know of my work and voice qualities through the contacts we had established from the ranch in Arizona. I gather they want me to help them give spiritual and psychic instructions to other groups who are more isolated but who can receive radio messages. It is connected with their project to establish a common unity among us to be passed along to the next generation. Not too different from what we were doing in Arizona at the school that we established just before 'the day the bottom dropped out.' They tell me I can do this work, but that even now I need some additional preparation here. All in good time, I guess."

"All right," Helen's voice intervened. I knew intuitively that she was feeling that this session should not become as prolonged as the one last October.

"I want you to move forward now, to the day that you die in this lifetime. . . . You will feel no physical pain and have no fear. Your conscious mind will not be disturbed by this knowledge. . . . It is not important for it to know when or even where this event occurs. But I do want you to focus in on the cause of physical death. . . . Again, let the images come as if in a dream, a vivid dream, a dream with no pain and no fear. . . ."

"Now, it is the morning of the day of your physical death. . . . What are you feeling? What is happening?"

Suddenly I felt overwhelming chilled again. It was like being back in that cold, clammy day I'd experienced during our first future progression session, only I knew I'd not returned to Arizona or to 1998. A sense of lethargy and rheumy weariness swept over me but without pain or fear. I struggled to put the feelings into words.

"I'm lying down, in a bed, I guess. My joints ache and I feel terribly cold, so cold. How I hate this damp chilliness!"

Clearly I was experiencing a terminal illness, probably something respiratory, as my lungs ached.

Helen broke in at once to take me beyond the physical departure point:

"Now you've died and left that physical body, that character you've known as Chet Snow. And you're floating just above the scene. . . . Now, what are you thinking? What are you feeling?"

"It's wonderful!" I whispered almost in awe. "Oh, Lord, what a relief to be out of that dreary time!"

Such was my initial response to leaving this lifetime, there in the future, sometime in the early decades of the twenty-first century. Mere words cannot do justice to my actual feelings of joy and release. Oh, was I glad to be out of that body and away from that situation! I noticed several people around my bed down below but I barely hesitated an instant before soaring upward from that murky material world into the most beautiful golden-white light I've ever seen.

What a difference from some of the other body "deaths" I've experienced during recent past-life regressions. This time I was just overwhelmingly happy to be free of Earth's physical ties. Everything down there seemed so remote at that moment. I wanted it to last forever. Surrounded by a golden haze of such pure love that I literally cannot describe it—there are no words—I felt transported beyond all the struggle and all the pain, releasing every bit of it to the universe as I flew "home."

If those who have what are known as "near-death experiences" go through a process as liberating and loving as this, no wonder so many feel cheated at being returned to their physical bodies. Could I have had my way at that moment, I'd never have returned to the "here and now" either!

Helen, however, was as usual more interested in research questions than in listening to me try to describe my flight to nirvana. Her next question broke into my blissful reverie, returning my attention to matters at hand:

"Now that you've died and left that body, I want you to review the purpose of that survival experience as Chet Snow. . . . Why was it important for Chet Snow to live through such drastic changes and to use his voice in such a manner? Also, for what purpose did the other survivors remain physically alive? What greater purpose does this experience serve?"

Almost as an afterthought she then added, "You may ask those entities who are around you at present to help you answer these questions. They are there to assist you. Go ahead and ask their advice, now."

As my ears heard these words pronounced, I became aware that there were indeed several other nonphysical beings next to me in that light. I guess they'd been there all along, waiting patiently for me to notice their presence. I got the impression that they had aeons of experience in welcoming new "returnees" for they seemed slightly amused to watch my reaction of amazed wonder at the sparkling beauty of it all. Their manner was amused but also infinitely loving and caring. Reassured, I turned to them to repeat Helen's questions. Even as I looked up, however, their answers came flooding into my mind.

What they communicated was both amusing and sobering. One thing I have learned from these sessions with Dr. Helen Wambach is that these nonphysical entities, or the collective unconscious or whatever source I seem to "tap into" for information in this altered state, whatever or whoever it is, it certainly has an unusual sense of humor! And catering to my or society's conventions about "proper" attitudes is definitely not a priority.

For you see, the answer I got to Helen's philosophical questions about the reasons for these future changes was that after the "shift," as it was called, there would remain basically two categories of humanity: the "garbage" and the "garbagemen"! Further, this answer was conveyed to me not only telepathically but olfactorily. Yes, by smell! And it did smell . . . awful!

So much for our high view of human life and our race's obsession with physical survival. So much for the lovely "New Age" vision of humanity's spiritual evolution following the "purging" of the planet. I guess that once a pound of clay, always a pound of clay, at least as far as the physical form is concerned. "Ashes to ashes . . ." did seem to be these entities' viewpoint about earthly human life.

Actually, once their little barnyard-style joke about Earth had been made on a nonverbal level, my nonphysical friends continued in a more serious vein. They explained that in fact the Earth is similar to a huge garden project and that in a material/physical sense it is now overdue for a fallow or composting period. Apparently we humans, with our natural bent to exploit the planet's natural resources and move them around, provide the best compost! Every once in a while, however, garden Earth needs a physical renewal period. So natural forces, combined with and hastened by human machinations such as offshore drilling and underground nuclear explosions, plunge the most overexploited areas into the sea for a rest. Some of the ocean bottoms, on the other hand, rise as new, naturally fertile lands.

At such times, which recur at the end of long natural cycles, those who remain in physical bodies are made up of two main groups. Some, stay to provide compost and labor to reseed the soil and replenish the Earth. This group remains primarily because they have certain lessons to learn about material loss, privation, survival and self-reliance. Dealing with drastic changes in their physical environment is the best and most effective teacher for them. In effect, I was told, this bunch has no other place to go at this point in their growth pattern.

The second group sticking around will be the garbagemen, or, if you want a more positive term, the gardeners. These are mostly volunteers who are interested in studying such world renewals or who wish to accelerate their personal growth by accepting difficult duty. Their task is to see that things are cleaned up and that the new land is used productively by the new humanity that arrives to populate it.

The gardeners will also help preserve essential spiritual and material knowledge, not so much for the Earth's immediate physical future but for those later generations to come. These new Adams and Eves will inherit the replenished garden as more humans return to physical bodies in the future. They will also assist in raising the total Christ consciousness of all Creation, not just this Earth or this material dimension. For as each earthly cycle revolves, progress toward a reunion of all that exists emerges. Apparently it takes good, well-worked soil for higher-level crops.

As for my own small part in all this grand design, again my nonphysical friends cited that my words and my voice could be a resource to assist this recycling process and to reassure others that seeming calamities do not signal an end to human progress. I will have something to say at just the right moment, apparently, and the means to say it. This was their assurance to me.

Finally, I was told that it wouldn't be so awfully long before I completed this physical exercise and could move on, passing once more through this marvelous, regenerating light. That seemed somehow the most reassuring thought of all!

The last thought I got before my nonphysical companions bade me a firm "Good-bye and good luck!" and sent my conscious mind swiftly back to full wakefulness, even before Helen could speak, was the following. It sums up this experience far better than I could otherwise, so I will share it here. They told me:

> *Now is once again a time of preparation and perhaps also of initiation. For this is the time to get the tools sharpened and to review good gardening techniques. The harvest is for tomorrow.*

* 2 *
Past-Life Regression to
Future Progression

From time immemorial humanity has been fascinated with attempts to foretell the future. Sages and prophets, seers and diviners across the ages have, with varying degrees of success, used a variety of rituals in the common attempt to know what tomorrow would bring. A rare few individuals have become enshrined as the great prophets of the major world religions. Others, like Michel de Nostredame of sixteenth-century France, better known as Nostradamus, continue to confound believers and skeptics alike with their arcane predictions that seem to match crucial historical events centuries after they were made.

Today, as humanity struggles to avoid self-destruction through nuclear holocaust or ecological suicide, and as we approach the turn of a second Christian millennium, speculations about the future are particularly popular. Everyone from "born again" Christians like Hal Lindsey to the adepts of numerous Indian gurus and the followers of such "channeled" entities as "Ramtha the Ram" or "Mafu" express their own personal visions of the Apocalypse just around the corner. Further, although these types of dire predictions still remain outside the mainstream of contemporary Western thought, many respected scientists and historians agree that an accidental or deliberate exchange of thermonuclear bombs between the superpowers could trigger a "nuclear winter" with the potential to extinguish all viable intelligent life on this planet. Even in the absence of this ultimate, violent scenario, the more subtle pressures of unchecked population growth and the continued large-scale pollution of Earth's natural resources certainly are producing major planetary problems for the coming decades.

Our current state of affairs includes persisting East-West tensions, widespread international terrorism, the continuing specter of mass starvation in Africa, the growing AIDS epidemic and increasingly extreme weather conditions, with record winds, rains and droughts across much of the Earth's surface. The ever-present threat of financial collapse and economic recession still preoccupies world leaders. Even our once unshakable faith in new technological advances in space has been compromised by the 1987 Challenger disaster and America's costly and largely ineffectual Star Wars militarization plans for space. Although certainly everything in today's world is not negative, as stories of individual resourcefulness and international attempts to secure lasting peace attest, many current trends should serve to make us stop and think as we near the end of this critical century. What's going on here? Are these religious fanatics and discarnate "entities" right after all? Is it time for the end of the world? Are we now awaiting only the arrival of the fourth horseman before Armageddon?

Taking a long, hard look at similar conditions and humanity's legacy of prophetic predictions prompted Dr. Helen Wambach to begin investigating the mechanics of future prediction back in the early 1980s. Already noted for her pioneering research into the mysteries of reincarnation, the California clinical psychologist became interested in this topic as a result of her earlier studies. For example, her previous work had demonstrated that when taken gently into a light "waking trance" state of consciousness via her own Wambach method of hypnosis, most people, indeed nearly 90 percent, proved highly capable of recalling events from previous lives in a number of historical periods. They were able to answer mundane but statistically measurable questions such as "Are you a man or a woman?" "What are you eating for supper?" "What clothing are you wearing?" and "What kind of money do you use to purchase supplies?" In a sample of around a thousand cases, the answers supplied by Helen Wambach's lightly hypnotized subjects were found to correlate to known historical facts such as population curves, sex ratios, race distribution and nutrition sources. The answers she received and her analysis formed the basis for her first book, *Reliving Past Lives*, published by Harper & Row in 1978.

In compiling the data for that book Dr. Wambach also noticed that nearly 60 percent of those participating in her research workshops reported that they had "been ahead" of her questions while in the light trance state. It soon became obvious that once in the "dreaming mind," as she called it, many people could bypass the linear aspects of Time and memory. In the high theta brain wave state as measured on EEG equipment, Helen Wambach's subjects apparently activated latent telepathic abilities. At some point the idea occurred to her that this seemingly telepathic condition might be tapped to get answers about the future as well as the past. As she once told me:

"I thought, 'Wouldn't it be interesting to go out and hypnotize thousands of people and see what they predict about the future? Why stick with just one prophet or seer when you can do it the democratic way and get everybody's opinion?' "

Therefore, shortly after the publication of her second book on prenatal memories and choices made by her subjects shortly before birth into this current lifetime (*Life Before Life*: Bantam Books, 1979), Helen began offering workshops featuring the possibility of "progressing" to one of two future time periods—2100 or 2300 A.D.—as well as "regressing" to a past life. As before, her technique consisted of helping subjects achieve a light "waking" trance and then asking them routine questions that could be compared statistically. Since, for the conscious mind at least, the future has not yet taken place, she focused on finding data about which a significant number of workshop participants agreed. She became, in her words, a "Gallup pollster of the subconscious mind."

As noted earlier, I first met Helen Wambach in early 1983 when I went to her for private past-life therapy sessions to help clear up some nagging personal problems. Progressing to the future, either in this lifetime or in one in the future, was far from my mind. However, as our friendship grew, I became increasingly interested in her project. When I undertook to progress forward personally to the late 1990s, the results both fascinated and appalled me. Being basically an optimistic individual, I was shocked to find my subconscious mind projecting me into such a cold, dismal scenario! I had never been to the part of Arizona which I so clearly "saw" during those sessions, and even today, several years later as I write these lines, I have not gathered up the courage to check out the exact physical landscapes, which still remain vividly impressed on my memory. For now, at least, I'm very willing to let that much of my potential late nineties "future" take care of itself!

Nonetheless, as I became more involved with Helen professionally during 1984 and 1985, I began to discuss her work with her at length.

Just how had she developed her unique techniques for obtaining statistically comparable data during large group workshops? What had gotten her interested in attempting to progress individuals ahead in their current life? Had anyone else come up with results resembling the rather nasty developments I had foreseen for 1998? The following material represents a summary of what I learned of Helen Wambach's views on these and related subjects covering her odyssey from past-life regressions to mental progressions into our "mass dreams" of the future.

Among the first topics Helen Wambach covered with me was her concept of hypnosis and hypnotic imagery. Many people think that hypnosis is an unusual, possibly dangerous condition imposed by stage magicians on gullible individuals to make them do silly things without their being consciously aware of their actions. Or they feel it is a kind of artificial sleep used by doctors and dentists to permit minor surgery with little or no anesthesia. In either case hypnosis is seen as involving a temporary loss of consciousness and control, usually followed by a memory lapse of what occurred during the hypnotic session. Both of these experiences happen, of course, but they represent only a small fraction of the mental processes involved in hypnosis.

Most psychological uses of hypnosis, in fact, occur at a semiconscious level where one remains quite aware of physical surroundings but attention is focused inward to images and impressions arising from the subconscious, usually in response to the therapist's questions rather than on external stimuli. Afterward it is fairly easy to remember what the mind's "inner eye" revealed, especially if the subject is given a positive suggestion to reinforce conscious recall. Thus, at this level of hypnosis, the experience is quite similar to a waking dream, both mentally and physiologically, as measured by brain wave activity monitored by equipment such as the electroencephalograph (EEG). That similarity inspired the title of this book: *Mass Dreams of the Future*.

Helen Wambach always stressed that during her regression sessions, subjects received direct mental images coming from their subconscious minds in response to her general, usually mundane questions. Due to the focused state of mental concentration achieved during this kind of hypnosis, subjects' responses well up from hidden levels of experience, seemingly without regard to the Time and Space constraints of the conscious mind. The information contained in these images is then translated by the brain into concepts and words that can be communicated externally, either aloud or on paper. She thus felt that the brain serves as a "reducing valve" that allows the experiences of nonconscious mental levels to be passed along to the exterior world.

It is only natural that, in this process of reducing what the subconscious mind brings up during hypnosis, the subject's responses are filtered and subtly colored by all the rest of his or her experiences, even those of which the person is not consciously aware. This is particularly true whenever the information retrieved touches something emotional, something that has caused pain or pleasure or that is anticipated to lead to suffering or joy. Likewise, when the words one utters are heard by a listener, the listener's brain also filters them according to the sum total of his (or her) experiences and he too "hears" through his own emotional patterns.

Therefore, in normal human communication, for both speaker and listener, the brain, which takes mentally produced direct experience and reduces it to expressible words, acts as a buffer. It separates us from reality that might otherwise be overpowering emotionally. So the brain links the mind, which actually experiences everything, and our conscious awareness, which receives only a selected portion of what the whole mind knows. Words further reduce and separate personal experiences from one individual to another even though they may deal in commonly accepted symbols.

It stands to reason that the interference between what the mind reveals through the subconscious and what gets "remembered" and put into words is especially great when we deal with the future. Why is that so? Well, for one thing, the conscious levels of our minds are deeply involved in our individual futures, as are our emotions. Together they are constantly planning and plotting what we say and do from day to day in order to bring us the most pleasure and least pain from any given situation, according to a complex set of rules laid down by whatever society we are in at the moment. That's their job, after all! That's what we have defined as "normal behavior," or sanity. Psychology exists to help people stay on this straight and narrow path because whenever we stray and our behavior or expressed opinions aren't "rational," according to the norms set up by our parents or our peers, we are considered eccentric or neurotic or, if things really get out of hand, psychotic. And we all know where that leads!

Therefore concern about the future is built into our minds' vast experiences across Time and Space. The quality of our current life and the survival of our organized set of conscious perceptions, what Sigmund Freud called the "ego," depends on how well our brains handle what our minds see as the present while also looking out for the future.

Consequently, throughout history human beings have been fascinated with the idea of predicting the future. Moreover, due in part to the dual hemispheres of our brains, we have two fundamentally different ways of consciously expressing what our minds know, including future predictions. Thus we either develop "right brain" imaginational and prophetic systems to tell us what tomorrow will bring or we set up rational "left brain" ways of collecting, organizing and comparing as much past and present sensory information as possible and try to predict from correlations among the data. Today we call the first kind of predicting "psychic" and the second "forecasting." They've had other names in the past, but it boils down to the basic difference of which part of the brain we're primarily relying on for answers.

In looking for ways to investigate the future, Helen Wambach began by dividing her search between reading future forecasts by such rationally oriented "think tank" groups as the Hudson Institute, the Rand Corporation and the World Futurists and delving into what modern psychic "channels" have predicted. She concluded, to her initial surprise, that although both groups failed more often than they succeeded in predicting near-term trends, the psychics' "batting average" was as high, if not slightly higher, than that of the forecasters! This seemed to be especially true when the psychic's predictions had little immediate personal relevance or impact. It appears as if the conscious mind or ego interferes more with what we predict when it feels we may be personally affected.

Rationalist left-brain future forecasting is less accurate than psychic predicting because it is performed solely by the mind's conscious level, where personal involvement with the future is greatest. Consequently, the forecaster's social needs, surroundings and shared expectations act to "contaminate" this kind of future predicting. Despite current claims to the contrary, it is far from objective. Dr. Wambach felt that all such forecasts, from economic trends to political and even technological predictions based on conscious-level analysis, are too influenced by prevailing socioeconomic interests and belief systems, which overvalue stability and gradual change. All such forecasters have a vested interest in foreseeing a future closely related to the immediate past and one that favors the interests of today's elites.

Thus, while not ignoring the efforts of popular future forecasters, she decided she would get a more balanced picture by looking at reports from the subconscious minds of a large number of ordinary individuals while in a light hypnotic state. Obviously, obtaining information about the future via hypnosis, where direct mental images are received through the subconscious, is closer to psychic prediction than to think-tank forecasting. Nonetheless, Helen Wambach's research background led her to seek a way to combine these two methods. By lightly hypnotizing large groups of people and asking them all the same questions, she sought to establish whether their answers to questionnaires filled out immediately after each session would form meaningful group patterns. She was interested in comparing ordinary things like foods eaten, types of clothing worn and housing styles. Any response patterns in these and similar areas could then be compared statistically, thereby providing a picture of what our future society might be like. They could also be checked against the stories of individual subjects such as myself, who made more detailed verbal reports.

Still, it was the group patterns, the evidence of "mass dreams" of either past or future conditions, that always fascinated Helen. She frequently told me that one of the most valuable lessons a lifetime of clinical psychology had taught her was that "words are a smoke screen." Real communication, she insisted, takes place telepathically, beneath the words. It happens when you suddenly "know" what someone is about to say next during a personal conversation. It happens when someone's joy and excitement or fear and pain leap out across a TV screen or in a face-to-face interview. It occurs when one recognizes one's own deepest feelings in another's story, knowing that despite surface differences, you've shared the same basic human experience or emotion. It also occurs during the "waking dream" state of hypnosis she used for both her group and individual past- and future-life progressions.

Helen felt that the evidence she had amassed during her workshops that at least half of her hypnotized subjects could pick up thoughts and feelings telepathically was one of the greatest discoveries of all her research. Right after bringing her workshop participants back to normal waking consciousness, she always asked them whether they had found themselves getting answers, in images or impressions, slightly before they had heard her questions. Consistently between 50 and 60 percent replied yes. Moreover, most were not the least bit surprised at this accomplishment, despite the fact that what they were doing—answering questions before they were heard—is normally considered quite impossible!

She liked to cite this "matter-of-fact" attitude toward their precognitive telepathic abilities by her subjects as an example of how, despite our conscious self-concept as logical, rational beings, underneath most people easily accept such precognitive powers as knowing answers before they are asked, intuition and "hunches." We are much more familiar with "psychic" predictions of the future (at least the immediate future) than we consciously realize. Our seeming inability to see further ahead under ordinary conditions may simply be due to the conscious mind's refusal to believe it is possible. And of course such inhibitions against seeing our personal future in this current lifetime may also be protective for the individual ego. We *think* we want to know the future, but perhaps at deeper levels of the mind we really don't. Our rational minds have a vested interest in maintaining our belief that they are in charge!

Consequently, when Helen Wambach began her future-life progression study in 1980, she never intended to progress individual subjects ahead during this current lifetime. Instead, she planned a study of potential future lives in time periods between 150 and 400 years from now. As in her book *Reliving Past Lives*, she offered group workshop participants a choice of five time periods, with instructions that their subconscious minds would choose one of those periods in which to explore another lifetime. The five periods included three from the past, the most recent being 1900, and two from the future, around 2100 and 2300 A.D. An absolute random choice, disregarding population trends, should therefore have led to 60 percent past lives and 40 percent future lives. Given the world population explosion of the past two centuries, which still continues unchecked, over half the subjects could have been expected to go to one of the future periods. Moreover, when offered a choice before the hypnosis session, nearly two thirds of workshop participants (62 percent) indicated their conscious interest in seeing a future lifetime.

However, from the very first groups an altogether different trend appeared. Although about 90 percent of the first two sets of workshop participants filled in data sheets indicating they had been able to experience a different lifetime, only 5.5 percent reported being alive in the 2100 A.D. period while 11 percent saw themselves in the 2300 period. Helen checked and rechecked those first couple of hundred responses but the evidence was clear: The hypnosis process was working but only a handful of the subjects were progressing to the future. The next several groups confirmed the trend. It couldn't be simply random chance.

Puzzled by this development, she enlisted the help of a friend and colleague, Dr. R. Leo Sprinkle, a counseling psychologist and associate professor at the University of Wyoming, to hold some identical workshops in the Rocky Mountain states. Dr. Sprinkle was already familiar with her technique, as he had helped with the earlier research into past lives. Helen now gratefully got him to check whether possibly, despite her precautions, her own subconscious mind was influencing the process telepathically and inhibiting subjects from "progressing" to the future. She reasoned that perhaps her own poor health (she already had heart problems and diabetes) or some unknown fear of seeing her own future was holding her subjects back. The results showed otherwise: Dr. Sprinkle's statistics replicated what she had observed among her own workshop participants. About 6 percent of his subjects chose 2100 A.D. while 13 percent forged ahead to around 2300 A.D.

And so it went, with similar statistics from virtually every workshop held across the United States. Helen was particularly interested to note that there was no noticeable distinction between California subjects, those from Dr. Sprinkle's groups in Colorado and Wyoming, and participants in workshops held in the Midwest and on the Atlantic coast. Everywhere, between 5 and 7 percent of the subjects experienced a twenty-second-century lifetime and from 11 to 15 percent went beyond 2300 A.D. Even a large (300 persons) group familiar with the future predictions of noted American psychic Edgar Cayce, and therefore logically interested in seeing whether or not they'd have come true by 2100 A.D., duplicated the initial findings.

These results puzzled and disturbed Helen Wambach. For one thing, they made attaining over a thousand research cases for the two future time periods nearly impossible. If only 20 percent of the participants found themselves alive in one of these two future time periods, then it would take hypnotizing some 10,000 subjects to reach that goal. That would require time and resources she simply did not have. Even so, between 1980 and 1985 she and her helpers hypnotized approximately 2,500 Americans to reach the number of cases used in this book. Helen and an assistant, Mrs. Beverly Lundell, held sixty-two group workshops, with Leo Sprinkle contributing a couple of dozen more. I also ran several in 1984–85 and again, after Helen's death, from 1986 to 1988. The results of this research are discussed in Chapters 5 through 8.

Initially, faced with this strange evidence of a possible decline of up to 95 percent of the world's population within a couple of generations, Helen's impulse was to stop the project. Reviewing the reports of those subjects in the first dozen workshops who went to 2100 A.D. gave her a pretty negative picture of life in that time period. This was especially true for those few who found themselves alive during the period closest to 2100 A.D. itself. It depressed her and made her want to stop right there. If everybody was going to go around imagining scorched earth, empty fields, pollution and catastrophes, she just wasn't going to ask them anymore!

But of course she couldn't do that. Her scientific curiosity was aroused. So instead Helen decided to hypnotize some levelheaded individuals, people whose psychological balance she trusted, to see what they would say about the near future—about the period before 2100 A.D. For some this might mean projecting them ahead in their current lifetimes. But, even though she quickly found several volunteers, Helen soon ran into trouble with this method also. She discovered that the first eight people put under hypnosis individually and sent ahead into the twenty-first century all found themselves "floating," feeling "light and free." These were symptoms Helen Wambach recognized from her past-life regressions as meaning that those subjects had already left their physical bodies, that they had died. None of them found themselves physically "alive" during this period. Then, deciding to risk suggesting that one of her good subjects progress to a specific date in the late 1990s, less than two decades away, Helen quickly had to bring her back to the present as the young woman found herself choking to death in a big black cloud. She gasped for air for a moment even after coming out of the light trance. It was an experience neither she nor Helen wanted to repeat.

As an experienced clinical psychologist, Helen Wambach believed in the general principle that one should not do anything to harm a patient. The same holds true for research subjects, naturally. So very cautiously she began working with a few trained psychics, people whose special skills made them less vulnerable to being shocked at suddenly finding themselves having left the material world. She began by moving them ahead almost year by year in an effort to pinpoint the origins of these presumed disasters. It was tedious and tiring work, especially since she didn't want to risk projecting them unwittingly to the moment of their deaths.

Helen also did a more general session with noted psychic author Alan Vaughan (*Patterns of Prophecy*, 1973), who had correctly predicted Robert F. Kennedy and Martin Luther King's assassinations in 1968. All this took place in 1981 and 1982 and was interrupted by her own serious health problems. She was in and out of the hospital several times with congestive heart failure and valve bypass surgery, and as a result she had no organized research notes of these sessions. One thing she did tell me concerning Alan Vaughan's trip into the future was that he found himself, sometime before 2000 A.D., living in a rustic cabin in Mendocino County, far north of San Francisco, out in the woods. It surprised him since he'd always been more of a city dweller!

Helen Wambach quickly discovered, however, that most of the professional psychics she projected into the near future proved unsatisfactory subjects. By their very profession they had a vested conscious-mind interest in their future predictions. Their egos would get involved because they wanted to be proven right to demonstrate the accuracy of their claimed psychic powers! They were nearly as mentally "contaminated" by their social situations and shared expectations as the rational "think tank" forecasters. Thus, most of them came up with contradictory general information, often ignoring questions about themselves and what they would be doing in the years ahead, talking about celebrity-type happenings instead. Except for the session with Alan Vaughan, Helen didn't find their contributions very convincing.

Consequently, when she was again well enough to continue her research, Helen decided to stick with nonprofessionals who had no more than an average interest in the future. She began working with two ordinary but stable subjects, a student and a housewife, and hypnotized them individually, going ahead by their birthdays. She had begun using this approach during her past-life regression study as she found that her subjects' subconscious minds focused on significant personal events like birthdays or important holidays, such as Christmas or New Year's Day, more easily than on impersonal time intervals.

Helen Wambach had already discovered in her work with the professional psychics that it was not good to ask questions about specific future events that might either disturb or overly involve the current ego personality. Questions such as "When does your body die?" or "Is there a time when your home is destroyed?" or "Do you have to move suddenly?" instantly cause a block of the flow of psychic information due to their emotional strain on the conscious mind. Instead, Helen found that moving her subjects ahead either year by year, from holiday to holiday, or by taking them to a specific meaningful date in the future (i.e., one's birthday in 1998), she could get them to describe what was happening directly with less ego interference.

She also found that it helped the process if she could begin by taking her individual subjects to a happy or at least neutral experience. It was important whenever possible to avoid starting with an emotionally depressing event. Again, birthdays or holidays like Christmas usually worked well. She would also try and ask specific questions requiring simple responses as they are the easiest for the literally oriented subconscious mind to handle. She found that as a general rule the more specific the question and the less important the answer to the conscious ego, the more accurate the response. Thus, for example, she found the following to be a good initial suggestion:

It's now the Christmas season ten years from now. You are preparing for the season by doing some preholiday shopping. You find yourself in a grocery store. Go over to the meat counter and look

at the price of meat. Now, tell me, what is the price of a package
of pork chops?

Few people get upset at the idea of Christmas or some other holiday
and shopping in a grocery store is not very threatening either. But they
tend to remember what they were doing on holidays and also where they
spent them. So Helen often began by taking subjects ahead to a specific
meaningful date in the future, usually a time associated with a major
holiday or the subject's birthday. This is why she decided to project me
ahead to that fateful birthday in July 1998.

When projecting someone into the near future, Helen usually began
by focusing on two specific things: prices and food conditions. These are
basic indicators of our civilization. Naturally, the subjects gave whatever
their experience was in those areas and described other, more personal
activities at the date suggested. Then they'd be moved to other dates
and asked similar detailed questions. Once, when watching a January
television news program, Helen saw how she might get some more general news items from her individual subjects, whose concentrated attention, characteristic of hypnosis, usually kept their answers limited to
immediate personal concerns. Television networks frequently broadcast
news retrospectives around New Year's Day, going over the previous
year's highlights. Helen wondered, could a subject's subconscious mind
give her information from future TV shows? So she asked them if they
could find themselves watching such a program in the future, and a few
did. This was one of the strategies she used during my progressions as
well.

Of course, as in all work with hypnosis, she knew she had to be very
careful with the exact words used when making suggestions or asking
questions. The subconscious mind is extremely literal. I remember that
during one of my own progressions with Helen, she must have slipped
and used a phrase like "January and the holiday period," which my subconscious took to mean the following Christmas, not the one just before
January! It took us awhile to straighten that out. Of course something
personally upsetting may have happened in the preceding December that
my subconscious was unwilling to reveal at that time. There are always
several possibilities why a hypnotized subject skips certain dates.

Whenever, as frequently happened in these hypnosis sessions taking
individuals to the near future, upsetting material did surface, Helen always gave her subject's subconscious direct suggestions to lessen the
impact. Thus, for example, when I went through the earthquakes in
Arizona in 1998, she ended that trip by telling me, "This material will

not disturb you. You will have a neutral attitude about it and think of it as a dream." This helped my conscious ego from becoming unduly concerned over what was perceived as a life-threatening future experience. She used similar techniques with all her individual subjects.

With the groups that went beyond their current life expectancy, to 2100 or 2300 A.D., we didn't feel that such direct suggestions were so necessary. But even there experience taught us to add instructions at the end that a white light would enter their solar plexus, the emotional center, and wipe away any negative physical, mental or emotional after-effects from the future progression. It must have worked because neither Helen nor I had anyone come up to us later and say that they were still overly bothered by what they had foreseen. Nonetheless, the experience has often left workshop participants with significant "food for thought" about where their current habits and patterns of living might be leading them.

Thus, having established a basic strategy for safely progressing a few stable individuals ahead into the near future, Helen began working with the student and housewife who had volunteered. At first things moved along pretty smoothly. Their lives were filled with the usual stuff—paying bills, wiping kids' runny noses, graduation and career plans and all that. One of them predicted Reagan's 1984 reelection, certainly not a projection from Helen's mind as she strongly favored Mondale, although the woman saw it as a much closer race than it actually turned out to be.

Projected to a grocery store before various holidays, the two subjects reported food prices edging upward but without any dramatic rise until about a decade ahead. One talked of having difficulties with her credit cards but she was unsure whether this was a general problem or a personal one. And then, when they were about fifteen years ahead, in separate sessions, each of these two subjects suddenly reported that familiar pleasant "floating" sensation that Helen had come to associate with the subconscious mind's experience after death. Both reported very positive feelings of release, as if quite happy to be out of their physical bodies and surroundings. But neither they nor she wanted to risk taking them back to the exact circumstances just preceding their transition.

At this point, as Helen later confessed to me, she felt stymied. Her strong suspicion was that some calamity must be approaching in the not so distant future, for here were at least three (these two plus the young woman who had woken up choking and coughing) relatively young people reporting being gone before the year 2000 A.D. Of course Helen was also familiar with the various prophetic and psychic reports, including those of Edgar Cayce, predicting dramatic Earth changes around the turn of the century. But what did it all add up to? She still lacked a coherent account of a future set of circumstances which could conceivably kill so many people that even a century later Earth would remain severely depopulated. It was around this time that she recalled how, about a year earlier during one of her frequent hospital stays, she had experienced a vivid dream or out-of-body experience in which she found herself personally "floating" in the air, witnessing a future scene, set some fifteen to twenty years ahead. This is how she described her vision to me:

> In this dream I was taken out of my body and into the future where I saw the image of a very favorite niece of mine, whom I feel is quite a mystical person, and she was already a young woman around her late twenties to early thirties. That's how I knew it was the future because at the time she was still a teenager. Anyway, there she was wearing a yellow rain slicker aboard a kind of research ship which I knew was measuring the depth of the water that had flooded inland on the New Jersey coast just south of New York City. I watched the measuring device, which was not different from what we have now, and it read 9.6 something. I'm not sure if it was feet or fathoms; the entire thing was pure subconscious psychic imagery like that experienced by near-death survivors and it never occurred to me to wonder about such things as measurement units. I just accepted what I saw.
>
> One thing I am sure of is that I recognized the place where she was taking the measurements. It was at the site of the Ocean Port racetrack, near where I used to live in Rumson, New Jersey. And I said to myself, "Oh, that's nice; Jennie is still here." And then: "The East Coast is not nearly as battered as the West," at which point I was awakened by the nurses and doctors jabbing me with stimulants and bringing me back into my body.

Helen also commented that she realized in the dreamlike vision that she was watching that incident with her niece from outside any physical form so she knew she would no longer be around when it occurred. She told me in 1984, just a little more than a year before her untimely death, that this didn't really bother her personally. She was just happy to see that a loved one was still alive. But she confessed that she had felt frustrated about not having more details about what might be happening in between.

It was a few months after she had reached the impasse with her two volunteers that I met Helen Wambach. As mentioned earlier, I initially consulted her concerning some personal problems that I felt might be related to some of my past lives. Exploring possible future catastrophes in the 1990s had nothing to do with it! Actually, this made me an ideal subject for Helen's purposes because my conscious ego therefore had little stake in what I might experience. Further, I know she was impressed with the detailed and apparently accurate reports of my previous incarnations that came out of our past-life sessions. As she once put it, I am one of those rare individuals with a "research bump" in his character!

Therefore, after we had explored several past lives and resolved what lay behind some of my current problems, Helen asked me if I'd be willing to participate in her research into the future. By this time she was also persuaded that I had a pretty stable personality and wouldn't become overly upset if I too found myself "floating off" before the turn of the century. I readily agreed and we held the sessions that have been described in Chapter 1.

Those sessions took me through the 1990s and eventually, sometime after the beginning of the next century, to what appears to be death from a respiratory ailment. Both Helen and I agreed that it would be better to leave an actual date of death for this lifetime vague in my conscious mind. Even though the subconscious mind knows we are immortal spirits whose existence continues beyond physical death, the conscious ego and the body know they are mortal. A frequent punster, she would often say, with a hearty laugh, "Your liver wants to live, after all!"

As my story in the Arizona desert unfolded, Helen at last felt she was getting a fairly detailed picture of what America might be like around the turn of the century and an approximate timetable for the foreseen changes. Using this information, she then held individual sessions with five other volunteers: another student, two housewives, a teacher and a cook. They came either as clients or as people who'd read her books or heard her talk about her research. Like me, they seemed to have been sent to her. As she once remarked, "I didn't put an ad in the *San Francisco Chronicle* for them."

Helen worked with this small number of volunteers primarily to satisfy her personal curiosity about what the near future might bring. She was also eager to see if the stories told by these individual subjects would match my experience. Her major interest, however, continued to lie in the larger group research project, taking hundreds of people to potential future lifetimes around 2100 and 2300 A.D. via hypnotic imagery.

Again she began the tedious process of progressing these subjects ahead individually almost year by year. And slowly but surely a pattern emerged from their separate reports. It basically confirmed the more detailed account presented during my sessions even though many small points were different. This is what Helen and I found most convincing about this aspect of her future research: Separate individual subjects presented a similar pattern of events. The dates on which these events happen were not always the same. The severity of changes seen also varied from subject to subject. Their personal location and individual experiences were obviously different also. Yet there remains an underlying similarity, including the fact that all of Helen's subjects, including myself, found ourselves joyously leaving our physical bodies well before our "normal" lifespan by today's standards should be over.

What are the main points that Helen observed in this pattern? All the reports begin by noting a significant inflation in food prices, especially meat and fresh produce. This dovetails with stories of unusual weather patterns that have wreaked havoc on crops and livestock production. One woman describes drought in the Midwest and Texas while another mentions freezing rain and severe winter storms in the Pacific Northwest. Another says that "the soil goes bad" in a part of Southern California after a couple years of unusually severe drought. The common denominator seems to be a shift toward extreme weather conditions, either very hot and dry or quite cold and damp. Devastating winds indicate the possibility that these conditions alternate in wide frontal patterns. This seems to mark the starting point for more serious earth disturbances that follow.

Next, Helen noted that several of these reports mention personal finance or credit problems. The stock market is no longer a relatively secure investment value as it swings up and down more wildly than heretofore. Financial crises intensify and bank failures multiply. A couple of the subjects report difficulties with credit cards, which become less versatile or invalid. This is coupled with an increasing scarcity of money in general and the widespread use of barter for small personal transactions. This seems especially true for those subjects who see themselves in rural or small-town settings. Interestingly, five of the six subjects report moving out of the San Francisco Bay area within the next decade, most to less urban areas such as Iowa, Arizona or Washington State. Two subjects mention receiving a new kind of U.S. paper currency as part of a governmental monetary reform during the 1990s.

Serious Earth changes, including increased volcanic activity and several violent earthquakes spaced around the world, are also part of the pattern. They disrupt communications and fan inflationary pressures. Gasoline is reported as locally scarce in rural California. Two of the subjects besides myself tell of hearing media reports about important shifts in the Pacific Ocean area, such as sea quakes, volcanoes and the sinking of land. The area around Japan is seen as very unstable. Tremors at Mount Shasta may signal renewed volcanic activity there also, although there is no mention of an actual eruption in any of the reports.

Unsurprisingly, political tensions remain high around the world as nations scramble to maintain their current living standards in the face of these and other problems. The Middle East continues to be a trouble spot, with one report of actual fighting in Jerusalem around the Temple Mount. Another subject sees newscasts of a fifth Arab–Israeli war. Political problems in Europe mount also, with social disruptions and strikes. Only one of these six subjects tells of dying in a nuclear explosion. She says this happens in 1999 in Europe. She is the only one of the six who reported living abroad at that time. Interestingly, it seems to be an isolated incident, not a nuclear exchange or the start of World War III.

Finally, there seems to be a series of these above-mentioned trends coming together and causing widespread destruction, followed by the subjects reporting themselves released from their physical bodies and unpleasant surroundings. It appears as if there will be a combination of natural and man-made disasters that together wipe out large numbers of people in relatively short order. The six subjects don't agree on the exact date of this general catastrophe but it seems to be sometime between now and the late 1990s. At any rate none of these individuals find themselves alive much after the year 2000 A.D., if they last until then. Helen once told me that my own account of dying somewhere in Canada in the first decades of the next century was the furthest ahead of the six.

The terrible implications of her subjects' findings, which seemed to confirm the reports of a severely depopulated planet in the twenty-second century, depressed Helen Wambach's usually effervescent personality. She became very torn over whether or not to go ahead and publish the results of this research. In the end it was the less than negative reaction from the subjects themselves that made her decide to associate me with her project and ensure its eventual publication. As she once said to me:

> Oddly enough my subjects have been far less uneasy than I have about these results. Perhaps this is partly because all of them report such wonderful feelings of release and joy on leaving their physical

surroundings. I know that Kenneth Ring in *Heading for Omega* [Wm. Morrow, 1984] describes this possible scenario as "taking us through Hell" but my subjects report otherwise, at least as far as their deaths are concerned.

Helen then went on to tell me the story of her young woman subject who had found herself dying in a nuclear explosion in Europe. She experienced her death as a choking sensation in the lungs, which were seared in the flames. As soon as she left her body, however, a big smile came over her face. Amazed at the change, Helen asked her, "Are there a lot of confused souls around you?" as that is what one might rationally assume in the event of a nuclear holocaust.

But she replied, "No. There are many around me here and we're all very happy and very relieved. It's quite a pleasant gathering. There are thousands of us. And we're free!"

This is not exactly our intelligentsia's view of a mass disaster. Nevertheless, it tallies with the kind of feelings all five of Helen's other subjects reported at their deaths, also apparently in some catastrophe. I too remember the joy of finally leaving Chet Snow's body behind when I found myself dying in that future Canadian bed. This experience agrees with that of many other hypnotized individuals after ending either past or future lifetimes. Those who have returned from a "near-death experience" where their bodies were clinically dead for a short time also frequently tell of forceful positive feelings of love and warmth as they reach the point of decision, beyond which there is no returning of their consciousness to their present bodies. So perhaps physical death isn't the unpleasant experience we fear it to be.

Helen confided in me that she often wondered why such positive feelings just after experiencing bodily death under hypnosis is so prevalent, especially among those subjects who die in catastrophes. She said she'd come to believe that it is because the people who will die in the forthcoming disasters will die quickly. They generally will die with their whole families because these cataclysms will be widespread. Our conscious, intellectual view of catastrophe as something horrible is one based on fear of losing our present physical body. Many people, however, are aware that the person who dies is not the one to feel sorry for; those who lose their loved ones are the ones who suffer most. If we experience large-scale disasters such as appear to be foreseen by these subjects and some contemporary psychics, there will not be very many grieving close relatives left alive.

Nonetheless, obviously there will be some survivors. Several of Helen's workshop participants whose stories are given in *Life Before Life* mentioned that they had chosen to be born at this time in order to help in Earth's transformation to the New Age. Apparently these series of disasters are part of that transition process. These survivors seem to know it in advance and already some are preparing themselves for hard times ahead. This is especially true of those now forming self-sufficient rural settlements. The Earth, after all, must be nurtured. There must be nurses and doctors for Mother Earth because it will not simply disappear.

Along with this hopeful viewpoint about reincarnation and the impermanent nature of physical death, perhaps the most positive information coming out of these subjects' reports of the upcoming future is that there will be no total annihilation of life on this planet. Global nuclear war, so feared by "think tank" forecasters, just is not foreseen by Helen's and my subjects. Rather, the Earth appears to be entering a period of profound evolutionary change. Some people seem to have known even before they were born that one of their purposes in being alive today is either to teach the truths of the immortality of the soul and transition aspects of bodily death or to become survivors and make the New Age a reality here on Earth in the next century.

Of course there are also many individuals now living who have never heard of New Age concepts like future lives, psychic energy or being able to experience things beyond their physical bodies. Our age is one of such blatant materialism that for many people these things seem frightening. One must be concerned for people like that, who are so locked into their physical selves that they can't even conceive of the mind or consciousness as something independent of material reality. They automatically dismiss the idea of its survival without a physical body or its movement through Space and Time. They are the ones so terrified of death that they count on the advances of modern technology to keep their physical bodies alive at any price. They are the ones who eagerly await artificial hearts or multiple organ transplants.

Helen often said it was her opinion that such individuals are prey to a subconscious fear that is abroad in our contemporary culture—a premonition that in fact death is arriving, is going to arrive, on a fairly large scale and it's like many people are putting up a last-ditch mental resistance. She called this resistance, expressed through the frenetic pursuit of purely materialistic goals and instant gratification, the "Apocalyptic spirit" of our age. It's almost as if our culture is currently stuck between the most intense fear of death we have ever known and an opposite, almost underground development—the growing realization that we are more than our physical bodies, that we are eternal, spiritual beings. Today we stand at a crossroads, with fundamental choices about the future fast approaching.

Although the results of Helen Wambach's individual near-future progression sessions with her other volunteers essentially confirmed the trends we had discovered during my visits to the Arizona ranch, they did not provide any better clue as to why the Earth may be heading into such a drastic transition period just now or why Apocalyptic premonitions should today lurk in the recesses of our subconscious minds. How are such hidden thoughts affecting us? How might they be shaping the kind of future reality we may have to live through tomorrow?

Helen wrestled with these questions for the last few years of her life, intrigued with the growing body of scientific evidence from modern physics and biology that all living material organisms are surrounded by a band of invisible radiations, something which has long been asserted by Eastern and traditional religious mystics who call it the "aura," or "halo." Ancient esoteric traditions associate the strength and vitality of one's aura with both physical and spiritual well-being. It is said to connect us with nonphysical energies that interact with our material bodies through seven specific bioenergetic transmission points located along the spinal column and known by their Sanskrit term *chakras*, a word meaning "wheel," presumably a description of the energy's spiraling, circular movement.

Until recently our materialist Western science scoffed at such concepts as superstitious or unfounded metaphysical speculation. Today the presence of an electromagnetic field around living objects has actually been detected and measured by techniques such as Kirlian photography. This latter is a process that projects high-frequency electrical current through an object set between two electrode plates in front of a piece of undeveloped film. As the current passes in and around the piece of matter, its interaction with the object's invisible energy corona is registered as an image on the film. No camera is required for such "photographs." The technique was developed by a Soviet husband and wife team, Semyon and Valentina Kirlian, in the 1960s, although the principles behind it date from the mid-nineteenth century.[1]

The Kirlians' most intriguing finding about these energy fields that surround all living matter, including human beings, is that their shape and color change in response to emotional stimuli. Thus, the corona discharge around the hand of a person who is relaxed and calm will change if that individual is angered or excited. Furthermore, Western researchers of Kirlian photography such as Dr. Thelma Moss, now retired from the faculty of U.C.L.A, also discovered that certain individuals (notably experienced psychic "healers") apparently can actually transfer energy from their own field to that of another by touching them. Scientifically controlled experiments demonstrated that after such therapeutic intervention, the healer's corona discharge was temporarily dimmer while that of the patient expanded and brightened. Attempts by ordinary "control" subjects to duplicate the feat failed.

Other experiments showed that disease can be detected as anomalies in an organism's corona discharge (or aura) before its body shows detectable physical symptoms, even with the help of electron microscopes. The Kirlians demonstrated that the energy field around a leaf from an apparently healthy corn plant set next to a blighted neighbor weakened several days before the plant showed any outward signs of having caught the withering blight. In addition, when part of a healthy leaf was cut away, its energy field image on the photographic plate remained whole long afterward. This may help explain what surgeons describe as "phantom limb" syndrome, when people continue to feel sensations from an arm or leg after it has been amputated. Perhaps in their electromagnetic "aura," people retain a whole body after a limb is cut off. The effect is different from the slower disease process that appears initially to invade through weak points in our energy field, thereby impairing our body's natural immune defenses, so that physical germs, often routinely present, become a health hazard.

What does Kirlian photography have to do with our "mass dreams" of the future and a possible Apocalyptic spirit running around in our culture today? In my opinion two things stand out. First, in areas dealing with the interconnections between physical and nonphysical realities, our space-age technology is beginning to show us that many "unscientific" traditional and esoteric concepts mask actual, ongoing processes affecting both our physical and emotional well-being. Therefore, we ought to look at what such traditional sources have predicted for our immediate future and how today's material conditions relate to the wider cosmos of Time and Space. My research into traditional prophecies has shown that many predict significant changes within the next quarter century.

Second, the evidence from Kirlian photography suggests that our physical well-being reflects the vitality of an invisible energy field (aura) around our bodies. This energy field is in turn affected by our most deeply held emotions. If this is true for individuals, it may very well apply to humanity as a species or even, by analogy, to the entire planet. This is less farfetched than it may seem at first glance. Our ancestors long considered "Mother Earth" or "Mother Nature" as a single, living entity. Today's astrophysicists recognize that the Earth is surrounded by an invisible electromagnetic field, which controls our climate and other life-sustaining conditions. Biologists and ecologists are more and more recognizing the unified, interdependent nature of life on this small ball of dirt hurtling through space like a rocketship. Contemporary theorists such as James Lovelock (*The Ages of Gaia*: Norton, 1988) and Peter Russell (*The Global Brain*: BM Noetics, 1988) argue that the Earth forms a single living organism of which we human beings are but one part. Their "Gaia hypothesis" suggests that the very planet we live on is an evolving being with its own ecological needs and priorities.

If a species or planetary consciousness does exist, then today's subconscious premonitions of impending catastrophes, as shown by this research, may mirror collective unspoken fears that only drastic, dramatic change can solve our current world order's many thorny problems. Even worse, the unexamined existence of this hidden mass Apocalyptic spirit may actually be pushing us unknowingly toward a future crisis which most of us would consciously desire to avoid were we aware of the process. This is one reason I feel it is vital to share the results of Helen's and my findings as widely as possible today while there still may be time to do something about them. It is only by facing our deeply programmed fears of disaster and choosing more hopeful alternatives that we can strengthen our overall collective human energy field and achieve the predicted forthcoming and required changes in planetary conditions in a healthier, more positive manner.

Helen Wambach felt there was an additional factor relating traditional prophecies about our near future to the condition of the Earth's "biomagnetic" aura. She was convinced that many of the upcoming natural upheavals foreseen by myself and her other subjects will be the result of a quickening of the vibration of Earth's energy field itself, regardless of human material or spiritual activity. They therefore must be recognized and accepted. Humanity can help minimize the physical damage by being prepared and by helping those most directly affected as the difficulties unfold.

Helen argued that the Earth and the solar system are spiraling through Time and Space in vast cycles, each of which lasts from 25,000 to 26,000 years. At two opposite points of these spiraling circuits we enter a sector of material reality bathed in cosmic rays, which increase the Earth's rate of detectable electromagnetic energy when we come into contact with them. This process is cumulative and requires several decades to become noticeable.

One of its first effects, however, will be to heat up the Earth's magnetic core, causing increased geophysical upheavals such as volcanoes and earthquakes. These will cause the much-feared global disasters that will reduce the planet's population. Eventually this energy shift to what Helen called "beyond the ultraviolet" will modify the energy fields of all of Earth's living organisms, including humanity, favoring the spread of psychic powers such as telepathy. Only those organisms that can adapt to such higher vibratory rates will survive in material form.

Helen Wambach readily admitted that she had no hard scientific evidence behind this future scenario, which, nonetheless, she felt was already beginning to take place. She told me that most of the ideas had been transmitted to her psychically during a profound near-death experience she had had while undergoing her heart valve bypass surgery. She clinically "died" twice on the operating table. It was while in these out-of-body states and later in a couple of profound 2:00 A.M. meditations in her Pinole, California, home that she was "shown" energy patterns entering the Earth at faster than ultraviolet speeds.

It would be easier to ignore Helen Wambach's rather fanciful idea that a progressive planetary energy shift is already in progress today if it were not echoed by other sources, both traditional and contemporary. As we shall see in the next chapter, the concept that human history moves in vast Time cycles, each of which lasts approximately 26,000 years, forms the basis for humanity's oldest known science—astronomic astrology. Our distant ancestors were aware of what we call the "Precession of the Equinoxes" and appeared to place a special emphasis on a series of catastrophes that most likely occurred between 12,500 and 13,000 years ago halfway around what is known as the "Great Tropical Year." This period also marked what modern scientists now believe was the end of Earth's most recent ice age. Some paleontologists also claim to have found recent evidence of at least local prehistoric disasters around 26,000 years ago, around the period when modern, Cro-Magnon man replaced his Neanderthal cousins.[2]

Contemporary psychic sources, most of which I doubt were familiar to Helen, also cite our solar system's current entry into new energy fields as among the reasons for a predicted shifting of the poles in the next few decades. The most fascinating of these accounts appears in *Through the Curtain* (De Voss, 1983), Dr. Shafica Karagulla's story of a series of educational out-of-body "night classes" experienced by her close friend Viola Petitt Neal, Ph.D., during the 1960s. As recounted by this experienced neuropsychiatrist, Ms. Neal, a philosophy teacher, found herself remembering having participated in several out-of-body "seminars" taught by discarnate spirits during her sleep. The subject matter ranged from developing psychic abilities, such as telepathy, to nuclear physics. Much of the material involved future predictions.

Gradually, Ms. Neal trained herself to maintain a dual state of awareness while still asleep. She could then summarize each class's content out loud while her consciousness remained out of her body. Dr. Karagulla thus was able to tape-record some of her friend's accounts directly while copying down remembered summaries of other similar "night classes." Several of these sessions, recorded in 1962–63 but not published until 1983 (i.e., after Helen Wambach's near-death experience!) discussed upcoming Earth changes in terms strikingly similar to those Helen used when telling me of her own out-of-body experiences. The following quotation from a November 16, 1963, "class" called "Cosmic Energies and Their Effect on Planet Earth," summarizes the basic story:[3]

> At this time, the solar system is moving through a new area in space where great cosmic streams and tides affect the sun and all the planets, first of all on the physical level. This has happened before in the time of Atlantis, approximately 25,000 years ago. These changes come in cycles of about 24,000 years [sic]. It is a cosmic spiral and cycle difficult for man to identify because he has not been able to span in his awareness such vast reaches of time. . . .

> These radiations will raise the frequency of the planet and affect consciousness. The actual substance, physical, astral and mental, is even at the present moment being raised. This means that the vehicles of expression for the human kingdom will of necessity be built of substance of a higher frequency. Therefore, automatically those Egos—or Souls—at a lower state of evolution will be unable to reincarnate.

> This will mean that for several thousand years those of a more evolved level will come into incarnation. Perhaps for the rest of this planetary life wave.

While it is not necessary to accept every detail of either Helen's or Viola Petitt Neal's account, their overall similarity is especially striking in light of the fact that neither one was aware of the other's existence. I was only introduced to *Through the Curtain* myself when a remarkable young American healer from Hawaii visited me in Paris in July 1988. This same basic idea, that the Earth is currently entering a new "energy zone," has also been expressed by channel Jane Robert's "Seth" entity in the 1970s and more recently by Ken Carey in *The Starseed Transmissions*.[4] It is clearly an idea that is becoming a part of our current "mass dream" about the forthcoming dawn of a New Age here on Earth, an era that has been anticipated with both hope and dread since the start of our current cycle of recorded human history.

* 3 *
Hunting for the Future, an Ancient Tradition

A burning desire to understand, predict and control the future has inspired the human race since history's dawn. Originating long before the organized keeping of written records, oral traditions and pictures on cave walls survive to tell us of our ancestors' attempts to fathom the mysteries of Time. Trying to anticipate our future position in Time's ever-flowing stream, and thereby hopefully improve it, has always been a uniquely human endeavor. It is one of the few things that has set us apart from the surrounding animal kingdom.

On this planet at least, only human beings question their origins and fate, seeking to expand their horizons beyond immediate material well-being and instinctive racial survival. Throughout history, in all corners of the world, men and women have taken time to ponder the nature of creation, life's first stirrings and the future lot of the universe. And from the beginning they have looked to the heavens for the answers. Both ancient spiritual authorities and modern astrophysicists share the assumption that events affecting our current fortunes began happening before this planet, Earth, that cosmic dust mote we call home, was formed. Further, both agree that any real grasp of the future depends on accurately understanding the past.

How did it all start? When we consider that the Earth we stand on is only one small planet, revolving around a rather ordinary type of star in a remote sector of this huge galaxy, the Milky Way, which is itself only one of billions of galaxies all speeding through the universe at a fantastic clip, we can only experience awe at the incredible circumstances that have led to our current conditions.

Is this existence merely the result of chance, the accidental union of countless bits of autonomous matter into the pattern of "things as they are"? Did it start with stuff just drifting aimlessly about across Time and Space? Or, instead, are we part of a larger plan, an ordered scheme of things, some kind of superdrama whose overall budget and proportions would make even a Hollywood producer blush?

If we accept the idea that such an interdependent and organized phenomenon as the material universe we inhabit is unlikely to have resulted from pure chance, then we are inevitably drawn into further questions about its origins and eventual fate. In what context does the unfolding of this drama we know as Time or history occur? Do the actors take an independent, co-creating role? Or are they more like puppets, whose thoughts and actions reflect the pulling of hidden strings? Furthermore, is there a fixed and final conclusion to this play? Is the future predestined, either relatively or absolutely? Or does this story, as a total work, transcend the boundaries of Time and Space within which all the intervening material drama takes place?

Any inquiry into these questions ultimately leads to looking at the character of Time itself. What is the nature of Time? Is it strictly linear, always moving from an unalterable past toward an unknowable future, or is it somehow circular, turning back in on itself, so that things are endlessly repeated in an "eternal return"? The debate over the nature of Time, crucial to any discussion of prophecy and future prediction, has animated philosophers for millennia because it has profound implications for how humanity views itself and its role in the unfolding of the universe.

On the one hand, our everyday observations of Time reveal an unmistakable linear character concerning the immediate future at least. No intelligent person believes that each action he or she takes at any given moment will duplicate itself indefinitely, thereby sticking him or her in an endless repetition, halting all progress. We expect tomorrow to be different from today and plan accordingly. The fact that tomorrow's events always arise fresh and new for us is a source of hope for those who expect something better from the future. Our common sense also rejects the notion that specific historical events clone themselves identically. No one seriously expects a duplicate George Washington to refight the American Revolution any time soon. We reject with horror the idea that atrocities like the Spanish Inquisition, Nazi holocaust or Khmer Rouge genocide will be exactly replayed in human history.

At the same moment that we deny a near-term identical "eternal return" of past events, however, we continue to depend on circular Time daily. We unthinkingly presume the infinite repetition of basic cosmic and physical phenomena such as the Earth's revolving around the Sun, the Moon's regulating the tides and gravity's producing weight and holding things together. Our future plans require the predictability of the basic forces of nature. If everything were always totally new and different from instant to instant, the universe would revert to chaos. Life as we know it would be impossible.

Thus, in our commonsense wisdom, we live in a hybrid kind of Time. For us Time reveals itself as cyclical, but sharing both linear and circular properties. Psychologically, experiencing Time as moving in cycles or spirals provides us with hope, for it ties future consequences to present-day activity. Viewed cyclically, Time creates the possibility of cause and effect, that basic foundation of all human morality. Cause and effect, known in New Age circles by the Sanskrit word *karma*, can only exist if Time revolves as a forward-moving spiral. If everything under the Sun isn't eternally new but is somehow determined by what has already happened, then we can hope to influence our future favorably by our current actions. If the past returns in the future, not identically or unchangedly, but in a modified form based on what has happened in between, then we mere mortals, passing actors on this earthly stage, suddenly become far more important. We become responsible for our future, for it is an amalgam of our past and present.

Great prophecy depends on this combination because it is ever destined to serve as a warning. The Biblical prophets have always presented either a picture of a modifiable future, provided current deficiencies are corrected, or an unavoidable future that will result because past warnings were not heeded in time.

The prophet Isaiah, for example, at first foretells an early death for Judah's weak and wavering King Hezekiah, whose kingdom has already been saved once by divine intervention against the Assyrians. But following the king's sincere repentance and supplication of Yahweh (the Lord), the Biblical prophet revises his gloomy forecast, announcing that fifteen more years have been added to Hezekiah's reign. Shortly thereafter, however, the self-assured king boastfully displays his extensive collection of gold and silver trophies to emissaries of another potential enemy, the king of Babylon. The king's misplaced pride leads Isaiah again to predict Judah's downfall. This time the prophetic sentence is without appeal, although its execution is delayed until the next generation (Isaiah 37–39).

The great prophets of classical antiquity also warned humanity through their reading of the future. Their prophecies reveal the all too human trait of overconfident pride as well, so that most admonitions to change were ignored. For the ancient Greek poet Homer, the tragedy of Cassandra, the Trojan prophetess, was that although her dire predictions were consistently accurate, no one listened to her while there was yet time to avert disaster. Her warnings therefore took on the character of the workings of implacable fate.

Perhaps the most famous ancient prophecy, which, while apparently avoidable, proved all too accurate, was that of the Roman diviner Spurinna Vestritius, who told Julius Caesar that "a great danger" awaited him around the Ides of March (March 15, 44 B.C.). According to the Roman historian Suetonius, Spurinna issued his prediction some time ahead, as a warning to the ambitious leader. The two men later met in the street on that fateful day. A scoffing Caesar derided the sage, saying that the Ides of March had come and he was feeling fine.[1]

"Yes," Spurinna is said to have replied, "but they [the Ides of March] are not yet gone."

Shortly thereafter the overconfident Caesar was assassinated on the steps of the Forum by his supposed friends Cassius and Brutus. He too had failed to heed the prophet's warning and so was caught in Time's web of cause and effect, or *karma*.

Perhaps the best description of cyclical Time belongs to the nineteenth-century German philosopher Georg F. Hegel.[2] He described man's Time perception as that of someone slowly climbing a winding mountain path. Imagine, he said, a cone-shaped mountain rising from a flat plain. A spiral pathway winds around the mountain from its base toward its peak. As one climbs up the mountain one necessarily returns to the same side again and again, although each time from a slightly higher level.

Consequently, the traveler whose gaze is fixed on the plain below will periodically see the same landmarks return to view, cycle after cycle, while he who looks only straight down at the path ahead will continually see new ground in front of him. For the former it may take generations to realize that although the same landmarks reappear, they do so from a new, higher perspective each time, implying that Time is progressive, not eternally repetitious. He who sees only the ground immediately ahead may never realize that in fact his path is marked by prior similar experiences. The wise man will understand that his progress up the mountain may be predicted and assisted by carefully observing both the periodic return of specific major landmarks below and the roughness or smoothness of the pathway currently being walked.

The same obviously applies to the student of future predictions. While remaining ever aware of the newness of each turn of Time's wheel, it is important to review what former sages have correctly predicted and to compare their landmarks with those currently in view. It is thus that one becomes aware of just how cyclical human history really has been despite clear evidence of cultural progress as well.

Our most distant forefathers were well aware of the cyclical nature of Time. Armed with carefully preserved records and surprisingly sophisticated measuring devices, they looked to the heavens for help in solving life's problems. To an extent hard to appreciate today, Earth's ancient civilizations depended intimately on the periodic renewal of celestial phenomena, the apparent rotation of the stars and planets around our Earth. The ruins of ancient astronomical observatories are among the oldest surviving relics of humanity, often dating back over 5,000 years. Scattered over the entire face of the Earth, these neolithic stone monuments attest to the importance our distant ancestors placed on accurate knowledge about the appearance and activities of specific star and planetary systems. England's well-known Stonehenge circle, estimated at nearly 4,000 years old by antiquities expert John Mitchell in *The New View Over Atlantis*, is the remnants of just one of these astronomical observatories of remote antiquity.[3]

All ancient cultures honored those star-gazing "magi" who as experienced astronomers could predict the appearance of specific celestial phenomena and as astrologers could interpret their influence on society. Even the Bible, despite a warning against overreliance on or pagan use of such techniques as astrology or divination, cites the arrival of the three Wise Men at Bethlehem as evidence of the supernatural nature of the advent of Jesus.

Evidence from dozens of ancient civilizations clearly indicates that this interest in the heavens was not just superstitious or meteorological in terms of crop plantings and harvests. Our ancestors were convinced that the planets and stars represented divine forces which personally intervened in human history. Humanity's oldest religious traditions clearly divide prehistory into the era of celestial gods and goddesses, when such superhuman interventions were commonplace, and more recent times when human priests and kings assumed divine prerogatives, acting as regents or substitutes for their absent celestial masters.

Moreover, virtually all such traditions predict the eventual return of that Golden Age when the gods directly controlled the destiny of the world. It was believed that the heavens themselves would reveal the signs and portents of that return just as the observed daily revolution of the Sun and annual cycles of the starry constellations acted as reminders and guarantees of that distant promise.

Thus, from our earliest days, human beings have focused their attention on the skies and devised ways to chart and record celestial activities across a band that came to be known as the "zodiac." The origins of the zodiac are lost in the mists of Time. Various experts have attributed its invention to several different ancient cultures but none have convincingly shown that their version was the original. The Phoenicians, Mesopotamians or Chaldeans, Egyptians, Indians and Chinese all had quite similar zodiacs, indicating a possible common ancestor. Pre-Columbian cultures in the Americas shared the belief in heavenly intervention in human prehistory and also had intricate circular zodiac and calendar charts although their patterns and signs differed from those in Europe and Asia.

The term "zodiac" itself derives from the classical Greek word *zodiacos*, which means "a circle of little animals." Some occultists trace the term back further to two early Egyptian radicals, *zo* and *on*, meaning "life" and "being." Both roots may be correct, for while our forefathers believed the stars represent living divine powers, from ancient times the constellations making up the zodiac have been represented by a variety of human and animal figures, each with specific symbolism. Thus, for example, the sign Cancer is symbolized by a crab, while its neighbor Leo is represented by a lion.[4]

The star configurations that make up the zodiac occupy a specific band of the sky, which, viewed from the Earth's surface, seems to revolve around our planet. In measuring this band astronomically, one starts from the Sun's apparent terrestrial "orbit." Our closest star describes a huge ellipse around the Earth, tilted at 23 degrees 28 minutes from the belt of the Earth's equator. This orbit is known as the "ecliptic." All of the known planets of the solar system trace their apparent terrestrial orbits within a band on either side of the solar orbit. This band, which is just under 17 degrees wide, is what we call the "zodiac." All the constellations that are represented as human and animal figures in the daily horoscope are visible within this band of 17 degrees around the solar ecliptic.[5]

Traditionally the zodiac has been divided into twelve sectors of 30 degrees each to form a perfect 360-degree circle. Each sector is assigned a specific representative, the twelve "signs" of the zodiac. As the Earth moves around the Sun, these signs succeed each other across the night sky. Because the zodiac's ecliptic is tilted in relationship to the Earth's equator, their two planes coincide only twice each year. These two points, where the Sun's apparent orbit is equidistant from the Earth's north and south celestial poles, are known as the two equinoxes because they mark those two points when the Sun sets directly west and hours of sunlight are equal to those of darkness. The vernal equinox (March 21–22) is the beginning of spring when the daylight hours once again outdistance those of night in the northern hemisphere. Symbolized by Aries the Ram, it was chosen by ancient astrologers, individuals who study the stars' influence on human affairs, as the starting point for each zodiacal year.

The Earth's orbit around the Sun is not its only major cyclical motion. It is matched by the planet's daily rotation on its celestial north–south axis. If either of these two repetitive cycles ceased, physical life as we know it could not survive here. Earth's rotation is not, however, perfectly symmetrical. Our planet wobbles around its axis, generating a circular tilt in reference to the heavens. This rotational irregularity creates another significant earthly Time cycle often referred to as the "Precession of the Equinoxes."

As viewed from Earth's surface, the Sun makes its annual revolution through the twelve signs of the zodiac, returning to its original sign with each vernal equinox. However, because the Earth's rotation tilts our planet's celestial north–south axis in a slow-moving circle of its own, like a wobbling top, the Sun falls a little short of making a complete 360-degree circuit of the heavens during one solar year. As a result, with each vernal equinox it crosses the equator slightly behind the place in the zodiac where it crossed in the preceding year. Thus, at each vernal equinox, the positions of the zodiac's constellations appear to have moved slightly backward. The equinox seems to be moving slowly in the opposite direction from the Sun's motion through the zodiac's twelve signs, forming an opposing cycle. It marks the extremely slow but inexorable reorientation of the Earth's celestial north–south axis, the planet's spinal column in a certain sense, from one pole star to another.

This cycle moves extremely slowly, for it takes the Sun approximately seventy-two years to lose one degree. As each sign of the zodiac contains 30 degrees, it requires about 2,160 years for the equinoxes to shift from one constellation, or sign, to its predecessor. An entire circuit of the zodiac, one complete "wobble" of this rotating Earth with respect to the constellations, thus requires nearly 25,920 years to complete. Put another way, it will be around 26,000 years before the constellations observable on any given night from Earth will return to their same positions on that same date.

This majestic Time wheel, called the "Great Cycle" by Dane Rudhyar, one of this century's most respected astrologers, is known as the "Great Tropical Year." Other traditional sources cite 25,827 years for this cycle or 2,152 years per astrological sign. Due to minor periodic fluctuations in the Earth's rotation, an exact figure is not known. The most widely adopted figures are 2,160 years for each sign and 25,920 for the Great Tropical Year.[6]

The 2,160-year periods during which the vernal equinox occurs within each specific sign represent the Earth's "Ages." According to long-standing astrological usage, each Age is distinguished by the characteristics of the animal symbolizing its zodiacal sign. Further, those who interpret the stars have long predicted important changes in human history each time the vernal equinox crosses the border between signs. These changes are thought to be progressively apparent as the border approaches. Thus astrologers usually assign every Age "dawn" and "twilight" periods, each lasting about 10 percent of the Age's total length, or around 216 years. These border periods, called "cusps," often are described as times of conflict between the natures of the two Ages when some characteristics of each Age manifest themselves at the same time.

Like any completed circular form, the Great Tropical Year has no natural starting or ending point. How can you tell where a circle begins? Every point along its circumference is identical. Thus, like the solar year, which Westerners customarily begin on January 1, or the zodiac, which astrologers conventionally initiate at the vernal equinox, the start of a Great Tropical Year is the product of an arbitrary selection process. Esoteric traditions, based on ancient Greek and Egyptian sources, have set the beginning of the Great Cycle at the point where the constellation of Leo marked the vernal equinox in the Earth's northern hemisphere, between 12,500 and 13,000 years ago. Although the exact reasons behind this choice have been lost, it is certain that the event must have been marked by impressive cosmological circumstances to have so affected our distant ancestors that they have kept that tradition alive for so many generations.

One ancient alchemist, Julius Maternus, said the Greek god Mercury (Hermes) disclosed that the sign Leo marked the creation of the world.[7] This is all the more intriguing when one realizes that the planetary representative of Leo is the Sun, whose creation led to the formation of the rest of our solar system. Furthermore, the oldest known astrological sky

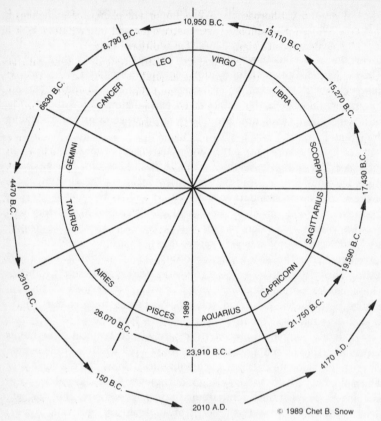

**"The Great Tropical Year
and the Zodiac"**

chart, copied on the ceiling of the Egyptian temple at Dendera in about the third century B.C., depicts the ancient heavens as they were visible when Leo marked the vernal equinox in the northern hemisphere some 12,500 years ago.[8] Could this, therefore, have been the lost Golden Age, the Age of the Gods? And, if it was, what is its relevance to ancient and present-day prophecy about the future?

Although it may be premature to identify the Age of Leo definitively with that of the Golden Age of the Gods, its relevance to prophecies about our present situation is easier to understand. Any student of astrology knows that the influence of the heavens always works in opposition pairs.

Thus, if one's natal horoscope reveals important planetary influences in the sign Aries, for example, a wise astrologer will immediately look in its 180-degree opposite sign, Libra, for additional data.

Further, heliocentric astrologers, whose predictions take into account not the sky's apparent revolving around the Earth but our planet's actual fact of orbiting the Sun, understand that whatever sign the Sun appears to be in at the moment, viewed from the Earth, its *actual* astronomical position *vis-à-vis* the Earth is exactly 180 degrees opposite, that is to say in the opposite sign. This is due to the circular nature of the Earth's orbit around the Sun. Where we place the Sun in the heavens, as seen from the Earth's surface, is in fact directly opposite (180 degrees) from where an observer on the Sun would place the Earth at the same moment. A heliocentric astrological calculation assumes that one observes the heavens from our star, not our planet. These are only two basic examples of what is a well-known astrological truth: The heavens' influences in human affairs operate like mirror images.[9]

How does this concern the future? Presently, as we near the end of the twentieth century after Jesus Christ, the vernal equinox is on the verge of passing out of the zodiac sign of Pisces, the Fish, into its predecessor, Aquarius, the water (or energy) spout. Because the boundaries of the star constellations that mark the 30-degree zodiac signs are arbitrary, and because the specific date of the Great Cycle's beginning is lost, astrologers can only approximate the exact year when we leave Pisces and enter 0 degrees of Aquarius at the vernal equinox. Dane Rudhyar estimates that this will happen in the year 2060 A.D. Other astrology works consulted have given 1950, 1999, 2030 and 2112 A.D. as the crossing point.[10] Scientists at the prestigious French Institut Géographique National have stated that the year 2010 A.D. marks the actual astronomical passage.[11] This can be considered the most accurate date. In any case, all contemporary astrologers agree that whatever the actual "zero degree" point, we are already well into the "twilight" of the Piscean Age with the Age of Aquarius about to dawn.

What does this have to do with the Golden Age of Leo, the Sun? Just the fact that Aquarius is the sign 180 degrees across the zodiacal circle from Leo. The Aquarian Age is therefore the celestial opposite of the Age of Leo. Hence, according to astrology, the two are vitally related. That is why for so long esoterics and New Age prophets have insisted on the radical character of the changes coming with the "dawning of the Age of Aquarius." The coming Aquarian Age is to be the mirror image —just how we don't yet know—of the fabled lost Golden Age of the Sun.

And if that Age was ushered in between twelve and thirteen thousand years ago with such awesome celestial and terrestrial happenings that humanity has preserved its memory in our oldest myths and oral traditions, then what can we expect as we prepare to move around the halfway point of the Great Year's cycle in just a few decades?

Before turning to what Edgar Cayce, one of the twentieth century's most accurate psychics, has said about the special character of the coming decades, as we slip into the Aquarian Age, let us look at what some ancient seers had to say about the different Ages of humanity and the cycles of Earth's history. There is also important testimony from the Great Pyramid at Giza, Egypt, to consider. As we shall see, experts who have studied the Pyramid mathematically feel that it is a calendar in stone, marking key historical epochs from 2600 B.C. to 4000 A.D.

Lord Acton, a British statesman of the last century, authored the famous saying that those who do not learn from history are doomed to repeat it. And in fact history does seem to repeat itself frequently when looked at in retrospect. The record shows that many, many World Ages and great civilizations have met violent ends from natural or human causes. The legends of virtually every known ancient culture bear witness to periodic major catastrophes, often so devastating that only myths and legends about preceding times survived. The Polynesians, for example, list nine succeeding creations and destructions in the Pacific, covering hundreds of thousands of years. The Chinese mention ten vanished ages (called Kis) from the world's beginning to the present "age of Confucius." Other Eurasian sources, including the Persians, Tibetans, and Etruscans, frequently mention seven perished epochs, each with a different sky configuration.[12]

In the Americas virtually all pre-Columbian cultures report a minimum of three vanished worlds and human races, ours being the fourth. The Aztecs and Mayas refer to four previous earthly civilizations, all of which disappeared in natural catastrophes. Among the most developed of these cosmogonies is that of the Hopi of the American Southwest. The Hopi are a small peace-loving tribe living in a series of pueblos near the "Four Corners," where the states of Arizona, Utah, Colorado and New Mexico meet. They consider their land and very existence as a people sacred.

According to Hopi teachings, as recorded in the 1960s by Frank Waters in *The Book of the Hopi*, the universal creator spirit was known as Taiowa. Taiowa means "The Infinite" in the Hopi tongue. The concept corresponds to the Hindu universal god Brahm. At the start of Creation, from Taiowa, "The Infinite," sprang forth "The Finite" or Sotukuang, the first manifested being and equivalent to the Hindus' Brahma. Taiowa also established Tokpela, meaning "the endless space."[13]

Through Sotukuang, whom the Hopi considered Taiowa's "nephew," a way of indicating nonsexual parentage, Tokpela (Space) assumed material form via the elements of water, wind and atmosphere. Then, in order to give material reality life, Sotukuang fashioned a female helper, Kokyangwuti, or Spider Woman. She created four human races, black, yellow, red and white, from spittle and clay. Sotukuang gave them a language, intelligence and the capacity to reproduce. In turn they agreed to recognize Mother Earth as their living relative and cherish it, living on it in peace and harmony.

Unfortunately, this primal Eden did not last forever, as rivalries erupted among the different races. Lies and jealousies, fostered by birds and serpent creatures, led to illness and dissensions. Mankind forgot its creator and stopped respecting Mother Earth. Sotukuang regretted his having created humanity and resolved to eliminate it. He agreed, however, to save those few who remained faithful, the Hopi's ancestors. He led them underground to a refuge through an anthill. Then he destroyed the first world by fire and volcanoes. According to the Hopi, he literally turned it inside out, making land where there had been oceans and vice versa.

Tokpa, the second world created through Sotukuang, was wide and flat. The Hopi's ancestors emerged and lived in harmony at first as this time they had telepathic abilities. A village system grew up and with it commerce. This proved Tokpa's undoing, for trade created material greed in the people. This led to social inequality and warfare. Again, most people forgot to honor their creators or the Earth and were ripe for destruction. The small pure remnant was taken to safety in the anthill as before. This time Sotukuang tilted the Earth's axis, calling on the poles to reverse themselves. The Earth's orbit swung wildly and it rolled over twice, freezing the planet in an icy shroud.

Nonetheless, Sotukuang intervened once more, creating the third world, known as Kuskurza, and settling it with Tokpa's survivors. An urban civilization quickly flourished, with important cities and a sophisticated technology. Telepathy, however, had disappeared. This time it would seem that sex was behind humanity's downfall, for an "evil woman" used it as a political weapon that led to a world war, including fierce air battles fought from flying "shields of hides" (the closest Hopi words for aircraft). When the war threatened to destroy the Earth itself, Sotukuang again acted against the majority of wicked humans. Having hidden his faithful followers in hollow reeds, he flooded the Earth in a great deluge. The survivors had to use the reeds as boats until dry land appeared.

Our present fourth Earth is Tuwaqachi for the Hopi. The name means "world completed." Their surviving ancestors were guided to the southwestern mesa areas by a "guardian" spirit, Masaw, whom they say settled them there as it was sacred ground. This territory will remain safe even if the fourth world is destroyed, as long as the Hopi maintain their traditional rites and ceremonies and honor the dignity of the Earth.

According to Hopi prophecies, though, Tuwaqachi is not the Earth's final form. Their entire creation cycle includes seven successive human worlds or civilizations (plus two heavenly ones). By their reckoning, therefore, we have three more worldwide disasters yet to come. In fact, their most honored seers state that signs of the fifth world's advent are already noticeable today to those who observe the Earth and its minute life forms closely. This may reflect, in very different language, the influx of new cosmic energies into the Earth discerned by the late Helen Wambach and discussed by Dr. Karagulla in *Through the Curtain*.[14]

The Hopi consider present times as highly critical in determining the fate of our fourth world, Tuwaqachi. One of their most important prophecies was carved on a rock cliff in the Black Mesa of Arizona around the time of Jesus, some 2,000 years ago. The meaning of this ancient petroglyph has been described in detail by Sun Bear, a Chippewa medicine man who studied with Hopi elders and who currently lectures around the world, attempting to convince people that we must stop misusing natural resources for destructive purposes such as armaments and wars. He is convinced that Hopi prophecies and those of other Native American traditions that honor the Earth are vitally relevant for both today and the near future.

According to Sun Bear's *The Bear Tribe's Self Reliance Book*, the Hopi petroglyph depicts the Great Spirit pointing to two divergent historical paths across this era. An upper path denotes that followed by our white culture and those Native Americans who adopt Western ways. A lower path marks that of Hopi spiritual traditions. At one point the two paths are linked by a vertical slash, which Hopi elders interpret as marking the arrival of European settlers. Shortly afterward two large circles represent the First and Second World Wars when conflict circled the entire Earth.[15]

A bit farther along the petroglyph a third circle marks what the Hopi call the "Great Day of Purification," marking earthly upheavals and the return of the Great Spirit. After this event the upper, modern, western path zigzags a short way before fading out, while the lower, Hopi spiritual path blossoms into the next, fifth world.

Hopi elders interpret this as a definite sign that our current civilization, following the upper path, is heading into trouble. They flatly predict that unless current superpower policies change drastically, a new world war will break out within the next quarter century, decimating those nations that have lost themselves in rampant materialism and that are fast exhausting the Earth's natural resources. This conflict marks the Great Day of Purification, for the Earth will then be purged by fire.[16]

The Hopi elders, like most truly great prophets, do not predict that this "great purification" is unavoidable, at least not yet. According to their legends, before the purging fires come again, Sotukuang will send a messenger called "Pahana," the "True White Brother," to make a last appeal to the nations to change their ways. Pahana will appear in a "light from the East," bearing certain signs and part of a broken Hopi religious tablet and accompanied by two companions (or groups of people). If enough people, led by the Hopi themselves, agree to restore traditional ways of caring for the Earth and for their fellowman, the global calamity can be averted. Sun Bear echoes this message. Since 1970 he and his white American wife have formed the Bear Tribe, the continent's first deliberately interracial tribe, headquartered near Spokane, Washington.[17]

Like most Native American prophecies, the Hopi predictions include several highlights marking the trail leading to the Great Day of Purification. Among those that Sun Bear considers already accomplished are the laying of a "silver thread" across the land (U.S. Highway 66, which goes from St. Louis to Los Angeles) and the building of "spider webs in the sky" through which "people will walk" (telegraph, telephone and electric lines and television transmitters).[18]

A dramatic and unexpected confirmation of an ancient Hopi prophecy came in 1969 when from the Moon's surface Apollo astronaut Neil Armstrong announced, "The Eagle has landed." Centuries earlier the Hopi had been told to expect "the eagle to walk on the Moon" shortly before the end of the fourth world. According to the same prophecy, a "house in space" would be our modern civilization's final major achievement before the Great Day of Purification. It is unclear whether this indicates the already built American space shuttles and Soviet Soyuz space lab or a yet-to-come orbiting space station. Regardless, this accomplishment is not very far away.

Among the special signs predicted to occur very shortly before the dawn of the new world cycle is the appearance in the sky of a large blue star, symbolized by the dancing of a special "Blue Star" Kachina (a masked, costumed traditional dancer) during Hopi ceremonies in their sacred plaza at Oraibi, Arizona. The 1981 discovery of a very distant but extraordinarily massive blue star over 3,500 times the size of our Sun and the largest star ever discovered may signal the fulfillment of this prophecy.[19] Sun Bear believes it refers to the 1985 descent of the U.S. ill-fated Sky Lab satellite, which emitted a distinct bluish glow when it fell into northern Canada.

Other students of the Hopi prophecies have associated the dancing of the "Blue Star" Kachina with the August 1987 "Harmonic Convergence" celebrations, although that has never been officially confirmed. In any case, this date and event were given special significance in Hopi lands. Hopi elders predicted that during the weekend of August 16–17, 1987, 144,000 people around the world would "dance in honor of the sun" and open themselves to a new awareness of the Oneness of all life. As a participant in that event, along with a few close friends, at a rural retreat center in southern France, I can personally attest to the powerful energies present.

Since the 1960s a group of traditional Hopi elders have been trying to address the United Nations with a disarmament proposal they claim could avert nuclear war. Denied the right to speak to the U.N.'s special session on disarmament in June 1982, they nonetheless submitted written proposals to that body. In those proposals they reiterated the crux of their prophecies, including one from Masaw, the "guardian" spirit in this world, who said that when a "gourd of ashes" would be dropped on the Earth great loss of life would follow and that the end of the "materialist way of life" would soon occur. Some of the Hopi have interpreted this to mean Hiroshima and Nagasaki. Others maintain that it represents a possible scenario for a nuclear World War III holocaust.[20]

Throughout their history the Hopi have been enjoined to maintain their ancient rituals and ceremonies as proof of their spiritual purity. Today their small tribe is badly split between "modernists," who want to exploit mineral resources on Hopi land for tribal profit, and "traditionalists," who see this as another proof of man's growing disrespect for Mother Earth. The struggle is seen by some as one more sign that Sotukuang will soon intervene once more to cleanse the planet of its troublesome human burden.

While this may sound to some like the picturesque folklore of a "primitive" people, designed to explain away its inevitable losing clash with modern civilization, recent archaeological discoveries ought to make us look twice at what the Hopi elders are telling us about the past and potential future of our hemisphere at least. In the last twenty years independent archaeological digs in Peru, Mexico and Arizona have uncovered physical evidence of a series of sudden Earth changes down to levels of over sixty feet deep. At each of these sites scientists have found superimposed layers of volcanic ash, glacial alluviations and muddy clay sediments separated by "ordinary soil," convincingly showing the order of the successive disasters. The latest of these cataclysms was obviously massive flooding, just as the Hopi proclaim. Furthermore, although the Hopi do not offer a precise date for this last world cataclysm, according to *The Bear Tribe's Self Reliance Book*, their elders estimate it happened sometime over 10,000 years ago—which puts it around the time of that mysterious zodiacal Age of Leo.[21]

The Hopi account of Earth's most recent "cleansing" by a great flood, which a lucky few survived in reed boats, concurs remarkably with the Bible's account of Noah and the Deluge. Moreover, as anthropologists have discovered, ancient records unanimously agree that within the human race's prehistorical memory the Earth was swept with raging waters that destroyed existing civilizations, leaving but a human remnant behind when they subsided. Similar traditions of this worldwide catastrophe exist among all peoples of all continents, including Scandinavians, Greeks, Egyptians, Hebrews, Sumerians, Babylonians, Persians, Hindus, Chinese, Fiji Islanders, Eskimos and native North and South Americans. The persistent myths of the fabulous antediluvian cultures of Atlantis and Shamballa stem from these traditions.

Furthermore, in almost every case local legends describe the survival process as one in which a warning of the impending calamity was given to a selected few, most often a single family, who then took steps to save themselves. Present-day humanity is their progeny. An accurate prophetic premonition of disaster therefore lies behind the survival of the direct ancestors of every living human being. You might say that premonition is in our genes! Is it so surprising then that, regardless of our scientific culture and rationalist sophistication, we remain transfixed by the possibility of another worldwide catastrophe in the future?

If there is reasonable physical and anthropological evidence for a great global deluge in our remote past, can we estimate about how long ago it took place? What do traditional and scientific sources say about the causes of this catastrophe? Is it likely to be repeated? These are huge questions and obviously exhaustive answers are beyond the scope of this work. A number of excellent books deal with the subject in detail, including Charles Berlitz's *Doomsday 1999 A.D.* (1981), Zecharia Sitchin's fascinating trilogy *The Earth Chronicles* (1976–85) and John White's *Pole Shift* (1980). These works show that although the evidence of a universal prehistoric Great Flood is overwhelming, as yet no authoritative, universally accepted date or direct cause for such a disaster exists. In light of the Hopi and other ancient sources, it is likely that more than one such global catastrophe has occurred in our distant past.

Despite the absence of a final verdict, recent geological discoveries and interpretations of ancient records have consistently tended to move the Great Flood's date back from those proclaimed by earlier generations. Traditional Western sources, cited throughout the nineteenth century, dated the Deluge according to the Hebrew calendar, which begins in 3760 B.C. Following the list of Adam's descendants as given in Genesis, Biblical scholars estimated the Great Flood as taking place 1,292 years later or around 2468 B.C.. This was its accepted age until twentieth-century anthropologists began deciphering the ancient writings of other contemporary civilizations and discovered that several were flourishing well before that date. These calculations, based on Middle East archaeological digs of the 1920s and 1930s and the anthropological evidence, indicated a date of 4250 B.C. for the Deluge. This date was based on the depth of mud layers found and Babylonian and Egyptian king lists.[22]

Non-Biblical Western sources, the Greek philosophers Plato and Heraclites, had already given significantly earlier estimates of the catastrophe that had inundated the lost continent of Atlantis. In *Timaeus*, Plato relates that Egyptian priests told a famous Greek visitor, Solon, of a fabulous civilization that had "perished beneath the waves" in "a single day and a night" in what was 9560 B.C. by modern dating methods. A century earlier Heraclites had already cited Atlantis in his writings, dating its demise at what was 9614 B.C. However, because Greek culture could only be traced back into the second millennium before Christ, most Western scholars considered these accounts as mere myths. They weren't taken seriously as possible candidates for dating the Biblical Flood.

In recent years, however, two developments have made these dates far more plausible and possibly pushed back the Deluge even further into prehistoric times, back to between 12,500 and 13,000 years ago. The first has been in-depth scientific sampling of the polar ice caps and the Earth's crust, using newly developed drilling techniques. These procedures have given us a far clearer picture of climatic conditions throughout Earth's geologic history than heretofore. They reveal that the planet's last ice age began about 75,000 to 77,000 years ago and not 250,000 years, as had been previously estimated. This most recent glaciated period was divided by a short warming trend after about 35,000 years, which lasted just two or three millennia. Then, around 38,000 years ago a much colder and drier period set in, which ended quite abruptly (in geologic terms) between 10,500 and 11,000 B.C. when our present, relatively mild climate was established. It is noteworthy that this period coincides with beginning of the astrological Age of Leo![23]

The second development was a less biased translation and comparison of ancient Mideastern texts, especially those of the ill-fated Sumerian civilization. This set of Mesopotamian kingdoms, which flourished between 3800 and 2000 B.C., is the oldest human culture whose written records have survived relatively intact. Indeed, amazed archaeologists have been forced by their findings to conclude that it was extensive and advanced from its earliest days. Furthermore, the evidence suggests that the Sumerians were more sophisticated than the group of better-known cultures that succeeded them. It is as if civilization in the ancient Middle East somehow declined rather than advancing in the slow, plodding progress so often presented as the way of history. Moreover, many Sumerian historical epics closely parallel those of the early chapters of the book of Genesis. Sumer has been clearly established as a major contributor to human history. Its impressive list of "firsts" includes the firing of clay in kilns, development of metallurgy, organized writing and record-keeping, law codes, medical treatises, divorce, agriculture and animal husbandry.[24]

Moreover, recent deciphering of ancient Mesopotamian texts has also established that the Sumerians had developed a twelve-sign zodiac several thousand years before the ancient Greeks. Further, the Sumerian term for zodiac, like its Greek descendent, already meant a "shining herd" of animals in the sky. The Sumerians correlated virtually all of their zodiac's twelve signs with the same human and animal symbols as those used by the Chaldeans, Egyptians and Greeks centuries later. Thus, the Sumerians developed astrology as well.[25]

As their civilization flourished between around 3800 and 2000 B.C., the Sumerians naturally emphasized the sign of Taurus, the Bull, whose constellation crossed the Earth's ecliptic at dawn on the vernal equinox during most of this period. Today we begin the zodiacal year with Aries, the Ram, whose sign crossed the vernal equinox during the next two millennia, the Greek and Chaldean era. Our modern zodiac, which also begins with Aries, was derived from those cultures. The Age of Aries was also the era of the Biblical Old Testament with its emphasis on the *shofar*, or ram's horn, and the Passover lamb sacrifice.

Evidence from a Sumerian clay tablet, however, now in the Berlin

museum (number VAT.7847), suggests that although the Sumerians began their zodiacal year in Taurus, they initiated their official list of zodiac
signs not with the Bull but with the sign "UR.GULA," or Leo, the Lion.[26]
Again an ancient source points to the Age of Leo as the origin of one of
humanity's oldest and most useful astronomical and divinatory devices.
The Sumerians apparently were aware of both the precession of the
equinoxes and some remote but extraordinary event in that earlier era
which led them to give the Age of Leo precedence over their own. This
event was, as shall be shown below, in all probability, the Great Flood.

Comparing Sumerian and Biblical stories concerning humanity's origins with the meteorological record, Zecharia Sitchin, a Biblical scholar
and an expert on ancient languages, has discovered significant agreement
among them about the timing of key events in early human history. In
his celebrated trilogy *The Earth Chronicles*, Sitchin argues that, based
on his research, the Earth's last great natural cataclysm, a worldwide
deluge, most likely took place at the end of the last mini-ice age, between
12,500 and 13,000 years ago, or around 10,800 B.C. This would put the
Bible's Great Flood, as we have seen, during the Age of Leo, halfway
around the Great Tropical Year's circle from that of the now-dawning
Aquarius.

A critical part of Zecharia Sitchin's reasoning that leads him to this
conclusion is that the great Flood was not "a single, sudden event, but
the *climax of a chain of events*."[27] He cites both Sumerian sources and
the book of Genesis to show that long before the Great Flood, Earth's
climate had turned harsh and cold and that men were struggling to survive
even in the lush fertile crescent. This was the last mini-ice age. A Sumerian epic poem estimates that the worst of this unpleasant prehistoric
period spanned some 25,000 years, matching the ice-age record from the
brief 38,000 B.C. warm spell to around 12,800 B.C. Later copies of various
Mesopotamian epic historical texts recount humanity's despair when con-
secutive harvests failed. Famine was rampant and the world's population
declined. Some people even reverted to cannibalism.[28]

Does the Bible record provide any parallel account? If one can accept
that mankind's first generations, the pre-Flood patriarchs, lived significantly longer lifetimes than we do, then the answer is yes. Several generations following Adam and Eve's expulsion from the Garden of Eden,
the book of Genesis quotes their descendant Lamech as saying that Yahweh (the Lord) had "cursed" the ground, clearly meaning that the fields
were not producing enough grain. Lamech then named his son Noah, a
word meaning "respite" or "relief," obviously in hopes of better times
ahead (Genesis 5:29).

Could just a few Biblical "generations" have spanned several thousand years (the duration of the last mini-ice age)? It seems impossible to us because modern human beings rarely live to be a hundred years old. However, a number of very ancient sources, including the book of Genesis, Sumerian clay tablets and Egyptian and Hindu legends about the Age of the Gods report that humanity's antediluvian ancestors lived far longer than we do. Thus, for example, all of the Biblical patriarchs from Adam to Noah are reported to have attained lifetimes lasting several centuries. The Biblical longevity record, held by Methuselah, was nearly 1,000 years. Moreover, Sumerian sources, cited by Dr. Sitchin, ascribe lifetimes of several *millennia* to their antediluvian kings! These lists closely parallel those of the Egyptian ruler-gods of pre-pharaonic dynasties such as Ra, Osiris and Horus, who also purportedly reigned for several thousand years each. Ancient Greek and Hindu legends likewise measure the earthly reigns of their gods in terms of millennia, not years and months.[29]

It is in fact probable that early Hebrew scribes underestimated the lifespans of their remote pre-Flood ancestors when committing their tribe's oral legends to writing rather than the other way around! Thus, although it seems fantastic to us, ancient reports make it quite conceivable that the Bible's Lamech and his contemporaries of the eighth generation after Adam either remembered or still had records of the milder, more hospitable climate that had divided the last global ice age several thousand years earlier.

It's also possible that Adam's descendants turned away from worshiping and serving their creator gods (whom the Bible calls the "Elohim," a plural noun in ancient Hebrew) after their appeals for help in restoring more favorable weather failed. The Bible record concerning humanity's early development is extremely abbreviated, but one possible hint about the effects of the climate change may be found in the story of Cain and Abel, where it was Cain's agricultural offering that was rejected, leading to his brutal fratricide (Genesis 4). In punishment, the Bible has the "Lord God" Yahweh (a singular noun in Hebrew, possibly a given name of one of the "Elohim") decree, "When you till the ground, it shall no longer yield to you its strength" (Genesis 4:12).[30] Cain and his descendants, "to the seventh generation" (i.e., until the time of Noah), were then marked by Yahweh (Genesis 4:13–15). Could this "curse" be the Bible's way of representing a long-term series of crop failures spanning several thousand-year "generations"?

Further, shortly thereafter, Genesis 4:26 mentions that during the generation of Adam's grandchildren by his third son, Seth, "men began to call on the name of Yahweh." However, the Bible is silent as to the nature of their requests. Perhaps it was for better weather and less harsh living conditions. We know from the geological data unearthed by modern scientists that the climate worsened from 38,000 to 13,000 B.C. instead of improving. Then, virtually "overnight" by geological standards, a temperate climate prevailed and the ice caps receded, flooding much of the Earth's lowlands.

The Bible, and especially the Old Testament, frequently associates adverse changes in natural conditions (weather, earthquakes, etc.) with God's righteous anger over humanity's moral failures. Thus it is not surprising to find that it cites the Great Flood as a punishment for our distant ancestors' willful disobedience. The book of Genesis tells us that the Lord Yahweh became angry about the increasingly frequent mixed marriages between the "sons of the Elohim," called "Nefilim," and the "daughters of men," whom they "found to be fair" (i.e., sexually compatible).

Apparently Yahweh felt that even long-lived humans should not breed with "the gods." When His orders were ignored He decided to annihilate the offenders once and for all. Humanity's willful miscegenation with divine beings (Were they "angels" or extraterrestrials from UFOs? The Bible never clearly identifies the mysterious "Nefilim,")* is therefore given as the main reason for the universal Deluge, which the Bible presents as Yahweh's way of cleansing the Earth of a disobedient and sinful human race (Genesis 6:1–7).

The Bible's account of man's relationship with his creator gods (Elohim) at this early stage of human history is very abbreviated. Archaeologists have discovered that other ancient civilizations left more complete records of their early history among their "myths and legends." Many of these stories contain similar accounts of human-divine sexual unions during the pre-Flood period of the Golden Age, usually with many more details. Thus in the Sumerian version, which is closest to that given in the Bible, the creator gods' leader, named Enlil, also became incensed over the genetic weakening of the divine strain on Earth through frequent intermarriages by his host of space-faring gods with nubile Adamic (earthly) females.[31]

---

* Dr. Sitchin translates the Biblical word "Nefilim" as "those cast down upon the Earth." He states that the word likely comes from ancient Sumerian sources where it was used to describe those ancient extraterrestrial "gods" who came down from the heavens and ruled the prehistoric Middle East. Sitchin also argues that the Biblical word "Shem," usually translated as "reknown," really meant "sky ship." Thus the "mighty men of reknown" (Genesis 6:4) were in fact the descendants of the astronaut "gods" and their human mates. (*The Twelfth Planet*, pp. 170–72.)

After a series of lesser measures, including plagues and induced famines, failed to reduce mankind to a suitably servile level, Enlil, like the Biblical Yahweh, despaired of his human creation and decided to blot it out along with its semidivine cousins. Things came to a climax with Enlil's orders to all the pure gods then living on Earth to abandon their human partners and half-human offspring and leave the planet at once, due to an approaching great planetary disaster. The Sumerian sources do not spell out whether or not this catastrophe was then caused by Enlil or was simply foreseen by him. (In general, the Golden Age "gods" of Sumer are far less moralistic and omnipotent than the Biblical Yahweh.) But they do make clear that Enlil decided to use the event to rid Earth of its human burden, for his orders to those pure gods living on Earth were to leave secretly, without warning the earthlings, or half-breeds.

At this point humanity's doom appeared to be sealed. But, the Sumerian tablets reveal, Enlil's decision was not unanimously approved of by his fellow gods. His chief rival for lordship over the Earth, a half brother named Enki (or Ea), disputed his judgment. Their rivalry was nothing new, and many Mesopotamian epics describe often turbulent conflicts between the two concerning territory, Earth policies and even moral issues. Moreover, the Sumerians generally attributed Enki with the scientific (genetic) knowledge that had led to the creation of humanity as a hybrid between native Earth primates and the "seed of the gods" in the first place. He was therefore, naturally, loath to abandon his own creation. Still, Enlil forced him to swear an oath not to reveal the future disaster to Earth's human inhabitants.

Maintaining the genetic purity of the gods' own race seems to have been Enlil's main concern. It is possible also that he and those gods who backed him feared eventual competition from a half-human and half-god race. The Bible's greatly abbreviated account of this pre-Deluge period tends to support this idea when it mentions that the offspring of the "sons of the gods" and the "daughters of men" were "giants, mighty men of reknown [Shem]" (Genesis 6:4). As noted earlier, Shem can also be translated as "sky ships."

The Sumerian god Enki overcame Enlil's forced promise by that classic ruse of obeying the letter of the law while betraying its spirit. According to the Sumerian texts, he cleverly suggested that his favorite human devotee (called Atra-Hasis in some texts, Utnapishtim in others) wait behind a movable screen inside his temple where he could not be seen. Then Enki proceeded to reveal Enlil's entire prediction of the Great Flood out loud, ostensibly talking to the temple wall but within his servant's hearing.

Enjoining the man to secrecy, he then laid out plans for the building of a huge submersible boat, big enough for his extended family, animals and foodstuffs. In fact, according to the specifications mentioned on the clay tablets, it must have resembled a large hollow log, as it was designed with sealed openings and the ability to "turn and tumble" in the flood waters. Noah's ark and the Hopi's "hollow reeds" shared similar features (see Genesis 6:14–16 and note that Noah's ark was to be covered with pitch both "inside and outside" so that it would be submersible).

Thus were the Sumerians' ancestors saved from extinction by the intervention of a sympathetic god in an account whose practical details are remarkably similar to those of Noah. Interestingly, the Sumerian epics also have the survivors land at Mount Ararat and offer burnt sacrifice in thanksgiving.

Charles Berlitz, in his book *Doomsday 1999 A.D.*, provides an extensive survey of other ancient people's accounts of the Deluge. Although they are too numerous to list in detail here, these stories include descriptions by the ancient Hindus of a Great Flood survivor named Manu who was saved by attaching a boat to a large intelligent fish, which pulled it through the waters to northern mountains; Mexican (Toltec) legends of a couple who took refuge in a hollowed tree trunk during a flood that lasted fifty-two years; and several South American stories of a few deluge survivors either floating to safety on rafts or finding refuge atop the continent's highest mountains. Ancient Egyptian tales add an interesting twist to the traditional Great Flood legend when they have Ra, the Sun God, promise an annual, beneficial mini-flood of the Nile after his plan to wipe out humanity in an uncontrollable deluge failed.[32]

As noted earlier, Zecharia Sitchin, relying primarily on ancient Middle Eastern sources, postulates that antiquity's Great Flood most likely occurred between 12,500 and 13,000 years ago, at the end of Earth's last ice age. If, then, the Deluge took place following several thousand years of increased glaciation, what exactly caused the sudden inundation? A theory based on samples of the Earth's crust taken during scientific expeditions to Antarctica and examined by Dr. John T. Hollin of the University of Maine, among others, may provide a possible answer.[33]

Examining core samples of sediments under the Ross Ice Shelf, these scientists discovered alternating layers of fine-grained sands and coarse, glaciated strata. The sandy sediments had to have been deposited by rivers at times when Antarctica was ice-free. Dr. Hollin concluded that, astounding as it may seem, Antarctica's geologic history seems roughly similar to that of North America, with alternating ice-age glaciations and intervening warm, temperate periods. His theory has been contested by other, more conservative geologists but not categorically disproven. And its data does seem to tally with that of the sediment samples found in Arizona and Mexico by other scientists and mentioned above.

The evidence further points to several abrupt shifts from one regime to the other within the short geologic period of the past couple of hundred thousand years. Apparently one of these shifts took place around 12,500 years ago, rapidly warming the "frozen continent" and possibly creating a massive tidal wave as ice sheets up to a mile thick broke up and slid into the seas. Swedish scientists have also gathered evidence that the Earth underwent a reversal of its magnetic field during the same period, stabilizing about 10,400 B.C.[34]

Zecharia Sitchin categorically states in *The Twelfth Planet* his opinion that the Deluge resulted from these disturbances, which he feels may have been provoked by the unusual passage of a twelfth body of our solar system within the orbit of Mars. Ancient Akkadian texts, undoubtedly copies of Sumerian originals, indicate that the constellation of the lion (Leo) "measured the waters of the deep" approximately twelve to thirteen thousand years ago. According to the same sources, the Age of Leo was also accompanied by the sudden appearance in the sky of a bright, fast-approaching heavenly body called the "Lord whose shining crown with terror is laden."[35]

This planet, which Sitchin christens Marduk, after the ancient Babylonian god of war, may circle our Sun in a highly eccentric orbit outside the ecliptic plane of Earth and the other planets. The presence of such a planet or large comet, still undiscovered by modern science, would account for certain known but inexplicable anomalies in the orbits of the "outer planets," especially Uranus and Neptune.

In a 1987 article in *Discover* magazine, John Anderson of the NASA Jet Propulsion Laboratory is cited as having revealed that recent observations from the Pioneer 10 and 11 spacecraft as they fly by the "outer planets" tend to support such a theory. He believes that "the only object that could easily fit the available data would be a planet, about five times as massive as Earth, that circles the Sun in an eccentric orbit perpendicular to those of the other planets."[36]

Another recent hypothesis about a possible companion "dark star" to our Sun has been extensively discussed by paleontologist David M. Raup in *The Nemesis Affair*. This theory contends that the periodic approaches of a small dark star to the inner solar system throws thousands of comets and meteorites into collision courses with the Earth (and other planets) as it passes the Sun's "Oort cloud," which is filled with such objects. This star, nicknamed Nemesis after the Greek goddess of misfortune, could pass through the inner solar system about every twenty-six million years, thereby provoking the massive extinctions of animal and plant life on Earth discovered in recent paleontological research. These extinctions, including that of the dinosaurs some sixty-six million years ago, seem to occur about every twenty-six million years. Dr. Raup notes that, according to this hypothesis at least, Earth should be "safe" from Nemesis for several more million years.[37]

It is thus unlikely that Nemesis could have been responsible for the Great Flood. A potential "planet X," with a perpendicular orbit of a thousand or more years, is, however, a much more likely candidate. It is possible that such a "twelfth planet," which Sitchin feels was represented on Sumerian astronomical charts, could periodically approach the Sun, thereby disturbing the inner planets, including Earth, provoking natural upheavals and climatic disturbances. This is precisely what he feels happened during the Age of Leo, causing the redoubtable prehistoric Deluge and the end of the last ice age.

Although some of Sitchin's other sweeping astronomical generalizations and conclusions about the formation and behavior of the solar system may be contestable, his association of the Great Flood with the end of the last ice age seems tenable regardless of exactly what triggered the catastrophe. As has already been pointed out, considerable differences of opinion exist as to what might have been the direct cause of such a cataclysm. John White, in his book *Pole Shift*, discusses the prevalent theories in detail.[38] It does seem likely that either displacement of at least part of the polar ice caps or a shifting of the Earth's poles must have been involved. Any event of the magnitude required to thaw the Antarctic and flood all but the world's tallest mountain ranges would certainly have marked important changes in climate and mean temperature distribution. It could have been associated with a cometary or planetary "near miss," even though that is far from certain.

Further, if current astrological data about the timing of the precession of the equinoxes is correct, this relatively sudden climatic shift took place when dawn at the vernal equinox was crossed by the constellation of Leo. This constellation, as recorded by both the ancient Sumerians and Egyptians, marks the starting point of the ancient zodiac. Thus for them it represented an important beginning period.

Could it be that our remote ancestors, the Flood's survivors, henceforward observed that terrible catastrophe as the end of an old world and start of this present one? The evidence points in that direction. If so, this demonstrates the tremendous psychological impact the event had. Some legends assert that the world's ageless pyramids were later constructed both as astronomical observatories, so that the heavenly portents of future catastrophes could be noted, and as possible refuges against another flood.[39]

From time immemorial men and women have been awed and inspired by the sight of the Great Pyramid and its two smaller neighbors rising above the plain of Giza in Egypt. Considered one of the Seven Wonders of the ancient world, the Great Pyramid (and its neighbor, the lion-shaped Sphinx), have attracted more scholarly attention than any other ancient artifact. A virtual science of "pyramidology" has developed in the past two centuries as archaeologists, astronomers, mathematicians, and even biologists have explored, measured and hypothesized about the structure's origins and possible special energy-producing properties.

Among the most intriguing theories concerning the hidden purpose behind the construction of this artificial mountain is that, in addition to being a sophisticated astronomical observatory, it also represents a veritable "calendar in stone" whose geometry offers an overview of human history covering thousands of years. This theory was first put forward by nineteenth-century scientists, including the Scottish astronomer Charles Piazzi–Smyth, who measured the Great Pyramid's internal passageways. Along with William Petrie, he discovered that they were designed around a special measurement unit he called the "pyramid inch," equal to 1.00106 of our inches, and its multiple, the "sacred cubit" (25 pyramid inches). Based on these measurements, the Victorian-era scientists theorized that special events in world history, including the life and passion of Jesus, were accurately predicted by the geometry of the Pyramid's corridors.[40]

Even though Piazzi–Smyth made some obvious mistakes, both in measurement and interpretation, one of the foremost contemporary students of pyramid lore, British author Peter Lemesurier, has concluded that the Pyramid is based on highly sophisticated mathematical and astrophysical knowledge indicative of a civilization technically greater than the Egypt of the Pharaohs. He feels that scientifically accurate measurements of the monument reveal that its builders intended it as the blueprint of a master plan for Earth's future destiny. In his remarkable book *The Great Pyramid Decoded*, Mr. Lemesurier discusses the chronology of this plan outlined in Pyramid geometry and its relationship to historical events from 2623 B.C. through 3889 A.D., seen as the end of humanity's physical odyssey and graduation to higher spiritual dimensions.[41]

What is extraordinary about Lemesurier's painstaking analysis of the Great Pyramid, literally inch by inch, is his contention that it pinpoints the century between 1914 and 2014 A.D., the "cusp" between Pisces and Aquarius, as one of the most critical junctures of human history. This is a time when souls must choose whether to participate in humanity's eventual spiritual liberation and ultimate reunion with the Divine Creator or not. According to the Pyramid, this special transition period is characterized by the division of those individuals who seek to pave the way for the succeeding Messianic Age (Aquarius) and those who resist that advent, thereby creating a literal "Hell on Earth," or Apocalypse of war and destruction. Lemesurier feels that the Pyramid forecasts a brutal collapse of material civilization within three years of 2004 A.D. (i.e., between 2001 and 2007). As he puts it, "The bottom will fall out of the world." The nadir, or lowest point, of this cycle is predicted to occur in 2010 A.D., only to be followed by the return of the Christ 2,001 years after Calvary in 2034 A.D.[42]

According to Lemesurier's account, influenced by Biblical research and by the psychic readings of the American clairvoyant Edgar Cayce, the current scenario foreseen by the Great Pyramid represents a mirroring of the events preceding the Great Flood, which took place around 10,500 B.C.. At that time the previous material civilization of Atlantis was annihilated, possibly to preserve the Earth for humanity's ultimate spiritual regeneration.[43]

Lemesurier feels that even though the Great Pyramid's chronology effectively begins in 2600 B.C., it was actually built much earlier, probably shortly after the Deluge by Atlantean refugees. Citing various authorities to back this conclusion, he notes that recent research by Swedish scientists has revealed that the Earth's last known reversal of its magnetic poles occurred around 12,500 years ago, an event that coincided with the rapid melting of the ice-age glaciers.[44]

Further, because the Mediterranean Sea of 10,500 B.C. lapped the edge of the Giza plateau, the pyramids' massive building blocks could have been easily transported by water from their stone quarries and floated into place. Edgar Cayce dates the Great Pyramid's construction between 10,490 and 10,390 B.C. as well. Finally, Lemesurier calls our attention to the enigmatic Sphinx, the sacred pyramids' great stone "guardian." Ancient peoples naturally associated such symbolic monuments with the ruling sign of their contemporary zodiac. The Sphinx portrays a man's head atop the form of a crouching lion. The lion was, of course, the symbol of that mysterious Age of Leo, which ruled the skies between 10,970 and 8,810 B.C.

Thus the Great Pyramid's esoteric geometry, if properly interpreted, provides us with a direct, tangible link between the ancient catastrophe of the Great Flood and the Apocalyptic events so widely feared and predicted for the near future. If true, the Pyramid's prophecy in stone indicates that we still have much to learn about the real nature of Time and the cyclical recurrence of similar events. Is there some overall "master plan" for the human race? What about our valued free will and daily struggles with both moral and material issues? If at some level of existence the most likely future course of action can be foreseen by thousands of years, how does that fact influence our own "mass dreams" of that future's unfolding?

Although certainly we must admit that we do not as yet have final answers to these questions, which have been debated by theologians and philosophers for centuries, it seems clear that, as already mentioned, if such a disaster occurred, then we are the direct descendants of those who lived through it. Our genetic ancestors, therefore, were those who acted on their prophetic premonitions, Divinely inspired or not, and thus survived. Furthermore, due to astrology's emphasis on the organic relationship between the zodiac's opposite signs, or ages, there is no doubt but that our current passage from the Age of Pisces into that of Aquarius again raises the specter of massive planetary upheavals such as took place during the Age of Leo, on the other side of the Great Year's cycle.

At our current level of understanding we cannot be sure of either the exact timing or relationship of such cosmic events. Nonetheless, our inherited genetic "memory" combined with an eventual subconscious awareness from our own past lives associating the upcoming Age of Aquarius with tribulations experienced in the ancient Age of Leo form an increasingly potent psychic force today. Our "mass dreams" about the future, both conscious and unconscious, reflect this stress. Deep within us we are more and more aware that the world now stands at a crossroads.

Whether this awareness propels us toward materialistic hedonism, depressive despair, or a renaissance of spiritual growth and unity remains to be seen. As any psychoanalyst knows, the popularity of such expressions as that attributed to France's pre-Revolutionary King Louis XV, "*Après moi le déluge*" ("After me, the Deluge"—Think about it!), reflects underlying popular wisdom. The age-old patterns of the stars make it clear that at this very moment fundamental choices are fast approaching for planet Earth and her human passengers. The ancient spiritual traditions of the human race, across the face of the entire planet, also point toward the coming century as one of unique potential for metaphysical growth and expansion if we so choose. It is therefore up to each one of us to use the energy being liberated during this special era as wisely and constructively as possible. The choice is ours alone to make.

* 4 *

"Channeling" the Future Today:

The "Ageless Wisdom" and Edgar Cayce

As we move rapidly into the forthcoming Age of Aquarius, symbolized by the pouring out of life-giving energies (the "water of life") from an apparently bottomless urn, our culture is once again opening up to the concept that there is more to reality than what can be perceived by our five physical senses. Today more and more people in the Western world are seeking guidance and advice from nonphysical sources. Although many rely on such traditional methods as prayer or meditation, increasing numbers are accepting the spiritual advice of self-defined nonphysical entities speaking through the medium of someone in an altered state of consciousness. We have even adopted the term "channeling" to express this process.

Psychic channeling about everything from how to succeed in the stock market to where to move in order to avoid the predicted California earthquake has become widely popular. As shown by the overwhelming commercial success of actress Shirley MacLaine's recent books, starting with *Out on A Limb*, and the influence of such contemporary "channels" as Jach Pursel ("Lazaris") and J. Z. Knight ("Ramtha"), providing information from nonmaterial, psychic sources is one of today's growth industries!

This phenomenon, broadly defined, is hardly new, however. All the world's great religious and philosophical traditions stem from inspired

83

texts or sayings whose origins are attributed to discarnate spiritual sources communicating through a human disciple or prophet. The Bible, after all, is considered by our Judeo-Christian culture to be "The Word of God." Moslems believe that Allah personally dictated the Koran to the prophet Mohammed. The special role of the in-trance utterances and actions of the oracle, shaman and faith healer in native cultures is also well documented.

One sure sign of this subject's universality is the extensive number of names we have for those who receive such special information. In addition to the terms already mentioned, such as channels, mediums and prophets, we identify seers, visionaries, initiates, adepts, gurus, medicine men, masters and mystics among those privileged to communicate directly with the spiritual realms. Other, less flattering, names given self-styled psychic channels have included daydreamers, fortune-tellers, hysterics, schizophrenics, fakirs, mythomaniacs and charlatans. Doubtless every reader can think of additional synonyms in current use.

The concept of spiritual trance channeling is ancient. What seems to have changed in today's context, however, is the more and more widespread nature of this heretofore highly selective process. In the past only a few special individuals claimed direct contact with the gods or higher wisdom. These unusual people, after careful testing of their "calling," were set apart from the mass of society and called upon to lead specific, regimented life-styles. Celibate monastic orders, shamanistic ritual dress and behavior and the renunciative vows of yogis are among the role models that have been assigned to the world's traditional psychic channels.

Today, on the other hand, we find outwardly ordinary people of all ages and from all walks of life, businessmen and housewives, students and retirees, suddenly spouting tomes of spiritual wisdom and advice. Corporation executives and stockbrokers have used the meditation and visualization techniques taught by several channeled "entities" to enhance profit margins in the increasingly competitive business world. The teachings and future predictions of "Ramtha," who identifies himself as the prototype of the Indian god Ram, have led literally thousands of people to leave California in order to avoid the forthcoming big quake he has predicted.

Channeling's current popularity is, moreover, merely part of a larger extension of personal contact with levels of reality beyond the ordinary tangible world, within American society, at least. Since the 1975 publication of *Life After Life*, Dr. Raymond Moody's revolutionary study of what is now known as the near-death experience, or NDE, tens of thousands of Americans have reported personal brushes with death in which their mental consciousnesses remained alive and alert outside their physical brains, which were registered as temporarily dead by sophisticated medical equipment. The reports of what these near-death survivors experienced while outside of the physical world closely coincide with what the channeled discarnates describe as the passage to the "Other Side."[1]

These previews of what lies in store for all of us mortals have led to a number of fascinating studies, including Drs. Osis and Haraldson's comparison of how people from two very different social and religious contexts (India and America) perceive their continuing consciousness outside the body as they cross the threshold of physical death. The cultural context seems to affect only the identification of spiritual symbols such as Jesus and Mary or Vishnu and Kali and not the experience itself. In addition, University of Connecticut psychologist Dr. Kenneth Ring, an authority on the subject, has organized the International Association for Near Death Studies (IANDS) to do further research in the field, as well as to help survivors cope with the spiritual awakening that often accompanies the near-death experience. His 1984 book, *Heading Towards Omega*, is a classic study of the impact that this psychic "bolt from the blue" can have on ordinary people whom Dr. Ring feels may be precursors of humanity's next great evolutionary leap.[2]

Personal contact with the spirit realm has not been limited to those involved in a life-threatening incident that pushed them to the brink of physical extinction. The general public's attitude and experience concerning the hereafter have also undergone important changes in recent years. For example, a 1980 Gallup poll found that 71 percent of Americans now believe in life after death. In 1986 a poll by the University of Chicago's National Opinion Research Council reported that 42 percent of American adults feel they have had personal contact with someone who has died, usually a relative. That's nearly half the adult population of the United States, or some 65 million people! Seventy-eight percent of those reporting such a personal psychic experience said they saw the dead person, 50 percent heard their loved one speak, while 18 percent actually carried on a conversation with the spirit of the discarnate individual. Even more amazingly, the same poll divulged that 30 percent of the minority who deny an afterlife nonetheless felt they had experienced a personal contact with someone who had died.[3]

These statistics, approximately valid for all the modern Western nations, reveal today's growing interest in and direct experience of psychic

and spiritual phenomena by ordinary individuals. This trend coincides
with the growing numbers of reports in recent decades of other paranormal phenomena such as the manifestations of the Virgin Mary around
the world, succeeding waves of UFO sightings and spontaneous out-of-
body experiences (OBEs). All these events form part of our current
worldview at a time when more and more people are seeking alternatives
to our culture's materialist and supposedly objective recipes for the meaning of life and the nature of reality.

People today sense that material satisfactions and the evidence of
our five physical senses fail to describe our human condition adequately.
They are searching for personal meaning in life and for a spiritual connection to life's Source. In the West, at least, many have become suspicious of traditional cultural and religious institutions, which they see
both as indecisive and as controlled by dogmatic elites. They naturally
seek to learn from those who claim to be inspired by an eternal wisdom
that transcends mortal limitations. Because this is so, it is vitally important to look at what a few of today's best-known psychic channels have
to say about our world and its future. For, regardless of any evaluation
of the accuracy of the messages thus given, they definitely form part of
our "mass dreams" about who we are and where we are headed.

Whether or not they have directly acknowledged its influence, virtually all modern psychics have based their advice and predictions on a
set of philosophical concepts that Dr. Jon Klimo has dubbed the "Ageless
Wisdom" in his well-researched book, *Channeling*.[4] Because this rather
special worldview has been such an important influence behind recent
channelings, including those about the possibility of a future Apocalypse,
it is important to review some of its major precepts. Therefore, before
turning to the predictions of psychics such as Edgar Cayce, I want to
offer my own interpretation of what the Ageless Wisdom philosophy says
about the nature of reality. Further, even though I cite a few specific
examples for some points, overall what follows is my personal understanding of this vast subject at this time. It should therefore not be taken
as necessarily representing the exact position of those psychic channels
mentioned in this chapter.

The term "Ageless Wisdom" itself stems from the channeling of Alice
A. Bailey. Between 1919 and her death in 1949, this Englishwoman,
originally a member of the Theosophical Society, wrote eighteen volumes
covering virtually all aspects of metaphysics, providing a thorough and
highly sophisticated spiritual doctrine labeled the "Ageless Wisdom."
These works were, she claimed, telepathically dictated to her by a Tibetan

lama, Djwhal Khul, or D.K., himself an initiate of a benevolent spiritual hierarchy that controls our Space-Time dimension.

Aart Jurriaanse, a South African student of the Bailey teachings, has compiled several anthologies around specific themes. Among these is the *Prophecies of D.K.*, 1977, which discusses her channeled information concerning the forthcoming New Age. I recommend it to those interested in further study of her viewpoint on human history. The definitions of the Ageless Wisdom that follow, however, are my own and only generally correspond with the Bailey material.[5]

Practically all modern-day channeled sources agree on several key philosophical concepts, commonly known as "New Age" but which in fact have existed for thousands of years. Underlying this Ageless Wisdom is the idea that there exists only one unified, living and creating Being. This Being, a conscious and multidimensional spiritual force that can be called God, Allah, Brahm, Universal Mind, the Creative Forces or "I Am Who I Am," is inhabited by self-aware participatory units that co-exist on many different "planes," or energy levels, of which our material universe, including Time and Space, is but one. Each conscious unit of this Divine Being shares in its living, creative potential at some level of awareness. They (we) are therefore co-creators of different dimensions of reality with the Universal Being or Mind which is God, another name for All That Is or the "Ultimate Reality."

Relations between the individual co-creating units of Ultimate Reality are governed by a series of universal laws. The First Universal Law, often stated "As Above, so Below; As Within, So Without," confirms the fundamental unity of all life. Usually attributed to the ancient Egyptian god Thoth, known in Greek as Hermes Trismegistus, it states that the workings of the Whole, on any level of reality, are necessarily reflected in all of its component parts. Thus, every dimension of reality, including our material cosmos, reflects the principles of the Divine Being at its level of awareness.

Human beings, therefore, at our level of awareness, are a reflection of God and co-creators of our dimensions of reality with the Universal Mind. This is what is meant by the Biblical phrase "made in God's image." A corollary to the First Universal Law is that, whether aware of it or not, all units of consciousness share in the Universal Life Force eternally. We have an immortal "higher self," outside Time and Space dimensions, which identifies us with God. This higher self has traditionally been known as "the soul," although some channeled teachings use different terminology.

According to the Ageless Wisdom philosophy, humanity shares more than one level or dimension of All That Is. We are, of course, most conscious of the material, Time-and-Space-delimited universe in which we live our daily lives. Even here, channels such as Edgar Cayce tell us, our physical bodies, with their diverse component organs, glands and cells, mirror the makeup of the wider universal cosmos. Similarly, even our limited conscious mind shares a spark of Divine wisdom and the capacity to love.

But we are more than just "flesh and blood." At the most sublime, we are immortal spirits, united through our higher selves with the God Force itself. Even the Bible, which is often cited against this overall philosophy by Christian fundamentalists, categorically states, "You are gods, sons of the Most High, all of you" (Psalm 82:6); Jesus himself quoted this phrase approvingly when accused by self-righteous Pharisees of blasphemy in claiming to be the Son of God (John 10:34).

If at one level through the spiritual higher self we are God, co-creators of Divine Reality, nonetheless we remain ego-bound individual human personalities while living within the Space-Time universe. For each of us, the ego, or "lower self," has allowed itself, through free will, to separate its desires from those of its parent soul. It is, therefore, a sad mistake to confuse the two dimensions and let the lower self ego think it ought to be given divine prerogatives. This is, of course, one definition of insanity and a cause of much evil. It is most definitely *not* what the true Ageless Wisdom teaches, although some unscrupulous gurus and channels have deliberately mixed the levels to con the gullible.

Fortunately, most of us are animated by a third, intermediate, level, or dimension, of human reality, that of the mind. The human mind, according to virtually all channeled sources, mediates between our lower and higher selves through what is commonly called willpower, or the Will. Another term for this intermediate agency might be conscience. It is the mind that holds the lower self's inherently selfish egotistical desires within reasonable bounds, at least most of the time. It is the mind that can, under certain conditions, contact the oft-hidden higher self with its eternal wisdom and unconditional love.

Although exact definitions vary from source to source, the human mind is generally acknowledged to operate at two distinct levels during our physical lifetimes. These are, of course, the conscious mind, which guides our waking thoughts and is usually amenable to reason, and the subconscious mind, which surfaces during dreams, in some altered states and which follows its own inherent logic. Both levels are influenced by our emotions. A third mental level, the supraconscious, is also mentioned by some psychics such as Edgar Cayce. Not normally accessible to waking awareness, it shares qualities of the higher self or soul, and apparently is in continual contact with all other units of consciousness of its own level of reality. This is what the Swiss psychiatrist Carl Gustav Jung referred to as the "collective unconscious." The highest forms of channeling come from this dimension. The wisdom of the collective unconscious forms what Hindu sages call the *Akashic Record*.

Although our basic identity is contained within our higher selves, in eternal co-existence with God, somehow our human mental and even spiritual consciousnesses have become disconnected from their original Divine Source. The exact reasons and circumstances given for this separation vary among the different channels, as do moral interpretations. The popular "Course in Miracles" states simply that as souls we have lost our way for a short time while undertaking a cosmic journey of self-discovery. Edgar Cayce, an earlier, more Biblically inspired psychic, has said that our curiosity about the material levels of reality that we were co-creating led some souls to enter into material forms. The emotional thrills derived from sensual pleasures then trapped us spiritual beings in physical dimensions to the extent that we forgot our higher identity. We thus became subject to the selfish, carnal and mortal nature of the lower self.[6]

Jane Robert's channeled "Seth" entity ignores the moral implications of such a division. It states that as the Ultimate Reality is "inconceivably multidimensional," each of us is experiencing his or her current physical, mental and spiritual separation from the rest of his or her identity deliberately, as a spontaneous, creative act. In any case, "Seth" argues, this separated self is but one aspect of the Whole Being, operating in isolation here in the physical Space-Time universe for specific reasons. These reasons include learning how to manipulate energy consciously so that we may become more complete co-creators with the Universal Mind.

Regardless of whether this separation of ego consciousness from the higher self and Universal Mind is morally accountable, the Ageless Wisdom channeled from spiritual sources throughout history agrees that human beings exist within the material universe with its Space-Time relationships for one definite purpose. According to these sources, the ultimate goal is a complete self-reunion, or the reintegration of all our fragmentary consciousnesses within the single Ultimate Reality of All That Is. We seek to rejoin God and perfection. At some level beyond Time and Space this union is already realized (because it has never been broken;

that is God, of whom we remain a part), but from our human viewpoint
we need the mediation of Time so that we can align our Wills with those
of our higher selves, thereby achieving self-enlightenment, perfection
and liberation from this darkened material world of reflections and illusions.

Aligning the conscious Will with God's takes discipline, or willpower.
It can be accomplished only through Time. It might be likened to the
process by which an amnesia victim slowly refamiliarizes himself with
forgotten surroundings until his true identity is suddenly remembered.
Enlightenment is recognizing the real inner self at all levels of consciousness. This is the analogy presented by the discarnate source of "A Course
in Miracles." We need Time in order to remember who we really are.

The concept of using linear Time for spiritual growth leads to another
basic concept of the Ageless Wisdom now being channeled through so
many individuals into public awareness. I refer to the Universal Law of
Karma, or cause and effect, with its corollary of human reincarnation. If
we are really spiritual beings operating within the material universe
because we need Time and Space experiences in order to recover our
true identity, then the idea of reincarnation becomes obvious and practical. In fact, from this perspective, limiting our chances for enlightenment or salvation to just one physical human lifetime seems unnecessarily
harsh and cruel. It is hardly the kind of thing one would expect of a God
Force universally described as loving and parental. God's love for us as
spiritual souls consists of allowing us Time and Space in which to grow
at all levels into the perfection we already are in our highest selves.

Moreover, the concept of the reincarnation of the soul is among
humanity's oldest religious beliefs. It is found in virtually all spiritual
traditions and was banned from our Judeo-Christian heritage only in the
sixth century on orders of the Byzantine Emperor Justinian. Nor should
this idea be confused, as it often is in popular writings, with that of soul
transmigration between human and animal bodies. All ancient religions
distinguished between these two concepts, giving a higher place to human
reincarnation. Transmigration remained a lower, more vulgar interpretation of the oldest traditions.*

---

* A few channels, including Edgar Cayce, have indicated that animals do also have souls
and that they can reincarnate within the animal kingdom. Some have also stated that
occasional transmigrations of originally animal souls to human form have occurred in unusual
cases. Most, however, say that once in human form, we continue to reincarnate as human
beings.

The concept of human reincarnation is a corollary of the Universal Law of Karma. Again, this law forms part of almost every spiritual tradition known on Earth. Simply stated, it says: One cannot escape the consequences of one's actions. Each of us must bear the ultimate responsibility for who and where we are at this moment. It is not always pleasant to face up to this reality; most of us would prefer to blame someone or something else for our present predicaments. But denying a law doesn't change it; nor does it keep one from suffering its effects. In a way the Law of Karma parallels Newton's Second Law of Physics: For every action there is an equal and opposite reaction. We may not like this law either, especially when we stub our toe or smash in our car's fender, but we don't deny its existence in organizing our everyday living.

Furthermore, if we accept what channels such as Edgar Cayce tell us, this law, combined with reincarnation, is in fact both just and loving. As an integral part of this Space-Time universe we inhabit, it provides a framework for us to use to practice exercising our human willpower until we gain the character and skills required to transcend this material and mortal level of reality. Without the possibility of reincarnation, man's inhumanity to man would be truly monstrous, as so much surface-level injustice has always existed in this world. Could we long survive in a universe in which every thought and emotion that we emit were instantly translated into concrete action? We need Time's buffer; it is a blessing!

According to the Ageless Wisdom philosophy, even accidents and inequities here are part of a larger plan designed ultimately to reunite us with ourselves in God. Whose problem is it if, at a lower self or ego level, we would prefer shortcuts or cheating to the rigors of prolonged mental and spiritual training? The quickest way from your home to the grocery store probably cuts through several other buildings. It would be great not to have to go around the block to get there. Yet who seriously entertains the idea of walking or driving through those walls just to avoid a few extra steps? We all might enjoy the glory and fame that accompany the winning of a gold medal in the Olympics. But we also know that behind every medal lie many years of laborious preparation and personal sacrifice.

The laws of karma and reincarnation do not operate in a vacuum; they are accompanied by the apparent educational nature of this entire Earth experience. Edgar Cayce, the American photographer whose extensive trance channeling between 1910 and 1945 set the stage for the current explosion of this phenomenon in the Western world, put it this way:

Life is continuous. . . . And though there may be only a few short
years in this or that experience, [all lifetimes] are one. . . . There
has been given to each soul that privilege, that choice, of being one
with the Creative Forces. And the patterns that have been set as
marks along man's progress are plain. . . . The passage of a soul
through Time and Space . . . is for the purpose of giving more and
more opportunities to express that which justifies man in his relationships one with another; in mercy, love, patience, long-suffering
[and] brotherly love. These are the fruits of the Spirit. . . .

                                    [Edgar Cayce reading No. 938-1]

Thus the Ageless Wisdom now being channeled through so many
ordinary people tells us that our mortal earthly lives, with their many
experiences of pain, suffering and joy, exist to teach our souls true love,
wisdom, patience and self-discipline. In his recent popular book *The Road
Less Traveled*, Dr. M. Scott Peck argues that discipline is the means to
human spiritual evolution. Further, our evolution's ultimate goal is
love—not the emotional, ego-bound merry-go-round of sexual attraction
and possession which so often passes for love here on Earth, but the
selfless, unconditional love of the higher self and the Universal Mind, or
God.[7] As I was once personally "told" during a deep meditation: "Love
is the universal lubricant linking all dimensions or levels of All That Is
into one united Whole."

True love from the soul level is a willingness to grow, to go beyond
whatever limitations the egotistical Lower Self has imposed on us from
this or other incarnations. It is our choosing to strive for self-perfection
without demanding it in others in return. And to do all this joyfully! It
is the kind of uncalculating giving that is cited as an example in the
famous Biblical quotation of John 3:16:

For God so loved the world that God gave His only begotten Son,
that whosoever believes in Him should not perish but have eternal
Life.

This example of Divine love is certainly not limited to orthodox Christians. The precepts of Ageless Wisdom teach us that by its very nature
such Divine love is endless and unconditional. We have it whether we
want it or not, just as we have the material Space-Time universe for our
childish egos to play in until we grow up sufficiently to transcend its
boundaries. This can and will occur only when we are able to put our

selfish personal desires aside long enough to accept grace or Divine destiny, the last element of the Ageless Wisdom, as it is given to us.

Paradoxically, although we must work to perfect and discipline our willpower if we want to grow spiritually, only when we stop seeking enlightenment for ourselves can it be given to us. All great spiritual teachings stress this final requirement to "let go and let God!" However, not until we have disciplined the lower self and its appetites, obviously not an easy task or there wouldn't be so many of us here on the Earth today, can we truly understand what this means. The mind must carry us lifetime after lifetime and cycle after cycle as we grow, but in the end its values and beliefs must give way to an acceptance of Divine grace, knowing that the ultimate decisions come from beyond the individual ego. To paraphrase Carl Jung, such grace appears synchronistically, without apparent cause, but always at just the right moment. It remains a miracle every time, no matter what the circumstances are. Let us welcome it!

This extended discussion of the Ageless Wisdom currently pouring from numerous trance channels or mediums may at first seem somewhat removed from a concern about the future. Nonetheless, the concepts given above are crucial to understanding what these same channeled sources have to say about how the human race negotiates this Space-Time classroom known as "life on Earth." It is particularly crucial to understand that all channeled sources agree that our fundamental nature is spiritual, not physical. Our souls inhabit succeeding physical bodies and personalities much as most of us wear clothes and live in houses. They also agree that we are here in this earthly plane for a distinct purpose—to learn how to handle the powerful energies of love and creation more wisely. The plastic nature of this Space-Time reality provides a laboratory for our experiments. It is one in which we directly bear the consequences of what we have created together through history.

The Ageless Wisdom philosophy insists on the *conditional nature* of future events. What will happen to us tomorrow, both individually and collectively, depends on our choices today. Ultimately, therefore, we are each responsible for our future. We share this responsibility between the conscious mind, which directs our willpower, and the higher self, or soul consciousness. This higher dimension of self, existing outside Time and Space, is connected through the collective unconscious, or *Akashic Record*, which remembers all thoughts, emotions and actions ever considered. Through it our souls construct future material circumstances according to the Universal Laws, including that of karma.

If the future is continuously being created, then how do we account for premonitions and precognition, those eerie flashes of correct fore-knowledge that erupt spontaneously in dreams and even at odd moments of waking awareness? How do we explain the uncanny accuracy of the predictions of seers such as Nostradamus or the Biblical prophets? It is at this point that we must recall Ageless Wisdom's precept that our Space-Time universe is just one of many levels of being within a vast multidimensional Ultimate Reality. It is a created construct designed to operate according to definite laws or principles. While the laws of Space-Time relativity, including linear Time, generally apply within the material universe, human beings, through the mind, can occasionally transcend this limited perspective. We can, therefore, catch glimpses of what "Seth," via channel and author Jane Roberts, has dubbed the "Spacious Present," in which all events are simultaneous.

What we see in such cases need not be considered a rigidly fixed and predetermined future but the most probable outcome of all the untold multitudes of already expressed choices of all the self-aware components of the Ultimate Reality. Prophetic accuracy depends on the seer's ability to translate what his spiritual higher self or discarnate source knows to be the obvious consequence of all past and present circumstances into a set of specific future events that will then unfold in this dimension within linear Time's limitations.

Because some occurrences have a greater human impact than others, either emotionally or materially, they seem to stand out as more fixed or solid. It is therefore generally easier for clairvoyants to forecast upcoming conflicts, wars or natural cataclysms than more placid, or ordinary, events. The psychic "volume" of such happenings is somehow louder. Also, many channels indicate that as we advance through linear Time toward what has been predicted, our choices narrow considerably and conditional future events become progressively more and more inevitable. The conditional future therefore becomes fixed at some point before it actually happens.

Finally, contemporary psychic sources such as "Seth" warn us that just as Space is made up of different material particles, so is Time composed of moments of unequal importance. This is not an easy concept for our conscious minds to accept for we are used to thinking that each unit of Time is uniform. One minute equals any other minute. Still we do recognize that some moments have greater psychological significance than others; these are the ones we most easily remember, such as a first romantic kiss, scoring the touchdown that won the "big game" or winning a lottery jackpot. Our colloquial language even has the phrase "a pregnant moment," indicating one in which we anticipate something important is about to occur.

From a perspective outside the Space-Time universe, such moments themselves, separate from any physical event, apparently can be distinguished from Time's ordinary flow. Meaningful incidents are more likely to happen during such turning-point periods. These special intervals in our Space-Time's history seem to accompany the cyclical patterns discussed in the astrology of the passage of the Great Tropical Year (see Chapter 3).

It is at this point that today's contemporary psychics join up with all of the venerable philosophical and religious prophecies underpinning our culture's current Apocalyptic spirit. As the Earth cycles its way out of the Age of Pisces into that of Aquarius, astrologers and seers foresee crucial changes just ahead. Virtually all modern channels agree with their judgment that we are now reaching a critical crossroads period in human history. They tell us that the next quarter century or so will determine whether or not most of us are able to "graduate" from this particular earthly classroom into other levels of the Ultimate Reality.

Further, many channels indicate that this special "pregnant moment," unequaled in many thousands of years, is likely to include significant upheavals on material, emotional or psychological and spiritual levels. As noted above, the extent and severity of these convulsions, often compared with birth pangs, are conditional. They will depend on how we as individuals and groups react to the changes the psychic channels foresee just ahead. The quicker we are able to shed our ingrained selfish habits and learn cooperation with the Earth's natural forces, the easier the upcoming transition is likely to be.

Nonetheless, even if most of the human race stubbornly clings to its ego identity and refuses to adapt, the resulting natural and man-made cataclysms will cleanse the planet and prepare a new Golden Age so that the cycle of human development through Space-Time can be renewed. Which path we choose is up to us. In a psychic reading given in the 1930s, Edgar Cayce said:

> Hence the two influences that are ever before thee: good and evil, life and death. Choose thou!
>
> [Reading 262-119]

All the psychic channels who discuss humanity's future emphasize the crucial nature of the spiritual choices before us today. Some limit themselves to this dimension, only mentioning in passing, if at all, the possible material consequences of our stubbornly refusing to change. Jach Pursel's "Lazaris" and Ken Carey's "Raphael" in *Starseed Transmissions* tend to adopt this attitude. Other channeled sources, like Jane Robert's "Seth," take a more amused, detached, psychological viewpoint about our concern for the immediate material future, arguing that we are all creating alternate Space-Time realities every day through our thoughts.

Several of the best-known channels, including Edgar Cayce, Ruth Montgomery and J. Z. Knight's "Ramtha," have, however, offered specific future scenarios for our world as we make the transition to the twenty-first century and the Age of Aquarius. They are joined by less-well-known but equally convincing testimony from "Hilarion," channeled by Toronto businessman Maurice B. Cooke and from the spirit guides inspiring Dr. Verna Yater, a psychic from Santa Barbara, California.

Edgar Cayce, the only son of a evangelical Christian "gentleman farmer" from Kentucky, lived between 1877 and 1945. Known widely as "America's Miracle Man," he was among the most celebrated of this century's psychic predictors. The story of his life and work has been the subject of several best-selling books, including Thomas Sugrue's *There Is a River* and Jess Stearn's *The Sleeping Prophet*. Thus it is not necessary here to do more than touch on a few highlights of his life that influenced his prophetic output. In 1932, during the Great Depression, he founded the Association for Research and Enlightenment (A.R.E.), an organization dedicated to psychical research and spiritual development at the grass-roots level.[8]

Today the A.R.E., headquartered in Virginia Beach, Virginia, has over 50,000 members worldwide and supports an extensive library, including a computerized collection of all of Edgar Cayce's psychic channeling, a small collegiate-level academic program, numerous conferences and lectures around the United States and a health clinic in Phoenix, Arizona, devoted to nontraditional therapy using Cayce's methods. Thousands of "Search for God" study groups meet weekly to discuss practical applications for daily living of the spiritual principles described by Edgar Cayce's Higher Self.*

---

*Between 1909 and 1945, Edgar Cayce gave 14,256 trance-channeling sessions, known as "readings," for some 6,000 people. Stenographically recorded and transcribed, these psychic readings total 49,135 pages. Computerized and indexed into over 10,000 subjects, it is by far the largest amount of channeled material from a single psychic source in existence. Copies of most of the readings are available through the A.R.E. at P.O. Box 595, Virginia Beach, VA 23451. Reading numbers are given in parentheses in the text where appropriate. The Edgar Cayce readings are the exclusive property of the Edgar Cayce Foundation. Quoted by permission.

Even though his formal education ended at fourteen, Edgar Cayce gained phenomenal success at psychic medical diagnosis and nontraditional therapy in an era when such were both rare and suspect. His ability to diagnose and prescribe successful treatments for life-threatening ailments that had baffled doctors won him fame and even a grudging acceptance from the American Medical Association. Medical experts who worked with him or who investigated his diagnoses and prescribed treatments estimated that his physical-health readings attained between 85 and 90 percent accuracy.[9]

Entering into a deep, self-directed, hypnotic-like trance, Cayce claimed his subconscious mind, through his soul consciousness, had access to a source of universal knowledge that he called "God's Book of Remembrance" from which he could read. He was referring to the *Akashic Record*, which his channeled source said is written "upon the skein of Time and Space" (1549–1). While in this deep trance state, Cayce's soul could communicate directly with the higher self, or soul, of the person for whom a diagnosis was requested (3744–2). He then channeled this information into spoken words, which his wife, Gertrude Evans Cayce, or his longtime secretary, Gladys Davis Turner, recorded verbatim and later transcribed. Cayce himself, like many other deep-trance channels, had no conscious recollection of his channeled utterances.

Although the vast majority of Edgar Cayce's celebrated channeled "readings" concerned healing ailments of the physical body, about 2,500 of them were specifically given to inform individuals about their psychological and spiritual development throughout several lifetimes here on Earth. These transcripts, known as "life readings," introduced many middle-class Christian Americans to such Eastern concepts as past lives, reincarnation and karma. They were designed to help those who sought his assistance to understand present-day relationships, talents and failings better in the light of similar episodes they had lived through previously.

A committed evangelical Christian noted for having read the entire Bible once for each year of his life, while in trance Edgar Cayce nonetheless presented the basic precepts of the Ageless Wisdom outlined above, which his soul claimed had found its highest expression in the life and original, unadulterated teachings of Jesus, who became humanity's Christ, or Messiah. Cayce urged everyone, Christian or not, to find common spiritual ideals and to apply them together to realize the human race's age-old dream of a harmonious and loving world. Only through such a united effort will we attain the perfection of body, mind and spirit that is our birthright and the precondition for reunion with God. As he told one woman in a life reading in 1938:

> Oh that all would realize . . . that what we are—in any given ex-
> perience or time—is the combined results of what we have done
> about the Ideals that we have set!

> The soul of each individual is a portion then of the Whole, with the
> birthright of Creative Forces to become a co-creator with the Fa-
> ther, a co-laborer with Him. As that birthright is then manifested,
> growth ensues. If it is made selfish, retardments must be the result.
> [1549-1]

And to a young man in 1941:

> Thus it becomes each soul . . . to know the Author of its Ideal,
> spiritually, mentally, materially. The spiritual is the life, the mental
> is the builder, the material is the result. . . .
> [622-6]

In addition to his medical advice and past-life readings, Edgar Cayce
occasionally discussed the future. In this way he once warned a friend in
April 1929 to cash in all his stocks and bonds as the market was about
to crash; six months later "Black Monday" occurred. Similarly, in the
mid-1930s he correctly predicted the beginning and end dates of the
Second World War, which he saw as the karmic consequence of the Allies'
harsh treatment of defeated Germany and Austria in 1919 and the failure
of the League of Nations. Interestingly, for several years his "sleeping
self" reassured anxious petitioners that America might avoid involvement
in the upcoming conflict if the nation that has "In God we trust" on its
money would only "act as it prays." [1598-2 and 3976 series]

But on August 31, 1941, three months before Pearl Harbor, the die
was apparently cast. In a channeled reading that day Cayce's higher self
warned that war was imminent and that nations heretofore considered
as friendly (i.e., Japan) would soon become enemies. Men on both sides
had failed to use their willpower to build the cooperation and trust that
alone could have averted the final break with the Japanese and kept the
United States neutral. [3976-26]

This example is important for it indicates how Cayce's channeled
source viewed the conditional nature of future world events. Squarely

placing the responsibility for the breakdown of world order on contemporary individuals, Cayce's source indicated that some events, such as the outbreak of war in Europe in 1939, could be predicted with relative certainty several years ahead of time. The war was part of a karmic pattern begun decades if not centuries ago. Other aspects of the war, such as Japan's sneak attack and America's entry, were seemingly viewed as much more conditional. They could have been altered up until just over three months before they actually occurred. Finally, however, these events also became inevitable for, as Cayce had earlier stated:

> Man's answer to everything has been power—power of money, power of position, power of wealth, power of this, that or the other. This has never been God's way, will never be God's way.
>
> [3976-8; see also 364-1]

Nor, the Cayce readings point out, has man's misuse of power been confined to human relationships such as politics. Edgar Cayce and all the other important contemporary psychic channels repeatedly remind us that we live in a truly holistic universe where the condition of each part affects that of every other part. Further, they tell us that this marvelous Space-Time construct was created specifically for the evolution of consciousness, or soul, development. Therefore the condition of the very elements of nature themselves reflects our race's level of soul maturity. Thus, like it or not, we are each responsible not only for the health and well-being of our human neighbors and the ecological balance of plants and animals but also for the continuing rhythm of such impersonal "natural" forces as winds, rains and sunlight! [See reading 417-7]

How can this be so? In an unusual reading focusing on sunspots, areas of temporarily lowered thermonuclear activity on the Sun's surface visible from Earth and which affect our weather, Edgar Cayce argues that all components of the material Space-Time universe "are *one* in their various stages of consciousness or of activity. . . ." So-called natural forces, such as the Sun, Moon and planets, share this consciousness but without free will. They "have their marching orders from the Divine and they move in same. Man alone is given that birthright of free will. He alone may defy his God!" [5757-1]

Therefore, in exercising our free will to defy God through "anger, jealousy, hate [and] animosity," we human beings disrupt natural forces as well as human relationships. Thus, according to Cayce's Higher Self, sunspots and other natural anomalies, such as cyclones, volcanoes and earthquakes, are "a natural consequence of that turmoil which the sons of God in the Earth reflect upon same . . . [because] thy *mind* is the builder!" [5757-1; emphasis in the original]

This cause-and-effect relationship between the human psyche and forces of nature has been termed "biorelativity" by Dr. Jeffrey Goodman, the geologist-anthropologist author of *We Are the Earthquake Generation*, which explores Edgar Cayce's channeled predictions of significant geophysical changes by the end of this century. He notes that virtually all so-called primitive peoples incorporate this concept in their worldview. Native Americans such as the Hopi stress man's duty to "walk in balance on back of the Earth Mother" so as to maintain our environment's ecological well-being. Otherwise, their spiritual traditions say, in self-defense she may act to rid herself of an intolerable human burden, as in the Hopi "Great Purification."[10]

There is no doubt but that Edgar Cayce's "Earth changes" predictions are among his most famous psychic prophecies. Given during a series of life readings in the early 1930s, they single out the forty-year period from 1958 to 1998 as the beginning of the transition from one major human cycle of evolution to another. Cayce's psychic source foretold that this transition would be marked by increasingly severe geophysical disturbances in and around Earth, including a pole shift that would radically alter the planet's climate. These "Earth changes" would accompany, and mirror, widespread economic, political and spiritual upheavals as humanity unconsciously prepared itself for the New Age. All this physical and psychic energy would culminate in nothing less than the Second Coming of the Christ to usher in the Golden Age of Aquarius.

A summary of the major physical aspects of this transformation was given in the following reading of January 19, 1934:

The Earth will be broken up in the western portion of America. The greater portion of Japan must go into the sea. The upper portion of Europe will be changed as in the twinkling of an eye. Land will appear off the east coast of America. There will be upheavals in the Arctic and in the Antarctic that will make for the eruption of volcanoes in the torrid areas, and there will be the shifting of the poles—so that where there has been those of a frigid or the semitropical will become the more tropical, and moss and fern will grow. And these will begin in those periods in '58 to '98 when these will be proclaimed as the periods when His light will be seen again in the clouds. As to times, as to seasons, as to places, *alone* is it given to those who have named the Name—and who bear the mark of those of His calling and His election in their bodies. To them it shall be given.

[3976-18]

Clarifications to this general list indicated that changes in the South Pacific seabed's condition and the eruption of Sicily's Mount Etna volcano would signal the general start of such upheavals, which would proceed gradually, punctuated by sudden shifts such as was predicted for northern Europe. Eventually, however, major seismic and volcanic activity was predicted to destroy Los Angeles and San Francisco, inundate the Mississippi River valley as the Great Lakes drained into the Gulf of Mexico, and flood much of the Carolina and Georgia coasts. A rise in the ocean water level of several feet was indicated, as most northern hemisphere coastlines would go underwater. New York would be destroyed in a following generation along with much of South America. A specific sign that the California disasters were imminent (within ninety days) would be new significant eruptions of Naples' Mount Vesuvius or Martinique's Mount Pelee. [270-35, 311-18, and 1152-11]

As mentioned above, Dr. Jeffrey Goodman's *We Are the Earthquake Generation* discusses these predictions fully, putting them in their biorelative context. John White's *Pole Shift* investigates what Cayce had to say about a forthcoming displacement of the Earth's axis, tilting the continents and possibly thawing the polar ice caps.

In addition to the reading quoted above, the Virginia Beach seer mentioned a future pole shift in two channeling sessions given in 1933 and 1936. In the first [378-16], after predicting that lost records of Atlantis would be rediscovered in Egypt and Mexico shortly before the end of this century, Cayce stated that the shifting of the poles would begin by 1998, the same year that the Christ Spirit would again enter the Earth. In the second [826-8], when asked what major changes were due for the years 2000 or 2001 A.D., he replied, "When there is a shifting of the poles, or a new cycle begins."

In a third 1939 reading [1602-3], he indicated that the changes begun in 1998 and associated with the new cycle of Aquarius would be more gradual than cataclysmic. From this Mr. White concludes that the predicted tilting of the Earth's axis may begin in 1998 and continue through at least 2001 A.D., giving most of humanity time to adjust, despite the obvious upheaval any such event would cause. This would be in keeping with Cayce's stress on the educational and biorelative nature of all such natural happenings. Cayce's source corroborated this hypothesis by adding that the coming Aquarian Age will overlap the end of that of Pisces, "as in the natural sources" and as we ourselves adopt new patterns of thought and behavior without entirely giving up old ways. The reading further predicts that we will only "begin to understand [this] fully in 1998." (1602-3)

Nor, according to Cayce's supraconscious source, will the upcoming pole shift be the first in human experience. John White notes that in a 1932 reading it was stated that 10.5 million years ago Earth's current polar regions were "tropical and semitropical regions." The Sahara and Gobi deserts were verdant and fertile and the legendary Garden of Eden lay in what are now arid mountains and deserts near the Caspian Sea. [364-13] The "sleeping prophet" made another reference to an apparent prehistoric pole shift approximately 200,000 years ago when the lost continent of Lemuria (or Mu) sank into the Pacific Ocean. [364-4; A-1]

The most recent such "turning of the axis," according to Cayce, occurred during an Atlantean crisis involving enormous beasts overrunning the Earth in around 51,000 B.C. Here Cayce claims that "nature, God, changed the poles and the animals were destroyed," thereby saving that ancient civilization. (5249-1) He does not mention a pole shift in connection with the Great Flood of 10,500 B.C., which finally sank Atlantis, leaving us to speculate that another cause, possibly the planetary "near miss" hypothesized by Zecharia Sitchin and discussed in Chapter 3, was at fault.

Among the significant social and political changes that the "sleeping" Cayce foresaw for the period between now and the first decades of the next century was the birth of democracy and the return to religious freedom in Russia. He flatly predicted that "out of Russia comes the hope of the world" after it trades its current atheist Communist philosophy for an alliance with the United States. [3976-10 and 3976-29] As for America, founded on the Divine principles of freedom and equality, it must be careful to expand those concepts to all of humanity. For, he warned, if Americans do not accept "the closer brotherhood of man, the love of neighbor as self . . . [then] again must Mongolia, must a hated people, be raised." [3796-15]

These predictions about comets and pole shifts echo one of the famed Renaissance seer Nostradamus's enigmatic predictions that a "great King of Terror" will appear in the sky in the summer of 1999. They also remind us of our personal responsibility to practice the "Golden Rule" if we are to bring about the Golden Age. For, according to Edgar Cayce and most of his channeling successors, we still have time to avert such disasters as a runaway comet or future pole shift.

The "sleeping prophet" even hinted that he may return to assist in smoothing out the transition process. In a 1934 reading he predicted his own next incarnation here on Earth for 1998. At that time he will return as a "world liberator," helping those still-unenlightened souls to understand the meaning of the New Age, which will include the Second Coming of Christ. In this way he will play a role similar to one he described he had once known in Egypt as the priest Ra-Ta. During that past incarnation some 12,500 years ago he had been instrumental in transferring the spiritual wisdom of wrecked Atlantis to Egypt. [294-151]

On another occasion, in 1936, he dreamed of a second eventual rebirth in 2100 A.D., a time when he saw himself astounding contemporary scientific investigators with his accurate recall of what he had accomplished more than 150 years earlier as Edgar Cayce. At that time he also noted that New York was being rebuilt after destruction "either by war or an earthquake" and that the West Coast of the United States was in Nebraska! [294-185]

Dr. Mark A. Thurston, director of educational services at the Edgar Cayce association's (A.R.E.) Virginia Beach headquarters, offers a different yet quite intriguing interpretation of Cayce's predictions concerning the dawn of the New Age. In his *Visions and Prophecies for a New Age*, Dr. Thurston asks us to consider the sixty-year period of 1940 to 2000 A.D. and asks, "Will it be more like the years 30–90 A.D. or the years 1490–1550?"[11] These eras were, respectively, the period of Jesus's ministry and organization of the early Christian Church and the flowering of the Renaissance and Age of Discovery.

Dr. Thurston reminds us that during both of these epochs, humanity's future worldview was radically altered. Columbus's historic "discovery" of America in 1492 and the Copernican revolution in astronomy changed Western society almost overnight. The world's leading authorities heralded the dawn of a new era. In contrast, the immediate impact of the changes of 30–90 A.D., as viewed by contemporaries, was practically negligible. Most secular and even spiritual leaders ignored what had transpired among a handful of Jewish zealots in a minor Roman province. Even the spread of Christ's revolutionary message of love and salvation among the lower classes of the Roman Empire was viewed as only a minor disturbance to the all-powerful Imperial system.

Today we view that same period quite differently, however. We recognize its long-term historical importance. As Mark Thurston says,

"A relatively small group of people went through a quantum jump in consciousness evolution [between 30–90 A.D. but] it took hundreds of years for that experience to be recognized and accepted by the mainstream culture in which they lived."[12]

A similar pattern may unfold from the apparent breakthrough in trance channeling and spiritual enlightenment now sweeping parts of the Western world, even if none of the spectacular, cataclysmic events foreseen by so many contemporary prophets takes place. In any event it is clear that our conceptions of the future are currently being shaped by the messages coming through the subconscious minds of many individuals, themselves influenced by what America's "sleeping prophet" began predicting over half a century ago.

5

Mass Dreams of
2100–2200 A.D., Part I:
Life in Space and a Budding New Age

According to New Age or Ageless Wisdom thinking, psychic channels and seers mentally "step outside" of the Space-Time level of reality in order to receive their previews of the future. They therefore temporarily disassociate themselves from the conscious mind's linear Time limitations and its preoccupation with present circumstances to look ahead. Despite its seeming mystery, this ability is not a rare phenomenon even though, as with any art, it seems to come more easily to some people than to others.

Across the ages great spiritual teachers and well-known psychics such as Edgar Cayce have unanimously told us that everyone can look into dimensions beyond linear Time if they are willing to submit to the necessary mental discipline. Although most of us admit to occasional precognitive dreams or hunches, few are really willing to spend the time and effort required to go further. For one thing, we lack self-confidence that one lone, individual mind can give us valid results. The Time-bound belief system of the conscious mind, absolutely essential in everyday life, hampers our attempts to go beyond its barriers and view the potential events and circumstances that, so the psychics tell us, we are unwittingly creating with each passing moment.

These two concepts—that we are creating our future reality right now in the present and that at some level of consciousness the mind is aware of this creation and can therefore foresee what will happen—spurred Dr. Helen Wambach to begin her pioneering research of mentally "progressing" average American subjects into their potential future lifetimes between 150 and 400 years from now. Having already demonstrated to her satisfaction that the "dreaming mind," as she termed it, the part of consciousness that becomes accessible when electromagnetic brain wave activity falls to between 7.9 and 8.3 cycles per second, can accurately describe past-life scenarios, she set out to see what would happen when it was asked to scan future lives.

Consequently, she began hypnotizing large groups of volunteers during a series of workshops in the early 1980s, suggesting that while in a light trance they review one of five possible lifetimes other than their current incarnation. The choices offered included three past lives: around 100 A.D., in the eighteenth century, and around 1900 A.D., and two future lives, either about 2100 or between 2300 and 2400 A.D. The suggestions given and questions asked were similar to those she had already tested in the research that led to her two best-selling books on reincarnation, *Reliving Past Lives* and *Life Before Life*.

In view of the large sample required for statistically significant results and because her physical health was already less than perfect, Helen soon sought help. Her friend Beverly Lundell became her workshop assistant and traveling companion. A colleague from the Association for Past Life Research and Therapy (A.P.R.T.), Dr. R. Leo Sprinkle, a licensed counseling psychologist in Wyoming, agreed to perform identical future-lives research in the Rocky Mountain states. His results were tabulated with her own data.

Between 1980 and 1984, Helen Wambach personally performed several dozen research workshops in major American cities such as New York, Chicago, Seattle, San Francisco and Los Angeles. It was toward the end of this period, as her health rapidly worsened, that I joined the project and, in addition to my own future-life progression, discussed in this book's concluding chapter, analyzed the preliminary data for her. I also led a few research seminars. Altogether, by the end of 1984, over 2,500 volunteers had participated in our joint research efforts.

In March 1985 I wrote and presented at the First International Congress on Alternative Therapies in São Paulo, Brazil, a first analysis of what those subjects who reported reincarnating in the 2100 A.D. era had said. This study, "Beyond the Millennium: New Age or Brave New World?" was later published in *The Journal of Regression Therapy*.[1]

Even as Helen Wambach and I were discussing how to combine these results with those of the subjects who went to 2300 A.D. and with the reports of the handful of volunteers, including myself, who had progressed to future dates in the 1990s, her health took a radical turn for the worse. She passed away in Berkeley, August 18, 1985, on her sixtieth birthday, following a massive heart attack. The entire project came to a grinding halt. It remained "on hold" for the next two and a half years.

During the period 1985–87 I was busy with other activities connected with my own regression therapy practice and some cross-cultural past-life research in France. Nonetheless, I remained fascinated by what had been glimpsed during the future progressions, both into the near-term possibilities of the 1990s and those relating to lives more than a hundred years from now. Therefore, as I crisscrossed France and the United States, performing workshops similar to Helen's so as to gather further past-life data for my own study, I occasionally would offer subjects the choice of progressing to 2100 or 2300 A.D. as well.

I also developed alternate techniques for helping people project themselves into the future, including that of "seeing" future events through someone else's eyes if they found that they themselves did not incarnate in a physical body during the time period specified. I found that, in the right depth of trance, many people could visualize a future lifetime lived by someone else's body and recognize the difference between what they were receiving that way and their own future incarnations.

This was an exciting development, for, as mentioned in Chapter 2, one of Helen's and my biggest problems with collecting future-life data, especially for the 2100 era, had been that only 4 to 5 percent of our hypnotized subjects reported finding themselves alive in new physical bodies during that period. The rest either reported "floating," out-of-body sensations or chose other time periods. These percentages doubled for the 2300 A.D. era but still came far short of what would be normally expected, even if the choice were due to random chance. Finding that, given the proper suggestions, most subjects could receive similar information even as somewhat detached outside observers meant that eventually the amount of future data could be increased without having to hypnotize literally tens of thousands of individuals. I intend to work on this concept further in future workshops in order to gather additional comparable information.

At the time, however, this was merely an interesting bit of secondary information as my focus was on my own research into French and American past-life recall experiences. Consequently, I never made any concerted effort to gather a lot of new data about 2100 A.D. or other future time periods. Still, after being contacted in 1987 by Helen Wambach's daughter and her literary agent about finally writing this book, I found to my astonishment that I had collected nearly as many future-life progression cases to 2100 A.D. using solely my methods as the three of us (Drs. Wambach, Sprinkle and myself) had so laboriously come up with earlier!

In the workshops where I offered a "future trip" along with a look at a past life, I focused on taking participants to 2100–2200 A.D., as it was the period that interested me the most. Hence I now found that I had not only Helen Wambach's 2100 A.D. data to analyze but another set of reports about the same future time period. They proved surprisingly similar portraits even though the second batch had been obtained more recently (1986–88 vs. 1980–84), under somewhat different circumstances, and not all of the same topics were covered. Further, 31 percent of this second group of subjects were French, gotten from workshops I conducted in France as part of my cross-cultural past-life project. Although none of the absolute numbers involved are large enough to make definitive statistical comments, their comparison has led to some very interesting results that will be tested in future workshops over the next couple of years. Readers interested in sponsoring or participating in such workshops can contact me at P.O. Box 4452, Bluejay, CA, 92317.

Before looking at what these two groups of volunteer subjects progressed into a future lifetime report about the twenty-second century, it is important to understand the factors that seem to have made this data so hard to come by in the first place. Among the first noticeable results of Helen Wambach's original 1980–84 future-life study was her discovery, after just a few sessions, that far fewer subjects than expected reported finding themselves alive and in a physical body in *either* of the two future time periods offered (2100 and 2300 A.D.).

Later examination of all the 1980–84 workshop data gathered by Helen Wambach, R. Leo Sprinkle and myself confirmed that only about 5 percent of our approximately 2,500 volunteers experienced physical-lifetime events in the 2100 A.D. period, while about double that figure (around 12 percent) reported finding themselves physically "alive" in the 2300 period. These results were consistent within statistical norms from workshop to workshop and from researcher to researcher. Interestingly, they also seemed to be totally independent of the conscious desires of the workshop participants themselves, as expressed just before the progression. In addition, they also appeared independent of the subjects' current religious or philosophical beliefs.

An illustration of this relationship took place when Helen held a Chicago workshop sponsored by the Association for Research and Enlightenment (A.R.E.) in April 1983. The gathering consisted of a large group (225 participants) whose conscious minds knew of Edgar Cayce's celebrated prediction that he would reincarnate in North America sometime around 2100 A.D. As individuals interested in Cayce's work and often following his holistic health advice, it is natural to assume that many A.R.E. members would be interested in returning at the same time to witness the event. According to Helen, some of the participants even expressed this thought verbally before the workshop began.

Nonetheless, that group's future-life progression percentages remained at just under 5 percent for 2100 A.D. and at about 12 percent for 2300 A.D. The same thing was true for other New Age groups consciously interested in the dawning of the new Golden Age of Aquarius, so widely predicted as just around the corner.

What can be made of this surprising lack of response for the two future time periods and especially for the 2100 A.D. period? One answer may be that our subconscious "dreaming" mind tends to resist progressing to the future more than regressing to the past. This could be a result of unintentional interference from the conscious mind, whose belief in one-way linear Time may inhibit progressing to what it believes to be a still-undetermined future. Or this phenomenon could be related to the Law of Karma, which states that one's actions and attitudes in each lifetime are accountable in succeeding incarnations. In the Bible the concept is stated this way: "For whatever a man sows, that he will also reap." (See Galatians 6:7.)

The Law of Karma coupled with human reincarnation implies that we live physical lifetimes in order to have certain learning experiences. Perhaps we have more to learn from what we perceive as the past than from the future. Many of Edgar Cayce's psychic "life readings" tied his clients' present-day circumstances to key events from their previous lives. Cayce explained that such connections resulted from karma, or cause and effect. Although he only very rarely brought up the topic of future lives, other than describing his own projected reincarnations in 1998 and again around 2100, he never denied their existence. Indeed, he often told his clients that they would have to return to the Earth many times to complete lessons still unfinished.

Because he so rarely gave explicit future-life information, perhaps Cayce felt that those seeking his assistance were not yet ready to know what might lie ahead of them, influenced as it undoubtedly is by how their present-day lives were unfolding. Like all truly wise spiritual teachers and psychic channels, he stressed learning to live each day as a complete experience without worrying unduly over either one's past or future predicaments. We need to use information about past or future lives mainly to help us improve how we live out *today's* challenges and opportunities.

Another explanation for the few future lifetimes reported by Helen's and my hypnotized workshop participants is that the very newness of the idea of assisting people to progress to possible future lives makes it more difficult for untrained subjects to experience them. This explanation follows the ideas of Dr. Rupert Sheldrake's morphogenetic field theory, also known as the "hundredth monkey effect." This theory will be discussed in more detail in Chapter 9, "Is the Future Already Past?"

Basically, Dr. Sheldrake, a British biologist, hypothesizes that learning any new skill becomes progressively easier as more individuals, even if separated in Time and Space, pass through the same learning process. If one accepts this idea, then it would be easier for the subconscious mind of hypnotized subjects to regress to past lifetimes than to move forward to future ones simply because the process of past-life regression has already been experienced by so many more people. Thus, taken logically, the earlier success of Dr. Wambach's own past-life research in which thousands were regressed to the past via hypnosis could ironically have contributed to the difficulty she found in trying to take new subjects to the future!

Still other explanations abound, including perhaps the most hopeful one, which argues that the small numbers who see themselves returning in 2100 and 2300 A.D. indicate that few of those who volunteered for this project will need to return to physical bodies beyond their current lifetime. I've personally heard this idea expressed by numerous individuals interested in New Age concepts, many of whom believe and desire that this is their own last time around the wheel of rebirth. That certainly is a comforting thought! I know that the idea that I'd have to face being born and growing up all over again in another body soured me on the concept of reincarnation at first.

Unfortunately, however, this wish-fulfilling solution fails to account for the interesting fact that, according to our research results, significantly *more* subjects return to the flesh *after* 2300 A.D. than in the earlier 2100 period. It also is at odds with Edgar Cayce's life-readings data in which he indicated that all but a handful of the 2,000 or so individuals who received such readings would have to return to Earth to continue their "studies" beyond their current twentieth-century lives. It therefore seems likely that many of those now alive who hope to avoid having to re-don human bodies in the future are going to be disappointed. At best Helen Wambach's and my research indicates that most of us will be taking a lengthy vacation from garden Earth while it is replenished and refurbished. Eventually, though, we will have to return to physical level reality to continue our spiritual growth.

Of course the most obvious explanation for the small numbers who find themselves returning in the 2100 A.D. time period is also the simplest. Somehow at that juncture, just over 100 years from now, far fewer physical bodies or "vehicles" will be available than exist today. This assumes that for some reason, as yet unknown, our Earth undergoes a severe drop in population between now and then. As Helen once pointed out to me, this thesis most readily explains the discrepancy between the data reported for 2100 and 2300 A.D. as well. It stands to reason that if there were an important population drop in the late twentieth or early twenty-first century, its effects would be far more clearly visible in the 2100 A.D. period than 200 or more years later.

According to this idea, humanity could be making a comeback from some Apocalyptic disaster by 2300 A.D. It hardly needs to be added that this explanation also agrees with the numerous prophetic predictions concerning an upcoming twenty-first-century Armageddon or other Apocalyptic scenario. Even scientific forecasters admit that we currently stand on the brink of ecological disasters that are becoming increasingly difficult to reverse unless we act now.

Before rashly adopting such an unpleasant hypothesis, however well it might seem to fit overall facts, both Helen and I felt it essential to investigate the actual data sheets filled in by those workshop participants who had reported physical lifetimes in the 2100 A.D. time period. Because of the tiny percentage of subjects who reported future lifetimes in this period, when their subconscious minds were asked to choose between five different eras, initially there were just under 100 data sheets covering 2100 A.D. to work from. These came from the first set of future-lives workshops conducted by Drs. Wambach, Sprinkle and myself.

As mentioned earlier, these first twenty or so workshops were conducted across the United States between 1980 and 1984. They included around 2,500 participants in all. Obviously, virtually all these subjects were Americans. Although specific sociological data was never taken, these volunteers can be assumed to follow about the same profile as those who have been described in Dr. Helen Wambach's two books. The majority were from white, middle-class backgrounds with about 65 to 70 percent being women. Their ages ranged from the mid-twenties to retirees in their seventies.

I personally conducted the second group of around a dozen workshops between 1986 and 1988 in several U.S. cities, including Los Angeles, Atlanta, San Francisco and Toledo, Ohio, and in such French towns as Paris, Bordeaux and Aix en Provence. Again, most participants were from the white middle class with two thirds being women. Their ages ranged from twenty-two to seventy-two, with most being between twenty-five and forty-five years old. Thirty-one percent of this group were French; the rest were Americans. Although these groups were much smaller than those of the 1980–84 workshops, averaging only about ten participants per group, the specific focus on the 2100 era and the possibility to experience it "vicariously" produced 65 data sheets complete enough to be analyzed.

As self-selected volunteers, neither group can be said to reflect an average popular cross section in terms of current conscious-mind beliefs. As volunteers in future-lives workshops, doubtless they had a greater-than-average interest in future studies and ideas, for example. Most were certainly familiar with, if not believers in, the concepts of reincarnation and karma. Almost all had already had the experience of recalling one or more past lifetimes while in a light trance state, often in preceding sessions during the same workshop.

Nonetheless, their stories do represent a fascinating and hitherto untapped source of data about our possible common future. In some ways they resemble the responses given in opinion polls. Their descriptions of the twenty-second century can be compared with each other for obvious points of agreement or discrepancy. They can also be compared with other, consciously devised future scenarios, notably those of scientific forecasters, and with the predictions of present-day psychic channels. Finally, the reports of those American subjects who participated in the first set of workshops, held between 1980–84, can be compared with the strikingly similar results discovered among the answers given by my own French and American workshop subjects who either saw themselves returning to a future 2100 A.D. lifetime or who witnessed that period through the "borrowed eyes" of another.

Even before Helen Wambach's untimely death in 1985, I had already begun a preliminary analysis of the first 100 data sheets that describe the 2100 A.D. time period. Looking over these reports, whose dates given range from 2080 to 2250 A.D., I soon found intriguing news. Contrary to popular futurist "think tank" analyses, virtually none of those participants who reincarnate around 2100 A.D. describe a future world basically similar to ours today only bigger and better. In fact, a majority report conditions with definite negative connotations, either in terms of material or psychological/emotional well-being. Furthermore, the few (just ten) sheets describing conditions of the late twenty-first century (2080–2110 A.D.) depict physical desolation and ruins far more insistently than those that seem to take place a half a century later. Still, there are too few reports from the pre-2100 period for a real analysis.

Gathered between 1980–84, these first hundred reports of future lives around 2100 A.D. reveal several important correlations. The first is the sex or gender ratio, already discussed for past-life cases in Helen's book *Reliving Past Lives*. Once again, even in this smaller sample, the male/female ratio works out to nearly 50/50 with 50.6 percent female lives reported from a total sample of 79 who report their future gender. Forty-six percent of these subjects see themselves returning in male bodies. Thus the approximately 50/50 gender ratio of human populations seems to be predictably constant over time even though 80 percent of the 79 subjects tabulated are currently women. Again, as with the past-life data, this indicates that a number of subjects found themselves in future bodies of the opposite sex.

Naturally this basic sex/gender ratio was one of the first things I looked for when examining the second set of 2100 A.D. reports, made by my French and American subjects between 1986–88. Here I had a total of 65 data sheets with the future life's gender indicated. Two thirds of them (44) are women in their present lifetime. In this group 50.8 percent of the 2100 A.D. subjects report lives in masculine bodies, while 43.1 percent say they are female in the twenty-second century. As with the first group, these figures are much closer to the 50/50 ratio than the current gender distribution of the workshop participants. They thus confirm the 1980–84 data on this point.

Furthermore, as seen in the fact that neither of the 2100 era male/female figures given above add up to 100 percent, a fascinating third statistic must be mentioned. Of the 65 subjects from the second set of workshops, four (6.1 percent) state that their future-life body's gender is either indeterminate or androgynous! This tallies with three reports of androgyny given by Helen Wambach's subjects. One subject from her workshops even mentions having a sex change (male to female) during the 2100 A.D. lifetime!

Despite their limited numbers, these seven androgynous cases for the twenty-second century are very revealing and completely different from what people report for lifetimes remembered from the past. Neither Dr. Wambach, who regressed over 10,000 individuals to past lives before her death, nor I have ever come up with even one "sex change" case or androgynous body during our past-life research workshops. Yet both sets of independently gathered reports about the 2100 A.D. era include small but significant numbers of such "third sex" individuals.

As the entire transsexual concept has only become possible among today's generation, I find that data like this is very supportive of the hypothesis that such past- and future-life "memories" represent something more than just psychological fantasy. Why, if such experiences be pure mental creations, wish-fulfilling or otherwise, would anonymous subjects in independent groups with different researchers divide into nearly equal male/female gender ratios time after time? Why would "third sex" or androgynous reports be found only in future-life data and never among past lives? Such things provide food for thought!

The following table (Table 5-1) illustrates the gender ratios for the two workshop groups. It includes current participants' gender and the gender perceived for the 2100 A.D. era lifetime.

Another key overall statistic reported by the workshop participants concerns longevity. In contrast to recent historical trends toward a longer average human lifespan, the mean age of death reported for those 48 participants in the first 2100 A.D. group who were able to pinpoint this factor is just 62.4 years. It is slightly higher (70.4 years) for the 44 subjects from the second 1986–88 group, who gave an age of death for a combined figure of 66.2 years. By way of comparison, the World Resources Institute estimates that between 1980–85 average life expectancy worldwide equaled 64.6 years. This figure includes such high-mortality areas as Africa (49.7 years) and Asia (57.9 years). In Europe and North America today one

Table 5-1. Sex/Gender Ratio for 2100 A.D. Future Lives

Categories	1980–84 Workshops	1986–88 Workshops	Total
Males today	16	21	37
Females today	63	44	107
Total today	79	65	144
Males 2100	36	33	69
Females 2100	40	28	68
Androgynous 2100	3	4	7
Total 2100 A.D.	79	65	144

can expect to live 73.2 and 71.1 years, respectively.[2]

Still, within this picture of a twenty-second century where the overall life expectancy approximately equals today's, subjects give a broad individual range. Reports vary from accidental death at just 14 years old for the youngest to dying of "old age" at 152 for the oldest case. A novel and thought-provoking response comes from seven participants (five in the first group, two in the second) who state that they simply did not die at all! And 24 others (25.5 percent of the total of the two groups' reports) say that they *chose* to die after completing all essential life tasks. Apparently, if the reports by those progressed into future lifetimes are valid, by 2100 A.D. some people will have mastered the voluntary mental control of bodily functions and thus can "will" them to cease. To these, keeping a worn body functioning apparently is less important than accomplishing desired goals and then "moving on." The other major causes of death reported include violence, including murder and execution, disease (several mentioned respiratory ailments) and accidents. In this area, as in the other categories investigated, I found no significant differences in the data given by the two workshop groups (1980–84 vs. 1986–88).

One of the inconveniences of "polling" the subconscious about either past or future lifetimes is that the data thereby obtained must be immediately written down on preprepared data sheets. This is because as soon as subjects return to ordinary conscious awareness they rapidly forget the information that has appeared while they were in their light trance or "dreaming mind." With individuals either direct questions can be posed and answered verbally while the subject is still under hypnosis or further details can be gotten through personal conversation immediately after the person is awakened. This is obviously impossible with groups.

Thus, although the questionnaires devised by Helen and myself were prepared precisely to elicit as many recalled factual details as possible, most participants filled them in only partially as some events mentioned either had not been experienced fully during the trance state or had already slipped out of conscious awareness during the few moments between the end of the session and the filling in of the questionnaire. In this respect such memories are similar to those of dreams occurring during natural sleep. As soon as one fully awakes much of the dream scenario fades and can be recalled only with effort. Consequently, although nearly 100 percent of our subjects recalled the sex/gender of their future-life bodies, fewer individuals in each group provided detailed answers for most of the other questions asked.

Consequently only 72 of the 100 reports of 2100 A.D. lifetimes, drawn from the 1980–84 batch of cases, were complete enough to provide data for more detailed analysis. Similarly, I was able to use a total of 61 cases from the 1986–88 batch. When added together, therefore, they total 133 subjects overall. As mentioned earlier, this relatively small number of cases makes it impossible to label them representative samples of today's American population in any true statistical sense. As social scientists, both Dr. Wambach and I were fully aware of this when we first looked at the available data. Nonetheless, as many psychological and historical studies draw significant conclusions from far fewer reports, I feel that these 133 cases do provide a basis for a preliminary glimpse into our current culture's "mass dreams" about possible future realities. As such, comparing them for internal similarities and differences can be both interesting and instructive.

Satisfied that the 133 cases available from the two groups of workshops were enough for a beginning analysis at least, I was then faced with the obvious question of how to go about comparing these reports of future individual lifetimes clustered around the suggested target of 2100 A.D. Outside of gender and longevity, what common denominator could be used as a basis for comparison to detect identifiable patterns? Examining the data sheets carefully, I found that one of the first key groups of questions had asked subjects to give their perceptions of their future-life surroundings such as climate, environment and housing. Nearly every participant had filled in this section, at least partially. Here was a relatively impersonal topic area that could provide comparable information.

Having already noted that most of the data sheets contained distinctive descriptions of different physical habitats, I decided to divide all 133 of them accordingly. Starting from the description of the outside environment in which each subject found him or herself, I discovered, to my surprise, that all the data sheets could be fitted into four distinctive general categories or types. These were: (I) "In-space" habitats off of the Earth's surface, either in space stations, spaceships or in experimental colonies on other planets; (II) seemingly New Age communities on Earth, usually in the mountains or near the ocean shore; (III) "Hi-tech" urbanites, mostly living in artificially enclosed or underground cities; and (IV) "rural survivors" in nineteenth-century-style villages along with six "urban survivors" living in the rubble of once-great cities.

The following table (Table 5-2) gives the numbers of cases from each of the two groups of workshops according to the categories listed above.

Life in a spaceship or a space colony off of the Earth marked the most salient characteristic of the first group. This group of 35 cases was dubbed "Type I." It represents 26.3 percent of the total of 133 reports

Table 5-2.   Future-Life Environments for 2100 A.D.

Category Type	1980–84 Workshops	1986–88 Workshops	Total Both Groups
I (In-space)	18	17	35
II (New Age)	14	10	24
III (Hi-tech)	22	19	41
IV (Survivors)	18	15	33
Totals	72	61	133

tabulated. A majority of the 35 Type I subjects (52 percent) reported living in an artificial space station orbiting high above the Earth's atmosphere. The next most numerous group (26 percent) found themselves aboard spaceships. These were apparently interplanetary shuttles, although, in a couple of cases, an interstellar spaceship was specified. Two found themselves in terrestrial colonies or experimental stations on Venus and Mars, while six others (17 percent of the group) gave less specific indications such as "on another planet" or "it seems like an asteroid" or, in one case, simply "not on Earth."

In addition to their nonearthly environment, most subjects categorized as Type I agreed on the kind of clothes they found themselves wearing. Seventy-seven percent said that their clothing consisted of a one-piece, tight-fitting uniform or jumpsuit, often described as "metallic-looking" (usually gray or silver). Many of these mentioned that this outfit included boots. A smaller group (17 percent) saw themselves in more loose-fitting belted tunics or robes. As might be expected, there were a few highly individual costumes described as well. One spacefaring young woman reported standing in high gold-lamé boots, wearing a white mini-skirt and long-sleeved blouse, brought together by a broad gold belt. A flowing cape and gold skullcap completed the outfit. Another report, from a male living on an orbiting space station inside a bubble, described an atmospheric protection suit with wide fins on the feet.

Another group of questions asked focused around the eating of a typical evening meal. Here again there was a fairly broad consensus among Type I reports even though 23 percent gave only vague indications of what they were eating. The majority of those who did reply (40 percent overall) described their typical foodstuffs as either artificial and pre-packaged or pills. "It looks like butter quarters in plastic blocks," said one; "hi-tech, hi-protein minerals and vitamins, served in cubicles on a plastic tray," reported another. Six individuals commented that their food was "bland." Others (20 percent) mentioned a variety of fruits and vegetables as staples of their daily diet. One even saw what he described as "meat loaf," adding, "It's probably synthetic."

As for eating and social arrangements, reports of communal dining were common (34 percent), although several of these added that family groups ate together in community dining halls. Six individuals (17 percent) ate only with their families around them, while an equal number saw themselves eating alone. One woman even found herself nursing as a baby at her mother's breast!

Continuation of some sort of family structure was specifically mentioned in several cases, but one young man reported feeling intense loneliness aboard his spacecraft. Reflecting on this future life while looking out his spaceship's viewing port, he stated:

> I was looking at a star and feeling alone. Perhaps a sense of loss or mournfulness. The starship seemed like my home or assignment but I didn't feel I belonged. Maybe I am a soldier far from home?

Another, happier soul commented that her experience was "Buck Rogers all the way!" She was the one wearing the white miniskirt and gold-lamé boots cited above. Still another individual, who saw himself in a suit and helmet, described constructing an "enormous irrigation rig" with others of the space colony. His work there gave him a feeling of immense satisfaction.

A few of the Type I data sheets provided more details concerning the architecture of their space-station environment. One commented that her colony looked like "layers of buildings with lights and windows." Another, dated 2150 A.D., described a circular, intertwining space station with connecting arms around a central "garden unit" devoted to growing trees and vegetables for the colony. This was echoed by a report of living in a "great wheel in the sky." One woman said she found herself in "something spherical" at the top of a tower. It seemed connected to other similar circular buildings by passageways. Someone else said his colony had a "mushroom-like shape with stem"; it was "all lit up like a lighthouse."

Asked where supplies came from, 33 percent of the Type I reports indicated spaceships' storerooms as their source. Four subjects mentioned that the ships were crewed by extraterrestrials, the rest did not specify. As for the money used to pay for essential items, 51 percent reported using some kind of universal credit system based on one's signature or handprint instead of money. Thirteen (37 percent) failed to answer this question. Only three individuals (8 percent) saw any coins or tokens.

In order to get additional data concerning the possibility and commonness of space travel in the future, Helen and I included a set of questions asking our subjects to describe any "incident with a bright, shining light" that they might find. The questions were very general so that those participants whose subconscious minds took them into a past life could also answer them. Naturally, we also expected that some subjects would not find any such incident at all. The results of those who went to the 2100 A.D. period were generally in keeping with the kind of overall environment in which they found themselves.

Twenty-four of the 35 Type I subjects, or 69 percent, mentioned such an incident. Of these, 54 percent (13 cases) described some kind of spacecraft as the "bright light." All of these descriptions were positive in tone, including those five who stated that the craft had an extraterrestrial crew. One of these said simply, "The ship came to connect with us. We were ready." Another report of an incident with a spaceship indicated it was a power source. That woman subject said, "The spacecraft came and shed light and energized the entire unit and the garden unit took a growth spurt."

Five of the "In-space" participants (14 percent) reported contact with a telepathic light beam, or ray, that either expanded their level of consciousness or imparted an ethical or spiritual message. Through such a ray one subject said, "I could materialize creative thoughts," while another felt a "luminous spiral" transport her "into another dimension." A third reported that the light beam gave him a "deep feeling of security," as if all was well with the world. One final Type I participant remarked that the bright light was in fact an exit sign on his spaceship!

Other significant comments from this group included one by an individual who found herself directing a space shuttle. "This was a limited, unhappy life at the time I saw it," she said. "Our living space was just that, it was not a home." Another, a man living on a space colony named "Gaylord," felt differently. "There was an impression of beauty about the place. We are very happy at our achievements." A third subject commented, "I became aware that my current life [in the twentieth century] is to prepare me for this future one."

Finally, there was this suggestive comment from a woman who situated her future incarnation as sometime between the twenty-first and twenty-second centuries. There she found herself on a large spaceship orbiting the Earth. On the back of her data sheet she remarked:

> We were part of a communication system spanning around planet
> Earth and connected up to other galaxies. Our task is to monitor

groups to leave Earth during the shift of the axis. . . . I had many successful trips to Earth collecting human beings. I had completed my life's task.

In order to give readers as personal a glimpse as possible of the kind of future lives envisioned by those 2100 A.D. subjects who found themselves in a Type I space environment, I have chosen three reports as examples. Two are drawn from Helen Wambach's 1980–84 workshops, and the third from one of my 1986 French groups.

A young woman from one of Helen's workshops in the Midwest found herself returning as a male inhabitant of a "space research colony" that seemed to be located in the Asteroid belt between Mars and Jupiter. Describing the atmosphere as "pleasantly cool and airy," the man's initial vision was limited to a "rather bare" observatory room. A clear bubblelike porthole, however, provided a glimpse of the stars against the black velvet backdrop of space. The "bright light" proved to be a distant star, apparently gone nova. The young man's duties included studying its energy spectrum with quite sophisticated equipment.

Dressed in a "metallic but soft and stretchy" one-piece jumpsuit, the researcher described his white boots as coming equipped with "jet-propelled buttons for antigravity movement." Brown-skinned, with cropped black hair, he mentioned his "strong, well-cared-for" hands and "medium build." Later he found himself eating in what appeared to be a small communal dining room next to a blond woman whom he felt was his wife. A teenaged son sat nearby, while a few other adults took what looked like "prepackaged airline meal trays" from a machine in the corner of the room. Eaten with a single plastic "fork/spoon" utensil, the chunks of warm food reminded him of cubes of butter but were surprisingly tasty.

Asked to go for supplies, this space-colony dweller "walked down a long windowless hallway" to a storeroom. There an "Oriental-looking girl" provided him with several boxes, which he carried back to his laboratory. No money was exchanged; his signature was all that was required. He felt that a "universal charge" system handled payment. He also reported "knowing" that these prepackaged boxes of equipment were shipped to the colony via large space freighters, possibly of extraterrestrial origin. Food and water were manufactured (recycled?) locally in a central hydroponic garden unit that also served as a kind of recreational park when colony residents wanted to relax among more natural surroundings and greenery.

The seemingly placid surroundings and bland routine described by this Type I scientist seem to have masked underlying political unrest and intrigue, however. When asked to describe the circumstances of his death, he reported being "executed by lethal injection" while still in his early forties. Apparently he was involved in some kind of conspiracy against the prevailing political system. Unfortunately, the details of the incident were unclear. Nonetheless, Helen's subject reported feeling that this future life was "left incomplete" by such an unnatural and premature death. It seemed likely that this soul would have to return for further human lifetimes to complete its learning experiences.

The second Type I scenario came from a Southern California housewife who reported a 2100 A.D. life spent as a spaceship pilot. Given Helen's suggestion to "look down at your feet," she found herself in a "young, Oriental male body" dressed in long, narrow, silver boots and a one-piece silvery flying suit with gloves. A form-fitting golden helmet with an adjustable clear-plastic face mask completed the outfit. Although the body seemed youthful, the subject reported feeling that it was really quite elderly. Some artificial means were used to keep the exterior appearance young.

This subject's initial impression as a spaceman was looking out of his craft's cockpit into the docking bay of a much larger space vessel. Side portholes let in artificial light. The front of the man's ship was a large triangle that could apparently be darkened or made translucent as required. Reclining on a "pilot's couch" directly under the now-clear triangular viewpoint, he was carefully steering his ship into its berth using a "clear ball that pivots." Other similar craft were lined up in rows around the huge docking bay of the mother ship. The activity was routine: "I've done it many times," the subject wrote.

This spaceman's occupation seems to be that of a shuttle pilot, for the answers to the series of questions concerning his home life revealed that he had a studio apartment in a row of square buildings set in what seemed a dome-covered city in Siberia. His evening meal consisted of "just wafers and stuff." He shared it with another, smaller individual who had "grayish skin" and wistful childlike eyes. Perhaps it was an extraterrestrial humanoid; the impression was not completely clear. In any case, the two acted as if they knew each other well. The smaller person was said to have "a sweet face."

Unfortunately, this person was unable to recall going for supplies so that information is missing. Drifting in and out of conscious awareness often happens during such group progressions and in past-life regressions as well. His eventual death came from an in-space accident. Apparently a careless misstep during some kind of spaceship maneuver knocked him off balance and he fell down a ladder, crushing his chest. Death arrived as a welcome relief, for by that time this space pilot's life had become a boring routine, seemingly devoid of family or any other significant emotional ties. As we shall see, such feelings of dissatisfaction with the emotional quality of life in the 2100 A.D. period were also common among subjects who found themselves in Type III Hi-tech cities, which seem to be related to the Type I spacefarers. This subject concluded: "It was a very limited and unhappy life by then [time of death]."

In an interesting final comment this subject told Helen Wambach (who had mentioned her own out-of-body insights during recent heart surgery to the group) that she also had undergone a near-death experience in 1975. "It felt so good that I didn't want to return," she noted. Several unexplained serious illnesses in recent years had made her realize that she was still longing to return to what she had found in her NDE. As she put it, "I guess I keep going back and knocking on the door, asking 'Can I come in now?' " Until the time of this 1984 progression at least, the answer was obviously still "No." Her progression experience to 2100 also indicates that she still has more physical human lifetimes ahead of her.

The third Type I report chosen came from a forty-year-old Frenchman with a diploma from Paris' prestigious École des Beaux Arts. Part of a group that I progressed to the future during 1986, his data sheet was one of the seven (4.9 percent) that reported 2100 A.D. lives in an androgynous body. As such I thought it interesting to describe further. For convenience I will use masculine pronouns for his story.

Like most of the other space travelers, Pierre (not his real name) found himself wearing tight-fitting metallic clothes and flexible boots. "His" dark hair was cut short, apparently to fit under a space helmet, which he did not have on at the time as he was already inside a "space platform" orbiting the Earth. Unable to detect any visible secondary sex characteristics, such as breasts, he reported that he felt his body was essentially androgynous. Gender didn't seem to matter very much.

Invited to "look up and become aware of your surroundings," his initial view was along a "vast curving corridor without viewports," which separated the station's spherical working and living "pods." Apparently he was heading "home," for he next described his quarters as being two small interior rooms with "artificial windows" looking out on illusory holographic outdoor scenes that could be changed to suit one's mood. The climate-controlled atmosphere could also be altered from cool to warm as desired. Apparently he lived there alone. Meals were eaten in a communal dining room. While there he saw other station personnel, noting that he felt closest to an older man whom he took to be his work supervisor. All the food was processed and tasted "bland."

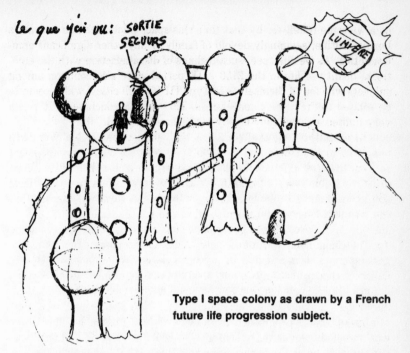

Type I space colony as drawn by a French future life progression subject.

"Gliding along illuminated corridors" to an equipment depot was Pierre's response to the question of how he traveled to get supplies. Like many other Type I subjects, he reported obtaining some sealed plastic-looking cartons there. Whatever he needed was apparently inside; perhaps it had been previously ordered. He registered receipt of the boxes on his wristwatch computer. The supply system seemed automated.

Unlike the other two Type I reports given above, however, Pierre's 2100 A.D. death was nonviolent. It involved some kind of illness whose most notable symptoms were skin ulcers and sores. Although no age of death was given, the sickness described seemed more likely to be space-related than due to old age. He reported a feeling of "liberation" on leaving his future-life body.

The second 2100 A.D. group (Type II) represents what I would like to think of as the budding of a New Age here on the Earth. All of the twenty-four subjects in this group reported living on the planetary surface and having unrestricted contact with a natural environment. Nine (38 percent) described green, rolling hills covered with trees and shrubs. Four indicated living among high mountains (the Andes and Himalayas), with another three next to the ocean. Three described a planned urban environment and one a desert monastic-style retreat. Five others gave less precise descriptions of their surroundings but their reports clearly showed them living in a natural Earth setting. Consequently they were included in Type II.

Virtually all of these New Age dwellers used highly positive descriptive adjectives when commenting on the climate and environment surrounding their communities. Fourteen (58 percent) specifically mentioned finding themselves amid "green" or "lush" lawns and gardens while half (twelve cases) described their environment as "pretty" or "well cared for." In general Type II subjects indicated living in temperate climes with fresh, breathable air. Warm sunny weather or brisk ocean or mountain breezes were frequently cited on their data sheets. The following two comments were typical:

> The climate was warm and moist, always comfortable. The landscape was clean and free from litter; it looked well-groomed with trees and shrubs carefully and skillfully landscaped. The buildings are beautifully planned; a simplistic but artful architecture.

> I was in the mountains—windy and cool. It was summer; many trees and heavy foliage. There were steep valleys and rocks with small flat areas. It was a school for children in a conventlike complex; wing-shaped modern buildings jutting out of the mountainside. . . . I was a teacher in the "school of the healing sisters."
>
> (Peruvian Andes)

Glass, marble, limestone and concrete were all mentioned by Type II subjects as materials used in constructing buildings of a wide variety of styles and shapes. The most common characteristic was mention of incorporating open space or greenhouses into construction (43 percent). Achieving a harmonious marriage of technology and nature was clearly important to those reporting future lives in New Age environments. Nearly two thirds of them (63 percent) also indicated that their living areas were somehow planned units, designed as part of a larger organized community. Special teaching and spiritual roles were likewise mentioned in about half of these reports.

Those who found themselves living in sylvan Type II settlements on Earth during this period reported being dressed quite differently from the Type I space explorers. Seventeen of the twenty-four subjects in this group (71 percent) saw themselves wearing loose-fitting garments such as long robes or tunics. These were accompanied most often by sandals (sometimes plastic) or soft shoes. The dominant colors reported were white (30 percent), gold (17 percent) and blue (14 percent). Only a small minority (17 percent) wore more tight-fitting clothes, including jumpsuits or even shirts and slacks. One woman saw herself barefoot in a swimsuit. Two failed to describe their attire.

Asked about a typical evening meal, one third (8 cases) of the 2100 A.D. New Age subjects had no recollection or didn't answer the question. The rest reported a variety of foodstuffs. Eight (33 percent) said that fruits and vegetables made up their diet, while three others saw fish as part of their evening meal. Only one reported having meat (a "meat stew"). In addition, there was one report of a "bland, synthetic, potato-like vegetable." The most original comment came from a woman who said that in her spiritual community food was eschewed in favor of a musical "energy disk," which gave off nourishing vibrations.

Even though a majority of the Type II participants indicated that they lived in a planned community, family units continued to be widespread. For example, ten (42 percent) mentioned eating at home with their family. Another seven (30 percent) said they ate in communal dining facilities. Some of these reports mentioned the presence of family members along with others at the meal. The rest made no particular mention of where they ate or with whom.

When asked where they got their supplies, most (42 percent) Type II subjects indicated that supplies were kept in a central or communal storehouse. Five subjects (21 percent) mentioned markets or grocery stores and one saw herself at a modern-style shopping mall. The most common item purchased was food (ten reports), including the "energy disks" described above. A signature-based credit system was used as money by seven subjects (29 percent) while five saw coins, bills or "pyramid-shaped" objects being exchanged. The others did not give any indication about how they paid for the supplies they received.

Asked to describe an experience with a "bright, shining light," only five of the 24 Type II participants either failed to find such an experience in their 2100 A.D. lifetime or didn't answer the question. Six others (25 percent) reported seeing some kind of spacecraft in the sky. Their experiences, all positive, were similar to those reported by the Type I data sheets. Three said that the ships brought supplies and two of these commented that such was a commonplace occurrence. The other three described the experiences as special visits to Earth by highly evolved extraterrestrial beings who came in the ships to teach humanity greater spiritual wisdom.

Nearly half of the New Age group's reports (42 percent) emphasized the light's special guiding, or spiritual, character. One subject said a "shaft of light" poured through a high temple window during a religious ceremony. Another saw Jesus at the end of a magnificent white light beam. A woman from one of my California workshops said the light marked "higher spiritual enlightenment" for humanity. "You are light" was the message received by a man who felt the experience was designed to raise human consciousness by the "raising of our vibrations." For others in this group the light represented "wholeness," "the Source" and "the Divinity." It brought "an overpowering sense of love and confidence."

Thus, if one includes the three people mentioned above who saw extraterrestrial teachers descending from spacecraft, over two thirds of the Type II subjects who reported encountering the "bright, shining light" characterized it as profoundly spiritual and uplifting. By comparison, only 14 percent of the Type I space explorers gave the experience any spiritual significance. Of the remaining three New Age subjects who answered this question, two saw the Sun, while one pragmatic individual watched a helicopter landing with supplies.

Of the four 2100 A.D. environments discovered, those who experienced Type II New Age life-styles were by far the most satisfied with their future surroundings. Nearly all (79 percent) the spontaneous comments from this group about their future life experience were positive. The following remarks are representative:

> I felt very positive and contented about my surroundings. . . . It was sad to leave.

> The voice of the Supreme Being gave me instructions as to lead or teach the people of the town and how to divide the work, food. . . . The comfort of the light was overpowering with hope and confidence.

> I said "good-bye old man," on leaving my body. . . . I then went to a much more *crowded* place!

Only one subject made a specifically negative comment about her future New Age life-style. She said, "I was somewhat depressed and I felt a cold environment in my home." Interestingly, hers was the only Type II data sheet to report an accidental death (at the young age of 35). The average lifespan reported for the New Age group was much longer: 92.4 years. By comparison, Type I subjects averaged only 75.5 years, while the mean lifespan for Type III was just 59.8 years during the 2100 A.D. period.

The New Age life-styles enjoyed by the Type II group in this era can best be described by a couple of examples taken from the personal accounts of our workshop participants. Therefore, I have chosen two individual accounts, one from a 1983 workshop led by Helen Wambach and one from a 1987 workshop I gave near Los Angeles, to present in more detail here.

A delightful complex of "spherical and tall, white stone" buildings set among a "lush rolling lawn" with fir trees dotting surrounding hills greeted one of Helen's 1983 workshop participants when asked to "look up and see your surroundings." She had already noticed that this 2100 A.D. lifetime would be lived as a slender white male with "short, curly and dark" hair and "long, artistic hands."

Realizing his name in that future life was "John," there was an "aura of peace and serenity" about him as he walked along a smooth stone path clad in sandals "with straps up the legs to hold them on" and a soft, loosely draped muslin tunic whose folds fell to "about mid-calf." A beautiful "deep-blue, almost violet" sky, punctuated by an occasional small puffy cloud, stretched overhead. It seemed like a crisp, clear morning in early spring. The exact location of this idyllic spot was unclear and didn't seem to matter: "Although on Earth, I don't think it is anywhere we know of today."

Asked about his encounter with the "bright, shining light," John reported seeing "a golden flying saucer with a bright metallic sheen" where the sun shone on it. "It was hovering overhead." A "friendly, familiar" voice from the saucer spoke inside John's mind, greeting him by name. It was a profoundly spiritual experience, yet apparently commonplace, for although John listened intently and almost reverently, his pace did not slacken. "It was instructing me about some lessons I was going to pass along to others in the town: things like how best to share our resources and how to cooperate more fully in some joint project."

John's own living quarters, high up in one of the towers, were as harmoniously arranged as the landscape below: "Everything was set in different shades of off-white, with marble floors and draped wall hangings and low, comfortable couches to sit on." He shared them with his mate, a good-looking blond woman, two young children and an older man, possibly his wife's father. Their evening meal consisted of fruits and vegetables, eaten by hand from gold-colored plates. Although the family didn't seem to eat a lot, the meal was "completely filling" and "tasted great." John felt "comfort and well-being" in his home.

Apparently a scholar, John found himself traveling in a small one-passenger hovercraft, "unlike anything we have today," to a nearby library bookstore for his supplies. There he traded an "oddly shaped metallic coin" for some "books and writing materials." The library was built "like a geometric [geodesic?] dome" and contained books, "printed on soft plastic," and audiovisual materials. "Everything was strangely quiet, as if we didn't need to talk out loud to be understood," he said.

According to Helen's subject, the end of John's life in the twenty-second century was as calm and deliberate as the rest. "I'm eighty-five and it's time to go," he noted. Thus, although "old age" was listed as the cause of death, it would seem that, as was widely reported by others living Type II life-styles, John chose to leave his physical body when he felt it had served its purpose. Death was seen as a necessary and desired transition, neither a tragedy nor a great relief.

The story told by a middle-aged California housewife who attended one of my 1987 workshops shared many of the features that "John" reported but with its own distinctive character. This woman described the outside environment as "warm and beautiful." There were "colorful flowers" everywhere and "thick green lawns," all irrigated by "an elaborate water system." People wore a mixture of long, loose, flowing garments and short belted tunics, usually with sandals.

Nonetheless, it seemed as if most living quarters in her part of the Earth were either underground or "somehow shielded from the Sun's rays, as if they were harmful to our skin." This subject, who reported being a "strong but slender," brown-haired woman named "Rhonda" in that lifetime, noted her skin was very pale, as if seldom exposed to sunshine. This aspect of her report resembled those classified as Type III, all of whom were set underground or within artificial domes. Everything else, however, was more like the Type II New Age life-style.

One of the suggestions that I gave participants in some workshops that had not been raised by Drs. Wambach or Sprinkle involved asking them to "move backwards in Time, still in the same body and lifetime, to about the age of twelve." This gave me the chance to know more about the subject's vision of his or her future childhood and family life. Rhonda found herself as a skinny young girl sitting in her family's apartment. It was bright and cheerful. She was apparently playing some kind of game when suddenly her mother called her. The command was passed telepathically from one room to another. It seemed like their natural way of communication.

Later, taken forward to a "normal, typical day of your life as an adult," she reported waking up between two other individuals in a very large ultramodern bed that could be recessed into the floor at the touch of a button. It was wide enough so that three or four people could sleep in it. Dining arrangements were also more communal than in John's town; people met in a "huge central dining room" with "large glass tables" for their evening meal. A wide variety of foods was available: "I could have anything I could think of" was Rhonda's comment. Apparently most dishes were what we call "finger food," for she ate the meal with her hands off of small glass plates.

Asked to go to a moment when she was performing a routine occupation or activity, Rhonda found herself teaching history and geography to a classroom of young people. Required documents could be obtained by teleportation and charged to a computerized credit system. She also reported being involved in the political and spiritual leadership of her community as well. At one point she experienced being on a raised stage with several other officials, leading some kind of important public ceremony. She later commented that her main purpose in that life was "to be free, to have many mates and enjoy leadership experience."

Like most others who inhabited Type II communities in this era, Rhonda reported living a long and pleasant life. Her death, at "over 100," was again marked down to "old age." As with John, it seemed to have been a preplanned event as she saw "many people" around her when she finally left her body in 2239 A.D. Her feeling just after death was one of being free to soar off to new adventures.

One of the last questions both Helen Wambach and I asked our workshop participants was to estimate where they felt their future lifetimes took place. As mentioned above, all Type I subjects reported lifetimes spent primarily in space or on orbiting space stations, other planets, etc. Of the Type II respondents, nearly half (46 percent) either had no answer or felt their New Age settlements were located in areas unknown today (possibly now under water?). Among the others, specific geographic locations mentioned included the Rocky Mountains, the Himalayas, Greece, the Peruvian Andes (two cases), Finland, a Pacific island, Ireland, New Hampshire, western Africa and two locations in the southeastern United States (North Carolina and the Florida panhandle).

Although never asked about their perception of the overall size of their community, a half dozen of the Type II subjects made spontaneous remarks that they noticed only a sparse population in their vicinity. Some indicated that there was something of an isolated feeling to their life. A typical comment was:

> In general, it felt lonely; not many people around although it was civilized, not chaotic.

Other parallel remarks included:

There were not a lot of others around. . . . I felt there was a small population only.

Not a lot of others around though I had a sense of sharing this place with two or three people. It was some sort of command research [computers or technical] or communal living area removed from the general population, if there is such a thing.

Similar comments were made by subjects classified as Type IV "survivors" as well, including the following: "Few people, apparently a lonely life." One gets the overall impression from many of these reports of the 2100 era that there are large unpopulated areas of the Earth's surface in that time period. This merely reinforces the fact that only about 5 percent of our workshop participants experienced a future life in this time period.

The following remark by a 1986 subject who is now a Southern California journalist but who found himself observing the early 2100 A.D. period through a young woman's eyes may shed some light on this general impression. After describing a spiritual healing ceremony involving people who wore large crystals on their heads, this subject commented:

Except where the people with the crystals were, the planet seemed dark, polluted and toxic.

It's possible that this brief description indicates that the few sylvan Type II environments described will be created and maintained by their inhabitants' positive mental attitudes. This concept, known as "biorelativity," was introduced on page 100 and is more fully discussed on pages 214 to 216. It may be used by Earth's spiritually evolved "gardeners" during the forthcoming Age of Aquarius when telepathy and other mental powers will apparently be more intense and widespread.

The above-quoted comment about the use of crystals to maintain natural, pollution-free surroundings, combined with the clear evidence of a smaller planetary population in 2100 A.D., should make us wonder about what the rest of the Earth will be like at that time. Are the "lush, well-kept" Gardens of Eden described by our Type II subjects small oases of green amid an ecologically ruined planet? In under 150 years from now will Earth's environment blossom only where human thoughts and lifestyles are consciously attuned to nature? A look at the other two types of future civilizations foreseen by Helen's and my workshop participants for the next two centuries may shed light on these possibilities.

6
Mass Dreams of 2100–2200 A.D., Part II:
Hi-Tech Cities and Primitive Survivors

If the Type II communities discussed in the last chapter herald the dawning of a future New Age on Earth, then the next group, named Type III, or "Hi-tech," apparently represents the simultaneous triumph of a cold and mechanical future society devoted mainly to physical survival. Described by 41 subjects, this group was the largest of the four categories based on environmental surroundings (31 percent of the 133 cases). Also located on the Earth's surface, and beneath it, modern, Hi-tech survivalist Type III cities apparently will exist inside huge artificial bubbles or domes or partially underground, sometimes within natural caverns.

Only a smattering of the 41 Type III subjects mentioned direct contact with a natural outdoors environment. Several hinted that the external atmosphere was polluted or poisonous. Thus, six subjects (15 percent) said that they suffered accidental death by suffocation when their air supply suddenly failed outside of their protective cocoon environment, while two others reported death from respiratory ailments at an average age of only 44 years.

The mean lifespan for the entire group was just under 60 years, significantly lower than either Type I or II and even slightly below today's world average of 64.6 years. Interestingly, in terms of longevity, this group proved to be divided into two, nearly equal, halves. Of the 33 Type III subjects who provided the age at which they died, 18 (55 percent) reported dying before the age of 56. These subjects were either executed, murdered, killed in the air-supply accidents cited above or died of a variety of diseases. In the other 15 cases (45 percent), death did not arrive until the subject was 80 or older. Of these, ten reported dying of "old age"; three said they "chose" to die at that point as their life tasks were accomplished; one reported an accidental death and the other a stomach illness.

I feel it is also significant that none of the 2100 A.D. Type III reports described contact with any *natural* freshwater sources such as springs, lakes, rivers or even rain. Only two subjects mentioned water at all, stating that their town was located in a combination of natural caves and man-made domes beneath the ocean. Of the rest nearly half (46 percent) describe living in a city covered by a clear dome or bubble that protects it from the atmosphere. Ten (24 percent), including four of the above, also indicated that their city was at least partially underground.

The Hi-tech aspect of Type III society was reflected in numerous answers about buildings sighted and in general comments about urban design. "Plastic and utilitarian" was the succinct description given of one urban complex. Another subject said his domed city included "no super-fluous architecture." There were ten descriptions of modern-type rectangular buildings and three indications of steeply slanting roofs, possibly for solar-energy collector panels. Two of these were on building complexes half buried in the ground. Only seven Type III reports (17 percent) included descriptions of curved or spherical buildings.

Of the 11 Type III subjects who mentioned specific building materials, seven (64 percent) cited the use of metallic alloys, including gold and silver. Four, including two of the above, mentioned glass and clear plastics. One saw marble buildings and there was a lone report of buildings made of "stucco with tile roofs." That subject said his town was located somewhere in what was once Mexico.

As the question was never directly posed, it is impossible to say whether or not the external environment was actually noxious for all of the Type III inhabitants. Nonetheless, the data they did provide certainly seems to point in that direction. As mentioned above, six of these subjects attributed their deaths to some kind of lung disease or air-supply accident. It was obvious from reading these data sheets that these future "bubble dwellers" definitely preferred their artificial atmosphere to whatever existed outside.

Consequently, almost half of these subjects (44 percent) ignored external conditions altogether or reported that they could not see beyond their domed, artificial environment. Ten (24 percent) indicated the presence of green grass, shrubs and trees *within* the area of controlled atmosphere. Nearly all (83 percent) of the 23 who did mention outside climatic conditions used such terms as "rocky," "barren," "harsh" or "like a desert" to describe what they saw. Fifteen also said that the external world looked "hot," "sunny" or "bright."

From these reports it is clear that the planetary surface of 2100 A.D. seen by the Hi-tech urban residents is far removed from the idyllic setting enjoyed by those in the Type II New Age communities. Only four Type III data sheets (10 percent) ever mentioned grass or trees outside their domed cities. Even these subjects went on, without explaining why, to indicate that they did not live outside or above ground.

Perhaps in keeping with their perceived surroundings, Type III subjects were far less optimistic about their future lives in the 2100 period than either the Type II or Type I workshop participants. Negative comments about the quality of life and the lack of emotional fulfillment were frequent on Type III data sheets. A typical remark by one of Dr. Sprinkle's subjects, asked to describe her feelings about her house was, "My home seemed kind of desolate."

Others gave similar answers. For example, when asked to describe their feelings on returning home (after getting supplies) only five Type III subjects (12 percent) expressed positive thoughts such as "glad to be back." Typical responses ranged from indifference—"It's just a place to live" and "I felt unconcerned, neither good or bad"—to outright dissatisfaction—"I didn't like the coldness of that time" and "I felt sad, repulsed."

In one of my own 1984 workshops, a young woman teacher from Northern California saw herself living a hundred years from now as a young man with "long, thin fingers." The man's community dwelt in a mostly underground complex of modernistic rectangular buildings with slanted roofs. A constant wind swept across the area's desolate prairie, dotted with a few eucalyptus trees, "planted for shelter."

After witnessing his death at age 37 of an intestinal disease, which "shrunk the organs on the lower right side of the body," she provided this descriptive commentary:

I was happy to leave [at death]. . . . I didn't particularly like the group I lived with; it was for survival's sake only. There was no real communication among us. I was sterile and I loved only my few books such as Shakespeare's plays. I guarded them. . . . The others didn't understand about art and literature. Humanistic feelings were lacking. I knew I'd come back in the 2300s to work for a rebirth of humanism.

Another Hi-tech subject compared his future life to that of a "conscious, intelligent machine." Seemingly androgynous, even his name, "Synchnotron II," was mechanical-sounding. Everything in his "emotionally cold" futuristic city was built along "rigid geometric lines" with "no superfluous architecture." It was cold and barren outside with "very little vegetation." Food consisted of computer-dispensed "powdery nutrients" and was eaten in communal dining areas.

Apparently a politician, Synchnotron II stated that his purpose in that life was to "learn to deal with leading crowds." The evening before an election he saw himself giving an "impassioned, persuasive speech" to a large group of fellow citizens. At another point he found himself part of a city delegation establishing contact with a "higher-level, nonearthly civilization." Nonetheless, when he finally chose to die at the advanced age of 100, he retained a "frustrating feeling of wanting to do more" in that life. He felt he was "going on to new tasks" in future incarnations after death.

As a society the Type III cities of 2100 A.D. appear to be linked to the Type I spacefarers, some of which, like the shuttle pilot discussed earlier, apparently used Earth as their home base. Reports on clothing were similar between the two groups, with 59 percent of the Type III data sheets mentioning the same silver-metallic, tight-fitting jumpsuits and boots as standard daily apparel. About the same percentage of each group (30 percent) mentioned eating in a communal dining room. A somewhat larger number (41 percent) ate at home with just family members. Only one saw himself eating alone. Nine did not comment on this aspect of daily life.

Foodstuffs described by the Hi-tech urban dwellers were also similar to those described by In-space dwellers but more variety was noted. Of the 27 Type III individuals who listed the foods they were served at their evening meal, 41 percent (11 subjects) described artificial, prepackaged food or vitamin pellets. These unappetizing (to my palate at least!) foods included "food bars," "a rather bland pink paste from a tube" and a "grape-flavored drink." The rest cited more traditional fare, including eight who mentioned tasting fruit and vegetables and six who had meats and stews on their tables. One man saw himself eating a "steak sandwich," while the final comment came from a Frenchwoman who said the porridge in her bowl was "nourishing but bland." She added, "There wasn't much choice, however."

According to our workship data, the economies of the Hi-tech cities and spacemen also appear closely linked. Both groups, for example, mentioned large storerooms or storage vaults as their chief supply source. Forty-one percent of the Type III subjects saw themselves at such a depot, while a third of the Type I participants gave a similar answer. Several subjects in each of the two groups also said they received essential raw materials or food from a spaceship. Four Type I and two Type III subjects further indicated that the craft was crewed by extraterrestrials or a mixture of humans and friendly aliens. As for money, again the overwhelming majority of the 23 underground urban dwellers who answered this question (83 percent) reported using a signature or handprint-based credit system instead of cash or checks. The others described using plastic, aluminum and crystal tokens or "blue-colored dollar bills" as currency.

Like the other participants in most of Drs. Wambach, Sprinkle and my future-life workshops, Type III subjects were also requested to comment on an incident involving a "bright, shining light" or luminous object. Again, like most of those who found themselves living in space in 2100 A.D., the majority (52 percent) of the 25 Type III subjects who provided such descriptions said that they encountered some kind of spaceship. Four noted that these ships were piloted by extraterrestrials.

However, in contrast to the unanimously positive feelings these spaceship encounters elicited among both Type I and Type II subjects, several of the Type III reports indicated that the ships might represent personal danger or possible enemies. Thus one individual reported feeling "stress" on noticing the ship in the sky. Another said that its sighting frightened her. Her feeling was "Uh-oh, here it comes again!"

Eight of the other Type III inhabitants who experienced the bright light identified it either as the Sun (four cases) or merely as the artificial lights of their domed city. One said it was the glaring surgical lights she encountered on being born in a hospital! Four more gave the incident a spiritual or consciousness-raising character. One woman said she felt it was the "Christ Essence," which then took on the "transparent form" of a being. Someone else described the light she saw as giving her "a warm feeling inside." A woman living in a domed city under the ocean saw a giant crystal that lit up and energized her body.

Nevertheless, even among those Type III subjects who had a spiritual experience with the light, its message was not always well received.

Thus a woman in one of Dr. Wambach's workshops saw the light grow from a dim glow to become "all pervasive." She then said:

I felt it was penetrating my ignorance. It filled me with tears for I knew I could not avoid this destiny. I definitely did *not* like the man who was going to become my husband [in 2100 A.D.]. I had married him following some sort of order. It was an awful experience!

As noted earlier, all of the Type III settlements were located on Earth. Of the 41 subjects who reported living in this type of controlled, artificial environment, 17 could not provide even an approximate location. Among the 24 individuals who did mention where they felt they were living, 15 (63 percent) felt their city was within what had been the continental United States. Four, the largest number to agree on a single state, named Arizona, just where I found myself in 1998! It's possible Arizona came to mind because its sunny desert climate today most closely resembles their 2100 A.D. hot, dry surroundings. Four locations were mentioned twice. These were Louisiana–Mississippi, greater New York City, New England and Utah. Washington State and Oregon were also cited once. Other areas named by Type III participants ranged from Australia, England, France and Saskatchewan to Tibet and the shores of the Indian Ocean.

Other general comments taken from Type III data sheets describing the overall nature of that society included the following:

I was a technician overseer of a huge underground power generator.

I worked at a lookout and receiving station in the Rocky Mountains, checking dials on the control board.

And finally:

I was a recorder of changes in the environment in a small domed outpost in northern Saskatchewan. It was nothing to get excited about as a settlement. I got the feeling there wasn't much choice [about food or clothing] available.

Again I have selected three representative reports classified as Type III Hi-tech urban dwellers so as to give readers a better picture of the kind of society these progressed subjects foresee for the 2100 A.D. period.

The first was drawn from a 1983 workshop given by Helen Wambach, the second from one of Leo Sprinkle's 1984 workshops and the last from one of my 1986 French groups.

"Somewhere north of where New York City is now" was the location given by a woman in a 1983 workshop who reported finding herself living as a young, bald and albino-looking male with "pockmarks" on his face during the early twenty-second century. Looking down at his feet, the youth saw himself wearing narrow shoes that "look like they're made of white spun glass." He also had on a "white, lightweight, all-encompassing" body suit made of some synthetic material. "It is thin and seems disposable, almost like paper," he reported, "but at the same time it protects me from the outside environment somehow." The suit included a clear head-hugging helmet and detachable face mask for indoor/outdoor use.

Protection from "barren, dry and very warm" outside surroundings was apparently important to this youth and those who shared his habitat. "We live in an enclosed city or large village," the data sheet reported. "There is a tall complex of some kind near the center, and a series of domes that cover all the lower buildings." It was "cold, artificial-looking" and the young man didn't find himself terribly happy about returning inside, as if it were a duty to be alive at that time and place.

Once inside the domed city complex, he quickly found himself in a "small room reserved for my family" with his brother and mother of that time period. Apparently the two boys at least slept there. Their evening meal was taken in a large communal dining area with the "couple of dozen" other residents of their building. Everyone ate at long metallic tables covered with easy-cleaning plastic cloths. The food consisted of a "strange substance" that resembled "artificial dehydrated food bars, like those the [twentieth century] astronauts use." There were no utensils at his table as the bars could be eaten directly from their package.

Asked to go for some essential supplies, the albino man, now in his late twenties, saw himself standing in line waiting for "a army-like PX [post exchange] place" to open. It had a sign stating "Community Location Center" on it. A small portable "jet pack" on his back, complete with a "steering bar," enabled him to move about quickly and easily. Once inside he used a plastic credit card to purchase a supply of the same kind of food bars he'd seen earlier in the dining hall. A clerk took the card and punched it into a machine that registered the transaction. He also noticed some people nearby were bartering handicrafts for food and other items such as blankets and small plastic appliances.

Death for this twenty-second-century young man living in such a harsh environment struck early and swiftly. One day, while on a reconnaissance mission outside of the city's artificially controlled atmosphere, his protective body suit or breathing apparatus failed and he quickly suffocated. He was only in his early forties. Still, the experience was far from traumatic; indeed, Helen's subject reported feeling "calm, a bit surprised but almost happy to be free." She reported that "it was as if I had stepped out of a car or some other vehicle. That body wasn't really me."

A man from Colorado provided Dr. R. Leo Sprinkle with the following report on his future life spent as a "average-sized white male with black hair" somewhere in what is now Arizona. Like Helen's New York subject, this individual also first saw himself outside wearing a "one-piece jumpsuit that includes white shoes, a light ski-type jacket, [and] a round, transparent plastic helmet that is removed indoors." He was walking in the desert under a hot sun. No trees or other greenery was visible, only some "low brush" with a series of nearby hills leading toward a distant mountain range.

Ahead toward one side lay his destination: a small, "mostly underground" cubically arranged settlement covered by "a translucent plastic" domed roof sticking up slightly into the air. It was apparently a scientific or research outpost, part of a network of such settlements. This man, who later heard himself called "Blada," knew he lived there with his wife and perhaps a half dozen other co-workers. Once within the dome's air lock, it was apparent that its inner surface was covered with a blue coating as a protection against the Sun's ultraviolet radiation.

Having arrived home just in time for the evening meal, Blada soon joined his wife, a "pretty chestnut-haired woman," in the outpost's communal dining area. The other workers, mostly younger people in their twenties and thirties, soon arrived. Dinner consisted of a "prepackaged seafood or chicken and vegetable stew," supplied in what seem to have been self-heating sealed containers. Seated around one long table, Blada and the others simply opened the steaming packs and ate directly from them, using "steel spoons" as their only utensil. It was the future equivalent of an Old West chuck-wagon stew dinner.

Blada's experience with the "bright, shining light" occurred when "what looked like a small UFO" landed nearby to take him on a shopping trip for additional food packets and other supplies. He reported:

We traveled far but at very high speed to a much larger domelike structure. All the entrances and exits to these structures were

double, with bubblelike air locks. The supplies purchased were prepackaged food, unmarked except for color codes. I paid for them
with color-coded "orgone energy pellets," sealed in plastic. They
were similar in size and shape to a roll of coins.

Commenting on his feelings about returning to the settlement after
this expedition, he stated that while it was "not a difficult mission," he
was nevertheless "glad to be back." As noted above, his was one of the
relatively few positive Type III accounts. Perhaps this was because his
outpost, despite its harsh surroundings, was part of a larger "galactic
network of inhabited worlds." He also noted that "extraterrestrial contact
was a commonplace occurrence."

Even though satisfied with his home environment, that of a small
research center, Blada remained subject to the problems caused by the
noxious atmosphere in his part of the world. At age 84 he, too, succumbed
to a mechanical failure of his portable breathing apparatus while away
from the protected settlement. "I was out on a mission alone when the
helmet failed, so I suffocated to death," he reported. "It was momentarily
traumatic and painful but I didn't panic. . . . Then I was up and out and
into the colorless light from which all colors come. It felt good."

A forty-year-old licensed psychologist and massage therapist from
Paris provided the third Type III example. Progressed ahead to the
period around 2100 A.D., she soon found herself in a middle-aged man's
"rather tired and flabby" body. Dressed in a tight "shiny but silky" me-
tallic-blue jumpsuit, complete with matching boots and headpiece, he was
sitting in the "single, spacious, uncluttered room" where he lived. There
were no windows but he knew there was a "bleak and uninhabitable
desert" outside the city's protective dome.

In any case, he felt no desire to venture out to see. He was content
to remain at home with his wife, only child and her pet dog. Asked about
his feelings toward them, he replied that he was "used to" his wife, loved
his daughter, but "detested" the dog. They ate their evening meal, con-
sisting of "prepackaged dinners heated in a microwave wall unit," in
strained silence.

Later, asked to describe an incident involving a bright light, he was
standing outside, but still under the dome, watching the blinking red
lights of a spaceship as it flew by overhead. Such events were considered
"commonplace," but the incident still left the man feeling "strained and
stressful." Somehow he felt uneasy about what was going on in the world
beyond his urban molehill.

Nonetheless, despite the "closed-in" nature of the artificial underground city, it abounded with technological marvels. A "vast, ultramodern shopping complex," filled with "strange electrical and mechanical appliances" and transport devices, was just a short scooter ride along a recessed roadway from the family's quarters. Everything "gleamed and glistened" under the "rather harsh glare" of the overhead lights. A single plastic credit card was all that was required to make purchases. Sales counters boasted holographic displays of products that could then be ordered for home delivery via an "entirely automated" system. For those not really interested in buying, there were restaurants and entertainment facilities.

The level of material comfort indicated for this urban complex was far greater than that reported by either Blada in his remote underground outpost or the young man living near the site of today's New York City. When, at the age of eighty, he contracted a serious digestive disorder, modern hospital care was available. He saw himself wrapped in white sheets and visited by his wife. The illness was apparently too serious or his body too weak, however, and, like many of today's elderly, he spent his last days hospitalized, hooked up to an IV bottle that may even have been part of a policy of euthanasia. "The doctors are helping me to die quickly and painlessly using the IV fluid," he noted. This use of drugs may account for the man's unusual report of a feeling of "listlessness" immediately after the spirit left the physical body. Most Type III subjects felt relief or at least a release at that moment.

On the back of her questionnaire this French psychologist left a final comment that summed up her future Hi-tech experience. It echoes the sentiments of a majority of those in this group. She wrote:

> During the whole time I was in that enclosed city I felt an overall tension in the air. This was accompanied by a kind of loneliness or feeling of isolation among the people. In fact, the only serene moments came when I was alone. It was as if life's purpose there was mere survival despite all the technological benefits. It wasn't at all what I'd imagined the future to be.

The last group, Type IV, was harder to compare, as it consisted of reports describing 27 rural and six urban settings of a primitive, nontechnical or a post-disaster nature. I decided to label them the "survivors." As in Types II and III, all subjects reported living on Earth. Most gave indications of direct contact with the outside environment but, unlike the Type II New Agers, their surroundings were rural farms or old urban ruins. In contrast to the modernistic Hi-tech reports, Type IV subjects described buildings and transportation settings that appear to be a throwback to around the end of the nineteenth century.

Saving the six urban cases for last, the 27 rural "survivors" reported environments ranging from temperate, green and moist (48 percent), usually with fresh running water nearby, to arid and barren deserts (22 percent) and hilly or snowy mountainous terrain (26 percent). One case was not specific enough to be tabulated. The buildings described were mostly what could be called "traditional," including eight log cabins, five wood-frame and five stone, clay or brick homes. Two mentioned living in a cave, while one described a white marble kind of complex with red tile roofs. The rest gave less specific terms such as "a farm" or "a primitive kind of place."

Type IV clothing was equally diverse, with cloth pants, shirts and skirts predominating (45 percent of the 27 rural cases). A significant minority (33 percent), however, did describe themselves wearing long, plain white or ivory-colored robes, not unlike those described by a majority of the New Age subjects. One man said he found himself in the plain saffron robe of a Buddhist monk. The cave dwellers saw themselves in furs and animal skins, and some of the others, notably those in snowy, mountainous areas, also reported coarse, heavy outerwear and flannel clothes as well. Footgear included shoes or boots (33 percent) and leather or rope sandals (33 percent). The others said they went barefoot.

There seemed to be less variety in the social structures represented among the Type IV rural survivors, with 78 percent (21 of 27 subjects) eating at home with their families. Another 11 percent, including seven of the nine who wore robes, indicated they took their evening meal in a communal dining room. The rest either gave no response or said they ate alone.

As for food, Type IV was the only group in which meat, fish and game dominated the diets described (46 percent of those answering), along with fruits and vegetables (also 46 percent). Beef, chicken and rabbit were mentioned among the meats consumed. Vegetables eaten included squash, beans and Brussels sprouts. No exotic or artificial foods were described by anyone in this group, urban or rural.

Among the twelve rural survivors who answered the question, nine got their essential supplies from some kind of market or general store. The cave dwellers hunted for their necessities. The one report that came closest to describing a modern life-style mentioned a grocery store. Food was the primary supply item received in 82 percent of these rural cases, with one report of kerosene as well. One person just saw himself piling up boxes on a wagon without looking inside.

Payment for this group was limited to traditional coins (38 percent said gold coins and an equal number mentioned silver or copper ones) and paper money (27 percent). One woman who saw herself dressed as a Native American paid for her supplies with black stones. No Type IV subject mentioned a signature or credit system for obtaining desired goods. Nor did any mention extraterrestrial contacts.

When asked about their experience with the bright light, half (13 cases) of the Type IV rural subjects either found no such experience or just ignored the question. This was the largest percentage of any of the four groups not to answer this question. Of the 14 who did answer, not one saw a space vehicle and only one woman said that she saw what looked like a prop-driven airplane. The majority found their light in natural occurrences. Three subjects said the light was the Sun, while two others sighted a "bright star" at night. One saw what he took for a falling meteorite and another saw some air balloons take off from his village green. Three reported spying artificial lights such as streetlamps or light bulbs.

Finally, three of the Type IV subjects associated the bright light with a positive spiritual experience. One woman, living as a man in the twenty-second century, said it was "a minimal experience, like a warm, golden loving feeling." Another simply said, "I felt the presence of God."

The future life-style envisioned by most of the Type IV rural survivors seemed made up of the basics, with few frills or even modern conveniences. Asked about how they traveled, 52 percent of those who responded mentioned walking or driving a horse and wagon. Only four said they used machines—a jeep, a truck, a scooter and a car. Among the more exotic methods for getting around cited were dog sleds, snowshoes and an ox cart. In like manner, all of the tableware described was either metal or wooden. Only the person who saw a "modern grocery store" mentioned eating with a plastic spoon.

Despite this rather simple way of life, commentaries by Type IV subjects were basically positive, although eleven individuals (40 percent) commented on the seeming isolation of their settlement. Essentially these data sheets present a picture of an uncomplicated but rather lonely life-style scattered among small hamlets, religious communities and farms. Typical comments included:

> I walked by the lake [near her town] to die peacefully [at age seventy]. [After death] I viewed the scene. Not many people there. That life was peaceful but lonely.

Another said:

> The landscape was barren, like the aftermath of a forest fire or a
> devastated area. . . . A rigorous but pleasant, warm climate. . . .
> Few people, apparently a lonely life . . . This was in Saskatchewan.

Of the ten rural survivors who described their feelings when returning home from getting supplies, seven made positive remarks such
as "Neat, I liked the place" or "I feel happiness, peace." Two felt indifference. One remarked, "Ho-hum . . ." Only one of the few cave dwellers
indicated dissatisfaction. He felt "unhappiness" in returning to his lonely
cave in a world he felt had been destroyed in a nuclear war.

The cave dweller's despair was an exception. The following comment
by a young woman who apparently lived in some kind of isolated spiritual
community was more typical of what these twenty-seven Type IV rural
data sheets indicated:

> I lived in an adobe building with rough-hewn walls in southern
> Arizona. We wore long, flowing robes and gold-colored sandals.
> There was a central market arcade with the houses grouped around
> it. I felt peace and contentment there. [After death of "old age"] I
> floated out of my body, feeling fruition and that I knew what it was
> all about at last.

Asked where they might have lived this 2100 A.D. lifetime, Type
IV subjects indicated locations scattered across North America, Africa
and Asia, with one hardy soul ending up in Antarctica. Five mentioned
U.S.A. sites, including the Black Hills of South Dakota, Montana, California and Arizona. Four said they were shown central Canada but indicated that its climate was warmer than today. The Russian Steppes,
Mongolia and the Himalayas of India and Tibet were mentioned by four
others. Africa, Israel and "the east coast of South America" completed
the list of Type IV rural settlements.

Two examples of the data sheets describing a future rural Type IV
life-style should give readers a good picture of the kind of conditions that
were most frequently mentioned by this group. The first is from one of
Helen Wambach's 1983 workshops and the second from a group progression I led in Aix en Provence in the spring of 1986.

"I know this is the future but it's confusing because so many things
looked like straight out of an old Western," Paula commented at the
bottom of her questionnaire. A secretary from the San Francisco area,

she had seen herself during her progression to 2100 A.D. as a slender, dark-haired young woman whose face reflected a mix of Caucasian and Native American features. Sometimes barefoot, sometimes wearing soft leather moccasins, she had on a "long, loose-fitting light cotton" dress that appeared to be made of unbleached muslin.

Although she was certain that her village, "more like a small frontier town actually," was located in Canada, the weather was much warmer than it is there today. The environment was clean and wholesome. A small pond lay in a nearby clearing, surrounded by "a stand of pine trees" that blended into a larger forest. Patches of plowed fields lay between fallow meadows in the opposite direction. There seemed to be some animals grazing out there as well.

This pastoral scene came to her while standing in the garden, about fifty feet away from her home. The house itself was a "good-sized log cabin, built with some kind of mortar in between the tree trunks." It had a rough wooden porch out in front and two windows with what looked like "old-fashioned glass panes" in them. The roofline was peaked. A big stone chimney took up most of one end of the house.

Moving inside when asked to "go to a time when you are eating your evening meal," the young woman found herself in a big room that served as kitchen, dining room and living area all at once. A stone hearth dominated one side. Half of it looked like a traditional fireplace, although there was a "metal and glass door." The other part had a "funny-looking black stove" set into it. This metal stove, which appeared to burn wood and whose exhaust pipe fit into the chimney, also had "an oven on one side" and a flat cooking surface with "three places for pots" or skillets.

The meal itself consisted of "fish and what tastes like potato pancakes." She shared the rough wooden table with her husband, a "big blond man," and ten-year-old son. They ate off of "pewterlike plates" and used simple metal utensils—forks, knives and rather large spoons. The meal was "tasty and good" and she noticed that they took time to give thanks to God before eating.

When asked to go for supplies this rural homesteader saw the whole family traveling via horse and wagon to a "general store" where they purchased "sacks of flour, salt and a bright yellow sun bonnet for me." A small gold coin "with foreign lettering on it" was used to pay for the required supplies. The village's main street was a "dusty dirt road" lined with "other log buildings" housing various stores and public meeting places. Although primitive, things looked well cared for and the people walking or riding around town seemed "busy and prosperous." Paula said she felt good about the life she led there and reported being "happy, peaceful" on returning to her log cabin home.

Life on the frontier, even in the future, is hard and often short, however. Somewhere in her late thirties, with her son now a teenager, Paula's future self was killed in a riding accident: "A horse threw me," she wrote. The year 2180 A.D. flashed through her mind. Any feelings of regret about leaving her family behind disappeared as soon as her spirit separated from the body. She reported feeling "lightness and peace" while spiraling upward "toward God's presence" through a light gray mist. Although short, it had been a "full and enriching life, especially in the spiritual sense."

A somewhat different picture of a relatively isolated rural life in the twenty-second century was reported by a young French housewife living in Aix en Provence. Her bare feet and ankles appeared "dark, long and narrow" sticking out from under a "long pale robe, partly woven from silver thread." The "tall and gaunt" body was, however, definitely masculine and appeared old, as attested to by gray hair and a "wisp of a white beard."

My name is Chalmik, she wrote, and I'm something like an astrologer or soothsayer in a small village in Mongolia. My skin, and those of the people around me, is yellow. We live on a high plateau where it's cold and dry. There's a continual chilling wind blowing across the steppe, coming down from tall mountains not too far away. It's mostly flat grassland but dotted with some big trees here and there.

Asked to describe his home, "Chalmik" said he lived in a "low, spread-out" house made of clay bricks and painted white. It contained "one enormous room" partitioned by a multicolored curtain strung across one corner in front of a sleeping alcove. He shared this space with his wife, a "tall, dark-haired Oriental woman," four children, ranging from infancy to their early teens, and his elderly mother. A bit later in the progression he noted that his mother's death, apparently of old age, was "the most emotionally moving" event in that lifetime.

The family ate their evening meal together, sitting on low hassocks around a central platter on which were heaped cooked grains, vegetables and fruits. They used their fingers or short dagger-type knives. Dinner was a "rather noisy affair," punctuated by slurping some kind of "soup or warm drink" from wooden bowls, the licking of fingers and heated discussions of daily activities. Relations between Chalmik and his oldest son were obviously strained. This added tension to the domestic scene.

Chalmik's happiest moments came when he could be alone outside surveying the heavens and charting the courses of the stars and planets with the aid of "a surprisingly sophisticated" portable telescope set on a tripod. It was apparently a family heirloom, just as his profession was an inherited calling. Indeed, the quarrel with his teenaged son concerned the youngster's "disrespect" for that tradition. The flash of a falling meteorite (or orbiting spaceship?) "in broad daylight" caught his attention one day. Later he noted that seeing bright lights pass overhead was a "fairly common" occurrence. He never saw anything land near the village, however, and reported no extraterrestrial contacts.

Items not grown or made by hand within the village, whose chief occupation seemed to be sheep herding, were obtained at a seasonal outdoor bazaar. It was held just outside a larger town set near the base of the mountains, about a day's journey away by foot. Chalmik and his two sons traded cured sheepskins for "buttons and metal tools." He also consulted with his astrologer peers, discussing weather patterns and the meaning of the strange "falling lights" in the sky.

Taken to the last day of that future lifetime, my French subject wrote that one evening when out studying his beloved stars, Chalmick suddenly felt a "sharp, stabbing pain" in his back. Twisting around, he realized that he had been knifed by his disgruntled son. As he fell to the ground his last thought was "how ungrateful, I'm leaving him everything." Then his spirit left the body, rising upward toward the heavens. The year 2197 flashed into his mind as the date of death.

The fourteen workshop participants whose 2100 A.D. stories fit a rural survival pattern were grouped together with six urban future-life reports that also exhibited survival-level life-styles, seemingly a generation or two after some catastrophe had ruined their once-prosperous cities. These six Type IV urban survivors said that their future lives will occur in what had been Moscow (two reports), Cairo (two reports), Manhattan and Los Angeles. These were by far the most unappealing accounts given by workshop participants who progressed into the 2100 A.D. period, with the possible exception of the post-nuclear "cave dweller" mentioned above. I nicknamed them the "urban rubble pickers" based on their environmental and life-style descriptions of survival in what they saw as the ruins of a former civilization.

In all six cases the climate and physical environments experienced were stark and desolate. The first Moscow survivor, a woman from one of Helen Wambach's workshops, provided the most complete report. Apparently a female soldier wearing a green uniform with numbers on the chest, she described that city's environment as "foggy, gray, flat, wet . . . nearly lifeless." The other Moscow case, from a young Frenchman, said the ground looked "irradiated, dry and stony." The air smelled stale and was hard to breathe. He was living in what he perceived to be underground storm sewers.

An American portrayed the Manhattan of 2090 A.D. as having "no plant life. . . . The tops of the buildings were damaged and there were piles of rubble, stones and pebbles underfoot." The two reports from Cairo both cited the overwhelming dryness of the desert atmosphere, with hot, biting, sand-laden winds. One lived in a communal settlement in the desert. The other said there were "very few survivors; it seemed to be after a cataclysm."

In retrospect the report of a San Francisco man who felt he was living among the ruins of Los Angeles was perhaps the most optimistic of the six. This California disaster survivor said:

> I see islands, perhaps what's left of California. The weather is strange, with fog and clouds and lots of purple in the sky. There are many overgrown ruins on the other islands.

Life in these six devastated areas was hardly pleasant either. The New York City post-holocaust survivor saw himself:

> walking down the street entirely alone . . . dinner is some type of red meat with a bone and I eat in a dark basement-type place with a man who has a cap on and red mottled marks on his face. . . . I also have red mottled marks all over my hands. . . . The entire experience left me feeling depressed. I really don't want to come back anyway, much less to a war-destroyed place like that.

In the hovels of what she described as Moscow, the woman soldier in the green uniform reported:

> The marketplace is a set of ramshackle buildings with many people; many are sick and all are dressed shabbily but me. I wear a coarse green uniform-style shirt and jacket and long skirt. It has numbers on the chest. The buildings are brick, square, red and white with three stories. They seem very small, with sloping roofs. I die at

twenty-eight, shot by my husband. My feeling on leaving the body is one of acceptance.

The other Moscow survivor also found himself in the military. He described his experience in these terms:

> I had a strong, heavyset man's body dressed in a dark green military uniform, topped with a black commando-style cap. I was wearing tall black boots. My skin was white. The air stank and was heavy; it was hot and dry. We were underground in what looked like a drainage sewer. There were mostly men around. I think we were searching the area. My throat felt like it was on fire. It was horrible.

This young man, who was in one of my 1987 workshops, popped back into full waking consciousness in the middle of the session, choking and coughing. Such abreactions are highly unusual because all workshop participants are given suggestions that they will experience their past or future lifetimes only as if dreaming and not as current reality. As soon as he became fully awake and back in the present, of course, his throat pain ceased and he was able to relax. He later told me that his parched throat and an overwhelming desire for a drink of cool water had interrupted the experience.

The two Cairo survivors, from two different 1987 workshops, gave less detailed descriptions of their post-disaster conditions. One, a young Frenchwoman, merely described the desolate and parched environment, remarking that there seemed to be "very few people alive." The other, a man from Atlanta, received comfort from his experience with the bright light, whose message was that "no matter what was to come, I had nothing to fear." He went on to state that shortly after this he was executed with a knife for some unnamed "crime against the community," possibly looting. He gave his age at death as just eighteen years old.

The fur-covered cave dweller, one of the rural Type IV survivors mentioned earlier, also noted that he died an early death, which he set at 2080 A.D. He identified his location only as "somewhere in the U.S.A." At the end of his data sheet he commented:

> I was unhappy in this life. I died a nuclear death and felt happy leaving the body.

Although several of the Type IV reports leave one with an uneasy feeling that these subjects were viewing the aftermath of some ancient catastrophe that crippled their ancestors' civilizations, I feel it is important to note that this last case was the *only* death directly attributed to the effects of a nuclear war among all of the 2100 A.D. reports collected in the two groups of future-lives workshops. In a way this "negative fact" of just one radiation death reported, combined with the relative scarcity of reports of large-scale physical devastation (only 6 out of 133 cases, or 4.5 percent) provides hope with regard to the likelihood of a future global nuclear holocaust. Apparently, if these reports are even partly valid, natural disasters and our inability to curb the human race's ongoing pollution of the environment will cause greater harm for future generations than any atomic blasts.

This then is the way the world of 2100 A.D. appears to the subjects who participated in various future-lives workshops held in the U.S.A. and France between 1980 and 1988. How should we interpret this remarkable data? Naturally, the easiest answer is either to ignore these findings altogether or to demean them as pure psychological fantasy or the product of overactive imaginations. This may well be the response of the intellectual establishment and classical futurists, whose forecasts tend to define progress in purely materialistic terms. Nonetheless, as a researcher and as a therapist who knows the value of alternate ways of viewing reality, I think that we need to consider them seriously, at the very least as testimony about mass perceptions of the world's future in the 1980s.

How probable is the advent of the environmental and social conditions described by Drs. Wambach's, Sprinkle's and my future-lives workshop participants? While saving a fuller discussion of alternate ways I feel we can view these graphic future "mass dreams" portraits until after the presentation of the 2300–2500 A.D. data, it is clear that several of the descriptions given above for the 2100 era are already developing today.

For example, of the 35 subjects that perceive what I label a Type I "In-space" environment, 52 percent indicate living aboard some kind of space colony or orbiting space station. Another 26 percent describe traveling around the solar system aboard space shuttles. Already, as of the late 1980s, both the United States and the Soviet Union have sent numerous astronauts into space, and the resumption of America's space-shuttle flights after the Challenger tragedy has demonstrated that humanity is going to keep its planned rendezvous with our sister planets in due time.

Moreover, in a press release timed to coincide with Discovery's successful 1988 mission, America unveiled plans for construction of a $23

billion orbiting space station to be completed in early 1998 and permanently inhabited as early as late 1996. This project, sponsored by the
United States and eleven other Western nations, is destined to "lay the
groundwork for a colony on the Moon or a manned mission to Mars,"
according to the September 30, 1988, Associated Press news release. The
orbiting station will feature pressurized laboratory units, "allowing astronauts to do research wearing ordinary clothes." Its construction will
require at least twenty-two space-shuttle flights over a period exceeding
three years. Buck Rogers may not be not so very far away after all![1]

As for the apparently somewhat isolated Type II New Age communities, examples of remote, mountaintop retreats have existed
throughout human history. Current examples of such planned, spiritually
oriented environments include Sun Bear and the Bear Tribe's interracial
group near Spokane, Washington, and the New Age settlements created
by followers of J. Z. Knight's "Ramtha" scattered across the Pacific
Northwest. Several similar projects have sprung up in the southwestern
deserts of Arizona and New Mexico where ancient "energy vortices" are
said to provide a beneficial influence, although I've yet to hear of a group
subsisting solely on luminous "energy disks" as one of the Type II reports
discussed in the previous chapter predicts. The largest of these energy
vortices are located near Sedona, Arizona.

An especially ambitious spiritual community project is under way at
Blue Mountain, high in the Rockies, just ten miles south of Colorado
Springs. Psychic Verna Yater, Ph.D., co-founder of the Santa Barbara-
based Spiritual Sciences Institute, purchased "tract No. Seven" on first
sight in October 1978, as she was already convinced that it was a sacred
spot, located on invisible energy "ley lines" connected to Machu Picchu
and the Great Pyramid at Giza.

Situated at 8,400 feet, the forty-four acre parcel is destined to become
a spiritual healing and retreat center. Dr. Yater sees it as one of twelve
"sacred citadels" that will provide emergency refuge and assistance for
North Americans during what she feels is an inevitable upcoming geophysical cataclysm in the 1990s. Already in use for summer spiritual-
healing seminars, the Blue Mountain center may someday provide shelter
for "thousands" of refugees. Preparations are currently under way for
providing it with alternate natural power sources, based on wind, water
and solar energy, and for underground shelters to protect inhabitants
against predicted gale-force winds, foreseen for a short period in 1995
when the Earth's rotation stops and the poles shift.

Dr. Yater and her colleagues insist, however, that the real benefits of the Blue Mountain center lie in the holistic healing and raising of spiritual consciousness work that is to be performed there during the coming years. "We're building it regardless of whether the predicted Earth shifts happen or not," she told me in a 1988 personal interview. "It is an opportunity for people to go to study, to advance their spiritual development and as a place of research."[2]

It is interesting to note that at least one Type II subject saw herself in just such a Rocky Mountain New Age center in the twenty-second century. Blue Mountain may prove the precursor of an entire way of life in the not so distant future.

Similarly, it is also clear that today's world is already sowing the seeds of the less pleasant Type III "Hi-tech," enclosed or underground cities, set in hostile, barren surroundings. It will not take a nuclear holocaust to bring our planetary environment to the brink of disaster; individual greed and lack of social responsibility are sufficient, particularly when combined with the understandable desire of the Third World to gain the material prosperity that only industrial societies have attained thus far.

Unfortunately, evidence of mounting ecological problems, even disasters, is commonplace today. In *Our Common Future* the special United Nations-sponsored World Commission on Environment and Development study cites six major environmental catastrophes that jeopardized our health during its tenure of just 900 days (October 1984–April 1987). These included the Bhopal, India, toxic chemical leak that killed 2,000 and injured 200,000 others; the U.S.S.R.'s Chernobyl nuclear reactor explosion and resultant planet-wide fallout, the effects of which are still being monitored among 170,000 people; the Basel, Switzerland, chemical solvents fire that polluted the Rhine River; a natural-gas tank explosion in Mexico City that killed over 1,000 victims; the African drought-caused famine that threatened some 35 million people with starvation, having killed at least a million already; and, finally, worldwide contamination of drinking water and inadequate food supplies that killed an estimated 60 million, mostly children and infants, during this three-year period.[3]

Two other looming natural catastrophes mentioned elsewhere in the commission's report and widely reported in the press in recent years are the depletion of the atmosphere's high-level ozone layer and the "greenhouse effect" resulting from mankind's abundant use of fossil fuels, whose burning releases excess carbon dioxide and certain other gases, thereby trapping solar radiation in the atmosphere and causing the warming of the Earth's surface.

The recent discovery of growing "holes" in the protective ozone layer over the polar regions means that more ultraviolet radiation, harmful to our skin, is penetrating into the atmosphere. If this trend is not reversed, specially treated sunshade domes, like those described by one of our New Age subjects in the last chapter, might be required for outdoor activities one day. The most alarming "greenhouse effect" would be significant melting of the polar ice caps, which could raise the world's ocean levels by as much as five to ten feet. This is more than enough to flood virtually all the world's coastal cities and major ports. It could account for Helen Wambach's future vision of her niece measuring coastal flooding in New Jersey, mentioned in Chapter 2.

The U.S. Environmental Protection Agency, in a 1983 report, stated that "changes by the end of the twenty-first century could be catastrophic taken in the context of today's world." Follow-up articles in such major American media as *Time* magazine, in October 1987, and *The New York Times*, July 19, 1988, underscore the seriousness of these brewing air-pollution problems already today.[4]

The worst of the matter, however, is that political and economic considerations have ensured that up until now only halfhearted palliative measures have been taken to counter these potential ecological disasters. It is a well-known political fact that as-yet-unborn generations do not decide elections. Nonetheless, if reincarnation does exist and if the future "mass dreams" of these workshop participants do represent their twenty-second century incarnations, then perhaps we need to consider more carefully just who is going to inherit this Earth after all! The bleak Type III Hi-tech reports were, after all, the largest single category in the survey.

In reviewing and analyzing the 2100 A.D. data sheets, I personally was most intrigued by the primitive, mostly rural survivors that I grouped together as Type IV. How, short of a global nuclear war, which would probably eliminate human society altogether, could so many people see their "future selves" living a nineteenth-century, frontier life-style? I wondered. A number of the Type IV subjects had similar thoughts when they returned to full, waking consciousness at the end of the session. Several commented at the bottom of their questionnaires that the conditions they had seen seemed more like a past life than something set over a century in the future. Still, the dates they received were consistently in the twenty-second century and many agreed that climatic conditions were different as well. Canada and the American Northwest were perceived as significantly warmer, for example.

It wasn't until recently, when I happened to pick up a book that included comments from the future forecasts made in the mid-1970s by the Club of Rome, a group of eminent European scientists and economists, that I began to understand that the conditions for producing Type IV societies already exist today. According to Janine Delaunay's *Halte à la Croissance?*, the Club of Rome's researchers established a series of twelve computer-generated models of potential global socioeconomic conditions for the period between 1900 and 2100 A.D. These dozen alternative "best" to "worst" cases of what the world might look like in another century were based on nearly 500 different items, ranging from population growth and environmental conditions to industrial and agricultural productivity. The models explicitly excluded any possibility of nuclear war or global catastrophes. They were based on existing observable, factual data and foreseeable trends alone.[5]

What do the Club of Rome's scientific and objective models project for the start of the twenty-second century? The first scenario was based on simply projecting current (1970) trends forward in time. This model predicted that, by the year 2000, world food supplies would be unable to meet minimum demands due to unchecked population growth; starvation and hunger would be widespread. Scarcity of energy and natural resources would precipitate a worldwide depression. Within thirty years population growth would begin to stabilize as billions no longer had the strength to reproduce. By the end of the twenty-first century not only would humanity's average standard of living have fallen below that of 1900 but lack of natural resources, especially energy, would keep it at a nineteenth-century level or lower for the foreseeable future.

Other cases that postulated that natural resources would become "unlimited" due to technological advances predicted that pollution of the environment resulting from unchecked population growth and industrialization would produce similar social and economic havoc by the mid-twenty-first century. Again, by 2100 A.D., the world's standard of living would have fallen to nineteenth-century levels. Even reducing polluting factors to 25 percent of those existing in 1975 and doubling world food productivity postponed the collapse by only a few decades. The twenty-second century result was still a standard of living below that of 1900.

The only two "satisfactory" scenarios, where the living standard remained almost at current twentieth-century levels, required immediate and draconian measures aimed at (1) stabilizing world population at 1975 levels, (2) halting industrial expansion and substituting a service-oriented economy, (3) recycling natural resources, (4) reclaiming lost cropland and rejuvenating forests and (5) reducing air and water pollution to a quarter of their 1975 levels.

Such overall socioeconomic controls of course implied the end of democracy and a degree of regimentation of daily life as yet unpredictable. The report concluded with the sobering warning that even these harsh measures would not be enough to forestall planetary collapse into pre-1900 conditions if they were postponed from 1975 to the year 2000 A.D. And, as mentioned earlier, it precludes the outbreak of a near-suicidal nuclear confrontation over who will control Earth's remaining resources and energy production. Nor, as it dates from the 1970s, does it include the impact of debilitating global epidemics such as AIDS or new outbreaks of influenza or measles.

Does this admittedly gloomy picture of life in at least parts of the Earth by the twenty-second century mean that we should all be heading for bomb shelters or Greenland or the Rocky Mountains tomorrow? Should we evacuate Manhattan, Moscow and Los Angeles immediately? Is it time to follow the Mormons' example and lay up a year's supply of food under the bed or in the attic? *Of course not.*

Even if the parameters seem set for a sudden drop in Earth's living standard and probably its population in the next century, many details affecting the timing and nature of the events that will cause these results remain open for conscious action and different individual options. All of today's psychic channels, as well as the messages of the Virgin Mary in her appearances at Fatima and recently in Yugoslavia at Medjugorje, stress the conditional nature of future situations. Because, as Edgar Cayce reminds us, "mind is ever the builder," we hold the key to what is going to happen to us in the future by how we think and act today.

Therefore, instead of blindly searching either for so-called safety lands to avoid the predicted coming natural cataclysms or for oblivion via drugs and alcohol or other unproductive forms of escapism, let us rather blend our joint efforts to raising human consciousness about our true immortal and spiritual identity around the planet. Let us begin *now* to take personal responsibility for our own immediate mental and physical environment. Let us begin again to "walk softly on the back of the Earth Mother," as the Hopi suggest.

Individual or collective prayer and meditation, if pursued sincerely and diligently, can work miracles. This has been proven throughout human history in times of crisis. It can be so again today if and as Earth's collected billions join together to build a positive common future and especially to avert a nuclear holocaust, which seems to me to be surely the worst way to solve our planet's many current problems!

As we shall see in the next two chapters, the reports from those subjects who progressed to the twenty-fourth and twenty-fifth centuries (2300–2500 A.D.) present a brighter picture of humanity's future further ahead. These reports indicate that in the two to three centuries following 2100 A.D., humanity seems to have broken the bounds of the solar system at last while also distinctly improving the quality of life back here on Earth as well. Nearly half of the 2300 A.D. subjects report lifetimes spent off exploring new worlds in outer space. Almost all of the others describe living on a regenerated, flowering Earth. Nonetheless, a majority of us are apparently still enjoying our lengthy vacation from physical reality and linear Time as only 12 percent of the workshop participants saw themselves in physical bodies between 300 and 400 years from now.

* 7 *

Mass Dreams of 2300 A.D. and Beyond, Part I:

The Outward Wave

Compared with the situation prevailing in the twenty-second century, humanity's future prospects appear to have improved by the period following 2300 A.D., according to Helen Wambach's and my "poll of the subconscious mind." The first evidence of this is the significantly larger number of workshop participants who found themselves "alive" again during this latter period. Of the approximately 2,500 individuals who participated in the 1980–84 workshops, conducted by Helen Wambach, R. Leo Sprinkle and myself, only 98 provided data concerning 2100 era lifetimes. Of these just 79 were complete enough to be compared against each other. These cases, along with those from my 1986–88 workshops, were analyzed in the preceding chapter.

For the 2300 A.D. era, however, the same 1980–84 workshops produced a total of 273 subjects reporting physical lifetimes plus ten who said they were alive in a kind of "energy body" without gender or most of the other characteristics we associate with material consciousness or life. This total of 273 reports of physical lifetimes lived around 2300 A.D. is nearly 11.5 percent, more than double the 2100 figure. Of these 273 cases I was able to use 258 in the sex/gender ratio analysis that follows (the other 15 were too incomplete). To these I have added twelve 2300–2500 A.D. reports coming from my own 1986–88 seminars, which, as mentioned in Chapter 5, focused on the 2100 A.D. period. These twelve

156

more recent cases include eight French subjects; all the others are Americans. Thus there were 270 cases for which present-day and future-life sex/gender could be compared.

Table 7-1 below provides the sex/gender ratios for these 270 cases from 2300 A.D. and beyond.

As can readily be seen from this table, once again the present-life gender ratio of men to women is heavily lopsided in favor of female workshop participants. As with the 2100 A.D. cases, 80 percent of the subjects who reported living in the twenty-fourth century and beyond are female today. This just reflects the fact that many more women than men attended Helen's and my workshops. This has consistently been the case throughout both our past- and future-life research. It reflects today's social attitudes toward these topics.

When the future lifetimes of 2300 A.D. are revealed, however, we find that again, just as for the 2100 A.D. cases, the disclosed genders orient themselves around the 50/50 ratio, which seems to be a universal human constant. Thus, in this sample of 270 cases, 135, or exactly half (50.0 percent) of the subjects found themselves inhabiting male bodies. The other half divided into a large female majority (42.1 percent of the total sample) and a handful (6.7 percent) of "third sex" or seemingly androgynous bodies. This larger sample, therefore, confirms the observations noted in Chapter 5 about the 144 cases from the 2100 A.D. time period. (See Table 5-1, page 114.)

A second positive trend in relation to the 2100 A.D. data has to do with the average lifespan disclosed by 174 data sheets from the 2300 A.D. time period. Nearly two thirds (64 percent) of the 270 subjects provided the age and cause of their future-life deaths on their data sheets. The average future lifespan revealed rose from 66.2 years for the 2100 A.D. reports to 73.1 years for the 2300 period. This figure would have reached

Table 7-1.   2300 A.D. and Beyond: Sex/Gender Ratio

Gender	Today	2300 A.D.
Male:	53	135
Female:	217	118
Androgynous:	—	17
Total Cases:	270	270

76.7 years if the 28 cases of space-related deaths were subtracted. As might be expected, the average lifespan of spaceship crews and space-station personnel (54.3 years) was the shortest of all the groups in this future period. Table 7-2, listing the environment-based groups, gives the average lifespan data for the 174 reported cases. Only those of the Type II "New Age" communities and Type V, "Beyond 2600 A.D.," exceed figures already common among today's Western industrialized societies.

As with the twenty-second-century data, the workshop subjects traveling to 2300 A.D. and beyond reported a wide range of lifespans and varying causes of their eventual deaths. The disclosed age of death for this group varied from only 25 years old (two cases: one a spaceship accident, the other, death in childbirth) to 400 years old (reported by a 2700 A.D. monk who said his "body wore out"). Not counted in these statistics were 12 exceptional cases, all from Type Ic ("Non-solar system") planets, where the subjects said either they simply didn't die at all but transmuted their body energy into another form or gave lifespans of 2,000 years or longer (two cases). Obviously, if these last two subjects' data were added to the rest, the overall average lifespan would have been significantly lengthened (to 101 years). The data, however, seemed too far askew from the vast majority of reports to be comparable.

Disease was the cause of death most frequently listed on the 178 data sheets where such information was given. A variety of illnesses, ranging from "radiation sickness" (two cases, including one in space) to heart failure (10 cases) accounted for nearly a third of the causes of death mentioned (54 cases, or 30 percent). Following close behind were 50 cases (28 percent) in which the subject reported choosing to leave his or her physical body voluntarily. Most of these voluntary departures took place beyond 80 years old, but one was mentioned at age 45 by a subject who said that it was "time to learn something new." Another, who reported his death at age 39, said "It's time to go!" As with the 2100 A.D. reports, many of the future-life subjects from 2300 and beyond indicated a serenity and flexibility in dealing with the dissolution of their physical form that is widely different from today's perceptions.

Old age, or phrases such as "no energy left" or "died in my sleep," accounted for 34 more cases (19 percent) of the 178 reported. The average age of these old-timers was 86.2 years. Still, one subject living on a space station orbiting the Sun remarked that his "old age" death at age 46 was not unusual as in space "everyone dies young; their bodies just wear out." As noted earlier, spaceship crews and space-station inhabitants gave the shortest average lifespan of any 2300 group.

Accidents and violence in some form or another accounted for the rest of the causes of death listed by the 2300 A.D. subjects (22 percent). Again, life in space was reported as much more hazardous than that on either Earth or Non-solar system planets.[11] Space accidents made up the majority (56 percent) of the 30 accidental deaths mentioned. The average age of their victims was only 33.3 years. The ten violent deaths included four murders (shootings, stabbings, etc.) and three executions, including one by lethal injection and another by a "laser beam" type weapon. Two subjects reported battle deaths while one spaceship pilot apparently committed suicide. In his report he said he died when he deliberately "plunged the ship into the Sun," possibly to avoid capture by the enemy.

It is interesting to note that no violent deaths were reported either on Non-solar system planets or among what seem to be two types of evolving New Age communities here on Earth. As with the 2100 reports, the highest number of deaths by violence (six cases, or 17 percent of the group total) was found among the 2300 A.D. version of the Type III Hi-tech futuristic domed cities (labeled Type IIIa). Along with those who find themselves in the aftermath of future military conflicts (Type IVb), the enclosed urban environment described by the Type III subjects in both future time periods seems to be the least pleasant and most violent of any of the future-life scenarios envisioned by these workshop participants.

After gathering sex/gender ratios and average-age and cause-of-death statistics, I again decided to analyze the future data sheets according to the surroundings in which the subjects reported finding themselves. Unlike the 2100–2250 period, which was relatively compact, I found that the data for "2300 A.D. and beyond" covered a longer span of time. Therefore, in order to maximize comparability, I took out the dozen reports that dated from beyond the twenty-sixth century and made them a separate category. There were also seven 2300 A.D. data sheets in which although the future-life gender was identified, the subjects had been unable to recall any further details of their lives. Putting these nineteen data sheets aside, along with the ten that discussed an alternate kind of life in an "energy body," gave me 251 reports to be categorized according to environment.

Table 7-2, below, provides a summary of the 2300–2500 A.D. groups that I was able to discern among the 251 data sheets examined more carefully.

As can be seen by this table, most of the basic environmental categories reported for 2100 A.D. continue to apply through the twenty-fourth

Table 7-2. 2300–2500 A.D. Groups

Categories	Male	Female	Androg.	Total	Avg. Age at Death
Ia In-Space	32	20	4	56	54.3 yrs
Ib Solar Space Colony	8	5	0	13	65.8 yrs
Ic Non-solar System Planet	18	20	2	40	62.2 yrs
Total Off-Earth:	58	45	6	109	59.2 yrs
II New Age	14	38	0	52	99.6 yrs
IIIa Hi-tech	18	10	8	36	56.7 yrs
IIIb Hi-tech Evolved	12	6	2	20	70.9 yrs
IVa Rustic	12	12	0	24	59.8 yrs
IVb Survivors	8	2	0	10	71.8 yrs
Total On-Earth:	64	68	10	142	74.3 yrs
General Total:	122	113	16	251	69.2 yrs
V Group Beyond 2600 A.D.:	9	2	1	12	152.1 yrs

and twenty-fifth centuries. Nonetheless, there are significant changes as well. To keep comparisons between this and the last chapter as easy as possible, I have used the same Roman numeral types I to IV to represent the same basic categories, although splitting Types III and IV into two sections each for clarity. This chapter is devoted to Type I, humanity's "outward wave" into space. Types II to IV, those who find themselves returning to the Earth, will be discussed in the next chapter.

Due to the evolutionary nature of human society during this period, however, and especially its surge outward into interstellar space, I have also subdivided Type I into three groups. Thus, Type Ia ("In-Space") represents those 56 subjects who reported living either aboard a spacecraft or on space stations orbiting the Sun. Type Ib (Solar Space Colony) shows the 13 reports of life in space colonies on other planets of our solar system, including the Moon. The 40 Type Ic reports are descriptions given of life on "Non-solar System Planets," apparently scattered throughout the galaxy.

Taken together, these 109 "not-on-Earth" data sheets make up almost half of the total 2300 A.D. sample (44 percent). This is practically double the percentage of Type I "In-space" reports from the 2100 period (26 percent). Furthermore, in 2100 there were only two Non-solar system accounts, each about a future life aboard an intergalactic spaceship. Suddenly, after 2300, literally dozens of reports of men and women living a wide variety of life-styles on faraway planets with such unusual names as "Alpha," "Centor" or "Zert" appeared. One subject said his future-life location was known simply as "Galaxy 28975."

These reports testify to an apparent outward wave of human beings across the cosmos during the flowering of the Age of Aquarius. Whether or not this exodus is one of reincarnating souls, freed from Earth's schoolrooms at last, or a science-fiction-style human "conquest of space" in physical bodies is not entirely clear. Given the nature of the reports, which reveal such characteristically human traits as violence and war during some of these future lifetimes, the latter is more probable. Certainly Types Ia and Ib, space colonization within the solar system, represent a real material likelihood for this time period. And at least one of the interstellar reports suggests that there could be physical contact between Earth and human civilizations on planets beyond our solar system as well. When asked about her experience with the bright light, this subject from one of Dr. R. Leo Sprinkle's workshops, stated:

> My name was "Tia" and I lived in a huge golden pyramid on an island continent [of a Non-solar system planet]. One day a ship came to the center of the island. Aliens from the Earth emerged. I felt sorry for them as they had experienced a great blast.

Another individual, from one of Helen Wambach's workshops, commented that for her the common denominator between Earth and other civilized planets was their tree populations. On her 2300 A.D. data sheet she wrote:

> I had the impression that the trees had some connection to outer space. It had been scientifically proven that trees were a transmitter from the Earth to other planets and had become revered. Therefore logging had become extinct and our heat and housing were synthetic.

Similarly, 44 of the 142 participants who found themselves reborn on Earth during the 2300–2500 era mention seeing spaceships as their experience with the "bright, shining light." Six, four from the "Hi-tech" urban centers and two rural dwellers, specifically state that they received supplies from such ships. Seven other data sheets from Earth dwellers mention meetings with extraterrestrial beings. Most of these get-togethers seem to have been positive occasions, with the aliens providing advanced technical knowledge or spiritual wisdom. A typical report stated that such encounters were "routine."

One woman, however, did say she felt "uncomfortable" in the presence of a "thin alien being," while a man said he "didn't like" some non-human visitors he encountered in his communal dining hall. None of the 2300-era subjects identified the origin of the extraterrestrials, although one report from 2100 A.D. mentioned contact with humanoids from a planet in the Pleiades star system.

It should be noted here that all such references to these "encounters of the third kind" were offered spontaneously. Our subjects were never specifically asked about extraterrestrial contacts to avoid planting such a suggestion in their minds. Further, as the workshop format offered them a choice between regressing to a past lifetime or moving ahead to a future one, both Helen and I felt that the questions needed to be sufficiently general to apply to all time periods.

If accounts of alien encounters were relatively rare among these data sheets, descriptions of human spacefaring were common. As mentioned earlier, nearly half of the participants who went to the 2300 A.D. time period described living off of the Earth's surface. Even among those who remained here, approximately half mentioned either riding in or sighting a spacecraft as an everyday event. It was nothing out of the ordinary. As with the 2100 A.D. data, only those who saw themselves in Type IVa rural communities seemed divorced from a human civilization, which by 2300 extended far beyond Terra's local boundaries. And even of those two dozen Type IVa "Rustic" cases that were set in a rural environment, two cited receiving supplies from a spaceship and three others said they used a "flying car" or a hovercraft when going shopping.

The most space-oriented subjects were, naturally, those living and working either in spaceships or on space stations orbiting the Sun. They are grouped together as Type Ia "In-space" on Table 7-2. The 56 Type Ia data sheets represent nearly one quarter (22 percent) of the 251 cases tabulated for the 2300–2500 A.D. period. Of these, half (28) gave their age at death. The youngest (today a Frenchwoman teacher who was 42 at the time of the workshop) reported dying as a young man at age 25 in a fiery crash between two spaceships off the planet "Xenon" in 2340 A.D.; the oldest (an American housewife today) said she chose to leave her (male) physical body at the age of 100. The overall average lifespan of Type Ia was just 54.3 years. Even in the future, apparently, space remains a hostile environment for human beings.

For analytical purposes these "In-space" cases can be combined with the 13 Type Ib, "Solar Space Colony," that relatively small number of subjects who found themselves living in encapsulated space colonies on the Earth's sister planets, including the Moon. If the data provided by our workshop participants can be believed, sometime by the twenty-sixth century the human race will have established inhabited research colonies on several planets, including Mars (three cases), Venus (two cases), the Asteroids (two cases), Uranus or one of its moons (one case), Pluto (one case) and the Moon (four cases).

None of their descriptions, however, seems to indicate mass human migration to the other planets circling our Sun. Apparently the harsh environments of our planetary neighbors makes them permanently unsuitable for life in physical human bodies. Thus, twelve of the thirteen Type Ib subjects specified that their artificial Earth-like environment, that in four cases included trees, was protected by a huge dome.

The average lifespan for the space-colony residents was 65.8 years. The youngest reported it was "just time to go" at age 44 (Pluto colony), while the oldest died peacefully at 85 of "old age" in an interior garden after a rewarding life as a scientist on Mars. This individual, a California woman who participated in one of Helen Wambach's 1983 workshops, described her future Martian life in these terms:

> My name was "Jabal;" I was an astronomer. There were only a very few people in the glassed-in town, which mainly served to support the observatory. My strongest impression was how deeply I loved my wife [of that life time; current identity not known]. She predeceased me by 20 years or so and I never remarried. I saw the year 2364 as the date of death.

When asked to look down at his hands and feet, Jabal noticed he was wearing "soft, shiny boots with cuffs at mid-calf height." They had non-skid soles and no heels. The boots clearly were designed for indoor wear, as was the "silky unbelted tunic" whose folds overlapped the boot tops slightly. It was a light lavender or lilac color. The light-colored one-piece tunic contrasted with Jabal's dark, swarthy skin and short curly "Negroid hair." He was of slight build with long slender hands. A "large moonstone ring" was noticed on the left ring finger.

Jabal's initial look at his twenty-fourth-century Martian surroundings came from his observatory window. The landscape outside its protective walls was "red, rocky and barren." Mars looked like a rust-colored desert. The sky was a deep purple and several stars and planets shone brightly through the thin atmosphere, even in the midafternoon daylight. It was an ideal spot for an observatory.

The evening meal was taken in a collective dining room. Jabal described it as a "nourishing stew," eaten with a "white, Chinese-looking" porcelain soup spoon. His wife, "Rima," a "small, soft-spoken Oriental woman," and some of the town's dignitaries shared his table. Other observatory and support personnel ate nearby. The entire colony's population couldn't have exceeded a couple of dozen individuals. It was a "quiet, peaceful" existence with "mostly scientists and other scholars" in residence. There were few children. In fact, the birth of his own child there on Mars was noted by Jabal as the "most important event of that lifetime for me."

Essential supplies that couldn't be grown or processed within the dome-enclosed colony were brought in via space freighters. Airborne land vehicles, "like the small shuttles in *Star Wars*," were sent out to pick them up. Computerized wall units dispensed what had been ordered. A credit card registered payment. Jabal did not report seeing any of the mother ship's crew members. Perhaps the entire operation was automated?

The colony did have an "interior garden" where fruits, vegetables and flowers could be grown. It was while walking in this lone patch of green, his frail eighty-five-year-old frame "supported by a walking stick," that Jabal suffered his fatal heart attack. The incident was not traumatic, however; all he felt was a kind of "detached interest" in what was happening. The spirit simply separated from the body and the experience ended. The subject saw the year 2364 as the date of death.

"Jabal's" quiet, scholarly experience on Mars shared several features, such as communal dining and automated shopping, with the other subjects living in space during this time period, although the beltless tunic he wore was unusual. Actually, grouped together, most of the 69 Type Ia "In-space" and Ib "Solar Space Colony" data sheets revealed remarkably similar life-styles as measured by the responses given to questions regarding clothing, foodstuffs, dining facilities, shopping for supplies and modes of payment used.

For example, 84 percent (58) of these subjects described wearing a one-piece, tight uniform or jumpsuit, usually shiny or metallic. Silver and blue were the color combinations most often cited. Other similar descriptions included "a dark-colored flight suit," "a strange, metallic but soft, stretch suit" and "a black-and-silver space uniform with a silver comet on the breast." About one third indicated that their unipiece, form-fitting suit extended down to include their footwear as well. The rest described wearing separate but matching "metallic" boots. Several commented that their clothing was surprisingly warm and comfortable despite its metallic look.

Only one of this combined group (Jabal) was dressed in a loose, draped garment, while nine (13 percent) described wearing short, belted tunics, some over long pants, with leather or plastic boots or sandals for indoor wear. The last person reported having on more conventional attire, including heavy, brown corduroy pants. He had on thick leather boots as well for a visit to the space colony on the Martian moon of "Phobos."

Asked to describe a typical evening meal, 57 percent said their nourishment came from liquids, vitamin pills or processed, synthetic food. Six different spaceship crew members specifically mentioned a kind of "energy pellet" that was taken with water. Several reports indicated either that food was not considered very important ("no big deal") or that they found it "bland." "I had no feeling of eating meals," said a space-station inhabitant who drank liquids for food. Another said her food resembled a "Nutri-systems dried-egg omelet." One spaceman, however, saw himself mashing up something "probably synthetic" that he found "very tasty."

Nonetheless, 23 subjects (41.8 percent) also cited seeing a variety of fruits and vegetables at their meals, sometimes along with processed foods or vitamin pills. Seven others (13 percent) reported eating meat, mostly in stews or casserole dishes. A couple of the space-station inhabitants even found wine at their dinner table. A future life in orbit may not be so bad after all!

In terms of eating and living arrangements, nearly two thirds (64 percent) of the 55 Type Ia and Type Ib subjects who answered these questions reported sharing communal dining facilities with nonfamily members. One space-station inhabitant described a typical meal as "many of us eating at a long table." A report from one of the spaceships said, "I'm eating with two other crew members—a black man and a white woman." Another 25 percent of these "In-space" inhabitants said they ate alone. Only 7 percent found themselves eating with just other members of their family (spouse, children, siblings). All of these were among the 34 permanent space-station residents.

These figures are hardly surprising as a third of the total (22 cases out of 69) consisted of spaceship crews. Interestingly, none of the subjects living in the enclosed planetary colonies reported seeing just family members nearby either. All of them ate either alone (45 percent) or communally (55 percent). Still, if "Jabal's" testimony about his life on Mars is accurate, meaningful family ties will remain important in the 2300s, for some space-colony dwellers at least. In general this data suggests that family life as we understand it today is not common among the space explorers of the twenty-fourth and twenty-fifth centuries. It seems most developed among the permanent space-station inhabitants.

As mentioned earlier, when asked to describe the buildings around them, nearly all of these solar system spacefarers (spaceship crews aside) stated that their controlled environment was surrounded by some kind of domed enclosures. The architecture itself was described by 34 percent as "futuristic" or "tall, ultramodern" with prefabricated plastic and glass structures predominating. Six of the 34 space-station reports (18 percent) said their orbiting station resembled a huge wheel, with a central hub and radiating tubular spokes. Others mentioned precast concrete and translucent materials (24 percent). Four reports cited seeing rockets blast off from outside their domed habitats.

One series of questions Helen designed to elicit information about future travel and socioeconomic systems asked the hypnotized workshop participants to leave their future homes in search of some essential supplies. Fifty of the subjects living "In-space" answered these questions. Asked to describe how they traveled, half, mostly space-station personnel, simply said they went by spacecraft. Of the rest, 38 percent (19 cases) said they walked, while five others (10 percent) described riding some form of moving walkway or conveyer belt. One spacer said he entered a dematerialization chamber (such as shown in the TV series *Star Trek*) and was automatically transported to his destination. For him travel in the future was just "Beam me down, Scotty!"

As might be expected among people whose lives seem to be spent either aboard large spacecraft or within the confines of a space station or enclosed colony, most supplies came either from community warehouses (24 percent) or storerooms (19 cases, or 38 percent). Of these latter, five subjects said they dealt with some kind of automated dispensing machine in the supply.room rather than human clerks. Jabal's Martian observatory, for example, was equipped with a "computerized metallic supply dispenser" that issued him the "mylar-type blankets" he needed. Other supply sources cited included "spaceships" (24 percent), telekinesis (four cases or 8 percent) and "hydroponic gardens" (2 percent).

One person simply had the things she needed "brought to me." Supplies obtained from these various sources ranged from ordinary human necessities such as foodstuffs (20 subjects mentioned food), clothing and cosmetics to "Fiberglas-like" building materials, boxes with unknown contents (six cases) and a "strange plastic device" whose intended use remained a mystery to the conscious mind of the subject, who saw her future self picking it up in the space station's supply room.

Along with all the other participants, those reporting future 2300–2500 A.D. lifetimes in space were asked to describe an experience or encounter with a "bright, shining light." Forty-four of the Type Ia and Ib subjects (64 percent) responded to this question. Of these an overwhelming 84 percent (37 cases) said that the light came from a rocket or spaceship. As with the 2100 A.D. space reports, all of these replies were positive; many were "matter-of-fact" in tone. Space travel was clearly not a novelty to them.

Typical were comments such as "It is a source of transport to and from home" or "It's pretty commonplace" and "peaceful, the return of friends." "It's just the light from the star field; another large ship is visible," stated a spacecraft officer.

The subject who found herself in a space colony on Pluto remarked that to her the light was welcome. She said:

A spacecraft came to take me back home; it seems I've been on a retreat here.

Another individual added:

It didn't get really clear; my whole experience was connected with space. I was always traveling in space. I wasn't even sure if this globe [i.e., Earth] still existed.

Someone else spoke of the light as part of an interplanetary commercial network that transited her space station. She described it this way:

The light is a spacecraft. It's quite commonly seen here [at her space station]. It brings us sustenance and some supplies. Supplies are first brought to the space station and then transferred to Earth by smaller shuttles.

A final spaceship crew member said that the experience was exciting because:

Inside the spacecraft different creatures [i.e., extraterrestrials] were in charge. They were pretty much simian in appearance.

Six of the 44 "In-space" replies about the "bright, shining light" (14 percent) told of an experience in which they received needed information or an energy boost from the light. One young woman on an asteroid space colony said:

The light is the Fountain of Creation in the Heavens. It is showering us with creative light, colors, stars. We are turning this asteroid into a new mini-Earth.

Another woman, now from Paris, who found herself living in an orbiting space station in 2300 A.D., commented:

There was a stairway down which poured light rays. We walked up it to a spiritual spring and were refreshed. This was one of my happiest lifetimes.

Only the Martian scientist "Jabal" gave a natural explanation for the light he observed. He stated that it was the dim light of the Sun as seen from the surface of the red planet. Apparently he was watching as part of his scientific duties in the observatory.

Thirty-seven of the space dwellers offered typically short, pithy comments regarding their general feelings about life in their homes during this future 2300 A.D. experience. Their feelings about the kind of society they found themselves living in were mixed, although positive comments definitely outweighed negative remarks. Twenty-two replies (60 percent) were judged as positive, ten were neutral and only five seen as clearly negative.

The negative comments ranged from "It was an [emotionally] cold environment" to "It's sterile," "I feel indifference" and "It [home life] was nothing much." Neutral remarks included, "Mundane, not much excitement" and "I was just always on this space station; was it home?" One spaceship crew member said, "I didn't want to leave my home to go on the mission assigned. But I had to."

This last remark may be considered as describing a future premonition, for the individual went on to describe how his one-man ship had later been destroyed during a space battle while on that required mission. Naturally this incident also ended that future lifetime for him.

Far more prevalent were positive remarks such as "It was pleasant, almost exciting" or "I loved it!" Six individuals said they considered their home environment "peaceful" or "homey," while five more said they felt "happy" there. A few of the space crewmen expressed their feelings of "relief" or of being "tired" when they left their duty stations for a break in their quarters. Other crew members made remarks to the effect that while they felt "content" with their life in space, it was a rather lonely existence, without much family life. A couple of them stated simply, "I was always alone here."

One of Helen Wambach's male subjects who saw himself as a space-ship crew member voiced similar feelings when coming off space duty: "I'm tired, need to get clean and relax. . . . It's pretty lonely." In his 2300 A.D. future life he found himself as a "slender black male with strong arms and gnarled, callused hands." He was inside a pressurized space cruiser, dressed in a "silvery one-piece uniform with black and white" insignia and an "open V-neck" collar. "Metallic-yet-soft" boots that attached to his pants cuffs and a detachable helmet, not worn indoors, completed his attire.

The ship was some type of "scout ship" that operated between an orbiting space station and a spaceport near a "dome-covered city" on Earth. It was equipped to perform both shuttle and survey missions within the solar system. Living arrangements on board were communal but the craft was mostly automated; there were just four or five crew members. Foods were synthetic and either squeezed from tubes or swallowed like pills. Supplies were kept in a storeroom.

This subject was unable to recall the circumstances of his death, stating only that "it happened like a flash." Possibly it was a space accident. Type Ia "In-space" subjects had one of the shortest average life spans (54.3 years) of any of the various groups.

A more detailed report of life aboard a future military "spacecraft carrier" came from a woman attending one of Dr. Leo Sprinkle's 1984 workshops. Progressed forward into the 2500 A.D. time period, she found herself wearing "black knee-high boots, like English riding boots," and a one-piece black-and-silver uniform "with a silver comet on the breast." Long, light hair flowed over the shoulders of her tall, willowy frame. She was a woman officer, looking out from the bridge of a "huge ship, the space-going equivalent of an aircraft carrier." Other similar and smaller vessels were visible from the viewport, along with a "gleaming field of stars."

On her data sheet she described a dramatic incident from her future life in space in the present tense:

> We're part of a space armada, from somewhere closer to the center of the galaxy than Earth. It's not in this arm of the Milky Way at all. We're patrolling this sector, fighting against dangerous [alien] enemies who threaten the very existence of the human race. "Do we become cattle or do we fight?" is the battle cry I heard in our command caucus.
>
> I'm a military test pilot. I've been chosen to fly a special experimental mission that, if successful, could secure this sector of the galaxy. These fighter craft are to be launched from the space cruiser. I was chosen for this job because my reaction times are so much faster than the other test pilots. My lover, an officer on another spacecraft, objects to the idea of my flying such a hazardous combat mission but I know too much depends on it to refuse.

Later, when asked about an "important, emotional event":

> The enemy must have been aware of my experimental flight for I've been shot down [in space]. I've crash-landed onto a heavily jungled world. It's *imperative* that neither the plane nor I be captured by the aliens so I've destroyed the fighter with thermite. I only hope I can hide out until our forces can slip through the blockade and reach me. I'm not finished with life yet! *I have too much to do!* [Emphasis in original]

Dr. Sprinkle's subject then "blanked out" when taken to the time of her future-life death, likely not very far ahead of her last, desperate thoughts expressed above. Her final comment, obviously from a twentieth-century perspective, was: "This was a weird experience."

Before turning to those subjects who discovered new lives on planets revolving around other stars across the cosmos, a final remark is in order concerning the kind of solar system-wide human civilization that apparently included most of these spaceship and space-station personnel. Although over 80 percent of these subjects never indicated any other environment than that of space, there were thirteen cases where the subjects also mentioned either coming from or retiring to the Earth.

Despite the fact that few details were given about their second home on this planet (all cases that described Earth surroundings in detail rather than the space one were assigned to the appropriate Earth group), it seems clear that, just as in the 2100 period, the space explorers were in close contact with Earth's Type III Hi-tech urban cities and also connected to a lesser extent with the Type II New Age communities.

Thus, four of the thirteen subjects who were aboard spacecraft say they saw a dome-covered city either when landing on Earth or where they died. Seven of the cases mention having a home base in New England or eastern Canada and two in South America. One each said Europe and Asia. These locations tally pretty closely with where 2100 A.D. subjects located their Hi-tech centers and, as we shall see, where Type III communities continued to exist in the twenty-fourth and twenty-fifth centuries as well.

The most detailed of these reports came from another woman attending a 1984 workshop led by Dr. Sprinkle. Asked to "look down at your feet," Jackie discovered she was wearing "lightweight metallic boots" attached to a "silvery-blue jumpsuit that looks made from woven metallic threads." Her future-life body was that of a "large, lanky" man with "big hands" and "black, wavy hair." He was working in an orbiting space station, high above the Earth.

His experience with the "bright, shining light" was watching a big interstellar spacecraft, crewed by both humans and extraterrestrials, docking at the station's spaceport. It was a "common event" for such ships regularly brought Earth "sustenance and some other essential supplies." At the space station the items were transferred to smaller "Earth shuttles" and then ferried down through the planet's atmosphere. The process was largely automated, using conveyer belts and other machinery. "Nothing was bought; everyone was allowed a certain amount." Payment was registered by "a time-clock type of machine."

This individual seems to have accompanied such shipments from the station down to the surface for he stated that his "home" was an apartment in a "city in South America" that was "encased in a huge see-through bubble." Inside, the temperature was kept at a comfortable 72 degrees (Farenheit). There were even a few trees and a bit of grass within the dome. No mention was made of conditions outside this artificially controlled environment. The low white buildings, "made from a stucco type of material," had flat roofs.

Like many of the Type III Hi-tech subjects, who lived in similar urban settings, this individual reported eating in a communal dining area.

The meal consisted of "preprocessed foods, mostly from vegetable matter." Despite the artificial quality, it tasted "very good." Several other adults shared the man's table; he didn't seem to be strongly emotionally attached to any of them.

Death came at age eighty-five, of "old age." The year was 2375 A.D. It was "a relief" for the spirit to leave that body and thereby to "rediscover the freedom to be one with the Universe." The subject stated that her feelings about that future life, spent between the space station and enclosed city, were neutral. It was "mundane." "There was not much excitement to it." She sounded just a bit disappointed!

In addition to the 69 workshop participants who found themselves living in spaceships or in artificially enclosed space colonies within the solar system during the 2300–2500 period, 40 of our subjects reported future lifetimes spent under the completely alien skies of Earth-like planets scattered across the galactic way. With one possible exception, all of these subjects continued to inhabit physically human or humanoid bodies and live within recognizable human communities.

The lone anomaly was a woman from one of Helen Wambach's workshops who said her "future body" more resembled a large bear's than that of a human being. Because her perceptions were completely alien, she felt unable to determine if she was actually living in the future or if her experience was a "throwback" to something earlier. Nor did the other, socioeconomic-based questions make much sense to her. Nonetheless, she stated that the vision of this bearlike creature had flashed before her when Helen mentioned the time period around 2300 A.D. Thus it is worth at least mentioning here. Hers was the only nonhuman case among the approximately 2,650 participants in all the future-lives workshops organized by Helen Wambach, R. Leo Sprinkle and myself between 1980 and 1988.

Despite their shared humanity, the 40 participants' reports categorized as Type Ic "Non-solar System Planet" differed widely both in physical surroundings and in type of civilization. Their most frequently cited common feature was the appearance of curved or domelike roofs overhead. Thirty cases (75 percent) mentioned such domes either over individual buildings or enclosing whole communities. Half of the Type Ic cases also said the buildings they could see looked "futuristic" or "modern."

Thus the individual who said she was living on the planet "Alpha" described her surroundings as a "dome-shaped silver building with colorful stained-glass windows and high ceilings." Another subject, on an "unknown" planet, described a similar arrangement, saying the buildings were "marble or light-colored with curved roofs." A French subject said her futuristic surroundings were a "large city filled with luminous, tall, white skyscrapers."

One of Dr. Sprinkle's subjects, a Japanese-American today, found herself living as a Caucasian male with "brown curly hair" and "strong, large hands" in 2300 A.D. His home was on the planet "Centor." He described his futuristic city as made up of "mostly round or oval, domed buildings [looking like] Styrofoam but strong." Clusters of these enclosed structures were connected by a monorail shuttle system. Residents also used individual air cars for travel outside the urban complex.

Other frequently cited architectural features of these non-solar system communities were the use of transparent materials or glass (10 cases, or 25 percent), construction using some kind of metal, including steel, aluminum and silver (11 cases), and adobe or stone construction (four cases). One of the subjects living in an adobe-style city said it appeared "almost like pueblos, with dome roofs, large windows and many skylights." Another said her home was "made of brown mud or adobe" with "a huge domed public building nearby."

A minority (six cases, or 15 percent) indicated that their surroundings were either primitive or temporary. One of these subjects described her home as a "temporary shelter made up of branches and grasses gathered nearby." Another, who nonetheless saw himself eating with "a plastic fork/spoon combination," said his home looked "like a cavern." Finally, two said that they didn't see buildings at all; people lived outdoors and provided their own protection from the elements telepathically!

Descriptions of the surrounding planetary environments were equally varied, although again all fell within basically Earth-like contexts. The most common descriptive terms used were the words "hilly" or "mountains." Twenty Type Ic subjects (50 percent) described their landscape using one or the other of these terms. One of Helen's subjects, who said, "I don't think I'm on the planet Earth," called her surroundings "fairly stark, with mountains in the background. Farmland is all around." Another commented that the landscape was "rugged and hilly with a mild climate and dark skies."

Nineteen (48 percent), including half of the above, described their climate as "cool" or "mild," with several adding that it was "comfortable" or "pleasant." Ten specifically mentioned the greenery (25 percent), while five (12.5 percent) said they saw trees or forests. One even found herself on a jungle-style world. Only six (15 percent) found themselves in "hot" or "arid, desertlike" zones. Equal numbers (six apiece) commented on either the "beauty" of their environment or on its "desolate," "barren" nature.

Overall, however, the vast majority indicated acceptable living conditions and a basically pleasant natural environment. Therefore, I didn't find, as with the 2100 A.D. Type III cities on Earth, any clear relationship between the use of domed roofs and a hostile external atmosphere. This may have been true for three or four of the Type Ic environments, such as one described as "barren, red rock, a 'Garden of the Gods' desert terrain, like in a sci-fi movie," but not as a general rule. One woman, who called her planet "Cara," said it was a "beautiful garden, green with a very perfect climate, like what I imagine Findhorn to be."* Yet she and her identical twin and their families lived in one of the futuristic dome-covered cities described above. It's possible that domes were considered aesthetic there.

The same diversity noted in city architecture and descriptions of the environment extended into such social domains as clothing and dining arrangements. Throughout the future-life workshops four basic kinds of clothing have been noted among the different 2100 and 2300 A.D. environmental types. These are (1) tight-fitting, usually one-piece, uniforms or jumpsuits, (2) loosely draped long robes or gowns, (3) short, often belted, tunics or dresses, sometimes worn with leggings or pants underneath and (4) traditional shirts, pants, skirts and blouses.

The following graph (Figure 7-1) illustrates how different clothing styles marked the different environment-based groups of the 2300–2500 A.D. sample. Clearly the loose, robe-style garments predominated in the Type II "New Age" communities, while the tight-fitting uniforms or jumpsuits characterized both the Type Ia and Ib "In-space" groups and their Type III "Hi-tech" counterparts on Earth. The graph also points out the near absence of traditional pants and skirts except among the Type IVa "Rustic" rural dwellers. Tunics tended to be evenly split among the Type II and III inhabitants of Earth. Type Ic ("Non-solar System Planet") was the only group without a clear preference for one or another of these styles.

As shown in Figure 7-1, all of the 36 Type Ic ("Non-solar System Planet") subjects who described their 2300-era clothing found themselves wearing one or the other of the first three clothing styles: robes, jumpsuits or tunics. Only the traditional Type IV clothes were missing. Further,

---

* Findhorn is a New Age experimental and spiritual community in Scotland, noted for its extraordinarily productive gardens.

Figure 7-1. Clothing Worn by 2300 A.D. Groups

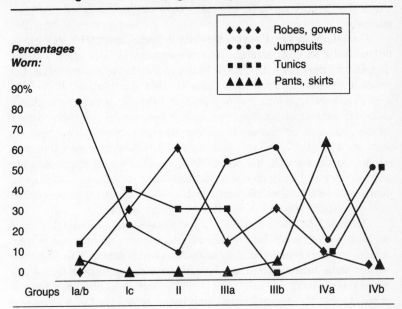

each style was almost equally represented among the Type Ic participants. Thus, 14 subjects (39 percent) saw themselves wearing short tunics or dresses; 12 (33 percent) were dressed in some kind of long and loose robes and the other 10 (28 percent) described having form-fitting uniforms or jumpsuits covering their bodies. Their footwear reflected the same patterns, with "boots" of one kind or another (42 percent) being slightly favored over either shoes (30 percent) or sandals (24 percent). Only one Non-solar system subject, whose primitive makeshift shelter was described above, saw herself continually barefoot.

The same diversity appeared in the eating arrangements of the Non-solar system inhabitants and in the foods they noticed at their typical evening meal. Thirty-two of the 40 Type Ic subjects answered these questions. They split exactly down the middle, with half the sample describing natural fruits and vegetables as their staple diet, with occasional mention of fish (6 percent) and cereals or breads (13 percent), and the other half finding nourishment in a variety of "energy pills" or synthetic, preprocessed foods. A couple of the reports indicated both vegetables and synthetic foods together.

Thus one subject saw herself eating "a tofu-like Jell-O and green beans" with a combination spoon/fork utensil. Another had a bowl of "soft, custard-style" substance to eat, while the person on "Cara" said her food consisted of "beautiful leafy-green vegetables and something like arti-chokes." One simply commented, "Food is immaterial." It should also be noted that of these 32 subjects none indicated seeing meat at their meals. In general, meat consumption in these future lives, whether on Earth or elsewhere, appears far below today's Western standards.

Dining arrangements also varied between large communal dining halls and individual family groups eating together. As opposed to most of the 2100 A.D. groups and those Type Ia and Ib "In-space" subjects in 2300, none of the Type Ic subjects said that they were eating alone. All were either dining in family groups (37.5 percent) or with others including more than just family members (62.5 percent). A typical scenario was that given by a subject who saw herself eating "breads and vegetables" with her future-life "brother, wife and nearby friends."

In fact, loneliness, or the feeling of being alone, an issue that came up frequently among the 2100-era reports, even in the New Age com-munities, was mentioned on only one of these 2300 A.D. period Non-solar system data sheets. This case, by a male who saw himself living as a woman in "Galaxy 28975" in the twenty-fourth century, included the comment that he felt "disappointment, incomplete, alone" on leaving that lifetime at only age 27, victim of a spacecraft explosion. As this subject also remarked that the future-life living quarters seen looked like "army barracks," these negative feelings may reflect a social alienation more than actual physical isolation from other people.

When asked about methods of travel, where they obtained supplies and how they paid for life's necessities, the Type Ic subjects living on planets scattered across the galaxy again reflected several of the different life-styles common to the 2100 and 2300 A.D. reports. Thus of the 34 individuals who described how they traveled, nearly a third (30 percent) said they went by space or aircraft, while 24 percent (eight subjects) said they walked to where they got essential supplies. Only two (6 percent) said they rode in motorized ground vehicles like automobiles, while four (12 percent) mentioned an instant "dematerialization transporter" resem-bling that used on *Star Trek*. Six others (18 percent) described highly individual flying belts or jet backpacks that propelled them through the air to their destinations. Finally, four said automated walkways connected their domed settlements to their supply depots.

Of the 28 subjects who described the places where they went for provisions, just over half (57 percent) described large storage warehouses or supply depots. One stated she found herself in a "big warehouse"

staffed by "Martian types [aliens] who are sort of slave workers." Another
found herself "pushing buttons in a large domed building. It was a com-
missary." Only three (11 percent) accounts would fit today's idea of a
supermarket or department store and just one mentioned an outdoor
market ("on a farm"). The last eight subjects (29 percent) said they got
their equipment either via "computers" or through automated systems
similar to those described by the Type Ia and Ib "In-space" inhabitants.

When it came time to pay for their purchases, 14 of the 33 Type Ic
subjects who filled in this data described using either credit cards or some
type of handprint or signature system that registered the transaction.
Eight others, about 25 percent, simply said they didn't pay for anything
but didn't elaborate. Taken together, these two answers accounted for
two thirds of the replies. The others included descriptions of various
tokens, coins and bills (30 percent) to two of the "outdoor primitives"
who bartered for foodstuffs.

The subject who saw herself as a future citizen of "Centor" provided
a good account typical of the kind of travel, market and monetary structures encountered by the subjects whose future lives were on planets
outside our solar system. She commented:

> We walked [to the supply warehouse] although there were conveyer
> belts and shuttles like monorails also. The supply depot was in a
> big dome-covered building with things hanging from the ceiling.
> People milled about aimlessly. We purchased food that looked like
> beef jerky but was softer and fruity, more like preserved, processed
> dates. We didn't use money [for the purchases] but plastic cards
> like credit cards. They didn't have letters or numbers, just raised
> dots and spikes, like Braille. There were different-colored cards for
> different purposes.

When asked about their experience with the bright light, 60 percent
of the 30 Non-solar system participants who answered this question described an incident with a spaceship. Ten witnessed a ship landing, while
five said they were watching a vehicle launch into space from their planet's
surface. Such events were described as ordinary. "It's common for spaceships to come and go," said one. As mentioned earlier, one Type Ic subject
even told of watching a ship land with "aliens from Earth," the survivors
of "a great blast." She felt sorry for them.

Of these 18 spaceship incidents only one was described in negative
terms. The same woman who saw the "Martian-type" slave workers at

the warehouse said she felt "like they [the Martians] were coming for me" on seeing the bright spacecraft in the sky. She said that to her the scene resembled the classic science-fiction movie, *War of the Worlds*.

The other twelve replies by Type Ic ("Non-solar System Planet") subjects to this question divided between "energy boosting" events involving a bright light (20 percent) and religious or spiritual experiences (17 percent). Just one individual cited a "natural" cause—a fireworks celebration. Thus there were two mentions of light being used to transfer energy between two people via their chakra openings (solar plexus and third eye) and two more in which bright colored lights apparently were used for healing. For the young woman on "Cara," a green light helped her leave her body at the time of physical death. "It was very smooth," she said of her transition. "I moved easily into the green light."

Of those whose experience with the light was more specifically spiritual, one described a mountaintop ceremony led by a golden-tressed woman in long "radiant" white robes. Drums beating around a bonfire heightened the effect. Another, who found herself on another planet in an environment reminiscent of the Type II ("New Age") communities on Earth, gave a detailed account of an outdoor meditation. She described it in these terms:

> At night the adults go outside and sit under a bright sky to meditate in a circle. Children come too, but [they] often fall asleep. The adults are in a state of group consciousness, seeming to draw power from the night sky and the universe. Spoken language is not necessary as psychic communication is quite clear and harmony with nature is acute.

This individual, from one of Helen Wambach's 1983 seminars, had earlier told of finding herself living that 2300 A.D. life as a "fair, sandy-haired young man." He was living in an "almost pueblo-style" group of buildings. Some of the roofs were flat; others were translucent domes. There were "large windows and many skylights" for light and solar heating. Although the surrounding landscape was "fairly stark with high mountains in the background," the village was set amid "rolling farmland and well-tended crops." The air was "moist, temperate and clear."

For clothing the pueblo dwellers wore "mostly synthetic and woven fabrics." Their sandals were made from bound fibers. The statement "No animals are killed for their products" was underlined on the data sheet. Cotton and wool were produced and bartered with nearby settlements.

Travel was by small "battery-powered" vehicles. Vegetarian meals of "bread, fruit and vegetables" were eaten communally off of "shining metal plates." The man noted that his "brother, wife and a couple of good friends" were at his table. Everywhere there seemed to be an atmosphere of goodwill, sharing and a "mutual commitment to the land and to each other."

Death, it appears, was understood as only a transition and nothing to be feared. The transfer, which took place in "November 2313 A.D. at age eighty-nine," was chosen when it was "time to drop that body." The event itself was described in the following beautiful terms:

> At the time of death, all friends and neighbors are gathered around, meditating and chanting. [They are] supporting my soul in its journey. There is no fear here, just understanding.

With such a send-off as this, it is no wonder that this participant described her spirit as "soaring" after leaving the physical body behind. She said she felt "pure love and peace" as she floated in that spiritual state at the end of the workshop.

Although this case was exceptionally inspiring, it mirrors the overall descriptions of these 2300 A.D. subjects living outside the solar system when they were asked to comment on their feelings about their home surroundings and general future-life experience. Twenty-six of the 40 data sheets answered this question. Of that number 70 percent (18 cases) gave positive feedback regarding their 2300–2500 A.D. adventure. Half of these used words such as "happy," "contented" or "satisfied" to describe their reactions to their future home environments. The others gave more individual responses, including the person who stated, "Everything was good, as it should be." Or another who said she felt "peace and love" in her future dome-covered home under a golden alien sky.

Most of the rest were neutral in their estimations, providing comments such as "I felt quiet there" or "I was ambivalent" when describing their environs. Only two, the individual whose quarters reminded him of "army barracks" and the one whose future life was troubled by Martian-like aliens, could be classified as actually negative.

The young man living on "Centor" remarked that he felt "quiet" and a bit lonely during this future lifetime. In his domed-in city, life was largely communal (he reported dining with strangers) and he didn't mention having any specific family ties. His was one of the few Type I reports indicating that the "experience with the bright light" was disappointing.

"I was waiting for a 'message' but didn't get one. . . . I didn't understand the lights." This plus his early (age twenty-four) accidental death in "some kind of air crash" undoubtedly influenced his overall impressions. After death his spirit nonetheless "spiraled upwards" through a dark mist into the light.

Before looking at the future-lives reported on Earth during the 2300 to 2500 A.D. period, two final reports from Non-solar system planets merit a closer look. Both came from women attending a workshop led by Helen Wambach between 1980–84.

The first thing Lee noted about her twenty-fifth-century life somewhere out among the Milky Way was that her future male body had extremely pale, "almost albino" skin. His hair, however, was black and curly. Of average height, he possessed a "rawboned physique" with "strong, expressive" hands. Clothing worn consisted of a "thick cotton sarong," loosely wrapped "from the waist to above the shins," and leather sandals. He also had on a long, tailless shirt, similar to the Filipino *barong*. The clothes were "comfortable and good-looking too."

The surrounding climate was extremely dry but "high yellow clouds" obscured the "Sun," deflecting any harmful radiation. The air was warm but not unpleasantly so. Looking around, the man commented that the landscape was "rocky, like the desert" with "no trees or green vegetation." He commented, "I don't think it ever rains here." Even the village where he lived was constructed of "brown mud or adobe" houses set around a "huge domed structure" that served as town hall, communal dining area and public auditorium.

About the only green things seen in this future environment on an alien planet were the green string beans noted as part of the evening meal along with some synthetic-looking dishes. Cutlery consisted of a "combination spoon and fork utensil," one edge of which also served as a knife. The man found himself eating in the community canteen next to a woman friend whose dark hair also contrasted with her very pale complexion. It was a "normal, pleasant" experience. Later they witnessed fireworks together as part of a local celebration. The fireworks were this subject's only encounter with a "bright, shining light."

Picking up essential supplies required traveling to a larger settlement. To get there residents used small yellow hovercrafts "about the size of a Honda Civic" that could travel either along the planet's surface, "some three feet off the ground," or up into space for interplanetary hops. Large dome-covered public warehouses served as supply centers. One merely had to show an identification card to receive what was needed;

purchases were marked against one's credit. This subject reported buying "dehydrated food."

This subject made no comments regarding a future-life occupation or career and replied "none" when asked what feelings came on returning home after the shopping expedition. She did note that it was "a relief" for her spirit to leave the body after it was caught in a violent earthquake and suffocated to death. The date given was 2475 A.D.

The other subject, a San Francisco housewife who attended an August 1980 workshop at Dolphin Farms, was among the very first of Helen's subjects to progress to a future lifetime. She, too, found herself living around 2400 A.D. on a planet light-years away from our Sun, but as a woman.

In that future life she had "an olive complexion" and "thick, short, reddish-blond hair." Her hands appeared "well cared for." She was clothed in a belted "white, knee-length dress" made of a "light, silky material that fell in soft folds" around her legs. "Soft, silver-mesh boots" completed the stylish outfit.

Named "Lana," her initial view of her surroundings was of "a dark globe in the sky with light coming from around the edges." It seemed to be a very large spacecraft either taking off or about to land. The event didn't appear to be all that unusual and did not upset her. She witnessed this sight while standing outside her home, set amid pleasant, rolling hills that were dotted with occasional trees. A "deep-blue sky with a few high fleecy clouds" lay overhead. She had emerged from "a rounded building that flowed from the nearby hillside." Made of some type of synthetic material, it looked windowless, when viewed from the outside at least.

Lana lived in that structure with her husband and one child. Family ties were close and important to her. A "warm, affectionate" atmosphere filled their home, making her happy to return indoors. The house was filled with plants and "unusual, ultramodern furnishings." Its interior was spacious and harmonious, as if the architecture were designed to promote good feelings for the inhabitants. The family ate their meals together around a "silver and glass table." The main course was "fish cooked in a lemony sauce," eaten with a "four-pronged fork" off colorful ceramic dishes.

During this future progression Lana never saw any transportation vehicles. She felt as if the concepts of "travel" and "supplies" didn't really apply to that time and place. "It was as if all I had to do was decide where I wanted to go and I would suddenly just be there," she said. The same was true of supplies: they, too, were brought home via teleportation.

Nonetheless, when asked how she paid for any supplies purchased, Lana did report seeing a "large coin with printed symbols on it."

Like several of our 2100 A.D. subjects, particularly those in harmonious New Age environments, Lana's death came from "natural causes" when she was around ninety years old. She reported being "ready to go," indicating an understanding of death's transitional nature. After a momentary "confusion" while leaving the body, she found herself once again on the "fluffy, puffy white cloud" that Helen Wambach so deftly used to transport her subjects across Time and Space. The year 2402 A.D. flashed in her mind as the date of death.

Lee's and Lana's stories, like those discussed earlier in this chapter, show that, for the participants in these workshops at least, twenty-fourth and twenty-fifth century lives on Earth-type planets flung across the *Via Galactica* appear much like human experiences right here today as we move rapidly into the world of tomorrow. Despite the varied styles of dress, architecture and socioeconomic organization described by the subjects for 2300 to 2500 A.D., most of their reports show common attitudes and human character traits that, it seems, will follow humanity even out among the stars.

For good or ill, individual emotional makeup appears to be a fundamental characteristic of the human species. Whether or not we succeed in using these basic attitudes and emotions to build a constructive, positive future, as shown in the majority of these Type I reports from the 2300 era, or allow them to continue to tear us apart, as witnessed by the few negative data sheets from this period, depends largely on our individual and collective human willpower.

* 8 *
Mass Dreams of 2300 A.D.
and Beyond, Part II:
Operation Terra

The preceding chapter provides a glimpse of what may be a diverse and widespread human civilization scattered across the cosmos through to the first part of the next millennium. The reports of these 109 workshop participants make it obvious that, for the "dreaming minds" of many of today's Americans at least, humanity's destiny lies among the stars. No longer confined to the solar system and space stations or enclosed space colonies struggling against the harsh atmospheres of our sister planets, as in the reports of the 2100 A.D. period, the human race is here predicted to fulfill many of the visions currently confined to the output of popular science-fiction writers.

Nevertheless, despite this fascinating and beckoning cosmic vision, we must remember that slightly more than half (57 percent) of the 2300 to 2500 A.D. data sheets found the workshop participants returning to future lifetimes here on Terra. What kind of societies do these subjects describe? What evolution from the lonely, separate and divided human communities pictured in the 2100 era has taken place? How do today's "mass dreams" about our own planet's future 300 to 500 years from now compare with those of the "outward wave" into space?

These are big questions and I can hardly offer definitive answers based only on the visions of these 142 subjects. More research obviously should and will need to be done to complete the picture painted by these workshop participants from the 1980s. Additionally, unlike the 2100 A.D. data, which divided sharply and clearly into four distinct environments with little overlap, these 2300-era reports from Earth proved more ambiguous. They tended to share more common characteristics, especially in their descriptions of their basic architecture, supply and transportation systems.

Still, the general prevailing social atmosphere of the different communities described remained distinctive. As will be shown below, a lot of elements of each of the three basic 2100 A.D. Earth civilization types (Types II, III and IV) described in Chapters 5 and 6 apparently will remain intact 200 to 300 years later. It is as if each of these future Earth cultures were now evolving separately but simultaneously, slowly approaching each other and each subtly changing in the process. Moreover, with a notable bunch of exceptions, which I have called Type IIIb, or "Hi-tech Evolved," each of the groups continued to depict its physical environment quite distinctly.

Just as the various reports of future lives aboard spaceships on space stations or in space colonies represented Type I "In-space," both in 2100 and 2300 A.D., so the data sheets described as Type II portrayed "New Age" civilizations in both future time periods analyzed. In the latter era all 52 subjects whose life-styles were categorized as Type II commented positively on their harmonious interaction with the outside environment. As in 2100, their surroundings were almost unanimously described as "green," "lush," "wooded" or "beautiful." Nearly a third included a comment indicating that the spot viewed was especially pleasant or beautiful. A "mild," "soft" or "temperate" climate was specifically mentioned by half of these 26 subjects as well.

Only four of the 2300 A.D. New Age reports, all set in Africa or the Middle East, used the words "desert," "hot" or "dry." No one in the group called his or her environment "barren" or "desolate," whereas half of those who found themselves in either the Type IIIa "Hi-tech" cities or among the ten Type IVb subjects classed as "Survivors" used such terms to describe their surroundings. Again, as in 2100, several of these Type II subjects (30.8 percent) mentioned being near the ocean or by natural sources of fresh water such as lakes and streams. Natural freshwater sources were never cited on the Type III data sheets in either time period.

The following comments are representative of how the Type II New Age participants described their surroundings in 2300 A.D.:

There are lush green trees and forests; a warm climate [near] the
sea or ocean. There's a gorgeous sky. The buildings are massive,
white and colonaded, surrounded by gardens . . . .

[Australia]

The landscape is woodsy and cool. Beautiful surroundings. There
are trees, shrubs, a small waterfall and stream. I see a white library
building shaped like this [a cutoff pyramid], as are the surrounding
homes. . . . It's welcoming and delightful.

["Canadian border" area]

This last description came from a California woman who participated
in one of Helen Wambach's 1983 workshops. She went on to discuss her
future life there in the 2300 period. Describing her womanly hands as
"tiny but well shaped" and her hair as "long, silky and blond," she wore
a "floor-length, soft-white dress" belted with a cord and "light sandals,
made of soft leather." Life in her "community of healers and teachers"
was both communal and family oriented. All the "low, white or buff-
colored" buildings were set among beautiful green gardens, around the
central library. Teleportation over short distances was commonplace.

People worked together at community projects and many were adept
at manipulating "crystal energies" as part of their contribution. This
woman, named "Jarna," saw "light emanating from [her] hands" during
one such energy transfer. Altogether, it was a "welcoming, delightful
and loving" place. Jarna commented that she had "much work to do"
during that busy lifetime dedicated to growth and service.

As can be seen from these two representative examples, buildings
in many of the Type II communities tended to be large and light-colored.
White was mentioned 18 times. This represented 36 percent of the 50
sheets giving architectural details. Marble and glass were also frequently
cited as building materials (24 and 20 percent) as were precast concrete
or plastic (24 percent each). Wood was still seen by some (16 percent).
Three subjects specifically described viewing roofs "like pagodas" or "Taj
Mahal" style temples.

Apparently, by 2300 A.D., these Type II communities will have
grown larger than in 2100, for a quarter of the 52 subjects mention that
they live in modern, futuristic cities set among rolling hills and verdant
fields. Sixteen (31 percent) say that the buildings incorporate curved roofs
or domes; most add that these are translucent. One of Helen's subjects

described her building as looking like a "dome, white like marble but letting in light. It had soft pastel colors inside."

Another said her city looked like this:

Buildings were white, [made of] a marble-looking plastic with molded plastic windows and skylights. The outer area [a square] was paved and filled with assorted colored lights. The lights were what drew me to this time frame. . . . Everything [buildings] seemed to be made of molded plastic.

[North Africa]

The larger, more urban environment mentioned by several of the 2300 A.D. Type II subjects was reflected in a greater variety in clothing styles noted when compared to the 2100 period. In the earlier period almost three quarters (71 percent) of the people wore long, flowing robes or togas, usually off-white. In the 2300 sample this costume was still favored by 61.5 percent of the subjects, including Jarna, mentioned above, but nearly a third (31 percent) reported wearing a short belted tunic, often over loose, comfortable slacks or shorts. A few (7 percent) even found themselves in the kind of tight-fitting jumpsuits that were usually associated with the Type I (In-space) or Type III (Hi-tech) groups.

Similarly, 57 percent of those 42 New Age reports from 2300 A.D. that discussed eating an evening meal described some form of communal dining arrangement. This was 27 percent more than had been indicated in the 2100 period. Mention of eating with just close family members fell slightly (from 42 percent to 38 percent), while the biggest drop came among those who saw themselves eating all alone. Only one Type II individual saw himself alone at his meal in the 2300 to 2500 period.

The following graph (Figure 8-1) depicts eating arrangements for all the 2300 A.D. groups. It reveals that by this time period a majority of subjects reported eating communally, often joined by family members as well, in all of the various socioenvironmental groups except for Type IVa, the "Rustics," practically all of whom continued to live and dine in small family units in their rural villages or isolated farms.

Nonetheless, despite some evidence that the New Age communities of the 2300 era, as reported by our workshop participants, will be bigger and more urban than 200 years earlier, their general aim of living in harmony with nature seems to have survived intact. This is reflected not only in their continuing highly positive comments about the physical environment and landscape surrounding them but also in their choice of foods. Forty-six of the 52 Type II subjects (88.4 percent) described their

Figure 8-1. Dining Arrangements by 2300 A.D. Groups

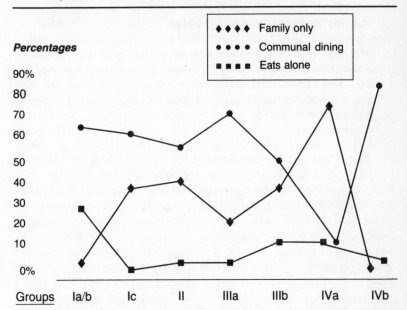

typical evening meal. Of these 38, or 83 percent, mentioned eating fruits and vegetables as their staple diet. Among those items specifically named were "oranges," "papayas," "corn on the cob," "peas," "beans" and "berries." Many just indicated "mostly fruit" or "fruits and vegetables."

About a third also mentioned whole-grain breads or cereal dishes as well. A "monk" who saw himself in a spiritual community in Argentina said the long communal table was laden with "dark bread, strong cheese and berries, eaten from wooden bowls." A few of the Type II reports (17.3 percent) mentioned fish. Jarna, for example, noted that a typical evening meal in her Canadian community included "corn on the cob and trout." Another woman whose future life was set in Asia said she was eating "Chinese rice with seafood and herbs" in a building with a "pagoda-style roof."

Only six (13 percent) discussed the synthetic foodstuffs or "energy pellets" so prevalent among the Type I space explorers. Two others said that eating was "not very important" for them as they were able to get much of their nourishment directly from light, air and other natural "energy sources." Just one Type II individual reported having meat ("steak") for dinner.

The brief descriptions of supply sources, money systems and modes of transportation given by forty of the Type II subjects came closer to the responses of their Type I space relations than their dining arrangements and foodstuffs. Exactly half of this group said that they obtained essential items from large, central warehouses or supply depots. Ten percent mentioned the kind of computerized, automated delivery systems cited by nearly a third of the "Non-solar system" subjects while 20 percent said their fruits and vegetables came from big modern grocery stores. Eight other individuals (20 percent) mentioned gardens or outdoor markets as food sources.

Methods of transportation were far more varied for the 2300 Type II sample than the descriptions given 200 years earlier. In that period most of the New Age communities were small villages in which people walked or rode small mechanized carts to their destinations. The more urbanized and sophisticated 2300 group cited all of the ultramodern travel modes such as spaceships, moving walkways, individual flying suits and hovercraft mentioned by Type I subjects. Only the *Star Trek*-style instantaneous transporter was missing. (Jarna's group may have possessed such a device. Her report of traveling was by teleportation. She said "I simply appeared there [at the supply center].") Ultramodern conveyances accounted for nearly three quarters of the Type II answers. The rest were divided between those who walked (22.5 percent) to their destinations and the two subjects (5 percent) who saw themselves on horseback.

The monetary systems mentioned by Type II subjects in 2300 A.D. also resemble those cited by several of the Type Ic "Non-solar System Planet" inhabitants as well. Although half mention the continued use of some kind of tokens (often plastic), coins or bills, just over 20 percent saw themselves using credit cards or signing for food and equipment, and nearly 30 percent simply said they didn't use money at all. As noted in the last chapter, 24 percent of the Non-solar system dwellers also stated they didn't have to pay for their supplies.

The answers to the questions concerning their general feelings about their future home and life and their experience with the "bright, shining light" definitely distinguish the Type II New Agers from most of their cousins on alien planets, however. Seventy-seven percent of these New Age community dwellers indicated how they felt about their home environments as they returned from their shopping expeditions. Their answers were overwhelmingly (97.5 percent) positive. Even the fairly common references to loneliness among the 2100 A.D. Type II subjects were totally absent in the 2300 to 2500 period. Only one woman said that she "didn't have any feelings" about her home life. I characterized this as a "neutral" response for it could have several meanings. There were no "negative" replies.

All of the other brief descriptions of how the subjects felt about their New Age communities were bright and uplifting. The words "happy," "peaceful," "good" or "comfortable" appeared on 28 data sheets (70 percent). Other less frequent synonyms such as "neat," "joyful" or "calm" were used on almost all of the others. A feeling of "peace and extreme love" was reported by one woman who situated her experience in a re-risen Atlantis. Another said she felt "contentment, happy and fulfilled" in her "white, colonnaded" settlement nestled amid "warm, lush forests" in Australia.

Several of these subjects also mentioned that they felt a sense of purpose about their 2300-era future lives. Like Jarna cited earlier, they were happy to participate in a working and sharing community. Thus one of Helen Wambach's 1984 subjects remarked:

> I felt safe and secure there [at home] but my job for the community was not finished for the day. . . . There was a friendly atmosphere to it all.
>
> [Alaskan coastal town]

Another woman who attended one of Leo Sprinkle's 1984 workshops made the following comment about her shopping expedition:

> I had gotten creative supplies for my profession [as an artist]. I felt calm, happy and ready to go to work now. . . .
>
> [Egypt]

This woman, who heard "Alena" when asked her future-life name, described the climate of her North African home as "warm, breezy . . . almost ethereal." The Sun shone down with a strong "white-gold light," but Egypt was not the arid desert we know today. There were "green grasses and palm trees" along with "well-tended gardens" nearby. The marketplace, to which Alena walked with her husband (called "my partner"), was set outdoors, bathed in the same all-pervasive sunshine as the rest of the area. The couple paid for their supplies with "coins and bills with buildings on them." Later they ate their evening meal at home with their daughter. It consisted of "fruit, nuts and cheeses," eaten with "silver utensils" off "large white china plates."

Asked about her experience with the "bright, shining light," Alena found herself in her artist's studio, part of the "white, stucco and tile Roman-style villa" her family shared. There, while meditating in search of inspiration, she saw "a white distant glow of Energy approaching with information." After being filled and inspired by the light, she concluded, "I gave profound thanks to the Energy and was prepared to go on with the day."

Alena's encounter with an inspiring energy source was not uncommon among the New Age reports from 2300 A.D. Fully half of the Type II participants reported a contact with a higher energy or spiritual source when asked about their experience with the bright light. On most of these data sheets, including Alena's, it was hard to distinguish between the two terms "energy" and "spiritual." The openly religious or specifically spiritual character of the 2100 A.D. reports had evolved into a generalized description of feeling "higher vibrations" or receiving information and nourishment from a "pulsing light." One woman expressed the light in her experience simply as the "God Source—Pure Energy."

A participant in one of my American workshops, who said she was gathered with others in a beautiful, natural-wood "church," described her encounter with the light in the following terms:

> It was a fulfilling experience. Everyone was hungry for more energy
> projected from that light to all of us.
>
> [New Mexico]

As mentioned earlier, Jarna remarked seeing light and energy emanating from her hands during a healing ritual. It was "an everyday occurrence," she noted. For another the bright light was the "Christ light," bringing peace and harmony to her and her family. A beautiful description of how one of Helen Wambach's 1984 subjects "met the light" on a hillside reminiscent of where Jesus taught was worded this way:

> I saw a large bright light surrounding a hill. I walked up the hill
> to communicate with a Higher Being.

This woman, who felt her future-life experience was set on a "resurrected Atlantis," described the climate there as "warm and soothing." Her large wood-and-stone house was fairly high up, near the mountainous center of the renewed island continent. It was set off by a stand of tall pine trees in front and a "large garden in back, outside the bedroom window." Named "Diana" in that future life, the subject saw herself dressed in a "long velvet robe." It was a "deep, rich cranberry-wine color." Soft, comfortable "cloth booties" were on her feet.

The house sat at the outskirts of a modern-looking community, nestled among the tree-dotted hills. Diana could therefore walk to a "large store in a shopping center" to buy groceries ("bread and vegetables"). She paid for her purchases with a few "gold coins with pictures on them." Later she saw herself eating "pudding" at home by herself.

Although she apparently lived alone in her later years, this future Atlantean also commented that she saw her (current) nine-year-old son back with her in this future lifetime. "He is a leader [in 2300], a very tall, well-proportioned blond man." She even gave a brief description of seeing the two of them together at a banquet, held in "a palace." She had dressed up for this special occasion in a "long blue evening gown, tied at the waist with a silver cord, with matching silver slippers."

Finally, at 200 years old, she decided it was "time to go on" and therefore willed herself out of the body. The transition was "very calm" and she was content. Her last comment was that this was a "rich, rewarding lifetime," filled with feelings of "peace and extreme love."

Although Diana's report was somewhat unusual (very few subjects described palaces or lived to be 200 years old, even in 2300 A.D.), her overall feelings of "peace," "love" and "contentment" were shared by nearly all the Type II "New Age" community residents. Her experience of the light as a vehicle of communication with a "Higher Being" also repeated a theme common to several of these data sheets, as noted earlier.

The rest of the Type II reports about the bright light were divided between those who observed the lights of various spacecraft (35 percent) and those for whom the light came from a natural, earthly source (15 percent). Thus, for one person, it was "like a sunset, fading into the horizon," while for a Frenchwoman from Bordeaux the light came from boats "taking our families to a religious ceremony." Another individual said it marked "a spacecraft that landed."

The South American "monk" mentioned earlier didn't say what the source of the light he saw was but commented that its appearance made him sigh sadly. "Maybe because I had to stay where I was," he added in a remark echoed by many of today's "near death" experiencers, as reported by Drs. Raymond Moody and Elisabeth Kübler-Ross in their books. Many who experience an NDE also report seeing a beautiful, loving white light with which they long to stay. Returning to their physical bodies is often seen as a required task.

The Argentine "monk's" reaction to the light, however, was not typical of the New Agers. Most felt very positive about their experience. One of Helen's Southern California subjects, whose wisdom and psychic talents have led her to organize an important spiritual community around her in recent years, found herself in a very scientific New Age community in the twenty-fourth century. For her the light signaled new birth, not death. She described her experience this way:

> My partner and I were being lifted into a large place [like a space-ship] to receive information and for "fusion" so that we might have another child.
>
> > [Location not given]

Several others of those who associated the light with spacecraft also gave a spiritual connotation to the event. One particularly vivid description of such an event came from another young Frenchwoman, originally from Madagascar. She stated:

> I was in a large stadium with what appeared to be thousands of other people. A bright white light came down from above, projecting onto the crowd, illuminating the entire stadium. Happy feelings of serenity and peace came over me. Perhaps we were seeing a space-craft land? It was a special, joyous event.
>
> > [Middle East]

This same subject completed her data sheet with a spontaneous comment that sums up the 2300 A.D. Type II experience beautifully:

> I chose the year 2300 but to me it looked more like a Middle Eastern life-style than the future, even though it was different, somehow. Everything appeared golden; I felt I was almost unreal; my body seemed ethereal, immaterial, very luminous. It was a very soft, peaceful, and pleasant life, one I'd like to experience someday. It seemed a Golden Age.

Nearly 60 percent of the Type II subjects gave at least an approximate indication of where they saw themselves in 2300 A.D. Twelve mentioned different regions of today's United States; seven situated their future lifetimes in Africa or the Middle East; four each were in South America and Canada, and the others in Australia (two) and Europe and Asia (one apiece). The last person located her New Age community in a resurrected Atlantis, between North America and Europe. Several others simply said they were somewhere "on Earth."

Specific American locations included three cases situated in either Arizona or New Mexico and two in the Colorado Rockies. One person saw herself at Virginia Beach, today the home of psychic Edgar Cayce's A.R.E. organization. The late seer himself predicted that this area would be spared significant damage during the geophysical cataclysms he predicted and would go on to become a major commercial center by the twenty-second century. Two others found themselves in Alaska; one of them remarked that "the coastline has changed" from the mid-1980s. Other states cited once included Wyoming, Minnesota, Washington ("near Seattle") and New Hampshire. Interestingly, none of this group mentioned California, even though about half were living there at the time of these future-life workshops.

North Africa and the Middle East were also mentioned on several data sheets, including those quoted above. Four said they felt they were in Egypt, while one person mentioned Constantinople (today named Istanbul) as the site of her New Age city. The small South African country of Botswana was cited once. Canada, including Saskatchewan and the Yukon, was home to four subjects, all of whom commented on the mild, temperate climate they found there in the 2300s. Three individuals were in the Peruvian Andes and one in Argentina, while, as listed above, the rest gave only the general designations of Asia, Australia and Europe. Many of these locations correspond with those already provided as Type II sites by those workshop participants progressing to 2100 A.D., while others, notably Egypt and Australia, were new.

These expanding communities labeled Type II, or "New Age," characterized by their cooperative life-style and harmonious interaction with nature, were not, however, the only human society envisioned by our workshop participants for the 2300–2500 A.D. era. Nearly as many subjects progressing to this time period found themselves part of what appear to be the descendants of the Type III "Hi-tech" urban culture already present 200 years earlier in the twenty-second century.

Again, as with those 2100 A.D. reports, the coexistence of a flowering Golden Age with the Type III's cold, artificial surroundings is hard to understand in the context of a single planetary environment. At the end of this chapter I will offer what I feel are a couple of possible explanations for this paradox. What is incontestable is that our workshop participants were clearly divided between the same two kinds of society in both future time periods suggested to them.

Further, as will be shown below, there definitely seems to be evidence of an evolution within each of these two social models over the intervening centuries. They appear to be converging toward one, more unified, planetary social order that will share the most positive characteristics of each group. Already by the 2300 to 2500 period a few reports, which I have named Type IIIb ("Hi-tech Evolved"), hint at the kind of overall society that seems to be emerging. The Earth itself also appears in better ecological shape by the twenty-fifth to twenty-sixth centuries.

Despite this hopeful evidence, however, the 36 data sheets from 2300 to 2500 A.D. that were grouped together as Type IIIa ("Hi-tech") continued to exhibit the same sterile, closed-in and violent characteristics as the 2100 A.D. Type III cities. Again, as in 2100, these Hi-tech urbanites lacked positive interaction with the natural environment outside their enclosed urban complexes. Fully three quarters of the Type IIIa data sheets reported lives led either underground (or underwater) or inside futuristic dome-covered cities surrounded by a hostile, barren landscape. "I was inside a domed area all the time," was one typical comment. Others such as "I didn't see much outside" or "This civilization is underground" echoed similar situations. One woman, living her 2300 lifetime as a man named "Eclah," remarked:

> The landscape was bleak, jagged, oblique. . . . Buildings were metallic, either flat-roofed or domed. We were in a very large, streamlined kind of tunnel; it was curving around . . .

Only a third of the group (twelve cases) mentioned the outside world at all, and of those that did, just one reported anything positive about it. The vast majority of reports used adjectives such as "barren," "hot" and "like a desert." One subject said his surroundings were "dry, rocky and dead-looking." From the safety of his domed city he wondered, "Does any life exist out there anymore?"

The lone exception was a woman hypnotist from Ohio who attended one of Helen's workshops. She found herself in 2300 A.D. as a man called "Miloko" living in a "campus-type setting" whose most prominent feature was a large dome-covered library. Blue-eyed, he also had "very pale white skin," "short black hair" and "slender, well-groomed" hands. Like most of the Hi-tech urbanites, Miloko wore a snug, "metallic gray" body suit that included "stocking-type boots." Although it "appeared coarse," this "uniform" actually felt "soft and loose" despite its close fit.

Apparently a scholar, Miloko found himself in his university's library at one point surrounded by a variety of ultramodern audiovisual equipment and also standard-type bookshelves. He also attended lectures in the auditorium "under a large domed roof." Other, flat-roofed, campus buildings, made of "sparkling, smooth, synthetic materials," appeared "grayish-white." He never traveled outside the university complex. Instead, all necessary supplies were ordered via a computer system. No money changed hands; "everything bought was recorded."

Miloko had a room in a university residence hall. Vegetarian meals were taken in a communal dining hall. Miloko noted "one male/female [androgynous?] close friend" nearby and also "another unknown person" at his table. Commenting about his somewhat solitary life there, he noted, "I liked my quarters but sometimes wished for a partner/wife." Eventually, at the ripe old age of eighty-two, he chose to leave his body. The subject noted that this transition included being "surrounded by friends who helped [Miloko] to 'let go.' " It was a "joyful" experience, after which the spirit "became a spiral of white light."

I have included this basically positive Type IIIa report here to remind readers that even within those future-life groups that seem generally unpleasant there are always exceptions. Nonetheless, even this essentially happy and optimistic subject failed to use any of the typical Type II ("New Age" community) words such as "green," "lush" or "beautiful" when describing Miloko's physical surroundings. No natural sources of fresh water such as a stream or lake were mentioned. In fact, Miloko never traveled outside his enclosed campus environment. And although he enjoyed what he was doing, he also experienced feelings of separation and loneliness during that lifetime (no "partner/wife").

The continuing highly technological nature of the Type IIIa enclosed environment was shown in the kinds of buildings described by these subjects. Again, ultramodern urban skyscrapers along with clear glass or plastic domes dominated the architecture seen. Twenty-two reports (61 percent) specifically mention domes or curved roofs, while almost as many (20 cases) describe futuristic towers. Precast concrete or plastic building materials were frequently cited (28 percent) along with glass (25 percent) and steel (17 percent). A minority of seven reports (19 percent) indicate the use of stone or adobe in either half-sunken, flat-roofed complexes or units built into hillsides.

Another noteworthy parallel between the 2100 A.D. Hi-tech subjects and their 2300 Type IIIa "cousins" comes from their average ages at death. The overall mean lifespan for the 2100 group was 59.5 years, far below the 92.4-year New Age average for that era. Similarly, the 26 Type IIIa subjects from 2300 A.D. who reported their age at death had a mean lifespan of just 56.7 years. This was the lowest average of any of the groups on Earth in that time period and only slightly above the spaceship and space-station crews' average of 54.3 years. In comparison, the average lifespan for the New Age group during 2300–2500 A.D. was 99.6 years.

Moreover, the causes of death cited by the two Hi-tech groups were remarkably similar as well. In both cases violent deaths, either by murder or execution, accounted for nearly 25 percent of the total. In 2300 only the Type IVb "Survivors," closely related to Type IIIa reports in other categories as well, also reported a murder.

Further, although never specifically asked about the air quality of their surroundings, just as with the 2100 A.D. Hi-tech subjects, six of the Type IIIa subjects (23 percent) attributed their deaths to respiratory problems. "Couldn't breathe" or "something to do with the chest" were typical causes given by this group. None of the Type II "New Age" participants in either time period ever mentioned lung or chest ailments in relation to their future lifetimes.

Clothing and footwear observed by Type IIIa subjects in the 2300 era also echoed the 2100 Hi-tech reports. Again, nearly 60 percent of each group found themselves wearing tight-fitting uniforms or one-piece jumpsuits, frequently described as "silvery" or "metallic." Styles seemed somewhat less militaristic than earlier, however, as another third of the Type IIIa group were dressed in short, belted tunics, sometimes worn with pants similar to those reported by many Type Ic ("Non-solar System Planet") dwellers. Boots were worn by 59 percent of the Type IIIa subjects, with 23 percent reporting cloth or plastic shoes and 12 percent sandals. Two saw themselves going barefoot inside their city apartments.

As with clothing, a slightly wider variety of foods was reported in the 2300 A.D. period than 200 years earlier. Energy pills and synthetic foodstuffs now accounted for only 31 percent of the meals described. This was down 10 percent from 2100 A.D. The rest of the 32 subjects who answered these questions cited breads and cereal products (38 percent), fruits and vegetables (37 percent) and meat and fish (13 percent) in their diets. (The total exceeds 100 percent due to multiple responses by some subjects.)

One item that seems to have become widespread among all three types of "advanced" cultures in 2300 is a combination spoon-and-fork eating utensil. It was independently reported by several subjects from Types I, II and III. Dining arrangements for Type IIIa were overwhelmingly communal (71 percent), with the rest eating just with close family members. Only one subject saw himself eating alone.

As in 2100 A.D., travel, supply and monetary arrangements in the Hi-tech cities resembled those of the "In-space" explorers. For example, of the 25 to 30 Type IIIa participants who answered these questions, 20 percent traveled in spaceships or aircraft and an equal number mentioned individual flying devices, some similar to the "jet backpacks" cited by some of the Type Ic ("Non-solar System Planet") subjects. The rest either walked or drove mechanized carts around their enclosed complexes. A wide variety of essential supplies including food, building materials and sealed boxes were obtained. Most (63 percent) came from large warehouses or supply depots. Other supply sources included spacecraft, automated delivery systems (17 percent each) and, for one person, a "market in a cavern."

Fifteen of the 26 subjects who described how they paid for their provisions (58 percent) described plastic credit cards or some form of computerized credit system. One said she had a card that "turned lighter in color as it was used." Another found his "fingerprints and voice" being recorded by a computer as he made his purchases. Ten others (38 percent) traded more traditional coins or bills for their supplies. Copper and brass tokens were mentioned as well as an unusual "six-sided metal coin with a hole in the center." One enterprising individual admitted he just stole what he needed.

Along with their artificial, closed-in environment and often violent life-style, significantly negative feelings about their future home and surroundings characterized both the 2100 and 2300 A.D. Hi-tech groups. Twenty-six of the 2300 Type IIIa sample gave short, often one-word, descriptions of how they felt on returning to their quarters after shopping for essential provisions. Only ten of these replies (38 percent) can be regarded as "positive," while the rest (62 percent) clearly expressed indifference or dissatisfaction. Still, even this was an improvement over the 12 percent positive responses given by Type III subjects who returned to Earth in the 2100 A.D. period.

Among the replies evaluated as positive were those indicating feeling "good" (four cases) and "comfortable" (three cases). One person said, "It was a home with my loving wife or companion." Another, whose comment was marked positive, was nonetheless more ambivalent. She remarked:

> I lived alone in a tall dome-shaped white building but *did not* feel lonely. (emphasis in original)

Several other Type IIIa subjects, however, did express feelings of loneliness or of disappointment with their future living conditions. One of Helen's 1983 subjects was a woman who always saw herself indoors during her 2400 A.D. lifetime. A very pale blond, she never walked

outside her "round-shaped" home, which was surrounded by "tall weeds."
She lived there with her husband and two children, a boy and a girl.

This woman's clothing, a "shiny, smooth outfit with a thick metal
belt" and "silken slippers with pointy toes," was typical of many Type
IIIa reports. "Leafy vegetables" and "something shaped like a potato"
were eaten with "very long, three-tined metal forks," which were "sturdy
and simply designed." The food was "not real great."

For this subject, who felt "isolated and alone" most of the time, just
visiting the neighbors was a big event. She commented:

> I feel really lonely [in this future lifetime] but I love my family. My
> little boy makes me happy. I like to watch the kids play [with their
> neighbors] when we get together. This life just seems drudgery
> otherwise. My only real happiness is my family.

Nonetheless, despite the apparent isolation, her community was clearly
part of the Hi-tech culture. Asked about a trip to get essential supplies,
she replied:

> I get into an air car all alone; it looks like it's made out of metal
> and plastic. The details aren't very clear. It makes almost no sound
> as it lifts off from a patch of level ground behind the house. My
> destination is a large round tower which resembles a silo, tall and
> metallic. I'm going to buy boxes of food; prepackaged things that
> will last a long time.

> I don't go [to the supply depot] often. It's a boring trip since every-
> thing is handled by machines and I don't see any other people. I
> just insert a charge card in a slot and the boxes are loaded into the
> back of the car. It's routine.

At the end of her data sheet this subject noted she "felt kind of glad"
to leave her future-life body at age fifty-seven after an unknown illness.
"My face is real ashen," she noted. Her son, "looking older now," was by
her deathbed. She set the year of her death at 2457 A.D.

Another subject who experienced similar lonely feelings said:

> Despite the others in my living unit, I always felt alone.

Half a dozen very short replies consisted of just one or two words.
They were made up of what I came to call the "four D's": "desolate,"

"dreary," "drab" and "disappointed." One of these subjects added at the bottom of his data sheet that his death (in a rock slide in 2505 A.D.) was "similar to previous nightmares and feelings of being crushed." He added that he felt "no accomplishments" in that lifetime. He was "disappointed" with his apparent lack of progress.

Other Type IIIa subjects felt oppressed by their artificial city atmosphere. One of these said that the city was "confining, restraining." Another said she felt "closed in" during the entire experience. Two reports displayed a more neutral indifferent attitude toward their surroundings. One man said it was "no big deal; it's my world." Another stated that returning home was merely "a banal event."

Their experience with the "bright, shining light" was also nothing terribly special for most of the 20 Type IIIa subjects who answered that question. Half of the group saw spaceships landing or taking off; it looked "similar to those seen on TV," said one participant, who wondered if her conscious mind hadn't influenced her vision. Such things were apparently commonplace for these subjects. One individual saw "a person airborne"; possibly they were using one of the flying-belt contraptions mentioned in other 2300 A.D. reports.

Six individuals saw naturally occurring lights such as the Sun, stars at night, balloons in the sky or a fire. One underwent a special "great initiation" ceremony that seemed to take place in space. The other two described "energy experiences" involving the telepathic sharing of information.

In addition to Miloko, whose story was discussed earlier, another of Helen's Type IIIa subjects found herself in a university complex. In that 2300 A.D. future life she saw herself living as a young female scholar named "Joanna" in a "large white building with marble pillars" covered by "a large dome." Her supply expedition was walking within the domed-over campus to the nearby library to borrow "some books and scrolls." Asked about her contact with the bright light, Joanna replied that she saw "a light beam from a glass-covered casket radiating back and forth to the heavens" through her university complex's transparent dome. The light apparently brought energy for the town.

When asked to locate their future homes on a map of the Earth, only about a third of the 36 Type IIIa subjects responded. Nine said they were in what is now the United States; two named European countries (Germany and Finland); one replied "the west coast of Australia" and the last one said "by the Black Sea." Two felt their future lives would be lived on a resurrected Atlantis or some other area now still underwater.

Of the future Americans, two did not name any specific state, two were in New England (Connecticut and "Maine or Nova Scotia"), and one each in Florida, Alaska, Virginia and California. The woman who saw herself living as Miloko on a dome-covered university campus said it was located in an "area built over the southern portion of the Great Lakes."

Before turning to those "Type IIIb" data sheets that seem to point to an evolution within the Hi-tech civilization toward a more harmonious and humane society, I want to quote one of my few 1988 American subjects who wrote an extended comment on the back of her Toledo, Ohio, workshop data sheet. I feel her experience, limited as it was, for her subconscious mind went on to "choose" to recall a past life from the first century A.D. rather than follow up on this future vision, contains most of the elements expressed less eloquently by many of the other Type IIIa subjects when progressed forward into this generally unpleasant Hi-tech life-style. Here is her report:

> I had two different experiences. The 2300 one didn't feel good but I followed it along with the other [the 100 A.D. past life] about a third of the way in.

> I was alone, looking at a very cold, tall and metallic-type city which you couldn't see into. The buildings were all close together, touching, no space between, no windows and reflective surfaces, a grayish-green color. I was tall and slim, all encased in a body suit, except for face and hands. It was one-piece, form-fitting, something like the luge teams wear in the Olympics. There was a huge empty space all around. Nothing green or growing, no trees, no other people; all was encapsulated in the city, I guess. I was not aware of my sex; it didn't seem important. My hair, head was covered with the body suit.

> I couldn't get further [into the future-life experience] but I know that I didn't like it there. Your questions about home and food irritated me. They didn't make sense or apply to me. . . . It was unimportant to this entity, almost as though it were a spirit occupying a body form only briefly, not needing food or shopping.

Such was the experience of a participant in one of the last groups I personally progressed to a future lifetime, either their own or one observed through the eyes of another. In many respects it typifies the overall impression given of these Type III or IIIa future environments. Note that this woman found herself "outside" the enclosed 2300 A.D. city, in a desolate, wasted landscape. She never really entered that future lifetime. Consequently, she had the feeling of being a "spirit occupying a body form only briefly." According to Ageless Wisdom and present-day psychics, this is our natural state between incarnations.

Nonetheless, this woman still clearly saw the tight-fitting, unisex body suit and tall, futuristic architecture described by the vast majority of Type III and IIIa subjects. Her gender was indeterminate and didn't seem important. (All of the androgynous cases reported came from either Type III or Type I environments.) Food, home life and shopping for supplies also seemed meaningless and she was unable to provide any details. In fact, she states that the questions asked about these topics "irritated" her. This puzzling "irritation," quite unlike the present-day personality of this individual, whom I happened to see for a private therapy session on the day following the workshop, spurred her to write the lengthy commentary quoted above.

How very different were the feelings emerging from the twenty reports from the 2300 to 2500 A.D. era that I labeled Type IIIb, or "Hi-tech Evolved"! I feel that these cases represent the emergence of positive, humanitarian characteristics among at least some of the future Hi-tech cities. While living basically Type III, Hi-tech and enclosed-environment life-styles, the Type IIIb subjects exhibited a much more positive outlook about their surroundings and human relationships in general.

The twenty subjects dubbed "Type IIIb" basically described living in futuristic urban complexes, most of which included domed buildings (60 percent) and/or modern skyscrapers (50 percent). They also saw themselves dressed mainly in the tight-fitting, one-piece jumpsuits common to Type I and III reports (60 percent), although 30 percent reported wearing the long, loose robes or draped garments associated with Type II communities. Footwear was split evenly between boots (50 percent) and either soft cloth (30 percent) or durable plastic (20 percent) shoes.

The diet of this group also reflected Type III tendencies, with 56 percent reporting eating fruits and vegetables at their evening meal, while 33 percent nourished themselves on vitamin pills and processed, synthetic foodstuffs. Meat was present at 17 percent of the Type IIIb meals reported. Dining arrangements for half of the sixteen subjects who answered this question were communal, while six others (38 percent) ate with just family members present and two ate alone.

The answers of these "evolved" Hi-tech subjects to the questions concerning transportation, supplies and monetary systems also paralleled those of the Type IIIa urban dwellers and Type I spacefarers. Fifty-seven percent mentioned aircraft or spacecraft when asked how they traveled. A quarter of them (26 percent) said they used some type of personal antigravity or flying device. They thus joined the 20 percent of the Type IIIa and 18 percent of Type Ic subjects who described using similar "jet backpacks," or flying belts. Two thirds (64 percent) of the Type IIIb group went to large warehouse buildings or supply depots to obtain essential provisions. Eighteen percent used a computerized automatic distribution system and the rest mentioned using a variety of modern stores and markets.

Half said they used credit cards or a signature credit system to pay for their purchases, while the other half used bills or coins. One Type IIIb report from a subject who said her futuristic community was located in Canada even cited using a "round coin with geometric cutouts in the center," quite similar to the "six-sided coin with a round hole in the middle" seen by a Type IIIa participant from "Atlantis."

One typical report from this group came from a retired woman artist who hosted one of my own future-life workshops in her New York City apartment in 1985. She found herself living a future life as a "curly, red-haired" man named "Jan" with "strong hands" and "long fingers." Jan's 2300-era life was spent in a "geodesic-domed" city filled with "wedged and triangular" architecture and tied together by a public monorail system. It had a "moderate" climate.

An "architect and urban designer," Jan found himself in a "huge warehouse complex" looking over construction supplies. Specifically, he was buying "materials for welding; they looked like laser-beam machines." He paid for them with small paper bills.

Jan's pale white skin was almost entirely enveloped in a "silver-gray coverall." This one-piece, utilitarian garment went from neck to ankles. Its pants tucked into "ankle-high silver boots" made of the same "metallic-looking but soft, flexible" synthetic material. He lived in a "futuristic apartment" with wife, son and daughter. Their evening meal, eaten communally with neighbors, was made up of "fruits and vegetables," eaten with a "stainless-steel three-tined fork." Everything in both his domestic and professional life was very modern and quite functional as well. "It was total communal living," this subject wrote at the bottom of her data sheet.

Jan's story, echoed by the other nineteen Type IIIb reports, clearly shows that in most exterior respects, these subjects' future lives reflect a life-style closely related to that of the Type IIIa Hi-tech city residents from the same future time period. Why not, then, merely group them together with the others in one large sample? What distinguished these reports from those of their Type IIIa counterparts? Simply put, these Type IIIb data sheets from 2300 to 2500, despite their descriptions of a Hi-tech, urban culture, also all contained specific references to ongoing, harmonious interaction with an outside natural environment depicted in positive terms.

Such descriptions had been completely absent in the 2100-period data and I admit to having been surprised at first to discover it when going over these reports of just 200 years later.

My New York friend's future-life story as Jan is an excellent example of this. Although clearly a Hi-tech city dweller, Jan nonetheless described the area outside his "geodesic" complex as set amid a series of "brown rolling hills" that led down to "wide green-and-yellow plains." It was apparently possible to leave the city and walk among the surrounding fields with little or no risk. The air was described as "brisk" and the climate "moderate."

As explained at the beginning of Chapter 5, when I began analyzing the 2100 A.D. data from the first group of Helen's workshops in late 1984, I deliberately chose to divide her subjects according to what they said about the surrounding landscape or natural, outside environment in which they found themselves in their future lifetimes. In part this was because nearly all the subjects who succeeded in progressing to the future gave at least a cursory description of their environments. But also, as social scientists, Helen Wambach and I agreed that these snapshots of future external surroundings were the least likely to be influenced by the subject's conscious prejudices or desires. All of their other responses, such as clothing, food, dining arrangements, etc., involved more socially determined circumstances. I wanted to start the analysis of their visions from as neutral a point as possible.

Therefore, when going through the 2300 to 2500 A.D. data sheets, a project I did not begin until late 1988, I was both surprised and fascinated to find a significant number that combined a Type III ("Hi-tech") society with Type II ("New Age") natural environment. For, even though only 30 percent made specific references to the natural beauty of their location or "clean" or "clear" atmosphere, all but one of this group either mentioned seeing greenery, trees and lakes or a moderate, mild climate. The lone exception, which I nonetheless included as Type IIIb, was that of a report of a community located in the Sinai (Egypt), a naturally hot, arid region. Even that subject mentioned being outside "in the desert" while traveling. She also loved her surroundings.

Later, when comparing this group's replies against others from this period, I was equally impressed by how closely the locations given by the ten Type IIIb participants who identified their surroundings agreed with the approximate sites of the Type II "New Age" communities. Thus, in addition to the Sinai case in Egypt, three Type IIIb reports were from Canada, including two that specified the Canadian Rockies (one said "the Yukon or Alaska"). Four more were from today's U.S.A.: Colorado, Utah, the Texas Gulf Coast and the rolling hills of one of the Great Plains states. The other two places cited were Spain and a "resurrected Atlantis." All of these spots except Spain and Texas were mentioned by Type II subjects from either the 2100 or 2300 A.D. periods as well.

Other interesting findings which support the idea that this group may represent an evolution of part of the Type III future Hi-tech society toward more humanitarian values came from the causes and average age of death reported. Of the eighteen Type IIIb subjects who provided this data, not one saw his or her future life ending in violence. Nor was there any mention of death by respiratory failure. Moreover, fully a third of the group reported leaving their physical bodies voluntarily (average age: 71). Remarks accompanying these reports included such phrases as "I'm off to learn something new" (age 45) and "Time to move on!" (age 82). There were two travel accidents (average age: 50), while the rest (50 percent) died of "old age" (average age: 79) or physical ailments (average age: 73). The mean lifespan for the entire group was 70.9 years, several years higher than Type IIIa's very low score (56.7 years) but still below Type II's near-century mark (99.6 years).

These "Hi-tech Evolved" participants' feelings about their home environments and their descriptions of the experience with the bright light also distinguished them from the rest of the 2300 A.D. Hi-tech urbanites or the Type IVb "Survivors." Of the fourteen Type IIIb subjects who described how they felt on returning home after getting supplies, none gave negative replies such as "dreary" or "lonely." Two had what I marked as neutral responses: "normal" and "so-so." The rest (86 percent) indicated they were enjoying their experience. "I love this place!" exclaimed the woman whose future life as "Kandra" in the Sinai Desert included a reunion with the soul who had temporarily shared her current life as a small daughter who died at the tender age of seven. "We came together again [in 2300] to experience love and connection," she wrote. Others remarked on their feelings of "peace," "warmth" and "accomplishment."

Each of these terms was used more than once among the Type IIIb
subjects.

> It's pleasant; I'm starting a fire [in the fireplace]. . . . We're in a
> sort of community outpost manning highly sensitive communications
> equipment

remarked a woman who saw herself as living as a man in the Rocky
Mountains of the Yukon or Alaska.

My retired artist friend whose future life as Jan was discussed earlier,
found that her present-day grown daughter will become her spouse in
2300 A.D. Commenting on that relationship, she wrote:

> [As Jan] I felt deep satisfaction in a life shared with others and was
> very fulfilled. We cared for each other in the deepest sense of the
> word. Our family life was warmly loving and sharing.
> [U.S.—Great Plains]

Sixteen Type IIIb subjects provided an account of seeing a light or
spacecraft during their 2300 A.D. lifetime. Of this number, six (38 percent) mentioned spaceship lights, while four others (25 percent) said they
saw aircraft. The other six described the experience as one involving
healing or telepathic energies. Among them was my New York artist
friend. Indicating that such energy sharing was a commonplace group
activity in Jan's geodesic-domed complex of wedge and triangular buildings, she commented:

> It [receiving the energy/light] was an ongoing experience, eagerly
> expected and received. The interrelationships gave us much plea-
> sure.

Another Type IIIb participant saw the light passing "between the
'third eye' of one person to the 'third eye' of the other" as a way of sharing
information telepathically. Yet another felt aware of "a tremendous energy" when witnessing the light. For her it was "like being consciously
able to materialize and dematerialize."

The existence of the Type IIIb group in the 2300 to 2500 A.D. period
seems to confirm the feelings of the Northern California teacher whose
comment about her dissatisfying, survival-level life in the twenty-second
century was quoted in Chapter 6. In that progression she foresaw another

future incarnation in the 2300s "to work for a rebirth of humanism" on Earth. Although we never explored this predicted return in another workshop, the kinds of values she hoped to teach, such as mutual respect and self-respect, living in harmony with nature, critical thinking and basic goodwill, seem to have become part of the experience of many of those subjects who found themselves living in a Type IIIb situation.

One of Helen's 1983 subjects, a young woman named "John" in her 2300 A.D. lifetime, made a typical Type IIIb report. After describing his Hi-tech living complex, including "houses raised from the ground, each on a single round pole" with "glass tops, like skylights," John went on to say that his dwelling was set among "green trees resembling Eucalyptus but with a kind of willow shape to them." He lived there with his wife, "a timid woman," and two sons. Family relations were "warm, not strained." The subject added, "I enjoyed being a husband and father in that lifetime."

Their food, a combination of preprocessed and natural vegetables, was eaten on plastic trays with the kind of fork/spoon utensil that showed up on several data sheets. Meals were eaten at home in John's community. The family's food and clothing came from a "big warehouse-style building" that was reached by means of an individual flying machine described as a "standing air-cycle." Purchases were paid for with "unusual-looking geometric brass coins." Contact with the light was seeing a spacecraft that looked "bright with dark silhouettes in the center." The experience was neither threatening nor uncommon. Life was generally good and uncomplicated. The setting was in what is today western Canada.

Eventually, by this time a "white-haired, white-bearded patriarch," John died peacefully at seventy-nine years old following the "failure of an internal organ." On leaving that future-life male body, this woman subject wrote on her data sheet:

I felt good, welcomed and free. It felt as if something important had been learned during that lifetime.

If the Type IIIb data sheets represent a possible evolution toward more positive, humane values by part of the futuristic Type III urban dwellers, the twenty-four reports from 2300 A.D., which I combined as Type IVa ("Rustics"), show that the lonely, primitive outposts of the 2100 period also appear to be changing. The data suggests that they are moving toward a more modern, technological life-style without, however, sacrificing the natural, land-loving character of their communities.

As noted in Chapter 6 when discussing similar reports from 2100 A.D., the main characteristic distinguishing the Type IVa reports from the New Age data sheets was their rural and rustic character, more reminiscent of a recent past (c. 1900) than of the future. In fact, several of the subjects who found themselves in such a life-style, in either 2100 or 2300, remarked that it more resembled frontier life than how they consciously pictured the future. One of Helen's 1983 workshop participants, a young woman who saw herself in a rugged male body in the future, commented:

> It seems like something out of on old Western. . . . I'm in a bar, bright lights, lots of people drinking. . . . The market is an old and gray, weathered wood-frame building. A young girl usually helps [wait on customers] there; she's got her hair in braids and wears a blue-and-white striped cotton dress. . . . [However,] we use chunks of metal or stone, not coins to pay for things. . . . I must be a trapper because I'm buying metal animal traps there.
>
> [Southern tip of Greenland]

This young man, whose name sounded like "Kenaweh" to the subject's conscious mind, lived at an outdoor campsite on the edge of a "lush pine forest" near a "clear blue lake" with "some rugged mountains off in the distance." His clothes, a simple "muslin shirt and green trousers, held up by a large leather belt," looked handmade. Apparently he lived alone some distance from town. His evening meal, a "salty beef stew with no vegetables in it," was eaten alone by a campfire. His only dishes were a rustic wooden bowl and metal spoon.

Kenaweh said he felt "tired" on returning to his campsite after his horseback ride into town for supplies. Later on he must have been caught in some kind of accident. The subject saw this future-life body with one foot amputated at the relatively young age of fifty-two. This shock, plus a "chest congestion ailment," killed him shortly thereafter.

Although definitely "Rustic," several elements of this subject's story point to its future, not past, setting. First, Helen's subject reported that it definitely "felt like" a future life. She even saw a death date of 2352 A.D. flash before her closed eyes. Additionally, its unusual location of southern Greenland, with a climate distinctly warmer than today, coincides with other reports that Canada and Siberia will also have more temperate weather in the future.

Furthermore, the subject's use of the term "bright lights" in the bar implies more than the smoky candles or gas jets of nineteenth-century pioneer saloons. The same is true of the metal animal traps and initially successful foot amputation. Data from other 2300-era Type IVa reports, such as the use of a "hovercraft" or a "flying car" when traveling, tends to support the idea that some types of modern machinery are available in that time, even in remote areas. Also, the use of "chunks of metal or stone" for money suggests people relying on the remnants of a formerly modern civilization rather than creating their own coinage. Finally, it is noteworthy that this subject saw "lots of people" in the bar; this kind of remark was totally lacking among the 2100-era rural Type IVa reports. It hints at a population increase during the intervening centuries.

Except for a few details such as the population increase noticed, the twenty-four Type IVa reports from 2300 A.D. resembled those from the 2100 era. Two thirds of the houses described were made of wood, adobe or stone. There were also four tropical "grass shacks," two tents and a "bungalow" mentioned. Two thirds of these subjects were dressed in a wide variety of traditional clothing, such as "suede leather pants," a "denim dress" and "cotton shirt and pants," although 25 percent wore short tunics or Type III body-hugging jumpsuits and two others the loose robes typical of Type II ("New Age") reports. While a quarter of the group went barefoot, an equal number wore soft leather or cloth shoes and most of the rest were in boots.

As with the 2100 A.D. "Primitives," none of the "Rustic" subjects in the 2300 era mentioned pills or synthetic, preprocessed foods at their evening meals. Various meats, including wild game, fowl and fish, accounted for 31 percent of the foodstuffs served. Fruits and vegetables were also found on most tables (67 percent), often accompanied by breads or grains (22 percent) as well as meat. Broccoli, mashed potatoes, peas, oatmeal and beef stew were among specific foods listed. Dining arrangements were overwhelmingly (83 percent) within family homes. Just two subjects reported eating alone and only one said he was eating with others who weren't close family members.

As for traveling, half of the group used horses and carts, five (20 percent) walked, and the rest (five subjects) rode in modern air vehicles such as those cited above. Old-fashioned stores and open-air markets predominated (77 percent), although two Type IVa subjects saw spacecraft bringing supplies and two others went to big supply depots for their provisions. Only the two people who got their supplies from visiting spaceships mentioned credit cards. The others either used bills and coins (50 percent) or some kind of small stones, "pyramid-shaped pieces" or "chunks of metal or stone" as payment.

Only half of the twenty-four Type IVa data sheets included a description of the "bright, shining light" experience. Of these dozen replies, four, including the two cited above, mentioned spacecraft while the other eight (75 percent) described a variety of natural ("the Sun") or mechanical lights, such as the "bright lights" of the saloon, a flashlight and "the light of a passing train." None of the reports mentioned lights or colors used as energy sources or in spiritual experiences. One subject, looking at the Sun, said, "I had no real encounter with the light." Another, seeing a spaceship fly by, commented:

It seemed natural. I knew and understood it.

However, the same subject added:

As it flew by, it caused me such upset that I slipped out of the experience [temporarily].

Sixteen individuals mentioned their feelings about life in these rural surroundings. Ten (63 percent) gave such positive answers as "peaceful," "happy" or "accomplished." One said he felt the "warmth and comfort of my family and grandchildren." Another said she felt "love" there. The only really negative comment was from a man who said he was "tired and bored." The physical wear and tear of this old-fashioned, hardworking existence accounted for the other four comments judged as less than completely positive. Two people simply said they felt "tired out," while another remarked that it was "a lot of work, but I'm strong and confident." The last comment was from a California man who saw himself living as a black woman on a riverboat in southern Africa with her husband. The subject said:

I feel content; I'm somewhat weary but I don't speak of it.

In addition to this man, who felt his future adventure took place in what is today Mozambique, just seven other Type IVa subjects were able to identify their whereabouts in the 2300–2500 A.D. period. As noted above, one said she was living as a man in southern Greenland. Another felt she was in Peru, while two others said Italy and the Montana hills. The final three individuals saw themselves in Australia. One noted in the margin of her data sheet that it seemed a "smaller body of land" than she remembered Australia as having today. It appeared more like a large island. Of these eight locations, just two, Africa and Montana, were also mentioned by workshop participants as sites of Type IV settlements during the 2100 A.D. period.

The last category, labeled Type IVb "Survivors," grouped together eight reports from subjects whose physical surroundings in 2300 A.D. were described as the "desolate," "abandoned," "destroyed" or "ruined" remnants of some future conflict. I also included the two data sheets from soldiers living in military camps or barracks for a total of ten. As far as could be determined, all of these subjects were living on Earth. Six identified their locations. Three were in Asia (two in China, one in Tibet); two in North America (Minnesota and "North American continent"); the final one was in Bolivia.

On reading these data sheets one gets the impression of devastated areas of ancient, half-forgotten destruction now being reexplored by soldiers or scientists. Only a couple of them give the impression that the person reporting was himself involved in whatever conflict had left these ruins. Nonetheless, a grim, foreboding pall seems to hang over the physical surroundings thus described. Half of these Type IVb "Survivors" called the landscape "barren" or "desolate." One woman said the atmosphere was "black and muggy." The man who found himself in the "destroyed ruins" of a formerly modern city somewhere in North America said there was a "thick haze, almost like a permanent fog" in the air.

None of these subjects described a flourishing environment, either urban or rural. Only the report of one of the two future soldiers indicated a "pleasant climate" over the "rolling land" surrounding his army barracks. The other said his military "camp" was in the mountains.

One of Helen Wambach's 1982 subjects, herself a Jungian analyst and regression therapist today, found herself returning in the twenty-fourth century in a "young, strong" male body dressed in a "lightweight, all-over uniform" that included "soft, supple boots" and "stretch gloves." Named "Brochal," this young man was part of a scientific team testing the "scummy waters" of a seemingly "dead lake," presumably for the residue of poisonous chemicals or radioactivity. The weather around the lake was "hot and humid." The area was "ruined, desolate" except for a few "stunted trees and greenish-yellow weeds." The subject identified it as being in Minnesota.

As might be expected, the buildings seen at such a location were falling apart. Brochal called the nearest one "an ancient corrugated-iron ruin." Only his team's own "small enclosed airship" looked modern and in good condition. He also noted that his group's rations of "fish and some kind of paste" were prepackaged in "round plastic containers." They ate nothing from the local, presumably contaminated, area. They ate with a smaller plastic version of the same combination spoon/fork utensil that was reported on several of the Type III ("Hi-tech") data sheets.

Brochal was not alone in calling the buildings where he found himself "ruins." Half of the ten Type IVb "Survivors" described similar damaged structures, calling them "abandoned" or "fallen in." One report mentioned living in a cave; another called a "log cabin" home. Tents, barracks and a stucco dwelling were also cited. None of these data sheets gave the impression of the sort of organized village life that abounded in the Type IVa ("Rustic") reports. Meals were either eaten alone (two cases) or communally (seven cases). Only one of these subjects mentioned eating with a close family member, a "nephew."

Still, in several areas such as "foods eaten," "clothing worn" and "supplies purchased," the group's data reflects surprisingly modern trends. The answers to these questions indicate that most of these Type IVb "Survivors" actually came from a Type IIIa "Hi-tech" civilization rather than a Type IVa "Rustic" culture. For example, none of these subjects wore conventional shirts, pants or dresses. Nor were they in the loose, draped robes typical of the New Age communities. Half of them reported wearing tight-fitting, metallic uniforms of body suits and the other half were in tunics and pants. Footwear was divided between boots (50 percent), shoes (30 percent) and sandals. Only one went barefoot. Canned or prepackaged foods were mentioned on four data sheets (40 percent) along with breads, stews and a kind of possibly synthetic "mush." Fresh fruits and vegetables were noticeably absent from their meals.

Eight of these ten subjects described traveling to get supplies. Three merely walked, one to "a nearby village's abandoned granary and storehouse," another to his military supply tent and the third to a "fisherman's hut." One soldier rode in a "horse and buggy" to collect ammunition. The four others, however, used space shuttles or aircraft! The man in the ruined North American city said that on such a journey in a "space vehicle" he "saw some trees and sunshine" in another location. He received prepackaged boxes of equipment from a "warehouse with a belt and a conveyer." Another individual reported using a "computer operated" dispenser. Six of these ten "Survivors" used credit cards as payment, a sure sign that they came from a more organized culture. The rest used a variety of coins and bills.

The young scientist mentioned above, Brochal, described his supply expedition thus:

Our group needed additional containers of canned food. I was delegated to go and get it. I used an aircraft to fly to a large warehouse some distance away. The depot was completely mechanized. One punched buttons to place requests; what was ordered was then brought on a conveyer belt. Payment was either by credit card or by using small, inscribed-plastic chips in various sizes and colors. I gave my card to a dark-haired woman at the checkout counter, made sure the boxes were loaded and returned to that deserted lake in the same air vehicle.

A final bit of evidence linking these ten subjects to Earth's urban cultures was that, despite their lonely and desolate living conditions, the average lifespan for the Type IVb group was a respectable 71.8 years. Indeed, two of these subjects reported living to nearly 100 years old and dying of "old age." Three others said they died either from "radiation poisoning" (two cases) or, in the case of Brochal the scientist, from "a disease contracted from the bad water." Even so, he lived until the mature age of 80, dying in his bed, "surrounded by [his] grandchildren." Natural causes took the others. As for the two soldiers, they both died violent deaths. One was killed by a bullet wound, apparently in battle, while the other was knifed by an unknown assailant.

Still, living among such ruined, desolate surroundings definitely marked most of these Type IVb "Survivors." Two thirds reported feeling "sad" or "not good" about their surroundings. Only Brochal indicated that, while he disliked the area near the lake, he nonetheless had "deep feelings" about his "mission" there. Other comments about their lives as "Survivors" included the remark "I'm happy we're both still here" made by a subject living as a man in Bolivia, apparently referring to himself and his future-life wife. Another subject, living with "a nephew" among the abandoned ruins of a Tibetan village, said, "I'm tired, sad about this life." Finally, one of the two soldiers said he felt "responsible" about his army career.

As might be expected from the descriptions of their clothing and general life-style, seven of the eight Type IVb subjects who mentioned their experience with the light said they saw some kind of space vehicle. Brochal said he was "invited inside a round spacecraft" by its (undescribed) occupants. The only non-spaceship report was vague. It came from the soldier who was killed by a bullet wound. He said:

I saw a type of light from the sky. Not very vivid.

I also noted that each of the seven subjects who saw a spaceship remarked that the craft was round. In every case the sighting seemed a routine event. Four said the spacecraft were "scout" or "search" ships, part of the general impression that most of these reports were by Type IIIa people sent into waste areas on specific missions from other, more hospitable locations.

One of Dr. Sprinkle's subjects, who said she was a man named "Bashu" living with his nephew in a ruined village in Tibet, even drew a small picture of a three-tiered, cup-shaped ship whose appearance was irritating. Bashu described what happened:

> I was standing on the side of a mountain, on a path. A spaceship was following me. I was angry. "Leave me alone," I thought. I was associated in the past with someone on board. I didn't want to be taken. I had a job to do, to raise my nephew. I hurried along the path, still angry.

This comment, in which the subject expressed anger at being followed, along with the fact that two of these ten Type IVb "Survivors" reported dying violent deaths, provides further evidence linking them to the Hi-tech cities analyzed earlier in this chapter. Anger and violence, while not typical of our overall data, nonetheless did seem to return regularly among three categories of 2300 A.D. environments: Types Ia ("In-space"), IIIa ("Hi-tech") and IVb ("Survivors"). A violent future space battle in another part of the galaxy and an example of how one of my own workshop subjects became "irritated" with certain of my research questions while observing from a Type IIIa future lifetime have been discussed earlier.

Several subjects from other workshops who found themselves in Type III and IIIa surroundings also reported being "annoyed" by certain of our research questions such as those about the "bright light" and about their "feelings" on returning home after going out for supplies. I had first become aware of this trend when talking over the initial set of 2100 A.D. data with Helen in early 1985. Some of the 2300-era Type IVb "Survivors" also voiced hostile feelings about certain of the topics on their data sheets.

On the other hand, few if any of the subjects who progressed to New Age futures ever expressed such vexations with the researcher's questioning, although such outbursts are not uncommon among past-life reports. These distinctions, although impossible to distinguish statistically, may provide an important clue about the origins of the other differences between these opposing future societies as well.

Dr. Helen Wambach and I are not alone in noting that hypnotized subjects, even in the light trance state that characterized these work-shops, very often assume personality traits of their past (or future) life persona. Cases demonstrating this tendency abound in professional jour-nals such as *The Journal of Regression Therapy*, for example. In deeper levels of trance the subject even takes on the emotional reactions of this "alter ego" to such an extent that he may temporarily loose awareness of his current identity. Somnambulistic amnesia is a widely recognized psychological phenomenon. One of the most famous contemporary cases involving the hypnotically induced "temporary takeover" of an individual by one of her past-life personalities was the "Bridey Murphy" story of the 1950s.

Perhaps, then, the examples given above, illustrating my observation that more Type III ("Hi-tech") and IVb ("Survivors") subjects reacted negatively during their future lifetimes to questions asked than those classified as Type II ("New Age"), suggest that the individuals who are "alive" in Type III future lifetimes are more easily annoyed or angered than their Type II counterparts. They feel and express hostility more readily. The future society that they describe certainly seems more an-tagonistic. (I am speaking here of the future-life persona as a distinct entity, although its presumed psychological disposition may reflect the character of today's subject as well.) While we cannot really measure this potential future character difference statistically, such a difference, if it exists, would also explain the Hi-tech and Survivors groups' virtual mo-nopoly on reports of premature violent deaths such as murder during the 2300 A.D. period.

It may even provide the key to understanding the puzzling coexist-ence of two or more contradictory natural environments on Earth in the same future time period. The connection between these two seemingly independent factors is what Dr. Jeffrey Goodman calls "biorelativity." This concept, introduced in Chapter 4, implies that there is a direct cause-and-effect relationship between the human psyche and such natural forces as earthquakes, volcanoes and weather conditions.

The idea that human emotions and beliefs have a definite impact on the environment also echoes the Old Testament view in which the Lord God Yahweh (Jehovah) deliberately caused storms, droughts and even the Great Deluge itself in reaction to humanity's stubborn disobedience to His Will. The New Testament claims that in reaction to Jesus's cru-cifixion, "the earth shook and the rocks were split," clearly a geophysical consequence of human wickedness (Matthew 27:51). Further, the very heart of the Universal Law of Karma is that we reap the results of what we have sown. Apparently, according to biorelativity, the more we "sow" discord and violence, thereby polluting our emotional atmosphere, the greater natural ecological pollution we will have to endure in the future.

America's "Sleeping Prophet," Edgar Cayce, directly linked violent sunspot activity to preceding outbursts of human "anger, jealousy, hate [and] animosity" here on Earth (Reading 417-7). Although not denying the basically cyclical nature of sunspots, which wax and wane about every eleven years, he claimed that the severity of their increase was controllable through the willpower of the human subconscious mind. This was just one example of how Cayce's readings indicate our individual and collective responsibility for our physical environment. "Thy *mind* is the builder!" he cautioned over and over again (Reading 5757-1; emphasis in the original).

Archaeologist Jeffrey Goodman, in investigating Edgar Cayce's psychic predictions of major geophysical upheavals around the turn of this century, found convincing evidence that human thought patterns or "thought forms" can affect the surrounding environment. He cites recent work with Kirlian photography as demonstrating that both plant and animal bodies possess detectable electromagnetic fields that can be stimulated into visible emotional reactions. Anger and hostility provoke what look like miniature sunbursts of red and orange leaping from the surface of such "aura" fields around human subjects. Dr. Goodman further found that controlled scientific experiments with plants by Delawarr Laboratories in England, among others, demonstrated that seeds that were made the focus of positive prayer showed up to a 52 percent growth advantage when planted—*depending on who was doing the praying*.[1]

Note that the impact of this positive mental stimulus (prayer) definitely seemed influenced by the individual who was providing it. If it can be assumed that all the participants in these experiments were praying the same amount of time, then some subconscious mental factor that varied from person to person must be presumed to account for the difference in results. Similar findings have come from experiments investigating the unusual abilities of psychic healers. The healer's ability mentally and spiritually to attune with the subconscious mind of his patient seems more important for lasting results than any ritual followed or any preexisting beliefs.

Dr. Thelma Moss, a psychologist and former professor at the University of California, Los Angeles (U.C.L.A.), measured the psychic energy emitted by dozens of psychic healers in scientific Kirlian photography experiments in the early 1970s. As previously mentioned in Chapter 2, Dr. Moss concluded that such healers actually transfer a detectable kind of electromagnetic energy to their patients. She reported that Kirlian photography may indicate the existence of a wordless interaction between people through "invisible and probably electrical means."[2]

These experiments, which confirmed pioneering Kirlian photography research into the effect of psychic energy projection on plants by Dr. Douglas Dean of the Newark College of Engineering and similar studies by several Russian scientists, such as Dr. Victor Adamenko, demonstrate that bioenergy transferral exists. Edgar Cayce and other psychics further assert that the kind and amount of "healing" energy available depends on the degree of spiritual awareness in both the healer and patient's subconscious minds. Cayce insisted that it is the quality of each individual soul's experience, acquired through many earthly incarnations, that determines its future heritage. By making positive use of our conscious willpower to overcome personal shortcomings, accomplish worthwhile goals and develop loving, caring relationships with others in this life, we are forging the circumstances of our future lives.

Edgar Cayce often said that anyone could perform the amazing feats of psychic medical diagnosis that he accomplished while in trance. Anyone can be a spiritual healer or grow the abundant kind of gardens that made Findhorn famous if they have spiritually prepared and properly disciplined their minds. This is, I feel, one of the most important teachings of the Ageless Wisdom philosophy and one that may account for the future coexistence of both the Type II "New Age" kind of communities, living in harmony with each other and with a beautiful, pristine natural environment, and the violent and encapsulated Type III "Hi-tech" urban complexes where the external atmosphere appears noxious. The forthcoming Age of Aquarius may very well be one in which some of humanity at least discovers (or rediscovers?) the power to mold the environment via collective thought processes.

I realize that this idea may sound farfetched for many of today's "realists." Biorelative effects might seem possible in individual cases, such as the psychic healers investigated by Dr. Moss, or for such limited experiments as those dealing with plants or Kirlian photographs of the human aura, but is there evidence that human thought-form transference could actually affect large-scale results among natural forces such as earthquakes or weather patterns?

According to Dr. Jeffrey Goodman, the answer to this question is "Yes"! In Appendix C, "Thought Forms and Biorelativity," to *We Are the Earthquake Generation*, he describes how his own research as a graduate student at the University of Arizona convinced him that at least three large groups of prehistoric peoples in the American Southwest had gradually been forced to migrate from their centuries-old homes when their culture became "disharmonious" with the local environment. Over an extended 700-year period (650–1350 A.D.), as each of these group's moral and spiritual levels declined and they began engaging in "disharmonious" activities like cannibalism, slavery and war, the rainfall and/or water table in their immediate vicinity dried up, reducing their numbers and forcing them to migrate elsewhere. At the same time other isolated neighboring populations, whose cultures did not exhibit hostile, warlike behavior, apparently flourished, with adequate water.[3]

Dr. Goodman found that each of the three areas studied, the Navajo Reservoir district, Chaco Canyon and Mesa Verde, followed the same basic "good guys = good environment/bad guys = bad environment" transition even though they had no connections to each other. Further, throughout the same time period the nearby Hopi tribe, whose traditional peaceful ethics of "walking in harmony with the Earth Mother" have prevailed until the present day, remained on their "sacred land" with enough water to sustain their quiet, agricultural way of life. The prophecies of this remarkable people are discussed in Chapter 3 of this book.

A more recent example of how trained human thought patterns, brought together in collective meditation around a single ideal, affected the surrounding environment formed the subject of Elaine and Arthur Aron's book, *The Maharishi Effect*. This book tells of how a group of adepts of Transcendental Meditation (T.M.), a mental and spiritual discipline first taught by an Indian guru popular in the 1960s named Maharishi Mahesh Yogi, gathered together at different Tehran hotels in 1978, during the height of the Iranian revolutionary street fighting there. Their purpose was to raise the spiritual vibrations of peace and of positive social change.[4]

For three months, totally unknown to anyone outside the T.M. organization, groups ranging from 30 to 200 meditators met together in various spots around the city. According to the Arons, day after day during this time it was conclusively demonstrated that there was less fighting and fewer casualties in the immediate vicinity around where the groups meditated than either before or after. Unfortunately, the new revolutionary government soon canceled all Western tourist visas and the group had to leave the war-torn country before they could gather enough meditators together long enough to hope to effect more widespread, lasting changes. They left Tehran and the rest is history.

Other scientifically controlled research into the psychological effects of Transcendental Meditation has been performed by Robert Keith Wallace, whose 1970 Ph.D. thesis at U.C.L.A. proposed that such meditative states formed a distinct state of consciousness, physically and mentally different from waking, sleeping or dreaming. Such research, by Wallace and others, has demonstrated that the regular use of T.M. over several months helped reduce hypertension and addictive cravings for drugs, cigarettes and alcohol, even among drug abusers. Regular meditation also proved more effective than ordinary rest in improving reaction time, in increasing visual perception skills and in combating psychological stress.[5]

What do biorelativity and T.M. have to do with the various future social and material environments described by the participants in Helen Wambach's and my workshops? While I want to make it clear that during our study of these future-life scenarios we never tried to correlate them either with our subjects' current meditation habits or with perceptions of meditation practices in the future, the clear distinctions between the Type II, III and IV future-life groups point to a much more active spiritual consciousness among those living in Type II ("New Age") communities. The use of regular group meditation, crystals and of other as yet undiscovered techniques of bioenergy transfer seem a logical and plausible explanation for the more positive and healthy environment experienced by Type II subjects in both 2100 and 2300 A.D. period.

At present I cannot confirm that this positive harnessing of human energy, leading to Type II solutions for humanity's future, will occur, but I certainly feel justified in saying that it *can* happen if enough people start actively preparing for it today. If, as Edgar Cayce and other channels of Ageless Wisdom assure us, we are continually shaping our future physical reality by today's collective thoughts and actions, then the time to wake up to the alternatives we have created is *now*. The choices between the kind of Earth represented by each of the Types II, III and IV societies are clear. Which do we want for our grandchildren? Which do we want perhaps to return to ourselves someday?

* 9 *

Is the "Future" Already Past?

"New Age" Physics and the Holographic Universe

One of the first things Dr. Helen Wambach noticed when starting her future-lives research was that only a few of her hypnotized subjects reporting being physically alive in either the twenty-second or twenty-fourth centuries. This initial discovery, later confirmed by similar results from both Dr. R. Leo Sprinkle's and my workshops, showed that, when offered a choice of one out of three past and two future time periods, only 4 to 5 percent of our workshop participants reported future lifetimes around 2100–2200 A.D., while between 11 and 12 percent saw themselves returning in the 2300–2500 A.D. period.

These figures are significantly lower than the 40 percent (two in five) probability of expecting a future life to be reported if the workshop results were distributed randomly by chance. They are even more startling if the rate of Earth's population growth since 1750 is taken into account as a greater number of future physical "vehicles" should be available, unless something between 1989 and 2100 is going to occur to reverse today's population explosion. Moreover, as previously mentioned, nearly two thirds of those workshop participants who were asked before the experience began said they consciously wanted to explore a future lifetime.

These glaring discrepancies in her expected results led Dr. Wambach to begin progressing a few individuals ahead in their current lifetime as discussed in Chapters 1 and 2. Their reports, including my own personal experience, set in motion the events that have led to this analysis of today's "mass dreams" concerning where the human race currently may be heading as a species. As already mentioned, the relatively small numbers of workshop participants who reported future lifetimes in the periods suggested makes all of this data subject to review and refinement by further research. Nonetheless, analyzing the reports from these approximately 350 subjects provides a fascinating preliminary glimpse of what the future may hold in store for us.

What general findings have come from this analysis? First, just as with Helen Wambach's past-life statistics, discussed in *Reliving Past Lives*, only a few of the future-life data sheets reveal obvious "fantasy" characteristics or clear-cut signs of ego wish-fulfillment needs. Hardly any presented obviously "impossible" future-life scenarios. Only one subject reported finding herself in a nonhuman physical body. A few others discussed having ethereal energy bodies that appeared human but were without material substance. These may represent an intermediate state between physical lifetimes. The vast majority, however, reported credible pictures of an evolving humanity, both here on Earth and (eventually) on other Earth-like planets.

Another important feature of this data that appeared, despite a smaller sample size than Helen Wambach's past-life studies, was the male/female gender balance, which again approached a 50/50 ratio. In both future time periods almost exactly half of our subjects reported being in male bodies. Slightly fewer saw themselves as females, while a small (7 to 8 percent) number felt their sex was androgynous or indeterminate. This near-equal male/female balance, required for continuing population replenishment, occurred despite the great (75 to 80 percent) preponderance of women attending these workshops. Further, it matches Helen's earlier past-life results, with the obvious exception of the "androgynous" cases, a feature not found in any historical time periods, including the three chosen by the other subjects attending the same workshops. Like Helen Wambach, I find this unconscious sex/gender ratio balancing among the strongest evidence that this data represents more than mere random reports of individual psychological fantasies.

Further, in addition to the overall gender balance, the future lifetimes of our workshop subjects showed a natural division, by description of their outside environments, into a very limited number of plausible and recognizable groups that apparently shared other common characteristics. I categorized them as Types I to IV, based on my initial 1985 analysis of the 2100 A.D. data.

Both Helen and I agreed at that time that the division of these 2100 A.D. reports into just four distinctive, internally cohesive groups was highly unlikely if the data came only from our subjects' speculative "imaginations." There were simply too many coincidences and too much parallel data among the reports. Pure fantasy would have led to a much wider range of possibilities. As for the idea that such reports might prove useful as psychological predictors of current personality patterns, Helen Wambach had already explored this theory when doing the past-life research for *Reliving Past Lives* and had found it inadequate.

Thus I decided to analyze the reports from the perspective that they did, in fact, represent at least partial glimpses of the future, using environmental conditions as my control factor. As mentioned in Chapter 5, my first study of the original bunch of 2100 A.D. data was published in 1986 as an article in the first issue of the *Journal of Regression Therapy*.

The most puzzling feature of the four types of future lifetimes discovered involved the obvious contradictions among the material environments portrayed as existing on Earth at the same time. In the 2100 period, at least, the descriptions of Earth's physical conditions by subjects in the different groups appeared nearly impossible to exist simultaneously. Their coexistence seemed to violate natural physical laws. How, for example, could the clear, clean and beautiful atmosphere indicated by Type II New Age community members co-exist on the same planet with the bleak, noxious and barren conditions described by those subjects who lived in Type III dome-covered cities? How could some rural towns apparently get by with only rudimentary, nineteenth-century conveniences (Type IV) at the same time people lived in highly sophisticated space stations (Type I)?

Perhaps specific, highly local conditions lay behind the seeming contradictions, I reasoned at the time. In any case, Types I to IV clearly typified the reports of subjects progressed ahead to the 2100 era, for I discovered the same four groups when later analyzing the data stemming from the dozen 1986–88 workshops in which I progressed subjects ahead to that time period and allowed them to view it either from their own experience or as an observer.

I was surprised, however, to find that these same four basic social and environmental types carried over into the 2300–2500 A.D. data, which I did not begin to analyze until the fall of 1988 in preparation for this book. Moreover, as discussed in the preceding chapter, except for the "Non-solar Planet" cases, absent in the 2100 period, each group, while still retaining distinct, recognizable features, showed signs of a common evolution toward a single solar system-wide human civilization that will be both technologically advanced and in harmony with natural spiritual principles. This is the most positive of the findings from our subjects' data.

For myself the emergence of these three or four simultaneous, yet seemingly contradictory, future environments in and around the Earth proved the most startling and thought-provoking result of this research. Let me explain. As mentioned above, if these reports were mere psychological fantasies, then they should have shown a much broader range of future types. Even contemporary science fiction provides a lot more than four or five futuristic social or environmental models.

Further, if this data primarily reflected wish-fulfillment or fear projections from our subjects' present-day personalities, then why did so few of them (under 3 percent) mention radioactivity or describe the aftermath of what might be a large-scale nuclear conflict? Or, conversely, why didn't more than about a quarter of them see themselves in Type II New Age communities? Surely most of our workshop participants, interested in psychic development and reincarnation, would consciously have preferred this kind of future over the others. Indeed, it may be more difficult for dedicated New Age believers to accept the possibility that the Aquarian Age's first few centuries will not entirely correspond to their hoped-for earthly spiritual paradise than for disinterested skeptics to concede that these "mass dreams" might contain the germ of truth!

Finally, these reports hardly describe the rather homogeneous, interdependent world, which modern future forecasters such as the Hudson Institute or the writings of popular futurists such as Alan Toeffler (*Future Shock*) tend to predict. Instead they portray a world that remains divided both materially and spiritually, with some people apparently living far more technically sophisticated lives than others. In this respect, at least, things appear to be not too far removed from today's global picture, in which some people continue to eke out a primitive, agricultural existence while only a short distance away others depend on microwave ovens and jet transports. The major difference, for the 2100 period in any case, seems to be the much smaller population indicated.

If the data from Helen's and my workshops can be taken as more than just individual fantasies, how can we explain not only the seemingly antithetical environments foreseen on Earth in a couple of generations but also the very contingency of mentally "tapping in" to the as-yet-unrealized future at all? Is there other evidence today that such "future memory," which seems to contradict the physical laws of a one-way linear Time flow, is possible?

An affirmative answer to this question may come from what seems, at first glance, to be a most unlikely source—the scientific and theoretical world of contemporary physics. One of the revolutionary discoveries of the "New Physics" is that the basis of what we have long thought to be a continuous, unidirectional and mechanical universe, reducible into ever-smaller individual parts, is in fact not deterministic or mechanical at all. Instead it seems to be an evolving process whose functions are frequently nonlinear. Our universe, which most of today's physicists term "Space-Time," is therefore more like a conscious, living Being in which the life of each part depends on the existence of the whole organism rather than the perfect machine envisioned by Sir Isaac Newton and "classical" materialist scientists.

Before discussing the ideas of contemporary scientists who connect a new, holistic view of our Space-Time universe with human consciousness, a few words about how the theories of quantum mechanics and general relativity developed are essential to understanding their impact.[1] The worldview of classical or Newtonian physics developed from a few basic principles established with the Renaissance and eighteenth-century Age of Reason. These principles were based on the astronomical discoveries that all visible bodies in the universe, including the Earth, are constantly in motion. Everything moves; everything changes. Further, as shown by Galileo and Newton, physical motion can be observed to obey certain invariable laws that can be expressed mathematically. These laws apply throughout the knowable universe, across what is known as Space and Time. All observable phenomena should, therefore, be reducible to the functioning of these "natural" laws, which could predict future behavior. It therefore became science's duty to formulate these laws and categorize all activity accordingly.

In performing this task the scientist can and should be a detached experimenter. For, as summed up by the French philosopher René Descartes, human logic is the basis for all reasonable behavior and behind all scientific observation. A perfectly objective opinion is not only possible but required for progress. The universe therefore can be compared with a gigantic mechanical clock whose inner workings, once set, infinitely repeat themselves. It is subject only to the inexorable decay of linear Time because, according to the Second Law of Thermodynamics, all processes eventually lose their internal coherency. Thus, with the Age of Reason, a neutral, objective "watchmaker" God who once upon a time constructed the cosmos and then left it slowly to wind down through Time's erosion replaced the Bible's intervening Deity, whose very human emotions of jealousy and love had inspired traditional Judeo-Christian history and philosophy. Understanding the material basis for reality became man's task and physics the queen of his sciences.

By the end of the nineteenth century most Westerners felt that their civilization had succeeded admirably at this self-imposed chore. A celebrated American theorist, A. A. Michelson, remarked in 1894 that in his opinion all that remained for future scientists was to "add a few decimal places" in refining proofs of previous discoveries. According to Fred Wolf, Michelson's British contemporary, editor Hugh Elliot, once wrote that reality was based on three fundamental principles. These were: (1) The universal character of natural law keeps everything regular, uniform and orderly. Thus all motion occurs across an infinite, unmoving Space through an absolute, constant flow of linear Time. Change occurs smoothly and continuously from one physical state to another without any gaps. (2) All events are caused by the interaction of matter in motion. Therefore any teleological notion of God or a supernatural purpose behind existence is nonsense. (3) All reality is material in nature. Nothing exists that does not display some type of physical manifestation. Even though many classical physicists refused to adopt such a strictly materialist, atheist position as Elliot, they all based their scientific work on these ideas.[2]

Among the natural forces perceived as being behind all local (earthly) and cosmic activity by Newton and his successors, three stood out as particularly intriguing. These were electricity, magnetism and gravity. Throughout the nineteenth century physicists concentrated on defining and relating these forces mathematically, often by experimenting with three of the results of their influence: the energies of light, heat and attraction. From the outset scientists were confident that one day they would break everything down into its basic component elements and that the resulting theory would prove a blueprint of the entire universe, making all the workings of nature understandable at last.

For over a hundred years significant progress toward this goal marked the history of physics. Most of the modern conveniences that we take for granted today, such as electric lighting and heating, telephones, radio and television, jet aircraft, computers and much, much more, have resulted from our civilization's success in breaking down the Newtonian material universe.

One of the most significant achievements marking this trial was British scientist Michael Farraday's discovery in the early nineteenth century that an electrical current produces a magnetic field and vice versa. Thus both electricity and magnetism, originally seen as separate forces, were shown to be properties of a joint electromagnetic force. This insight was followed in 1860 by James Clerk Maxwell's mathematical equations which proved that the process of transforming electricity into magnetism and back again occurred in regular, repeating oscillations or waves. These waves varied only in their speed or frequency (number of oscillations per second).

Although the existence of electromagnetic vibrations was demonstrated by sound mathematical theory, James Clerk Maxwell wondered about the physical properties of such electromagnetic waves. What would they resemble? Taking a cue from Thomas Young's earlier (1803) discovery that light, which Newton had seen as made up of individual particles, also displayed wavelike properties, Maxwell sought to relate light waves and electromagnetic waves into a single formula. To his astonishment, he found that the two types of waves became identical when their frequency was accelerated to the speed of light (186,000 miles per second). He thus demonstrated a mechanical model of light and showed that light was a form of electromagnetism.

It was soon shown that heat was an electromagnetic wave as well, vibrating at different frequencies. Radio waves were discovered by German scientist Heinrich Hertz in 1887 by applying Maxwell's equations to other frequencies, invisible to the naked eye. The Newtonian universe, originally thought to consist entirely of material built from tiny, separable particles, now began to be understood as a phenomenon of electromagnetic waves, vibrating continuously through Space and Time along an entire range of frequencies.

However, this developing view of reality was faced with several difficult problems whose resolution seemed essential to explaining how electromagnetic waves produce observable heat and light. How to relate these different forms of electromagnetic energy to each other was one of the first problems tackled by physicists at the end of the last century. Anyone who has ever lit a match knows that burning matter produces heat and light as it is consumed. Looking closely at any flame, one can detect different colors within it, ranging from blue to yellow and even red. When the match goes out both its heat and colored light disappear.

Finding the precise relationship between heat and light, each being a type of electromagnetic energy, turned out to be impossible, however, as long as physicists held to the Newtonian credo that all motion is continuous and regular. Classical physics had already demonstrated that hot objects vibrate faster than cool ones and that this frequency change is observed as different colors. Further, it was also known that higher frequency waves have shorter wave lengths due to the geometry relating

Time and Space (more waves will fill any given space if they vibrate faster in the same time, therefore each oscillation is shorter). If, as Newton believed, change from heat to light was continuous and regular, then all heat energy absorbed by a burning object should seek to transform itself into faster-vibrating light as quickly as possible. The light thus produced would also instantly pass from low-frequency red and yellow waves and be emitted as ultraviolet frequencies beyond the visible spectrum so long as sufficient heat energy remained.

This theory was called the "ultraviolet catastrophe." If it had been true, it would have led to a universe in which little or no separation of heat, light and other electromagnetic waves could occur. Everything would be instantly drawn to the fastest wave frequency that the reaction could produce. Physical life would be almost impossible. Obviously, as this hasn't happened in our experience, something was wrong with the basic assumption that energy changes form in a smooth, continuous manner with no gaps.

In hindsight the solution to this paradox is disarmingly obvious: Energy waves must change form discretely, jumping from one unit value to another without any in-between, fractional frequencies. In this way, as a material object heats up or cools down, it emits some energy at all the frequencies of which it is capable simultaneously. As it absorbs heat energy, the electromagnetic waves thus produced hop from one unit value to another, putting forth different colors (frequencies) of light as they jump. As these jumps are not continuous, they involve gaps in Space and Time (duration). All energy is not instantaneously changed. An interdependent process takes place. This process permits the kind of hodge-podge energy universe we live in where wavelengths of separate, discontinuous frequencies can co-exist while still undergoing change.

Moreover, as the various frequencies are in fact multiples of each other, a heated object can liberate more low-frequency waves than high-level ones. Such transformations take less energy. High-level ultraviolet radiations are therefore discriminated against in all but the most powerful transformations. This process allows our kind of material life to exist. Otherwise, intelligent life forms might be limited to pure-energy creations with no material existence at all.

Hence a match flame produces yellow, blue and invisible ultraviolet flames simultaneously, in that order, as long as there is enough matter to support the energy (heat) transformation process into visible light frequencies. The majority of light produced will tend toward the yellow, lower-frequency levels. Even when the amount of energy produced by the match falls below the level where it emits visible light, after its fire is "out," the same process continues, only at unit frequencies too slow to be visible. This is why coals glow red and then continue to give off invisible infrared heat even after they've ceased to emit visible light.

For such a process to exist, electromagnetic waves, including light, must behave in a way not predicted by Newtonian physics. They must transform their energy in unitary packets or, as Fred Wolf puts it, "lumps." Albert Einstein, who was intrigued by this idea, named these nonfractional energy lumps "quanta," which means "whole." Moreover, each of these invisible quanta (packets of light energy) must correspond to a multiple of some indivisible primary unit that remains constant throughout the universe. The energy emitted by a heated object must equal a multiple of this universal, indivisible constant and the light frequency observed. In mathematical terms this is stated "$E = hf$." In this equation "E" stands for energy, "h" for the indivisible unitary constant and "f" for the frequency of light emitted.

This formula, the foundation of quantum mechanics, was presented to the German Physical Society in December 1900 by Professor Max Planck, who later won the Nobel Prize for his theoretical contributions to quantum physics. Dr. Planck admitted that his famous formula had popped into his mind in a flash of inspiration, long before he worked out the mathematical proofs of its existence. He described it as a "lucky guess." The indivisible constant "h" has become known as Planck's constant. Its value is infinitesimal, being measured as less than 7×10^{-27} power.* Being so small, its indivisible unit value directly affects only the tiny, tiny subatomic level of material objects. Everything larger than electrons (which were discovered only in 1896) appears to exist continuously. Newton's observation of an orderly, uninterrupted universe was correct for the physical world he could see. But he was wrong to assume that the same visible characteristics result from ever-smaller replicas of an identical mechanical model.

Max Planck's discovery of "h" and its indivisible quality revealed that light frequencies are produced in intermittent chunks and not in an unbroken, mechanical manner. This tiny separation of their frequencies makes all the difference. If this separation didn't exist, neither would much slow-moving matter. Were the separation much larger it would affect the quality of our observable material existence since sizable objects in our universe would then wink in and out of existence as their energy

---

*That's less than 7 divided by a billionth of a billionth of a billionth!

quanta hopped about! The tiny size of Planck's constant "h" was just right to produce an intermediate set of conditions, those which underpin our apparently whole but actually discontinuous material reality. The machinelike "clockwork" universe posited by Newton and considered the foundation of all reality by nineteenth-century materialist scientists was found to be riddled with quantum-sized holes.

Although Planck himself was for a long time reluctant to accept the consequences of his discovery, his formula caught the interest of the twentieth century's most celebrated scientific genius, Dr. Albert Einstein, who believed it provided the definition of the energy of an undiscovered particle, the light particle. Like all the other physicists of his day, Einstein believed in a basically mechanical universe that could be divided into ever smaller pieces in the search for its innermost workings.

Not satisfied with Young's and Maxwell's mathematical demonstrations that light is made up of waves, he felt Planck's separate lumps of light were actually tiny granules or particles. But, according to Planck's formula ($E = hf$), the behavior of such light particles depended on their observed frequency, a wave process. The two aspects, wave and particle, couldn't be separated. So if Planck's formula were correct, light energy included both wave and particle characteristics. This was unheard of and distinctly unmechanical. Still, because other physicists quickly discovered that this formula could explain and predict accurately other mysterious subatomic behavior, it was adopted. Light was thereby acknowledged to be simultaneously both particles and waves.

Thus, as Newton's successors divided the material world into smaller and smaller pieces, going from visible structures down to molecules, to atoms and to subatomic particles, they eventually reached a level of reality where elementary particles do not appear to exist as separate physical entities at all but only as part of a dynamic process that involves their interaction as a vibrating light wave. Because Einstein had initially named these light energy packets "quanta," the rather incongruous term "quantum mechanics" was born to discuss their behavior. Physicists have since renamed Einstein's original light quanta "photons" and developed the science of photography from his theories, but they have continued to call the subject of subatomic physics "quantum mechanics." Today some scientists prefer the term "particle physics."

At this basic, infinitesimally tiny level of reality, elements such as electrons possess some of the properties of solid, material particles but they also behave like energy waves with no mass and only a hypothetical individual existence. Only their interacting process, represented by a quantum wave function, can be precisely defined and located mathematically. British physicist Dr. Paul Davies denotes this wave function by the Greek letter *Psi* (Ψ). Dr. Fred Wolf whimsically calls it a "qwiff." It is important to recognize that a qwiff or (Ψ) does not itself represent a specific physical event but rather *information about how a system of events behaves*. This distinction is of critical importance to understanding how quantum mechanics operates.

Within the equation that defines a quantum wave function, the location, velocity and indeed the very physical existence of each electron as an individual event can only be expressed as a tendency or probability. Whenever one attempts to trace the exact path taken by an individual electron within an atom, one discovers that, due to its intermittent quantum nature, it is impossible to predict its velocity and position at the same time. Each electron can "jump" out of its physical position at any moment, in a sense leaping out of material existence for an instant. Its reappearance can occur anywhere within the parameters defined by Planck's formula as it emits a detectable flash of light energy. Thus each electron's exact future path around the atom's nucleus remains a probability, not a certainty. Only the behavior of all the atom's electrons taken together as the quantum wave function (Ψ) is predictable. It is (Ψ)'s behavior which defines the nature of the atom.

Consequently, at its heart, our Space-Time universe was discovered to have a built-in wholeness in which the most basic individual units actually exist only in terms of the overall system's activity or function (Ψ). Instead of finding basic component "building blocks" behind a mechanical, "clockwork" universe, scientists could now only hypothesize about indeterminate "packets" of energy called "photons," which, when interacting as a qwiff, produce predictable results at larger than atomic levels. Everything smaller remains in the quantum realm of probability until human observation determines its exact existence.

A young German physicist, Werner Heisenberg, mathematically demonstrated the merely probable nature of unobserved subatomic behavior at any given moment in the early 1920s. His theory has become known as "Heisenberg's Principle of Indeterminism" or "Heisenberg's Uncertainty Principle." Following the lead of Danish scientist Neils Bohr, who first developed the quantum model of the atom, Heisenberg showed that *until someone actually observed an electron's path around the atom's nucleus*, it remained indeterminate due to its quantum nature. He concluded that "the path comes into existence only when we observe it."[3]

Put another way, Werner Heisenberg based his conclusion on the fact that individual electrons display properties of both particles (which have a definite position) and waves (which have specific rate of rotation, dependent on frequency). However, they do not display these properties simultaneously as an individual, only as a group process: the quantum wave function (Ψ). An experimenter who wishes to investigate the behavior of a single electron must therefore *choose* which property he wishes to measure. Observing an electron's present position makes its past and future velocity uncertain, while merely tracing its velocity leaves its present position in doubt. Which property the electron will display *depends on the observer's choice*. The human observer's decision therefore helps create the physical result observed.

Heisenberg's startling conclusion that the definition of quantum-level reality depends on human observation marked a radical departure from the Newtonian mechanistic worldview, which stressed the universe's well-defined order and its strictly material nature. Even Descartes's time-honored distinction between physical and mental processes seemed overthrown. How could mere human observation, a mental activity, operate to define material reality? If it does, what happens to the scientifically enshrined credo of the "objective" observer? How can nature be considered to follow universal, unchanging laws if human observation actually helps determine quantum-level results? What happens to cause-and-effect if the outcome of an experiment suddenly "pops" into existence at the moment of final observation? These are the kinds of questions that quantum mechanics has raised in today's scientific community. It is not surprising that Bohr's quantum model of the atom and Heisenberg's uncertainty principle of subatomic behavior continue to cause controversy among scientists despite their apparent mathematical soundness.

As controversial as young Werner Heisenberg's conclusions were, in fact he was simply applying the subjective implications of Albert Einstein's theories of relativity to subatomic behavior. It was Albert Einstein who, in two papers published in 1905 and 1915, first pointed out the relative, subjective nature of all human observation of external activity. It was Einstein who demonstrated that, due to the constancy of the speed of light, all observed motion in the physical universe is relative to the position and momentum of the observer. It was Einstein who first challenged the concept of a smooth flow of linear Time across infinite, empty Space.

According to Newtonian physics, Time and Space are both independent and fixed. The universe consists of a series of definite "instants," which are constantly changing but any one of which, if "frozen" in Time, would contain the same reality everywhere in Space. Thus at instant "Now," for example, the Earth and everything on it would be the same reality whether seen by a human being in New York or by an alien peering through an ultrahigh-resolution telescope from a planet circling the star Alpha Centauri. This seems to be common sense, for our minds easily conceive of a "same instant" occurring everywhere at once.

In his Theory of Special Relativity, Einstein demonstrated mathematically that this is not so. Why not? Simply because all physical activity (or energy) must be transmitted across Space for perception to occur. This transmission necessarily takes time. The rate of such transmissions are limited by the speed of light, which remains constant everywhere. Albert Einstein expressed this in his famous formula $E = mc^2$ where "E" equals energy, "m" equals mass and "c" equals the speed of light.

Consequently, Earth and its activities in the frozen "Now" instant proposed above would be different for a human observer here and an Alpha Centaurian. The latter would, in fact, observe as his present "Now" what an Earthling had experienced about four years earlier because it takes that long for light to cross the space between our solar system and Alpha Centauri's. We express these distances as "light-years," a familiar term for most people, although we seldom think that it means that "Now" is a relative, not absolute, concept. Its definition depends on who is describing the event as "Now."

Similarly, our common usage of the terms "past," "present" and "future" is also relative. The "present" for someone in Paris, France, is not exactly identical to that of a San Franciscan because they are separated in space by the time it takes light to travel between those two cities. Luckily, like Planck's constant "h," which regulates quantum shifts, the amount of time it takes light to fly around the Earth is quite tiny and we don't notice it. This time interval is even smaller between two people standing in a common room but it still exists nonetheless, thereby forever separating us in Time just as the quantum jumping of electron levels separates energy in Space. In fact, as Einstein's Theory of Special Relativity brilliantly demonstrated, Space and Time are joint properties of a single universal process that he called "Space-Time." The entire physical universe seems bound up in this Space-Time process so that no single "instant" can exist without reference to all of its fellows throughout the cosmos.

Furthermore, in his Theory of General Relativity, published in 1915, Albert Einstein demonstrated that Space-Time itself is not a fixed, objective state. Its properties are also relative to whoever is observing

them. Notably, Space-Time "curves" in relationship to the mutual attraction of material bodies, the force we know as gravity. Subsequent
experiments using radioactive elements with known decay intervals (which
measure Time like internal clocks) have proven that Time runs "slower"
out in space, where the force of gravity is smaller, than on Earth. Einstein's relativity theories introduced a Space-Time universe, which shares
joint properties that cannot be understood separately from the operation
of the whole system. It is thus more akin to a living organism, whose
overall nature of being alive is more than the sum of its interdependent
parts, than to Newton's marvelous but lifeless machine.

Shortly before departing what he called "this strange world," Albert
Einstein himself stated that our concept of linear Time is but a mirage:[4]

> For us believing physicists the distinction between past, present,
> and future is only an illusion, even if a stubborn one.

Although it was Albert Einstein's own theories of relativity that
inspired Neils Bohr and Werner Heisenberg to conclude that subatomic
reality is uncertain or only probable until an external observer defines
what has happened, Einstein himself was never comfortable with Heisenberg's Uncertainty Principle. His oft-quoted remark "God does not
play dice [with physical reality]" summed up his attitude. Thus, even
though he had helped define quantum mechanics, he became one of the
most powerful opponents to its indeterminate view of reality.

To prove his point Einstein joined two American physicists, Boris
Podolsky and Nathan Rosen, in publishing a famous article in 1935. It
was called the "EPR Paradox" after the authors' initials. In this paper
Einstein and his colleagues argued that either quantum mechanics could
not adequately predict the behavior of subatomic particles or that it
assumed information could move faster than the speed of light, an im-
possibility according to his well-documented Theory of Special Relativity.

A simplified idea of the reasoning behind the EPR paradox might go
as follows.[5] Quantum mechanics and classical physics agree that the group
process, or qwiff, of subatomic particles like electrons or photons is predictable and stable. Otherwise atoms would not retain their shape. Let
us assume that a group consists of just two such particles. They are
identical but act like mirror images of each other. Thus if one spins
clockwise, the other will spin counterclockwise at exactly the same rate
of rotation. Because their joint activity is fixed, knowing the rate and
spin direction of one automatically tells us about its "partner." In the

language of physics, they are "correlated." Further, they are spinning within the confines of an opaque box. Thus we cannot observe the precise location of either particle; we only know that they must be exactly opposite each other since they behave as mirror images.

Now, suppose we can divide the box exactly down the middle, leaving two identical boxes. We have thus trapped one particle in each side, still without observing which one is where. Then the two still-closed boxes are separated. One could even be sent to Alpha Centauri. According to quantum mechanics, either particle could be in either side of the box as long as it remains unopened. However, as soon as one side of the box is opened and the spin and location of its particle seen, the spin identity and position of the other particle in the far-distant side of the box is also instantly defined. Somehow the other particle "knows" what behavior to exhibit in order to make their joint process (the qwiff) balance.

It therefore is the act of observing one particle that determines the properties of its partner regardless of their separation in Space-Time. Further, it doesn't make any difference which particle is observed, its opposite has to be in the other side of the box. This is not too difficult to visualize in a spatial context, but if we try to visualize it as happening in Time, things are less obvious. It would be like saying that an event in the future (opening the side of the box on Alpha Centauri and observing which particle is there) could instantly define our present (the identity of the particle on Earth) or vice versa.

"How can this be?" asked Einstein, Podolsky and Rosen. If quantum mechanics is correct and each side of the box had an equal probability of containing either particle, then there had to be a faster-than-light transmission of information between them as soon as one side of the box was opened to ensure that the sum total of their activity remained the same. This is impossible according to the Theory of Special Relativity, which holds that the speed of light is always a constant. Faster-than-light travel would involve a violation of the integrity of Space-Time. Therefore, they concluded, the quantum mechanics picture of subatomic reality is incomplete and some further factor has predetermined which particle will be in which side of the box before it is opened and the observation is made. Einstein spent much of his latter years unsuccessfully attempting to discover exactly what this "further factor" might be.

A number of years later, in 1964, an American physicist, John Bell, developed a mathematical formula (Bell's Theorem) which described two basic conditions for reality that must be met if Einstein's Space-Time theory is complete and the EPR paradox is to be avoided. These are: (1)

material objects have definite and real properties that are independent of observation; (2) physical influences cannot exceed the speed of light. The first condition denies Heisenberg's Uncertainty Principle. The second restricts instantaneous effects to a single point in Space-Time. It upholds the irreversibility of physical forces through linear Time.

For over fifteen years various physicists worked to develop an experiment to test Bell's Theorem. Finally, in the summer of 1982, a team of French scientists, led by Professor Alain Aspect of the Optics Institute at the University of Orsay, reported a breakthrough. In their experiment, involving pairs of correlated protons shot in opposite directions down a tube and then measured simultaneously at some distance apart, Aspect and his team demonstrated that the two particles reacted in accordance with quantum mechanics' predictions. Regardless of which property was tested (velocity, spin or position), the two protons always displayed opposite, or "correlated," effects instantaneously. This was true even when the decision about which property to measure was made after the two protons were already speeding in opposite directions. Hence the reality of the results was not predetermined but occurred with the actual observation.

Alain Aspect's two detached particles somehow instantly "knew" which behavior to exhibit to maintain the integrity of their joint quantum wave function. They broke Einstein's law of special relativity. Even the elegant, apparently seamless geometry of Space-Time was revealed to be punctured with an endless series of tiny holes. Human observation is *not* neutral with regard to natural phenomena. Some kinds of information can flow from the "future" to influence the "present." Human perception and choice are inextricably linked to physical results.

Today, nearly a decade later, the world's scientific community is still arguing about the implications of this clear violation of the traditional principles behind our understanding of what the material universe is and how it works. According to Dr. Paul Davies, Alain Aspect's demonstration that quantum theory correctly predicts the behavior of correlated protons after their physical separation forces us to give up either (1) the assumption that nothing exceeds the speed of light or (2) the belief that there is an external physical "reality" that remains independent of our human perception of it. Thus either we accept that Einstein's Space-Time universe does not completely describe things or we give up our "commonsense" notions about an external, material universe independent of human consciousness.[6]

Choosing to retain Einstein's very useful findings about the uniformity of the speed of light and Space-Time geometry, Paul Davies offers the analogy of a computer system to reconcile quantum mechanics with the theory of relativity. Working computers consist of two distinct components known as "hardware" and "software." Hardware is made up of the system's physical machinery and logical support network (wiring, microchips, etc.). Software, on the other hand, consists of concepts that permit the system to accept data and solve submitted problems. It is made up of programs and calculation parameters. Comparing the computer to subatomic physics, he argues that "the particle is the hardware whereas the wave (Ψ) is the software."[7]

Consequently, a computer's operation can be measured either in terms of its hardware (electronic impulses, etc.) or of its software (formulas being calculated, etc.). Just as with a subatomic element, the choice of which property of the computer to observe determines the type of answer observed. Such answers, Davies reassures us, are complementary, not contradictory.

Further, the computer's two properties exist independent of each other. Thus, for example, if a computer's circuitry is accidentally destroyed, it naturally stops working and the program stops running. If the program is embedded in the computer, then it too will be destroyed. The program's concepts, however, can be plugged into another set of circuitry and calculations continue until the desired result is obtained. Similarly, a quantum wave function, (Ψ), which represents knowledge about the behavior of a unified system, continues even though individual component particles pop in and out of existence.

Dr. Davies then compares this computer analogy with the mind vs. matter duality of classical philosophy. Both the mind and the brain are required in order to produce perceivable thought. Similarly, measurement of quantum-level reality depends on the dual particle-wave nature of the electron. Consequently, the quantum mechanics and computer analogy can be extended to the realm of human consciousness.

Yet here Davies makes a key distinction. Classical dualism eventually reduced mental processes to a component of a larger material reality, leading to the still widely held thesis that the mind is merely the expression of the physical brain. For the quantum mechanics-computer-human consciousness analogy to be meaningful, however, this concept must be replaced by one that acknowledges our mind and mental "software" as qualitatively distinct from our physical brain "hardware." As Davies puts it, "Mind is *pattern* rather than *substance*. . . . [It] belongs to a higher descriptive level than the brain."[8]

Just as the quantum wave function defines the indeterminate-yet-real existence of its component particles, our minds give meaning to the material Space-Time universe surrounding us. Thus, Davies concludes, mind and matter are independent yet must cooperate in order to achieve perceivable, meaningful expression, an idea backed by the theories of other well-known contemporary physicists such as Stephen Hawking, John Wheeler and Douglas Hofsteader.[9]

Physicist-mathematician Paul Davies's conclusions about the special nature of meaningful reality where material forces and human consciousness are interdependent echo a paradigm known as the Anthropic Principle.* First put forward in 1974 by British cosmologist Brandon Carter and developed by his physicist colleague Stephen Hawkings, this worldview holds that the universe must be so organized that human beings can observe and measure it. Otherwise we could never be aware of it. Our existence is somehow written into the laws of physics or we wouldn't be here. Further, the existence of our kind of intelligent life is a rare, perhaps unique, phenomenon. Dr. Carter demonstrated this through a complex mathematical formula known as Carter's Inequality, which attempts to define the probability of the random or chance evolution of intelligent carbon-based life within the known lifespan of our universe. The probability is estimated as very, very small.

The "just right" nature of our universe has been confirmed by other scientific discoveries as well. As was mentioned earlier in this chapter, both Planck's and Einstein's discoveries of universal constants ("h" and "c") revealed that inexplicably they are exactly the right size to permit our kind of cosmos to develop. For example, if "h" were smaller, the universe would collapse, for atomic structure could not hold together. If it were larger, quantum-level uncertainty would overcome the material world's apparent continuity—everything would pop in and out of existence and no certainty or planning would be possible. Similarly, if the speed of light ("c") were faster, it is highly unlikely that stars and planets would have formed. If it were slower, the universe's viable living space would be much smaller, as Space-Time distortions would be magnified over less distance. Ultimately we would lapse into what is known as "solipsism," the condition in which each separate individual unit can experience only a private universe made up of itself, alone.

Other modern physicists such as Stephen Hawking, co-discoverer of the Anthropic Principle, and thought by many to be Einstein's mental

---

* Use of the word "paradigm" to describe a structured overall view of how reality works was popularized by Thomas Kuhn in his book *The Structure of Scientific Revolutions*, University of Chicago Press, Chicago: 1962. Coming from the Greek word *paradigma*, it means "model," or pattern. The word "anthropic" means "concerning human beings."

equal, agree that our peculiar universe is unlikely to have evolved from random chance. He has stated that if our universe did not exhibit a property known as "flatness," matter would never have coalesced into galaxies, stars and planets after the initial "Big Bang" got everything moving. The odds against the development of our kind of cosmological structure are apparently enormous. It seemingly must be endowed with purpose, one which includes our existence as an intelligent species. Speculation beyond this premise marks the boundary between physics, philosophy and religion.[10]

Thus we have seen that for "anthropic" physicists man is indeed the "measure of all things." Indeed, according to some, he is its creator. One prominent contemporary physicist, John Wheeler, Ph.D., professor emeritus at the University of Texas, has stated Hawking's thesis even more controversially: The universe's form and age exist as they do precisely because they provide optimal conditions for creating at least one intelligent life form, namely human beings. This creation alone is justification enough for existing material conditions. Thus Professor Wheeler avoids the philosophical issue of describing the universe's "first cause" in religious terms. Even anthropic physicists remain uncomfortable in acknowledging God.

Taking his cue from the Heisenberg Principle of Uncertainty, which regards the (human) observer as an integral factor in defining reality, Wheeler theorizes that our very existence as individuals somehow depends on that of all other conscious observers, however separated within Space-Time. In his view, therefore, the universe is brought into existence by the collective awareness of all observers—past, present and future!

This viewpoint is strikingly similar to that of ancient Oriental philosophers, who held that we constantly create reality through our mutual interactions with others. Similarly, recognition of this fundamental unity of all consciousness can occur in deep meditative states. Once experienced, this comprehension remains vividly alive. I personally recall one such occasion in which, while in a profound meditation, I was moved to ask the question "Who am I when I'm not being me?" The answer instantly flashed across my mind: "That's when you're being everybody else!"

I now understand this as a statement of the quantum nature of existence. If this concept be true, it is any wonder that our "dreaming mind" can pick up glimpses of the common future, which we are even now creating together and which is already past in relationship to other sectors of Space-Time, for instance, as it would appear if observed from Alpha Centauri?

Giving up an "externally real" or "unobserved" universe so as to salvage Einstein's Theory of Special Relativity and the speed of light as a limiting constant is only one of the possible paradigms of the "New Physics," however. A second viewpoint that has gained important recognition in both scientific and philosophical circles holds that Alain Aspect's separated particles did communicate at faster-than-light speeds after all. Therefore, according to this worldview, Einstein's Space-Time universe is merely a special part of a larger reality, many of whose basic properties remain to be discovered.

One of these properties is the ability to pass information through Space-Time faster than 186,000 miles per second. The commonplace name for this ability is "psychic" and its expression within the Einsteinian universe is called "extrasensory perception," or ESP. At this point scientists can only speculate how this expression relates to whatever lies beyond Time and Space.

One contemporary American physicist who, even before Alain Aspect's successful violation of Bell's Theorem, accepted the challenge to test scientifically the idea that psychic functioning can indeed break basic physical boundaries is Russell Targ, Ph.D., formerly of the Stanford Research Institute (SRI). In 1972, after completing pioneering research at Sylvania Corporation leading to the construction of a thousand-watt laser capable of cutting through steel, Dr. Targ joined SRI in a project "to help astronauts achieve greater rapport with their spacecraft" by developing their psychic perception.[11]

This project led him to "remote viewing" research, in which individuals attempt to describe distant locations selected at random while receiving only mental or psychic cues. Among his first successful subjects was New York artist Ingo Swann, who had already demonstrated his ability to draw maps or pictures of distant locations when given their geographic coordinates. An "experienced psychic practitioner," Ingo Swann helped Russell Targ design the initial remote-viewing protocols. Among his suggestions was that any test for ESP offer its subjects opportunities to learn something new and interesting. His personal experience had taught him that encouraging the feeling that success is not only possible but personally enriching enhances the mind's psychic powers. Targ described how the remote-viewing experiments operated in a 1983 interview in *New Realities* magazine.[12]

> Our remote viewing experiments involved one person sitting in a laboratory. Another person in the room would direct him or her to try and experience and describe what was going on with a third

person at some distant location. That makes it a combination of telepathy between the viewer and the person at the distant location; together with the possible clairvoyant perception of the distant place. This enabled the viewer to simply live out the future that they had described in the laboratory. We liked this particular protocol because it opened as many channels as possible and gave the viewer the greatest possibility for success.

Dr. Targ conducted similar psychic experiments in remote viewing for over a decade at the Stanford Research Institute. The highly successful results, which have been repeated by other research teams at Princeton University and the Mind Science Foundation as well as in the Soviet Union, have demonstrated that psychic remote viewing is a "genuine, repeatable" phenomenon. Human minds can exchange information psychically across Space-Time in direct contradiction of Einstein's theories.[13]

In fact Russell Targ's remote-viewing experiments have conclusively demonstrated that mental perceptions or "thought waves" are qualitatively different from the electromagnetic waves that make up the physical world. Physicists advance science by establishing and testing "limiting conditions" for natural phenomena. All physical processes, including electromagnetic waves, have been found to work only within certain boundaries. However, after a decade of psychic research Targ and his colleagues at SRI concluded that all known traditional limits fail to contain the mind's ability to send and receive information psychically. Even placing remote-viewing subjects in a submarine under 500 feet of seawater, a shielding that affects even the lowest electromagnetic frequencies, did not hamper their psychic perception of randomly chosen targets. In this respect "thought waves" seem to resemble quantum wave functions, which represent *knowledge about a unified system* rather than specific physical processes such as light or sound.[14]

One of the most intriguing findings of Targ's remote-viewing experiments, all conducted under stringent scientific conditions, is that psychic perceptions can bridge Time barriers as well as those of Space. In a 1984 intercontinental experiment, conducted by Dr. Targ with the cooperation of Soviet scientists, a Russian clairvoyant and healer accurately pictured a merry-go-round in San Francisco even though, due to time-zone differences, the "target" was not randomly selected until four hours later! In fact Targ feels that "precognitive" perception of the future is easier to achieve than remote viewing of spatially distant objectives. In an interview cited in *Brain/Mind Bulletin*, he explained:[15]

> People try to analyze the present. A future event, to be determined randomly, casts you adrift from every conceivable analytical strategy.

In this brief comment Dr. Targ points out one of the fundamental aspects of psychic functioning—its nonanalytical nature. As anyone who has experienced so-called altered states of consciousness can attest, ordinary logical connections and interests are usually unimportant under such conditions. The inner workings of the mind, which apparently achieve expression most easily via the brain's right cerebral hemisphere, operate much more through imagery and gestalt connections than intellectual concepts. This fact has been one of the major limiting factors in gathering analyzable and comparable data for either past- or future-life research. What seem reasonable questions and research categories to the conscious, analytical mind simply often don't evoke much response at its other levels. In fact, as mystics have attested for millennia, at its deepest levels the mind loses contact with Space-Time reality altogether and floats in a purely nonmaterial bliss beyond any physical or temporal boundaries.

It is through our intuitive and imaginative faculties that we human beings transcend the confines of the Einsteinian universe and experience the greater reality of "All That Is." What we have been conditioned into calling "altered states" of consciousness by materialist psychologists biased in favor of traditional logic is now being shown to reflect our true, awakened state of being and our connection to the wholeness of experience, which goes beyond intellectual distinctions such as "past," "present" and "future."

If, as both Alain Aspect's physical and Russell Targ's metaphysical research suggests, some kinds of information are transmissible beyond the limits defined by the relativity theory, then how do such phenomena relate to our Space-Time universe and its laws? Physicist David Bohm of the University of London and other noted contemporary scientists such as Karl Pribham and Ilya Prigogine suggest that we are part of a dynamic, holistic process that extends beyond the physical Space-Time universe and which may be linked to us through implicit, intuitive knowledge and creativity. Their concepts are supported by British biologist Rupert Sheldrake's revolutionary theory that evolutionary change occurs across intangible "morphogenetic fields," which develop future forms from past habits.

One of the most articulate spokesmen for this emerging worldview, which emphasizes our universe's holistic and lifelike character, is Dr. David Bohm, who suggests that behind the seeming uncertainties built into quantum-level behavior lies an implied order or universal oneness. Although subatomic particles appear to behave discontinuously when considered as separate individual units, in fact they display a hidden or "enfolded" unity that expresses itself through the quantum wave function (Ψ). This function, as previously noted, is a mathematical expression of knowledge. It describes a basic, indivisible aspect of reality that cannot be perceived or measured like ordinary Space-Time events but whose existence is implied by the stability of relationships within Space-Time. Ultimately, Bohm explains, the entire universe, from protons and quasars to living and breathing human beings, is one unified system that cannot be broken down and analyzed separately without losing its essential wholeness and dynamic quality.[16]

Further, even though the unified organization that defines Space-Time cannot be directly examined, examples of its basic properties abound throughout Nature. All dynamic, evolving systems contain evidence of this universal organization and unity. Instead of comparing the universe to the computer, which is still a machine, Bohm argues that it more closely resembles the hologram, a projected three-dimensional image in which each fragment is a true representation of the entire picture. We live in a holographic universe, a "holoverse."

Within our holographic universe each individual part contains all the essential information of the whole. Information is not passed along paths of linear Time but can be instantly "remembered" by individual particles, which are always joined as part of the overall, indivisible whole reality. Further, our universe itself is the holographic reflection of a surrounding "hyperspace," which may in turn reflect something bigger still. Reality therefore very likely consists of a series of holoverses rather like those beautiful, hollow, lacquered Russian dolls, each of which nests in an identical but slightly larger replica of itself.

Just what is a hologram? Holograms are three-dimensional photographs produced by lasers. The mathematical theory for holographic representation of objects in space was developed in the 1940s by Nobel Prize winner Dennis Gabor. However, it took twenty years for other physicists, including Russell Targ, to design equipment that could make them visible. The most difficult requirement was finding a way to restrict a light beam to waves of closely related frequencies and then project that "coherent" beam through space. This is necessary so that the hologram's image will accurately reflect the object being photographed. The development of laser technology made this possible and opened the way for the production of visible holograms.

Holograms are created by beaming a laser toward an object. Some of the light waves rebound off the object's opaque surface. Then a second laser beam is directed at the reflected light waves and the resulting "interference pattern," the area where the two sets of light waves intersect, is captured on film. Taken by itself, the exposed film appears as just a random swirl of light and dark lines. However, when a third laser is bounced off the film, it "resolves" the picture into a three-dimensional image of the original object.

As mentioned above, one of the most important properties of a hologram is that, when broken apart, each of its fragments reflects the whole image, not just a partial view. Each part contains all the information of the whole. Therefore, if our universe operates like a hologram, then Alain Aspect's protons and Russell Targ's psychics are not actually sending messages back and forth through linear Time so much as they are reflecting a deeper level of knowledge that unifies all parts of our indivisible, holographic Space-Time system. At this underlying, implicit level of reality there is no difference between what we perceive as "here" and "there" (location in Space) and "then" and "now" (location in Time). Past, present and future events are all part of the same hologram and therefore coexist simultaneously. We perceive them as distinct only because we also exist within the same holographic universe. Thus, from a quite different perspective, David Bohm joins Albert Einstein in labeling linear Time as a mirage. This idea is echoed by New Age author Richard Bach (*Illusions*, etc.) in his "novel" entitled *One* (1988) where he explores alternate or parallel lifetimes all occurring at once. It is an interesting concept.

As discussed above, visible holograms are the product of two sets of interacting coherent light waves bouncing off an external object and resolved by a third light beam's illumination. Holograms in general are an electromagnetic wave phenomenon. They are the result of wave vibrations. Further, since James Clerk Maxwell's work in the nineteenth century, we know that electromagnetic wave vibrations permeate the universe at many more frequencies than just those occupied by visible light. Consequently, invisible holographic systems made up of sound or radio waves, to name but two common examples, must also surround us. We simply don't perceive them unless they are properly focused. And, as David Bohm points out, other unknown wave vibrations may be responsible for what he calls "holomovements," or dynamic, evolving holographic systems. The interaction of these systems is what we perceive as Space-Time, the "holoverse."

If David Bohm is correct and we do, in fact, inhabit a "holoverse," made up of a complex system of interacting wave vibrations, and if one of the principal properties of holograms is that each part contains information possessed by the whole, then where do we fit in? Do we share holographic characteristics that permit us to "resolve" the chaotic, seemingly random events of Space-Time?

According to Stanford University's Karl Pribham, the answer is "yes." We possess a holographic model in our brains. The brain acts as the photographic plate that records the vibrations we experience and then our minds, through memory, sort and compare them. Finally, it presents us with the coherent picture that we call "external reality."

A neurophysiologist, Professor Pribham started out as a student of the late Dr. Karl Lashley, who devoted his scientific career to discovering specific brain locations for all human activities such as speech, hearing, appetite and so on. He was largely successful, but one key human function evaded him. That function was memory. Despite literally thousands of experiments, he was unable to locate a specific neurological complex responsible for memory traces. Memory apparently is a process that may involve the entire brain but which can be evoked even when virtually all of the cerebral cortex has been destroyed. Memory patterns seem to be equally distributed throughout the entire brain.

Although Lashley went as far as to acknowledge that recall appeared to involve a kind of "resonance" among a very large group of neurons, it was Karl Pribham who took the ultimate step of comparing the brain's memory capacity with that of the hologram, in which each part contains the whole image. In his *Languages of the Brain* (Brooks: 1977), he proposed that memories are stored in patterns of nerve impulses scattered across the entire brain, just as the hologram's coherent light waves scatter across the photographic plate. Further, he stated that our brain then "resolves" the scattered frequency patterns mathematically, thereby constructing what we perceive as external reality. Among other things, this concept helps explain why we sometimes experience "sensory overlap." Under certain circumstances, notably in altered states of consciousness, it is possible to "see" sounds or "hear" colors. In such states our holographic brain temporarily assigns the incoming information scatter slightly differently than usual, thereby allowing a different sensory perception to occur.

David Bohm's "holoverse" combined with Karl Pribham's holographic brain represents a milestone in our attempts to understand our human relationship with the rest of the cosmos. It links us with both the infinitesimally tiny world of the quantum and the unimaginably vast distances to the stars. However, despite Bohm's bold notion of ever-moving wave patterns forming evolving "holomovement" systems, the holographic analogy remains essentially static. An image is, after all, a fixed representation, even if by adding many slightly different images together and projecting them we obtain a movie. What becomes of life's dynamic process of evolution and change?

Classical physicists answered this problem by referring to what is known as the Second Law of Thermodynamics. Briefly stated, this law holds that all physical processes necessarily involve a decline in the organization of energy from an active, coherent state toward a passive, chaotic state. The ultimate state of disorganized, inert uniformity is known as entropy. For cosmologists it is the cosmic opposite of the universe's initial "Big Bang." For Newtonian physicists it is what will happen when the universal clock finally winds down. For us more ordinary mortals entropy is a cold cup of coffee that will never reheat all by itself.

Despite general agreement that entropy must eventually triumph overall, biologists and organic chemists have always been less enthusiastic about the Second Law of Thermodynamics than physicists. Studying living systems has provided them with many opportunities to see at least temporary reversals of entropy, for life tends to move in the opposite direction. Living organisms evolve from simplicity toward complex, active organization. Mere seeds or fertilized eggs are virtually formless. As they grow they acquire more and more form, complexity and order. They accomplish this by adapting to and cooperating with their environment.

The theoretical analysis of Belgian chemist Ilya Prigogine, for which he won a Nobel Prize in 1977, takes this commonsense observation a step further. He developed a set of mathematical equations which prove that even systems of so-called inert matter interact with their local natural environment like a living organism. They can thereby act as a catalyst to create new levels of more complex organization in direct contradiction to the Second Law.

Dr. Prigogine called such local catalysts "dissipative structures" for they consume available energy more quickly than nearby, stagnant systems. They seem, on the surface, to be speeding their entire established order toward destruction. However, actually their disturbance of the status quo forces meaningful change on their surroundings. The dissipative structure's entire environment may be forced to reorganize itself creatively in a more complex way to meet the catalyst's challenge.[17]

Further, Prigogine demonstrated that such positive change is not the result of slow, continuous growth. Instead, just as quantum-level reality suddenly leaps into being upon observation, so higher-level physical systems suddenly appear just when chaos threatens to overcome the old order. The original system is forced to reorganize to a more efficient stage in order to survive. Paradoxically, the whole order's capacity for positive evolution is directly proportional to its complexity because only complex, rather fragile systems are threatened by unruly "dissipative structures."

In applying his mathematical theory to our own sphere, Prigogine is optimistic. He feels that our Space-Time universe is extremely complex and delicately balanced. It thus provides an ideal setting for this creative process. Therefore, although entropy may be inevitable within a set level of reality, it cannot rule a living, dynamic process such as ours. Our universe is so organized as to include both static structures subject to entropy and active, creative systems. As human beings we are dynamic, living systems sharing physical qualities with our material environment and also original, creative consciousness. As we evolve within Space-Time there comes a moment when we too become "dissipative structures" within its fabric. Increasing social and ecological stress thus push our entire universe toward a crisis point from which together we can leap upward into a greater, more complex reality. In fact Prigogine feels that our entire universe is evolving along with us.

Ilya Prigogine's excellent model of a living, evolving universe led the Nobel committee to name him "the poet of thermodynamics." Squarely placing man and nature as equal partners in the universal "biodance" of interacting energies, his vision helps us reconcile our nightmares of a possible Apocalypse with the necessary, positive disruptions pushing us toward a brighter future. It helps us understand that the holographic brain does more than just catalogue and organize past experience. In conjunction with our minds and in cooperation with all of Nature, it actually creates progress.

A complementary theory about natural evolution has recently been proposed by British biologist Rupert Sheldrake. Known as the Hypothesis of Formative Causation, it offers a nonmaterial explanation of heredity, evolution, and memory within both organic and inorganic systems. For Sheldrake the catalyst factor leading to structural inheritance and evolving progress are intangible "morphogenetic fields."* In living organisms

---

* The word "morpho" means "form" in Greek.

these fields unlock and interpret the genetic codes within the DNA as each cell is created, ensuring that the species' "correct" features emerge. In inorganic matter, such as crystals, they bridge the gap between subatomic quantum uncertainty and the regular stability of larger structures such as atoms and molecules. These "M-fields" permeate our universe. In fact they may form the fundamental wave vibrations that interact to form the Space-Time "holoverse" itself.[18]

According to Sheldrake, structures evolve by repeating patterns instead of following invariable laws. Specific habit patterns are transmitted across both Space and Time, from the past to the present in Sheldrake's theory, via intangible, omnipresent M-fields. These fields, akin to electromagnetic and gravitational fields, are highly specific (each species has its own M-field and possibly even each individual) and contain information. Acting like physical and behavioral blueprints, they subtly influence structural development at all levels of existence through "morphic resonance," or the attraction of like to like. Thus, extending Sheldrake's theory slightly, we create who we are today by resonating with our own past habits via our morphogenetic fields since the like-to-like attraction is strongest with our own identities.

Furthermore, when an individual organism evolves by successfully adapting to its environment, its newly acquired qualities are automatically resonated back to its M-field and the M-field of its species. When enough individuals repeat the adaptation, thereby demonstrating its effectiveness, the new condition is instantly transferred from the species' M-field to all other similar organisms and it becomes what is known as an "inheritable characteristic" of the entire species. In this way the universe's M-fields both stabilize development and allow for positive change. Moreover, such adaptations are recognizable for, as they progress, it becomes easier and easier for individuals to "learn" the new pattern. Thus, even if M-fields themselves are intangible, we can test their effects on existing organic and inorganic systems.

In a 1983 interview Dr. Sheldrake provided several examples of what he feels are the effects of morphic resonance in improving learning skills among separate and genetically distinct populations. Among the most notable have been a series of independent psychological experiments testing the learning ability of laboratory rats. These experiments, begun by William McDougall, a Harvard professor, in the 1920s, clearly showed that later generations of rats more readily mastered complex skills (escaping from a water maze) than their predecessors, *even if they were neither genetically related to nor ever in physical contact with the previously trained rats.* The same skill was later shown to have improved among still more recent generations of even totally unrelated and un-trained rats.[19]

In another experiment behavioral psychologist B. F. Skinner had once conditioned large numbers of pigeons to provide responses by peck-ing at light panels, a complex skill that took a long time to achieve. Several years later another psychology team was amazed to note that their pi-geons, completely unrelated to Skinner's except by species, learned the proper pecking response almost immediately. In their paper they criti-cized the earlier researcher's procedures instead of acknowledging the possibility of a basic change in pigeon behavior. Similar tests have re-cently been performed with human subjects, demonstrating, for example, that it is easier for non-Turkish speakers to memorize ancient Turkish poetry, which has already been memorized by millions of individuals, than an equally long collection of Turkish nonsense rhymes.[20]

As mentioned above, the existence of intangible morphogenetic fields interacting with our Space-Time reality complements David Bohm's the-ories about the holographic nature of our universe and its hidden unity, which permits instantaneous communication between subatomic particles and human minds. Sheldrake's theory provides a possible glimpse into the underlying wave vibration processes that join together to create what we then experience as events within Space and Time. It also presents a plausible model for human memory, where past experiences are stored at the M-field level and therefore bypass the need for a physical or genetic link to reappear in human consciousness. With it we can more easily understand the mental process by which Karl Pribham's holographic brain resolves unfocused vibrational patterns into meaningful "real" events.

Moreover, even though Dr. Sheldrake has been very careful in his published writings to stress that his research deals only with physical consequences and not spiritual principles, the M-field theory obviously throws new light on the hypotheses of survival of bodily death and rein-carnation as well. Sheldrake's concept of morphic resonance may explain how distinct emotional and behavioral patterns are transferred from life-time to lifetime as it is logical to assume that his like-to-like attraction principle would be strongest with one's own past lives. Could our souls be vibrating energy wave forms, creating M-fields that receive infor-mation from our senses so long as we are physically "alive," storing and filtering it, learning from those experiences, and then projecting that information back into Space-Time in another human body? Such a hy-pothesis might explain how past-life "memories" can be tapped during so-called altered states of consciousness such as hypnosis.

Finally, taken one step further, this theory, which at first glance seems dependent on how the past influences the present, (i.e., on one-way linear Time), may in fact help us understand how past, present and future interact to create what we experience as "Now." We have seen that, according to quantum mechanics, our physical reality is based on probability where individual behavior is uncertain and only group processes are relatively fixed. Relativity theory has demonstrated that Space-Time events only seem to exist in linear temporal relationships due to our own participation within the Space-Time universe. If, as David Bohm and others suggest, our universe is enfolded in a greater, indivisible "Whole," then at that level Time and Space are simultaneous. Past, present and future do not exist as separable concepts. Everything simply is.

Sheldrake's hypothesis of formative causation simply extends this picture one step further by positing the existence of intangible, evolving M-fields surrounding and penetrating our Space-Time cosmos. From our perspective they seem to pass information only in one linear direction, from the past to the present. That is how we perceive their results consciously, because we are participants within the Space-Time level of reality. However, it is equally plausible to assert that information which transcends Space-Time must also transcend its property of one-way linear direction. If M-fields form a higher order of reality, they must be capable of instantaneous transmission from any point of Time or Space within our universe to any other. Otherwise, they too are caught in the relativity illusion.

How then do we relate to this information? What happens to our cherished concept of free will and the indeterminate future? I would propose that if we can view reality as a series of dynamic, evolving holograms, each enfolded within another, then at each level (within each hologram) events at other levels can only be perceived as probability functions. Thus, because our Space-Time universe enfolds that of quantum-level reality, we can only perceive individual events there as indeterminate or probable. We have to choose which behavioral property we want to examine in order to make an event definite. We can, however, define the quantum wave function (Ψ) as it is an abstraction, a process that transcends quantum-level events, bringing information into our Space-Time level of reality.

Similarly, when we attempt to discuss individual events at the M-field level, a dimension which transcends the Space-Time universe and enfolds it (and us as conscious participants), we can discuss them only in terms of probability functions (the M-fields themselves). We can measure field effects within Space-Time but we cannot define their individual capabilities completely because they extend beyond Space-Time limits. Thus, while we can demonstrate the physical effects of past habit patterns on present structures and conscious behavior without any intervening material transmission, we can talk about the influence of future habit patterns only in terms of their probable effects on the present. Our conscious minds' reliance on the useful properties of linear Time (cause and effect) limits our awareness of future influences on what we define as "Now." It thus preserves our free will, which is a conscious human function.

Nevertheless, we are more than our conscious, analytical minds. As holographic parts of a larger connected "Whole," we possess the entire system's hidden or implied information, including that about the influences of the future. Where? In the nonconscious levels of our minds, of course. Thus, when either in "altered states" such as meditation, dreams, and hypnosis or simply through the use of nonanalytical intuition as in remote viewing, we can glimpse potential future events that are already formed within the relevant M-fields. They usually do not even rise to a conscious level of awareness.

Then, and here the process is still little understood (it is certainly weaker than blind determinism), these M-field-level events subtly influence us through morphic resonance with conditions already set from the past so that we tend to set in motion those conscious actions that will bring about the potential outcome our nonconscious minds have perceived. We retain free will because such resonances are subtle and can be ignored through conscious effort. If so ignored, they either are overlaid by another set of "future" circumstances or possibly spin off into another parallel "holoverse thereby contributing to alternate or parallel lifetimes."

Nonetheless, all else being equal, we are usually nudged toward the future perceived by our nonconscious minds, souls or higher selves at the M-field level. Thus when the Russian healer chose a merry-go-round in Russell Targ's remote-viewing experiment, which was mentioned on page 239, his vision was subtly influenced by the M-field's recognition that the San Francisco team would "randomly" select that target several hours later. And vice versa, as morphic resonance transcends unidirectional Time. Similarly, a "psychic's" correct perception of the future is both a cause and an effect of M-field resonance among the nonconscious minds of all participants. Incorrect perception can result either from internal interference from the seer's own conscious mind or be due to the interplay of conscious free will by those involved. Such use of free will, however, requires energy and therefore is less prevalent than what we commonly call "destiny" or "fate."

This M-field transmission process is also obviously enhanced by deliberate creative visualization, which combines the directive quality of our conscious minds with the M-field information processed subconsciously. It explains how we can use our innate psychic powers to enhance our future within the conditions set by the general M-fields of humanity and of Space-Time itself. It also provides, in my opinion, our most viable hope for making what chemist Ilya Prigogine describes as an "escape to a higher order" as the tensions and imbalances of our current social and ecological systems push us toward the future crises predicted by prophets across the ages and by Dr. Wambach's and my future-life workshop participants. Obviously it will take concerted and collective conscious action to visualize more positive futures than those foreseen for 2100 A.D. by the subconscious minds of our subjects.

Combining David Bohm's holographic image with Ilya Prigogine's dynamic model of progressive evolution offers a final way to understand the emerging New Age paradigm of the holoverse and multiple levels of reality from quantum mechanics to M-fields. We can compare the universe to a living cell within a human body. The two share many common features that also often correspond with what happens at the quantum level.

Thus even though we can distinguish each cell as independent (a particle), its life (quantum wave function: Ψ) depends on its joint interaction with all the body's other cells. Each cell is part of a living chain of being. While it forms an indivisible living part of a larger, functioning organ, its own shape is defined by its smaller genetic components. Moreover, even though individual cells die and are replaced constantly, the body's life remains uninterrupted for a much longer time span. Finally, as we know from the continuity of genetic DNA material and cloning, each living cell contains a perfect representation of the entire organism, which can be reproduced starting from one single component cell. Each cell thus retains a consciousness of its entire parent form.

For those who support this emerging New Age paradigm, reality is like a unified, living and evolving organism. Just as our Space-Time universe, seen as a local "special case," the greater Whole itself is alive and somehow conscious. The quality of its existence therefore exceeds the sum of any mere mechanical components. Within the Space-Time universe, as human beings we experience the simulacrum, or image, of a hidden, implied order. Even so, as holograms ourselves, we contain the key to the larger, living cosmos according to the new paradigm, supported by Bohm and Pribham's holographic analogy, which echoes Ageless Wisdom's dictum: "As Above, so Below; As Within, so Without." Thus the

New Physics and Ageless Wisdom agree: It is within the barely tapped powers of our imaginative, intuitive and creative minds that we connect with greater orders of reality.

It is interesting to note that this point of view is remarkably similar to that expressed by California channel Jach Pursel's nonphysical entity, "Lazaris," during a telephone interview published in Marilyn Ferguson's *Brain/Mind Bulletin*. Stating "his" opinion that linear Time is a man-made convention, masking the timelessness of All That Is reality, "Lazaris" said that what we consider to be one-way cause and effect, running from the past through the present toward the future, actually is perceived in reverse from the spiritual dimension. Thus:[21]

> The vibrational frequencies which define events in the present are set up from future choices that come into the present against the backdrop of the past. . . . The effect in the chosen future leads to the cause in the present. [Therefore,] as you decide what you are going to become, the choice influences what you are.
>
> Your reality is a conscious creation, based on your observation. Life is a "conscious dream"—your creation. The extent to which you recognize that dream, you can change the dream of waking consciousness. Then you can direct [your life] with your eyes wide open.

This idea also parallels the wisdom of Edgar Cayce's psychic source, which constantly emphasized the value of the human Will in determining our individual futures and yet who also acknowledged that the nonconscious levels of the mind have far greater awareness than we can usually consciously perceive. We are therefore undoubtedly right now rehearsing the "mass dream" of our mutual future each and every day without realizing it.

Stephen Weinberg, 1979 winner of the Nobel Prize in physics, also agrees that it is through the mind that we demonstrate our unique human ability to transcend the Space-Time universe. In discussing how human beings relate to the discoveries of contemporary physics, he is quoted as having commented:[22]

> Electromagnetism is a "warble in the fifth dimension." Since we can control electromagnetic activity in the brain via the mind, the mind must encompass more complex dimensions than the fifth one. The fifth dimension is the last one that can be measured in Space and Time. The cortex of the brain keeps track of Space and Time so

when you focus your mind and stabilize the electromagnetic activity of your brain, you can begin to identify with other dimensions of reality, the area that physicists call "hyperspace." It is here that Space-Time considerations can be transcended. It is here that remote viewing, out-of-body experiences and past lives can be experienced. It is here that glimpses of visions of the future and of "other mansions" can be seen.

At this point just one question, but perhaps the fundamental one, remains to be answered. If we inhabit a living "holoverse," a system of wave interferences, each part of which reflects a true image of some external object that exists in a greater "Whole" reality, just who or what is sending these coherent energy beams into our Space-Time universe? If we are corpuscles or cells within a larger body, whose body is it? If, as mystics and channeled entities such as "Lazaris" allege, we are living within a dream's images, who or what is dreaming this dream?

10
Spaceship Earth:
UFOs, "Star People," "Walk-ins" and the Future

"We are not alone in the universe. A few years ago this notion seemed farfetched; today, the existence of extraterrestrial intelligence is taken for granted by most scientists."

Thus began the opening remarks of Lambros D. Callimahos, a highly qualified cryptologist for the Department of Defense, at a military electronics conference held in September 1965 under the auspices of the U.S. Air Force Office of Scientific Research.[1] Mr. Callimahos went on to explain that such noted contemporary astronomers as Sir Bernard Lovell have estimated that our own Milky Way galaxy contains about 100 million star systems likely to possess planets capable of supporting some form of organic life. As our galaxy is only one of over a billion galaxies scattered across the known Space-Time universe, the total number of potential life-bearing solar systems is immense. Therefore, according to this reasoning, the existence of other intelligent life in our galaxy is statistically a near certainty. It represents a completely opposite perspective to Dr. Brandon Carter's anthropic theory that we are probably alone in the universe, as discussed in Chapter 9.

Nor are astronomers alone in believing that somehow, somewhere among the vast reaches of interstellar space the scientists and philosophers of other intelligent species are struggling to understand the workings of nature and the meaning of existence. Man's search for extraterrestrial life and the possibility that even now super-civilizations are in the process of reaching out to contact humanity has been one of the most widespread cultural themes of recent decades. The extraordinary popularity of Stephen Spielberg's film *E.T.*, and Gene Roddenberry's futuristic *Star Trek* television series, among others, demonstrates the public's continuing interest in this possibility.

It is also clear that a majority of the modern world's people believe that some type of visual, physical or psychic contact between living human beings and unearthly creatures aboard "flying saucers" or "unidentified flying objects" (UFOs) has already happened and is still going on today. Public opinion polls taken in the 1970s indicated that already at least 51 percent of adult Americans believed in the validity of the UFO phenomenon and that a staggering 15 million United States citizens were convinced they had actually seen a flying saucer. Moreover, by the mid-1970s over 2,000 modern-day physical contacts had been reported and some 700 UFO landings that left visible, tangible evidence investigated. Obviously these figures would be higher today.[2]

In the four and a half decades since the reports of modern UFO contacts have become widespread, there has been a noticeable shift in public attitudes about these phenomena. In the 1950s the idea that technologically superior alien intelligences might be zipping freely around our home planet, appearing and disappearing at will, contacting and even "abducting" human beings from time to time for their own purposes, formed the basis of many horror stories and films. Mass UFO sightings caused terror and panic in a number of places, despite repeated government assurances that "natural" causes lay behind all such events, followed by the silencing or ridiculing of even credible witnesses.

According to some reputable UFO investigators such as Raymond E. Fowler (*UFOs: Interplanetary Visitors?*), our government's unwillingness to deal with the UFO phenomeron reasonably and openly has caused unnecessary confusion and hampered serious attempts to understand what UFOs may represent. Naturally concerned about the widely publicized reports of numerous violations of U.S. airspace by supersonic "flying saucers," which it was unable to prevent, the Air Force and the Central Intelligence Agency apparently devised a twofold strategy for dealing with UFO reports. At the end of 1947 our military leaders began a classified investigation of these aerial sightings to ensure that they did not pose a direct threat by any hostile power (especially the Soviet Union). Originally known as "Project Sign," this investigation was renamed "Project Blue Book" in 1952. Until Blue Book's official termination in December

1969, United States Air Force bases around the world compiled data on all known UFO sightings, particularly by air crews, and sent it to a central advisory panel headed by a respected astronomer, Dr. J. Allen Hynek. Whenever such sightings could be explained by reasonable alternatives, the Air Force was quick to do so publically. Documents on inexplicable cases tended to be buried in secret files "in the interests of national security."[3]

At the same time, once fairly certain that the Soviets lacked the technical capabilities displayed by the UFOs, the CIA ordered a media "debunking" campaign to persuade public opinion that the phenomenon was nothing more than the result of the wild speculation of a few misguided individuals. Apparently this was done to direct attention away from the government's inability either to explain or prevent UFO incidents. Throughout the 1950s and 1960s government experts highlighted the most ridiculous reports and basically ignored those by credible, technically oriented witnesses. Thus they helped create a public image of UFO contactees as "wide-eyed cultists, three steps in front of the men in the white coats" or "little old ladies fresh from the medium's parlor," according to the late Don Elkins, a former commercial airline pilot who studied UFOs for over three decades. Naturally, as with any widely publicized mystery, many UFO stories have proven to be unfounded or self-seeking. But others, including up to 10 percent of those from competent witnesses investigated by the Air Force's Project Blue Book, have never been adequately explained by accepted scientific principles.[4]

Ultimately this official military strategy of combining secrecy with deliberate ridicule has caused more speculation about the real motives behind our government's UFO investigations than it has discredited reports by reasonable UFO contactees. Many Americans suspect that federal investigators and military agencies know far more than they have ever revealed about UFOs, a view bolstered by the fact that a lot of documents still remain classified top secret."

By the 1970s, when nearly thirty years of UFO sightings worldwide and thousands of contactee reports failed to reveal any horrible alien invasion scheme, or any impending mass landing, and no official revelation that would lay to rest all doubts about the phenomenon was forthcoming, most people adopted a "wait and see" attitude. Even when Jimmy Carter, a duly-elected President of the United States and a former naval officer, publicly admitted he believed that he had once seen a UFO, no one flinched or seriously questioned his fitness to hold high public office. Mass indifference had replaced fear and animosity, although occasional reports of

unusual sightings or contacts continued to stir considerable public interest
temporarily.

Many people heretofore intrigued by the possibility of UFO landings
now became more interested in exploring whether they themselves might
actually be either genetically different "Star People," distant descendants
of ancient alien astronauts, or extraterrestrial "Walk-ins," highly evolved
spiritual beings voluntarily taking on physical human form to help humanity develop. Each of these concepts and their possible implications
for the future will be discussed later in this chapter.

Today, as we near the last decade of this millennium in a sadly divided
world whose political leaders seem incapable of solving our massive economic, demographic and ecological problems, yet another opinion shift
about UFOs has taken place. Many, many men and women around the
globe are now actively seeking superhuman intervention and help to
shepherd us through the difficult days that are perceived as being just
around the corner in our near future. Thus, José Arguelles, author of
The Mayan Factor, and proponent of the 1987 Harmonic Convergence,
is now calling for a massive worldwide appeal to any UFOs currently
patrolling Earth's vicinity to come down and help us clean up our environment. He has scheduled this event for December 31, 1989, the beginning of our last decade in this millennium.[5] Other UFO contactees, like
Tuella and the Guardian Action Publications group, have described alien
plans to evacuate large portions of Earth's population in the event of a
sudden natural cataclysm, pole shift or global nuclear war. Tuella's predictions are discussed below on pages 270–272.

This turnaround in public attitudes toward UFOs in the space of one
generation was captured by a perceptive 1980s cartoonist who depicted
two identical scenes of a UFO landing, side by side but thirty years apart.
In the first cartoon, labeled "1953," a terrified crowd flees the saucer,
crying, "Save us! Save us!" as they run away. In the second, labeled
"1983," the same frantic crowd has turned around and is now rushing
toward the craft, shouting, "Save us! Save us!" to its crew.[6]

Part of this attitudinal shift has been due to a growing change in the
kind of UFO contacts reported. In the last few years accounts of physical
UFO sightings and scientific, experimental contacts have been increasingly replaced by disclosures of psychic messages from intelligent, benevolent aliens. Ken Carey's *Starseed Transmissions* and more recent
Return of the Bird Tribes are excellent examples of these uplifting channeled spiritual "close encounters." These messages almost invariably repeat both a promise and a warning concerning the world's future. The

warning consistently tells us that our current path is leading the planet to turmoil and possible disaster unless we can act together *now* to stop man's inhumanity to man and raise human consciousness to higher levels. The promise is that we can and are receiving help from our "Space Brother" cousins who are watching out for us and who will ensure that spaceship Earth itself does not explode in a nuclear holocaust.

Similar prophetic messages have accompanied earlier physical UFO-contactee stories. Recently, as reports of psychic channeling have become more widely acceptable, it appears that telepathic contacts with UFO aliens have supplanted openly visible manifestations. It is possible that the current wave of UFO contacts through psychic channels forms part of the next stage of our evolutionary process. If this is correct, then in the coming decades we can probably expect a merging of the two types of reported alien visitations, with greater tangible evidence of their on-going presence backing up their telepathic or psychic messages. Such a development could help prepare us for the kind of commonplace, "routine" physical and mental interaction reported by several of Helen Wambach's progressed workshop participants for the 2100 and 2300 A.D. eras.

Just what are these "unidentified flying objects" that millions of Americans and other modern, supposedly rational people around the world have reported seeing or communicating with in recent decades? Where do they come from? Why are they appearing at this point in human history? What role do they play in the "mass dreams" of our planetary future?

Certainly one common misunderstanding about UFOs is that they are a uniquely modern, contemporary phenomenon. Most discussions of UFOs begin only with Kenneth Arnold's dramatic June 24, 1947, sighting of nine silvery, disk-shaped aircraft soaring over the state of Washington's famed Mount Rainier in a linear aerial formation at speeds estimated at up to 1,700 mph. Witnessed from the cockpit of his private plane in broad daylight, this incredible sight shocked the experienced mountain pilot, who reported his story to airport officials on landing.

A newspaper reporter was present when Arnold compared the antics of the round, shiny craft to saucers skipping across a lake. The phrase "flying saucers" caught instant media attention and the story spread like wildfire. Within a few days literally *hundreds* of similar stories were flooding newsrooms as fearful, excited citizens related seeing similar unidentified flying objects in Earth's skies. Soon even United States Air Force personnel, including trained pilots, began reporting strange incidents in which silent, glowing craft suddenly appeared in the sky, performing aerial feats impossible by known physical laws, only to speed out of sight when pursued. The Air Force began its official, mostly secret, investigation of UFO sightings, which was to last twenty-two years, hiring astronomer Dr. J. Allen Hynek as its main scientific consultant. A contemporary mass phenomenon had been born.[7]

However, despite popular beliefs, UFOs did not just suddenly appear "out of the blue" in the late 1940s. In some form or another they have been part of human history from its earliest beginnings. Until recent times, because we could not fly ourselves, we lacked an adequate frame of reference for categorizing them and therefore attributed typical UFO-type incidents to divine intervention, magic, or occult, diabolical powers. They eventually became the subject of orally transmitted myths and legends. Such legends, repeated around the world, continue to fascinate us despite obvious editing and distortions by later storytellers. Otherwise the propositions of those who, like German author Erich von Daniken (*Chariots of the Gods*, 1969, etc.), feel UFOs influenced ancient civilizations would never have stirred up such controversy.

Actually, even in modern times, well before 1947, inexplicable aerial incidents have been widely reported. Thus, for example, during 1896–97 thousands of eyewitnesses gaped at a series of cigar-shaped "airships" that suddenly appeared over the American West, being seen from Oakland, California, to Chicago. Such a "dirigible" manned by six "strange creatures" was even seen rustling cattle by a startled and angry Kansas farmer! In the early twentieth century a Russian explorer and his party reported that a large, shiny oval had sped by overhead as they were trekking in the Himalayas in August 1926. The strange craft made a sudden right-angle turn (a typical UFO movement) and disappeared behind a mountain peak. During World War II pilots on both sides reported strange glowing globes that appeared and zipped around over battle zones. Allied airmen even coined the term "foo fighters" for these weird, supposedly enemy, craft, based on a popular 1940s comic strip where the leading character, Smokey Stover, often quipped, "Where there's 'foo' there's fire."[8]

These relatively recent reports are part of a vast chain of eyewitness accounts of inexplicable aerial phenomena that lie scattered throughout human history. Thus Ruth Montgomery reports that even in far earlier times, when "nothing was supposed to be flitting about in our skies except birds," contemporary annals mention the sky "filled with cylindrical shapes from which emerged black, red, orange and blue-white spheres which darted about" (from a 1561 German source). Even Alexander the Great's army once cowered in fear before two "shining silver shields" that dived around its ranks during one of his campaigns. Other similar reports from the Middle Ages and classical antiquity make it clear that what we now call UFOs are actually part of a much larger phenomenon whose source may be as ancient as human life on Earth.[9]

If it is possible, as suggested by these and other ancient sources from around the globe, that UFOs or related phenomena have been monitoring human history for millennia, then why have contacts increased so dramatically in the past half century? What is it about contemporary times that has attracted the attention of so many of these extraterrestrial visitors?

Throughout human history UFO contacts have occurred in four fundamentally distinct although clearly related ways. (1) Most dramatic are what Dr. Hynek labeled "close encounters of the third kind," where men and women undergo what they experience as an actual physical meeting with alien beings and often are taken aboard an alien space craft. (2) Next are psychic contacts that do *not* involve a face-to-face encounter or visit to a UFO itself. This includes the channeling of entities who identify themselves as coming from different planets or solar systems and out-of-body experiences with such beings. (3) Other contactees, sometimes known as "Star People," feel that they are somehow genetically linked to extraterrestrials who long ago intermarried with human beings ("Starseed") or that their ancestors assisted ancient astronauts during previous visits to Earth ("Star Helpers"). (4) Finally, some contactees believe that although their physical bodies are entirely earthly, their original spirit or soul has voluntarily given up its place to the soul of a highly evolved being from another planet or star or from another dimension of reality. Such "Walk-ins," as New Age mentor Ruth Montgomery calls them, are here to help the human race during what is widely expected to be a difficult transition period in our spiritual evolution.

Most reported UFO experiences combine features of two or more of the four types listed above. Thus, for example, many individuals now channeling alien entities may have had a face-to-face contact whose memory remains blocked from the conscious mind. Others who have had "close encounters of the third kind" have discovered that their contact was not accidental—they exhibit physical characteristics or psychic traits linking them to possible extraterrestrial origins. Brad and Frances Steiger, who have most carefully investigated this phenomenon, have found that most Star People have had periodic psychic contacts from around five years old with "space cousins" monitoring their development. Others have found their bodies share the Starseed genes while their personalities have become spiritual Walk-ins. It is as if their bodies were prepared by their original souls for the "Walk-in" transition, which only occurred years later. Linear Time causality tends to be absent from many UFO experiences!

In order to explain both the wide variety and interconnectedness of contemporary UFO contacts, as well as their relationship to our view of the future, I have chosen a few examples drawn from the four categories listed above. Some of these cases have been discussed in print previously, while others, to my knowledge at least, are here presented for the first time. In each case chosen some important aspect of today's "mass dreams" of the future is evident.

Dr. Hynek's "close encounters of the third kind," immortalized by Stephen Spielberg's film, remain the "classic" UFO story today. From the early 1950s, when George Adamski reported meeting highly advanced humanoid Space Brothers from Venus in the Mohave Desert to the 1987 best-seller *Communion*, the story of Whitley Streiber's alien encounters in upstate New York, we have been enthralled by stories of how apparently ordinary people are suddenly thrust into exceptional circumstances with mysterious UFOs and their extraterrestrial crews. Such contacts often, but not always, include the telepathic communication of some kind of message, either personal or for humanity. Frequently they involve a medical examination of the body as well. Some people have felt that their physical makeups were somehow altered so that they could be followed for further study from a distance. A few contactees have even reported sexual encounters with human-looking aliens!

As thousands of these stories have unfolded, a UFO-alien typology has developed based on the common traits reported by many different physical-level contactees. It is noteworthy that the vast majority of such extraterrestrials are human or humanoid in appearance. New Age investigator and author Brad Steiger provides composite portraits of four such interplanetary visitors by artist Hal Crawford, who designates them by the Greek letters "Alpha" through "Delta" in *The Gods of Aquarius* (1976).

According to Crawford, "Alpha-form humanoids" are small (three feet to four feet tall) puckish creatures with large eyes, pointed ears and generally friendly dispositions, although rather shy. They usually have green or grayish skin. Their frequent visits to Earth over many millennia probably account for humanity's persistent myths about the "wee people" such as elves and leprechauns.

Crawford's "Beta-form" aliens actually include two distinct types. Both look human and could "pass" for modern men and women if properly attired. The first of these types are labeled "Beta" and "Beta-F" to distinguish between tall, handsome Nordic-like men and their statuesque, blond and very feminine counterparts. Since both represent a Western ideal of Earth's humanity, it is possible that their appearance is a mental image projected by the aliens to human witnesses rather than their actual physical form. The "Beta-F" females tend to be less frequently seen with spaceships than the "Captain Kirk" kind of men.

The second, also human-looking, "Beta-2" types have sometimes been tagged as the "Men in Black" by UFO investigators because such apparitions are usually soberly dressed in dark suits or uniforms. Their taciturn, threatening manner seems to match their clothes. They have often appeared to UFO witnesses after a physical-level encounter to tell them to keep silent about their experiences. They also share such physical traits as pointed chins, dark hair, thick lips and dark, vaguely "oriental" complexions. They usually are shorter than the fair, blue-eyed Beta types. Again, these may be image projections designed to intimidate or at least command respect. There is, after all, no guarantee that just because they have developed more advanced technology, UFO aliens are also superior ethically or spiritually to human beings here on Earth. In fact, the history of encounters between technologically advanced civilizations and less developed peoples on this planet certainly has revealed that advanced technical skills do not always imply higher ethical qualities as well.

The last two types, "Gamma" and "Delta," seem more the stuff from which nightmares are made than lovable *E.T.*-type aliens. "Gamma-forms" are generally large, hairy apelike creatures akin to our idea of Big Foot or the Abominable Snowman. They are usually met outdoors although similar but smaller creatures are sometimes encountered inside flying saucers as well. Their horrible stench and generally stupid behavior have led some investigators to consider them as biochemical servants or robots of other, unseen aliens. They frequently leave identifiable footprints behind after an outdoor encounter.

Their "Delta" cousins often share the foul odor associated with the "Gamma-forms" but are distinguished by their apparent ability to change their shapes at will. Reported suddenly to materialize before the horrified eyes of a human observer, they can "wink out" again just as rapidly only to reappear in another location instantly. About their only constant feature is luminosity—they glow in the dark. Their eyes emit strange radiations and they seem like a will-o'-the-wisp. Seemingly weightless, they appear more like projected images than material beings, although there is some speculation that this may be due to a faster vibratory rate than ours. They are possibly more interdimensional than extraterrestrial. Myths about ghosts and ghouls may sometimes have sprung from "Delta-form" encounters.

Regardless of the type of aliens met or exact circumstances, physical-level close encounters are usually accompanied by a memory block of the incident, apparently induced by the aliens. Physical rashes or scars and the unpleasant sensation of having unaccounted-for "lost time" may be the contactee's only clue that an encounter actually occurred. This uncertainty has left many such individuals mentally distressed, a factor that has led some skeptics to discredit all such accounts as being from unstable, unreliable witnesses.

Fortunately, in many cases these induced "mental blocks" can be at least partially overcome through hypnosis. Counseling psychologists such as Dr. R. Leo Sprinkle in Laramie, Wyoming, have helped literally thousands of UFO contactees disturbed by such physical-level experiences and memory loss to understand what happened to them. Dr. Sprinkle, who also conducted future-life workshops whose results are included in the analysis presented earlier in this book, is one of the foremost scientific investigators of the UFO phenomenon in the United States today. He has personally worked with over 300 contactees over the past twenty-five years and for the past decade has organized an annual UFO conference at Laramie, where the latest theories and experiences are examined. He has also carried out a survey of the psychic impressions of UFO phenomena by several hundred contactees. His sympathetic counseling and important investigative work into UFO matters was given national recognition by Ruth Montgomery in *Aliens Among Us*.

As a result of his investigations and, as he humorously puts it, "after long hours of neurotic contemplation," Dr. Sprinkle has concluded that "UFO activity [occurs] at several levels of reality" simultaneously. He and most other serious UFO investigators agree that such encounters are examples of a shared experience between human beings, inhabiting Space-Time, and paraphysical beings whose reality parameters overlap our universe but extend beyond it. Entities encountered may be either travelers through Space or Time or both. Their appearance in our sector of this universe at any given moment may be materially "real" or psychically projected as part of the holographic image we experience as material reality.[10]

Thus a UFO experience can be *both* physical and psychic. It is also usually deliberately educational. Encountering such paraphysical aliens precipitates change in the life of the individual contacted. Moreover, the repeated intrusions of aliens into history (as in ancient India at the time of Krishna or Egypt/Israel around the time of the Exodus) have often signaled an important transition affecting the entire human race. Whether their influence is more largely mental or material probably depends on individual circumstances for, from the UFO perspective, the two (mental and material) are complementary aspects of the same larger reality or indivisible Whole, as discussed in the preceding chapter.

Although hundreds of physical-level-UFO-encounter stories have been published since the early 1950s, I have chosen the unheralded tale of an Oregon housewife whose contacts with a being she labels "a self-styled UFO character who calls himself 'Hweig' " have endured for nearly half a century. Her story illustrates many aspects of the typical "close encounter of the third kind" and, coming from a very ordinary witness whose main preoccupation has been to lead as "normal" a life as possible, avoiding spectacular publicity, it remains quite believable despite the incredible events she describes. Further, I think you'll agree that Hweig provides some thought-provoking comments about today's world situation and our immediate future.

Dr. R. Leo Sprinkle put me in touch with Mrs. Ida K. (who prefers to remain anonymous) a few years ago as she had met Helen Wambach at one of the Laramie UFO conferences in the early 1980s. In the correspondence that followed she told me her "UFO story" and provided me with some of Hweig's comments about the future. It was during a 1980 hypnosis session with Dr. Sprinkle that Ida K. first "remembered" her initial close encounter with Hweig, which occurred shortly before Christmas of 1940.[11]

Recently married, Ida and her husband spent December the twentieth to the twenty-third driving from their Washington State home to Arizona for Christmas with relatives, accompanied by three servicemen traveling south on holiday leave and sharing expenses. Following a day and a half of routine driving, they dropped one passenger in Los Angeles. After servicing the car, the rest of them set out to cross the Mohave Desert during the cool night hours. Thus it was sometime around 11 P.M. on the night of December 22, 1940, that they passed through the sleepy town of Indio, civilization's last outpost before the Arizona border.

Shortly thereafter, dipping into a desert valley through some low, rocky hills, all four of them noticed a "deep red, unearthly glow" emanating from a large ball floating on the horizon. At first they thought it just a full Moon, rising huge and luminescent in the clear desert atmosphere. Then, without warning, the "Moon" disappeared behind a rock outcrop only suddenly to reappear, moving sideways toward their left. No ordinary "full Moon" could do that! It disappeared behind some more rocks and they could no longer see the unusual glow that had first attracted their attention.

At the next wide bend of the road the driver pulled over and the three men got out to investigate, leaving Ida in the car. A sleepy glance at her watch indicated it was "twenty minutes to the hour" (11:40 P.M.). She noticed her companions illuminated by the car's headlights; they seemed to be talking. Cold and tired, wrapped in a blanket, she waited for them to return, alternately drowsing and shivering in the chilly winter night. Finally, she stirred enough to snap on the light to look at her watch and see the time clearly. It was 12:20 A.M. Forty minutes had passed! It seemed unbelievable that the three men hadn't come back to the car yet. Ida guessed she had misread her watch earlier. At that moment the men returned. They had seen nothing. All agreed that they had wasted enough time and they resumed their journey.

As they drove away Ida noticed a "great white silvery disk" swiftly rising over the treetops. Although one of the men commented that it must have been the Moon after all, she remained skeptical for it was moving too fast and in an unnatural, oblique direction. But, too tired to argue, and thankful to be on her way again, she dropped the matter. The incident seemed closed.

The next day, at her sister's in Phoenix, Ida asked her husband what he had been discussing so earnestly with the two others while they stood in front of the car. Surprised, he denied anyone had ever left the parked automobile! When she insisted he simply said he couldn't remember anything unusual having happened. The incident seemed unimportant and so Ida all but forgot about it also for the next two decades. She did, nonetheless, look up the Moon's phases and discovered that the full Moon had been on December 14; only a silvery crescent would have remained visible a week later.

In 1940 virtually no one considered the idea of UFOs, despite the "Martian" panic caused by Orson Welles's "War of the Worlds" radio broadcast on Halloween two years earlier. Public disclosure of the World War II "foo fighters," Kenneth Arnold's highly publicized "flying saucer" sighting and George Adamski's tales of Venusians landing in the Southern California desert were still years in the future. In the meantime, Ida K.'s life resumed and seemed to follow its "normal" course for many years.

Therefore, even when the start of some strange psychic phenomena, including hearing phantom voices, interrupted her life a quarter century later, it took Ida a long, long time to accept that there was a connection between that strange December "Moonrise" and the subsequent events. In 1968, after using a homemade Ouija board and a pendulum without taking any of the precautions, such as protective prayers, and having a clear spiritual purpose recommended by experienced psychics like Edgar Cayce, Ida K. apparently awakened latent "channeling" abilities. At first she felt the friendly contact of the entity who later identified himself as "Hweig."

However, as she did not know how to control the flow of psychic energy through her, this benign contact was soon overshadowed by a series of frightening disturbances, including an attempted "possession" by a very unpleasant spirit. This psychic "attack" upset her so much that she sought psychiatric help. The incident had so scared her that, even after she recovered, it wasn't until November 1977 that Ida finally established a regular contact with Hweig through what she terms "telepathic writing." He used this method to inform her that their first contact had been as early as that December night back in 1940. Eventually, in April 1980, Ida sought Dr. R. Leo Sprinkle's help in recovering those "lost forty minutes" via hypnosis.

During their session Dr. Sprinkle gently regressed Ida back to the moment when the car pulled off the desert road. In her regression she discovered that after dozing off for a minute or two inside the car, she was suddenly awakened by two strangers urgently asking for her help. They said there had been an accident and that someone with her same rare blood type needed an immediate transfusion. Would she cooperate?

She was soon walking with them around the rocks to a circular craft. Taken into a round cabin, she saw an injured man (Hweig) lying down. She allowed the others to take blood from her arm. Then she felt as if something were pressed into each ear and the left nostril as well. Whatever it was went "way up, way up." It hurt for a moment but the pain quickly subsided.

The ship's crew, who appeared to her as tall human beings, speaking perfect English, thanked her for saving their companion's life. They promised to communicate with her "much later" for further assistance. Then they escorted her back to the car, where she suddenly found herself snapping on the light and noticing that forty minutes had passed. Her traveling companions returned to the car and they noticed the unusual "Moonrise" as they departed.

This hypnosis session seemed to confirm Hweig's affirmation of their initial contact in 1940. However, Ida felt the "blood transfusion" tale was impossible as she had no memory of any scar or needle marks. A few months later she wrote to Leo Sprinkle telling him that during a subsequent automatic writing session with Hweig, she had questioned the hypnotically revealed story. She said that he "admitted" that she had been led to believe someone vitally needed her help to get her to go willingly. Actual blood had never been taken and her memory had been altered at a level untouchable even by hypnosis. Also, she now felt she had had a "fiber optic" kind of implant in her brain to help them monitor her telepathically later. That was behind her partial memory of something being shoved way up her left nostril.

Although she later had X rays to try and "prove" this aspect of Hweig's story, they were negative. Nonmetallic material would not show up on them. Nevertheless, Ida remains convinced that something was done that has affected her physical senses and ability to receive Hweig's telepathic messages.

Among the most important of Hweig's communications, received since the early 1980s, has been a series of statements concerning Earth's immediate future. Even though he has repeatedly said he foresees future events in terms of "probabilities" not absolutes, his vantage point is such that, like Jane Robert's "Seth," he can see a "spacious present" extending further ahead in our linear Time than we can perceive in ordinary consciousness. Until now his future "previews" have been shared just with other UFO contactees and Ida's personal friends. Still, I feel they are thought-provoking and deserve a wider audience.

Like most channeled entities, Hweig predicts important challenges face humanity here on Earth in the next couple of decades. These will include significant geophysical changes and also social upheavals as outmoded structures collapse from within. He told a UFO contactee group that[12]

This is coming into focus faster than we believed possible. People must be strong. . . . The old is crumbling from its own activities. There will be [this] shock [because] the new must be brought from a stronger, perhaps wiser source. Not necessarily from us but through us from wiser people.

In a personal letter Ida K. shared Hweig's view of the future more extensively. It is worth repeating in its entirety here. Hweig says:[13]

There will not be any world wide single catastrophe such as the old Earth turning itself upside down and shaking everyone off into the abyss. There will be many localized catastrophes such as earthquakes, famine, wars, volcanoes, floods such as we have been experiencing in the past decade [1980s]. These will increase in the immediate future rather alarmingly. It may seem as if the whole world is in a state of destruction, but each of these calamities can be dealt with on a contained basis, though international help will be sought and utilized.

There will be no atomic war or World War III. The much touted "Battle of Armageddon" has been underway for several decades, the "cold war" is a major part of it. War is fought in the minds of men, battlefields are only the outward show. The tide has already turned toward Peace, [although] it will take decades more for it to become a reality or even very apparent. The factors that make for Peace are in place, it just will take time for them to show.

UFO contacts in the immediate future will be on a different basis than in the past. Much has been learned about the mental and emotional make up of Earth people, as well as the physical body, and in the times to come there will be less exploitation and more respectful approaches to "Earthlings." The little big-heads [Alphaforms?] who have been pretty rough in their examinations are not the "Masters." They are clones and sometimes robots, or those who have been programmed to act in specific ways, and do not have initiative. Very soon you will be having contacts with the "Masters" themselves, who are nearly identical physically to human beings [Beta-forms?]. Therefore UFO contacts in the future will be more satisfying and humans will be treated less like bugs to be researched and more like participants in a joint adventure.

Nonetheless, Hweig also has warned UFO contactees that some caution is necessary when approaching these phenomena, either physically or psychically. Not all contacts have come from ethically superior beings. Among the galactic confederation currently watching Earth and our species is a separate faction Hweig calls "the renegades," whose methods and purposes are at odds with the vast majority of the UFO forces. Most frightening or malicious occurrences, such as animal mutilations, have come from them. They form a kind of negative side of the UFO dimension but, according to Hweig, are so related to the positive forces that, from the human perspective, we can only distinguish the two groups by the effects of their interaction with Earth humanity. Hweig said he was confident that the influence of such renegade groups would diminish as higher-level contacts between humans and our galactic cousins develop. In the meantime it is important to "test" psychic contacts by the kinds of messages received and their effects on one's personal development and well-being.

Such is one contemporary American woman's UFO saga. How should we evaluate it? Did this friendly, middle-aged housewife really meet alien humanoids, who have subsequently changed her life, way back in 1940? How does her story compare with other "close encounters of the third kind"? While it is currently impossible to make a final judgment about the "truth" of her experience, I am convinced that she is neither lying nor fantasizing. Whatever happened, it was convincing and meaningful to her. And, as psychologist Dr. Leo Sprinkle and others have attested, Ida K. isn't given to flights of fancy or idle speculation. She has a balanced personality and is quite common sense oriented. Personally, I think the fact that she voluntarily sought psychiatric help when her initial "channeling" experiences overwhelmed her back in the late 1960s speaks well of her psychological equilibrium. Not everyone would have recognized that things had gone too far and sought professional assistance in time.

Furthermore, the account of her experiences, which I have edited for brevity, resembles those of many other UFO "close encounters." Typical features include (1) an initial incident at night in secluded surroundings, (2) "lost time" or partial amnesia, (3) personality changes leading to intense curiosity about the paranormal, (4) later psychic disturbances, seemingly unrelated to the earlier forgotten contact, (5) eventual memory recovery under hypnosis, (6) unsuccessful attempts to prove that some "real" physical alteration took place and (7) a message to be shared with others. Her story is unusual only in that the first incident happened before 1947 and that it took so long for the subsequent scenario to unfold. Also, Hweig's message is clear and concise, and, if one accepts the UFO premise, very credible.

Although Hweig has mentioned the existence of a galactic confederation of a number of inhabited planets working together in this and other, superior dimensions, he has not, to my knowledge at least, indicated holding a specific function within any kind of extraterrestrial hierarchy. Such is not the case for the many reports coming from individuals contacted by a group loosely known as the "Space Brothers" or the "Ashtar Command."

The first psychic contact with a "Space Brother" came in 1952 when George van Tassel received a telepathic message from "Ashtar, Commandant Quadra Sector, Patrol Station Schare" while out in the Mohave Desert near a spot known as Giant Rock, California. Ashtar identified himself as part of a spiritual "Council of Seven Lights," which oversees our universe. He warned humanity about the dangers of nuclear weapons and indicated that "Shan," his name for Earth, and the entire solar system is moving into a specially energized sector of Space. This upcoming transit meant that in the near future humanity would face several material and moral crises that could decimate our species unless we are able to develop a higher spiritual consciousness, or vibration. Ashtar's and allied flying-saucer fleets were monitoring our progress and, if required, would intervene to stop nuclear destruction of our planet. Van Tassel and others were exhorted to spread the Space Brothers' message of a return to universal law and brotherhood. To this end he founded a church centered around a curious dome-shaped building at Giant Rock that he dubbed the "Integraton," which was supposed to raise spiritual vibrations and prolong human life.[14]

George van Tassel's "conversion" by Ashtar and the Space Brothers would probably have had little more impact than that of similar California fringe "cults," who seldom outlive their founder, had not almost identical messages from Ashtar and the "Intergalactic Confederation" or "Interplanetary Space Command" erupted from dozens of other psychic channels across America over the next several years. Messages from these UFO connections have been received psychically by several hundred different individuals over the past four decades, using names like "Ashtar," "Monka" or "Hatonn," purportedly the galaxy's "record keeper," and referring to the same intergalactic hierarchical organization said to be headed by no less a personage than Jesus himself (often also called "Sananda" by these sources).

As Jon Klimo remarks in *Channeling*, such psychically channeled communications would fill volumes of printed material and deserve a separate study of their own.[15] Space Brother channels assert that their reports actually come from humanlike beings whose advanced technical and spiritual evolution permits them to raise and lower their electromagnetic vibrations at will. This, they explain, accounts for the typical instant appearance of UFOs in our Space-Time dimension and their equally abrupt departures. It also accounts for their ability to forecast the future, as their ships can "accelerate the particles which make up the atom" and by this "frequency shift" travel through Time as well.[16]

Whether these are genuine telepathic contacts with extraterrestrials orbiting high above our atmosphere in invisible craft or not, the Space Brother communications form a fascinating collection of very similar messages received independently by a large number of people. As such they definitely form part of our culture's underlying psychic pattern and their view of the future is part of our collective "mass dream" of the road ahead.

Perhaps the best known of the Space Brothers channels is Thelma Terrell, a young mother now living in Utah who writes under the name Tuella, given her by the Intergalactic Council. Like George van Tassel twenty years earlier, she claims to have been telepathically contacted by Ashtar, called "the highest authority for our hemisphere," in 1973. Described as the "Christian commander" of a fleet of 10 million beings invisibly circling our system for many millennia, he remains her primary UFO contact.[17]

Depicted as a tall, blue-eyed, blond (Beta-form alien), Ashtar loyally serves "our Beloved Lord and Great Commander, Jesus-Sananda," the "Great Space Being" in charge of Earth. Other prominent Space Brothers associated with the Guardian Action Group, which publishes Tuella's communications along with those of related psychics, include "Hatonn," "Lytton," "Monka" and "Andromeda Rex." All are said to be part of the "Interplanetary Alliance and Space Commands," comprising about 35 million UFO astronauts monitoring our solar system. I cite these figures to give readers a bit of the scope of the UFO phenomenon as reported by hundreds of Space Brother channels.

Tuella's communications from the "Ashtar Command," published in her 1982 book *Project: World Evacuation*, reiterate the basic Space Brother message that *now* is a critical time in Earth and humanity's history. Calling it "the midnight hour," Tuella reports that Ashtar forecasts a drastic "purging" of the planet through a series of natural catastrophes and man-made disasters, including the results of nuclear testing, in preparation for a physical renewal of Earth and awakening of those human beings spiritually evolved enough to participate in the superior intergalactic civilization.

Humanity's long history of selfishness and violence, combined with the purely materialistic use of modern technology, has unbalanced the Earth's vibratory field. The planet's polluted atmosphere, magnetic field and rocky crust, fractured by repeated underground nuclear blasts, have lost their natural equilibrium. According to these UFO sources, only the direct stabilizing intervention of external forces (i.e., the Ashtar Command) has staved off total disaster so far. This intervention is necessarily limited to the minimum required to keep the Earth itself from utter ruin. Humanity will have to live with such lesser consequences of its past actions as earthquakes, volcanoes and weather disturbances leading to widespread flooding, drought, famine and other natural catastrophes accelerate. Drastic losses of human life are all but inevitable as Mother Earth seeks to relieve itself of its intolerable human burden. All this is likely to be worsened by wars and revolutions as people selfishly scramble for increasingly scarce resources.

Furthermore, Ashtar and his colleagues repeat the idea discussed in Chapter 2 that the Earth is currently moving into a special sector of Space. They have told Tuella that the Earth's burden of negative selfish human vibrations is increasingly clashing with our planet's spatial environment as our solar system enters a sector of the universe where more high-frequency radiations penetrate our atmosphere. This gradual, cumulative spectrum shift is already causing increased stress under the Earth's tectonic plates. It will most likely be released through more frequent volcanic eruptions and massive earthquakes, especially in the regions of the Mediterranean basin and the Pacific "Ring of Fire" (which includes the west coasts of the two American land masses). A pole shift of approximately 14 degrees could also result from these pressures, putting the new North Pole somewhere in today's Pacific Ocean.

Thus, according to Tuella and her Space Brothers, we are heading directly for a New Age version of the Apocalypse. Nevertheless, in a promise reminiscent of that of the Bible's book of Revelation's Chapters 7 and 14, where God preserves 144,000 righteous souls from Earth's "great tribulation," Tuella's UFO friends reassure us that *up to 10 percent* of the human race whose superior spiritual evolution will benefit Earth's new Golden Age will be miraculously "evacuated" at the last moment. They will be taken aboard virtual cities in the sky for five to seven years, or until the Earth has restabilized.

An advance guard of this group, known as "Light Workers," is currently being prepared by UFO and other spiritual contacts. They will assist Ashtar and his intergalactic fleet in shepherding those still unawakened but spiritually developed individuals to safe havens where the pickups can occur. Much of Tuella and other allied channels' current work is alerting potential "Light Workers." They need to wrap up their earthly affairs, open themselves for vital communications from the spiritual realms and relocate to less exposed places, generally away from polluted cities, if that seems right. Eventually they are to form an alternate communication network, ready to function if and when standard links break down.

If Tuella's and other similar reports are accurate and invisible "UFO arks" are standing by to evacuate several million people, just how will their future passengers be selected? In the book of Revelation's Chapter 14, the 144,000 "elect" are described in narrow, sexist terms as "those who have not defiled themselves with women . . . and in their mouth no lie was found" (Revelation 14: 4–5). By this standard very few of Earth's current inhabitants, including most of the proponents of the New Age, or self-styled evangelist preachers either, would qualify!

Fortunately, our Space Brothers seem more understanding of human frailties than those who spout Apocalyptic rhetoric, even though their announced standard remains difficult enough to attain. Thus, according to Ashtar's colleague "Commander Alphon," channeled by one of Tuella's friends called "Lyara," "the boarding pass for all [who will be saved] will be 'love in the aura,' for without that, one cannot withstand the higher vibrational frequencies which will be necessary." Therefore, like Jesus and St. Paul in the New Testament, as well as modern sources such as Edgar Cayce and "Lazaris," the Space Brothers remind us that cultivating the vibration of unconditional love remains our only valid passport to the "Beyond."[18]

One of the most intriguing speculations that has developed from Space Brother channeling in the last couple of decades is that Alphon, Ashtar, Hweig and the other Beta-form UFO astronauts appearing to human beings, either physically or psychically, are actually Time travelers from Earth's own future rather than extraterrestrial aliens from other planets. Certain of the telepathic messages received by contactees like Tuella, Ida K. and others such as Rev. Diane Tessman of San Diego, California, whose UFO astronaut "Tibus" has specifically stated he is from the future, indicate that this is at least partly accurate. In fact Rev. Tessman (of the Starlight Mystic Church) feels she and Tibus are a "shared consciousness" of the same overall identity, just separated in Time.

Thus he may be one of her "future selves," returned psychically to help her through these challenging times.[19]

If in fact Tibus and Hweig and other Beta-form UFO astronauts do travel through Time rather than Space, then it's possible that there are genetic as well as spiritual ties between some contemporary contactees and their Space Brothers. Such DNA links may add to existing psychological and spiritual explanations of why UFO contacts frequently surprise totally unprepared individuals whereas others who long for such an opportunity are never called.

Another aspect of this genetic UFO-contactee relationship theory has come from psychic channel and healer Frances (Francie) P. Steiger. She claims that some people today share unusual genetic characteristics inherited not from the future but from extraterrestrial humanoids who visited Earth tens of thousands of years ago, interbreeding with primitive human stock and thereby accelerating our species' physical and spiritual evolution. She calls them Starseed. The most common physical anomalies shared by this group include low blood pressure, lower-than-normal body temperature, extra vertebrae or ribs, unusual blood types (especially Rh negative) and sinusitis. Sensitivity to light and electricity, keen hearing and a strong sense of personal responsibility also seem to characterize Starseed individuals.[20]

Other related individuals, whose ancestors or "past-life selves" assisted the ancient astronauts, received advanced psychic "imprinting" instead of genetic bonding. They are the Star Helpers. Together they form the Star People, a distinct group of humanity through the ages dedicated to lofty spiritual ideals. The most common recognizable Star People features, applicable to both Starseed and Star Helpers, are deep feelings of kinship with the stars and UFOs and an intense desire to use their varied talents and abilities to serve their fellowman. Anyone can discover they are a Star Person! Many of the readers drawn to the message of this book undoubtedly are part of this positive, future-oriented fraternity.

Frances Steiger, who with her ex-husband Brad Steiger, discussed this concept fully in their 1981 book *The Star People*, has since organized *The Star People Foundation* to assist other spiritually like-minded people to recognize their star-born heritage and to put their gifts to work more effectively. She feels that it is no accident that Star People have begun to awaken to their spiritual identity and to come together in recent years. A common message was imprinted into their souls eons ago according to the Divine plan for human evolution within the Space-Time universe. Today's release of that message, that *"Now Is the Time,"* in many people's thoughts, visions and dreams has been triggered by Earth's revolving passage through the cycle of World Ages, which was discussed in Chapter 3. It indicates that we now stand on the threshold of a new, higher cycle of vibrational energies and spiritual potential.

The coming rise in our system's frequency will affect us physically, mentally and spiritually. It will be preceded by a difficult period, during which the Earth will undergo a "great transitional shaking." Thus, like so many others, Frances Steiger predicts that:[21]

There is soon to be a time of cataclysms, of floodings, of vulcanisms, of massive geologic changes, of the collapsing of social and political structures [and] of the disbanding of many of the world's religions.

Star People are being awakened to their identity now so that as Light Workers they can help humanity through the transition as smoothly as possible. A routine of regular, daily meditation, renewing contact with one's immortal soul and spiritual guides, practicing tolerance and forgiveness and opening one's heart to the "unconditional love vibration that you are to give to all living things" needs to be established *now*, before the wave of change sweeps over the planet. Only by activating such discipline in their daily lives will Star People be prepared to find safe haven during the storm to come and to help others willing to listen and to grow.[22]

Frances Steiger's concept that many people alive today are either genetically related to ancient astronauts or somehow bear their psychic imprint reflects humanity's oldest and most widely held belief—that we are the deliberately created children of a greater, Divine intelligence whose origins are not of Earth. As discussed earlier in Chapter 3, myths and legends about the celestial origins of the human race are universal. Only the language used to describe the contacts experienced has changed in today's accounts.

Thus virtually all of the world's peoples trace their ancestry to the stars—to Divine beings who descended from the heavens and who either created humans on Earth, in their image, or intermarried with preexisting Earthlings. Many so-called primitive peoples have preserved oral histories of their ancestors' arrival on this planet from other star systems. To cite just a few specific examples, the Dogon tribe in West Africa believe they are descendants of beings from Sirius; the Cherokee retain legends of a former home in the constellation of Orion, while many other Native American peoples, including the Maya and the Hopi, claim kinship with ancient visitors from planets in the Pleiades. The gods of Classical Greece and Rome frequently produced half-human children, while Japan's Imperial family officially claimed direct descent from celestial ancestors until after World War II when the Emperor was forced to disavow his Divine status because it had provided the Japanese a basis for claiming racial and national superiority over their neighbors.

Stories of mythical interactions between heavenly gods and human beings form the basis for all the world's major religions, including the monotheist trilogy of Judaism, Christianity and Islam. Archaic, nontechnical descriptions of celestial boats and chariots fill the pages of Earth's earliest religious literature. Ancient Hindu, Tibetan and Egyptian scriptures all describe UFO visits and ancient wars in the heavens. Moslems around the world strive to perform at least one pilgrimage to Mecca's fabled *Ka'ba*, a black stone of extraterrestrial origin that some legends say was handed to Abraham by "angelic" visitors from the skies. Radical Shiite followers of Iran's Ayatollah Khomeini already made one attempt in 1979 to wrest its possession from Saudi moderates in preparation for their version of the coming Apocalypse.

Even the Bible is filled with allegorical accounts of what would be described as UFO incidents if they happened today. The Scriptures mention no less than three different types of spacecraft as vehicles for God's intervention into human affairs. The first kind is the fiery chariot that swept Elijah up in a "whirlwind." It was pulled by "horses of fire" (II Kings 2: 11–12). The prophet Zechariah recounts a vision of four similar heavenly chariots descending from between "mountains of bronze" (mother ships?). The angelic charioteers are commanded to "Go, patrol the Earth!" (Zechariah 6: 1–7).

The Lord's own "cloud" chariot is the most frequently cited Biblical spaceship. The Scriptures abound with descriptions of key heavenly interventions into Earth's affairs by Divine beings using celestial "clouds" whose carefully controlled movements leave no doubt as to their mechanical nature. Thus Israel's exodus from Egypt was monitored by a "pillar of cloud" that glowed like a "pillar of fire" in the dark (Exodus 13: 21–22). When Moses ascended Mount Sinai to receive the Ten Commandments, "the cloud covered the mountain." It looked "like a devouring fire" from down below (Exodus 24: 15–17). Later the prophet Isaiah saw the Lord "riding on a swift cloud" (Isaiah 19:1). Other Old Testament prophets such as Daniel also describe heavenly "cloud" chariots. In the New Testament, Jesus's Divine identity was announced by a voice from "a bright cloud" during the Transfiguration (Matthew 17:5), while at his Ascension "a cloud took him out of their sight" (Acts 1: 9).

The final type of Biblical UFO is disk-shaped and was described as a "wheel within a wheel." It was this heavenly craft that was so poetically evoked by Ezekiel, who saw it "spinning in the air" and who even was taken for a heavenly ride (Ezekiel 1:16–28). Ezekiel's story associates this craft with the celestial cloud and whirlwind, demonstrating the close relationship of these types of extraterrestrial ships to each other.

His description of the craft that picked him up is by far the most detailed account in the Bible of such a heavenly encounter. Long considered just a spiritual allegory, it recently inspired a former NASA engineer, Joseph Blumrich, to test whether or not the vehicle described in the Book of Ezekiel was technically capable of flying. To his astonishment he found that, when translated into modern terms, Ezekiel's account portrays a craft whose features and abilities closely resemble those of modern UFOs! Blumrich described his successful recreation of the Biblical "flying saucer" in *The Spaceships of Ezekiel* (Bantam Books: 1974).

In his introduction Ezekiel also called the glowing, circular spacecraft he witnessed "the Glory of the Lord." This is the exact expression used earlier by Moses to describe how God descended to the top of Mount Sinai for their meeting: "the Glory of the Lord settled on Mount Sinai" (Exodus 24:13) and by the prophet Habakkuk in a visionary prayer where he also cites the heavenly chariot with its fiery horses (Habakkuk 3:3). These references make it clear that the "Glory of the Lord" was the common designation for Lord Yahweh's space shuttle. Interestingly, this same term, whose original UFO association has since long been forgotten, reappears in the New Testament in Luke's description of the familiar Christmas story:

> And in that region there were shepherds out in the field, keeping watch over their flocks by night. And an angel of the Lord appeared to them, *and the Glory of the Lord shone around them* and they were filled with fear . . .
>
> [emphasis added].

Would our reaction to the sudden appearance of a brilliant UFO and an astronaut in a shining suit in the middle of the night be very different? I wonder. Regardless, I feel that it is a significant and hopeful sign to realize that, by the Bible's own testimony, the birth of the one we call "Christ, the Prince of Peace," may have been carefully monitored by benevolent extraterrestrial friends. Let us hope that God's fiery chariots are still "patrolling the Earth" for, if the messages of many of today's UFO contactees are right, we may soon need their help!

These Biblical references to what at least one contemporary engineer has demonstrated to be a technically sound spacecraft are echoed in other ancient literature around the globe, as shown by the research of Erich von Daniken and other followers of "ancient astronauts" theories. The venerable (c. 2500 B.C.) Hindu epic *Mahabarata* calls them *vimana* ("flying machines") and describes vast aerial combats using awesome weapons capable of wiping out whole cities in a single incandescent blast reminiscent of hydrogen bombs. The ancient Tibetan parchments *Tantyua* and *Kantyua* describe UFOs as "pearls in the sky," warning that such knowledge is a priestly secret.

Pre-Columbian cultures from both North and South America worshiped a pantheon of sky gods and goddesses who were said to have once streaked through the heavens in fantastic sky ships. The Navajo of Arizona, for example, have a legend about a fair-skinned, blond "god" who descended from a "cloud" in a "whirlwind" (just like in the Bible) in prehistoric times, giving their ancestors a code of moral and political conduct similar to the Ten Commandments. Other similar stories, including legends of the blond, fair-skinned Kate-Zahl (Quetzalcoatl) abound among Native American peoples. His description in these legends is reminiscent of the Beta-form aliens so widely reported in modern UFO sightings.

An Egyptian hieroglyphic text from about 1480 B.C., around the time of Moses and the Exodus, tells how the Pharaoh Tuthmose III and his troops witnessed "a circle of fire" descend from heaven with "an evil-smelling breath" (fumes) and "no voice" (silent). They fell to the ground in frightened obeisance to the divinity. Another, later portion of this unfortunately badly damaged and incomplete text recounts that the Pharaoh himself was temporarily taken up "into the middle" of the fiery ball.[23] Apparently this "close encounter of the third kind" went well, for Thutmose III later became Egypt's most-renowned military strategist, conquering Ethiopia and extending Egypt's superior civilization across the Middle East as far as the borders of Persia. Perhaps he learned something in that divine fire ball!

However, apparently Thutmose III insufficiently applied whatever spiritual counsel he may have received from his UFO contact for he is also considered by many Biblical scholars to have been the "great oppressor" of the Jewish people. His harsh policies, such as forcing the Hebrew slaves to make bricks without straw, inspired Moses to revolt and flee to the Sinai, where he had his own "close encounter" with Yahweh in the "burning bush." This physical-level supernatural contact inspired Moses to return to Egypt to lead the famed Exodus during the reign of Thutmose III's weaker successor, Amenhotep II. As has already been shown, at that time heavenly intervention favored the rebels.[24]

Ancient Astronaut and Star People theories are complementary in that both seek to explain the human condition and UFO contacts through some kind of prior "seeding" of superior wisdom in Earth's distant past that is only now coming to fruition. Best-selling New Age author Ruth Montgomery has investigated another facet of this intriguing relationship between human beings and the stars with the controversial Walk-in hypothesis put forward by her Guides. Although Walk-ins are by no means limited to extraterrestrial spirits, according to Ms. Montgomery's best-selling *Aliens Among Us*, we are currently experiencing a vast influx of highly advanced souls whose primary physical-life experiences have been spent on alien planets. They have voluntarily taken over adult human bodies, with the full consent of their former soul inhabitants, to help humanity make a critical transition, a "quantum leap in consciousness," up to a new, expanded holoverse.

In both Ruth's survey and other UFO or channeled literature, three star systems stand out as particularly important sources for these star-born beings now spearheading a peaceful invasion of Earth. They are Arcturus, Sirius and the Pleiades. As with the Space Brothers, many of whom are said to hail from one or another of these star systems, it would require a separate volume to discuss the human race's time-honored interest in these three sectors of the heavens adequately. All have been hailed as the heavenly abode of the creator gods by one or more of Earth's traditional cultures, with the Pleiades probably humanity's most globally acknowledged ancestral home.

Even though these "seven sisters," as they were known in Greek mythology, are only a minor, barely visible star cluster in the constellation Taurus, the most ancient of Earth's known observatories were set up to measure their passage across our skies. Aztec, Maya and Hopi calendars were based on the rising and setting of the Pleiades. One of its brightest stars, Alcyone, was long considered by several traditional cultures, including the ancient Chinese, as the great central sun of our galaxy, around which our solar system revolved.*

Interestingly, however, contemporary psychic Edgar Cayce seems to give that role to Arcturus, at least as far as the soul's spiritual de-

---

*The theory of Alcyone as our central sun seems to have originated in China, where astronomical texts over 4,000 years old mention the Pleiades. It was later restated by nineteenth-century German author Paul Otto Hesse in *Der Jungste Tag* (c. 1880), where he claims that our solar system revolves in a 24,000-year orbit around Alcyone, passing through bands of unusual high-level cosmic radiation emanating from that star every 12,000 years. Hesse stated we would next enter this zone starting in 1962. Orthodox astronomy disclaims all "great central sun" theories, however.

velopment is concerned. During a hypnotic trance his psychic source once
remarked:

> Arcturus is that which may be called the center of this universe,
> through which individuals pass and at which period there comes the
> choice of the individual as to whether it is to return to complete [its
> material-life experiences] there—that is, in this planetary system:
> our Sun, the Earth . . . or to pass on to other [solar systems]."
>
> (Reading 5749–14)

"Lily, Arthur and the Group," the spirit guides who communicate
through Ruth Montgomery's automatic writing, have called Arcturus[25]

> a leavening star, a force for good, and it is used for honing character
> and instilling in those who tarry there a desire to return to their
> respective planets and tell everyone what they have discovered:
> that each of us is something of God and that we are all one.

California channel Jach Pursel's "Lazaris" persona told Jon Klimo in
an interview for his book *Channeling* that mental images created on "his"
dimension are projected "down" through ever-denser levels of reality
until they reach our Space-Time universe. They then enter our system
via the double-star system Sirius, the brightest visible star in Earth's
skies, about twenty times as powerful as our Sun.[26]

The entity "Albion," channeled by psychic Page Bryant, agrees. She
says that "The Wisdom Teachings" call Sirius "The Central Spiritual
Sun." Furthermore, Albion predicts an unseen "spiritual energy blast"
from Sirius starting in 1990 and lasting about twenty-five years. This ray
of high-vibrating energy is slated to have its biggest effect in what Albion
calls the Earth's "Root and Spleen Chakras," which are identified as lying
under the Pacific Ocean—the infamous "Ring of Fire."[27]

Sirius has also been identified by Ruth Montgomery's guides as "a
planetary system where those who have completed their Earth cycles go
to learn how they may further serve humanity." Known in antiquity as
the "Dog star," it was revered by the ancient Egyptians as a powerful
heavenly divinity under the names Sothis and Isis. Its appearance in
ancient Egyptian skies marked the annual irrigating Nile flood.[28]

Ruth Montgomery's guides have further singled out Sirius and Arcturus as the jumping-off place for many of today's spiritually advanced

Walk-ins. They specifically told her about the Sirian souls who have entered the bodies of UFO contactees Joyce Updike of Colorado, David Paladin, a Native American artist from New Mexico, and Charlotte King, from California, whose extraordinary sensitivity to earth tremors has made her a "walking seismograph," and about Arcturian teacher and astrologer Frederick van Mierers and his friend and associate John Andreadis.

Of these individuals, all of whom are presented in *Aliens Among Us*, Frederick van Mierers seems to have the strongest feelings regarding a specific mission to unite Walk-ins and help prepare the next generation for the energy changes predicted for the upcoming New Age. He proposes that today's youth need to surpass our hedonistic culture by adopting a rather ascetic life-style, including a vegetarian diet, herbal remedies and traditional yoga disciplines in order to sensitize their bodies and minds to the higher-energy vibrations he feels are now entering the Earth.

Like most other New Age teachers, Frederick and John assert that we are "reaching the end of a grand cycle of the ages," greater than the traditional equinox precession that marks the passage between two signs of our zodiac. As energy is "transmuted to a higher frequency" when the unlimited "I AM awareness" (God) returns to Earth, only those able to function at these higher vibrational levels will be able to make the transition without undue suffering. We need to stop identifying with our limited thoughts of self and open our minds to the incoming higher consciousness of unlimited strength and unconditional love.

What we hold in the mind, at whatever level, forms a pattern that attracts similar physical events to us. We therefore need to clear out negative emotional patterns from the past and harmonize with others dedicated to rejuvenating Spaceship Earth and all her passengers. Walk-ins, like Star People and Space Brothers, seem to have appeared at this moment in history to help us bridge the gap between "I am only myself" and "I am also everybody else" awareness. Or, as Arcturian souls John and Frederick conclude in *Aliens Among Us*, "It is true that our space brothers and sisters have landed. And we are they!"[29]

Although UFO investigations are usually confined to discussions of our relationship with physical beings from outer space, including divine gods and goddesses, from our earliest days some men and women have also claimed to possess the ability to leave their physical bodies behind and travel to the ends of this Space-Time universe and beyond.

Records of such out-of-body experiences, known as OBEs, are among humanity's oldest surviving literature. The story of the ancient Egyptian Una's spiritual flight to the stars during an initiation rite is over 4,300 years old.[30] Initiation mysteries from the high civilizations of Egypt and Greece stressed the soul's ability to transcend bodily limitations and thereby gain crucial, sacred knowledge from other planes of existence. For our ancestors life was a continuum from the material to the spiritual, a single unbroken thread that connected All That Is at all levels of reality. Such knowledge was, nonetheless, considered "top secret" and jealously guarded by temple priests and occult initiates.

Today, after a long interruption in which Cartesian dualism and Newton's mechanistic worldview rigorously separated the material and spiritual worlds, quantum mechanics, parapsychology and energy-field theories have rekindled scientific interest in the borderlands between body, mind and soul. Freed from dogmatic religious interpretations and undue superstition and secrecy, serious investigations of OBEs and UFO encounters are now shedding new light on who we are as a species and our possible relationship to larger dimensions of reality.

One of today's pioneers in this radical venture of exploring non-physical dimensions out of the body is successful businessman and former audio engineer Robert A. Monroe. Today head of the Robert Monroe Institute of Applied Sciences, a consciousness research center tucked away in the foothills of Virginia's famed Blue Ridge Mountains, Monroe has dedicated his life to helping others discover their own gateways to "inner space." His "Gateway Voyage" and "Human Plus" experiential seminars have helped thousands of contemporary individuals, including a high proportion of nurses, doctors and scientists, expand their reality frontiers through a patented process that uses audio signals to harmonize the electrical waves of the brain's right and left hemispheres. Many people who have experienced these programs, including myself, have thus obtained meaningful encounters with what Monroe humorously calls "our nonphysical friends" or simply "INSPECS" (intelligent species), reminiscent of psychic-level UFO contacts.

Robert Monroe has told his fascinating personal story of how spontaneous out-of-body episodes, starting in the late 1950s, radically changed his outlook on life and led him to found the Monroe Institute in two best-selling books, *Journeys Out of the Body* and *Far Journeys*. Less well known is his 1958 telepathic alien "close encounter" that preceded his first OBEs and which he discussed with Dr. Jeffrey Mishlove during a March 1975 radio broadcast, "Mindcast." The story appears in Mishlove's

classic parapsychological study *The Roots of Consciousness*. It is based
on engineer Monroe's own careful notes, made immediately after the
contact.[31]

The incident took place in a small office Monroe had built on his
secluded Virginia land as a retreat from his busy Washington, D.C.,
business and social life. Alone there one evening, he first became aware
of a persistent 800-cycles-per-second tone ringing in the room. This was
followed by a heat beam from an external source about 30 degrees above
the horizon, which penetrated the office wall and hit his body without
burning it. As soon as it touched him he perceived the presence of "three
or four entities," who proceeded to examine him physically. He even
remembers having a metallic "cup" placed over his groin, a detail he was
astounded to find later in 1961 UFO contactee Barney Hill's story (see
John Fuller's *The Interrupted Journey*, published in 1966). The Hills,
who were taken from their car into a UFO, also reported hearing a high-
pitched noise just before their "abduction." They could remember details
of what happened only later under hypnosis.

Even though (like most first-time contactees) he never had the
impression of bodily leaving his office, Monroe clearly recalled the entire
incident. His memory was not blocked. He told Dr. Mishlove that he also
engaged in over two hours of telepathic dialogue with the beings in what
he has later come to call NVC (nonverbal communication), which he feels
is the basic "language" used by intelligent life elsewhere in the universe.
Most important, he felt as if his brain had been probed and his thoughts
examined. He later wondered if this had a direct bearing on his subsequent OBEs.

Although Robert Monroe personally feels there is a qualitative difference between his kind of out-of-body travel and physical-level UFO
contacts, his 1958 "close encounter" certainly resembles many unexplained UFO reports from the same time period. Clearly the event and
following OBEs have changed his life as well. In his second book, *Far
Journeys*, he suggests that Time travel is also possible while in the out-
of-body state because linear Time does not extend to other dimensions.
He even broadly hints that he has met his own "future self" from around
the year 3000 A.D., an INSPEC whom he calls "AA" from dimension
"KT-95," during several OBEs and that this series of encounters has been
instrumental in helping him (and others) break free from what he calls
our "time/space illusion," or TSI.

As today's foremost out-of-body explorer, Robert Monroe's comments about our current situation and most probable immediate future are intriguing. One of his perceptions about the Earth, viewed from outer space during an OBE, is that our planet is literally blanketed in progressively thicker rings of psychic "static." He calls it "the M-Band." This mental and spiritual fog, the result of human emotional vibrations, apparently keeps our conscious minds trapped in the TSI we have created. Only our inner awareness, liberated during dreams, meditation, OBEs and by some psychoactive drugs, can temporarily break through to the greater external "Whole" reality. Our souls, originally outside and free, became entrapped in this material illusion through emotional entanglements, even losing the memory of their true identities. Only an awakening of our spiritual sense and purpose, to be accomplished by unselfish consideration for others, i.e., through unconditional love, can help us attain what Monroe calls "escape velocity" and break the psychic sound barrier.

Additionally, as we know, the Earth and its attendant energy field are constantly evolving, moving through Space and Time (or Space-Time events swirl past us, the stationery observers—take your pick!) As it does it occasionally intersects with other energy fields also passing through our Space-Time universe. Such conjunctions are rare. According to Robert Monroe's OBE contacts, our solar system is just now poised on the edge of "a conflux of several different and intense energy fields arriving at the same point in your time-space." They informed him that this particular interpenetration of energies happens only once in about 87 million years, if that often. It promises to be a spectacular show full of "both danger and opportunity," with Earth's humanity in the starring role![32]

Consequently, Space- and Time-traveling INSPECs from numerous "nearby energy systems" are gathering in and around the Earth to study what's going to happen. Some, apparently, use physical-dimension spacecraft, which we term UFOs, while others project themselves psychically from other dimensions. It is even possible, as mentioned earlier, that some of these beings are from our own "future." Monroe's nonphysical source told him that we have "many" such visitors today. Their arrival in anticipation of a coming energy shift may well account for the increase in physical and psychic UFO contacts in recent decades.

In *Far Journeys*, Robert Monroe describes his contact with a group of superior beings capable of melding together into a single "Group Consciousness" or "Collective Intelligence." Monroe feels it is this Intelligence that manipulates our Space-Time reality from another dimension. These "super beings" only made themselves known to him after he had accomplished several out-of-body journeys. They told him that they are the ones who project the energy that creates our holographic universe. According to Monroe, these advanced beings say that the coming energy-field junction in Earth's vicinity will stress our planet's physical and electromagnetic forces to their limits. Therefore a wave of natural catastrophes such as predicted by Edgar Cayce and other psychics is a very tangible threat. Many possibilities exist that could cause widespread disruption and suffering, decimating Earth's population.

The true crisis of the near future, however, is not material but mental and spiritual. The opening of human consciousness to heightened creativity and wider realms of reality, seemingly what increasing our vibratory environment will accomplish, can be a two-edged sword. Like recent advances in science and technology, which have brought us both nuclear medicine and hydrogen bombs, such energy is neutral in itself. Its consequences, for good or evil, depend entirely on how we human beings use it. Once again, to use Dr. M. Scott Peck's terminology, we are confronted with a test of our collective and individual willpower!

Therefore, the real crisis will be within each one of us living today. In the words of Monroe's source, the coming shift "will offer human consciousness a rare potential to emerge rapidly into a unified intelligent energy system that will range far beyond your time-space illusion, creating, constructing, teaching as only a human-trained graduate energy is able to do." Or: "Humans will retreat as the dominant species on Earth until they no longer survive as active consciousness, eventually, in any form."[33]

Still, we do not face this crisis alone and abandoned. That is the eternal promise, repeated by world religions, psychics and even quantum physicists. Unseen forces, whether considered as UFOs, INSPECs, spirits, energy fields or saints and angels, constantly monitor and subtly influence Earth-level reality through our subconscious minds. We can, by "going within" and attuning ourselves to our deepest human values, those exemplified by humanity's great spiritual teachers, the basis of whose teachings has always been love and self-sacrificing service, invoke these forces for the common good. This is the true meaning of "atonement," a prerequisite for spiritual growth. At some basic level *we know what "right" and "wrong" are* in the different circumstances affecting us, no matter how deeply we have buried this knowledge from waking awareness. I do and you do too. Think about it!

Undertaking such an "internal spring cleaning" is never easy; the vast majority of us have invested much time and energy in creating all kinds of illusory thoughts, desires, fears and prejudices, possibly over several human lifetimes. As Jesus rightly remarked, it's much easier to perceive a speck in someone else's eye than to notice the log blocking one's own vision. Nonetheless, both outer and inner space explorers agree that *now* is the time to quit dreaming, to wake up and set our mental/ spiritual house in order so we can face whatever kind of tomorrow is all too rapidly heading our way.

11

"In His Presence"

"Now, I want you to let yourself yawn a big, comfortable yawn. . . . That's right. . . . Just relax and let your mind concentrate on my words. . . . Your eyes are closed and it feels so good to close your eyes. . . . The muscles of your face relax now and your breathing is easy and regular. . . ."

Once again I let the familiar, gravelly tones of Helen Wambach's soothing hypnotic voice resonate in my ears. I leaned back onto the soft pillow on her spare bed and let my conscious mind start drifting. It was already early December of 1984 and we were about to embark on a final voyage of future discovery together, this time investigating the possibility that I might have another earthly lifetime in the crucial twenty-first century.

Previous sessions had revealed that I will have departed from Chet Snow's body during the early decades of the next century and that I will not be among those individuals destined to return in either of the two time periods we had studied in our group workshops (2100 and 2300 A.D.). In fact when progressed to the twenty-second century at the end of one memorable session, I knew instantly that I was no longer in an Earth body. I had felt liberated yet at the same time very "thoughtful and distant," according to my post-session notes. In a measured, emotionless voice I hardly recognized as mine I informed Dr. Wambach that "the

286

conquest of Space in a physical body" didn't interest me very much and so I didn't plan to be around for that phase of human development.

I got the impression that I could choose to return to Earth later if I so desired, in order to "review certain things about human relationships," but that it wasn't really necessary and, if I wanted to, I could skip that final Earth incarnation and go directly to what I could only identify as "Level Seven"—something that made no sense whatsoever to my conscious mind but seemed obvious to the inner personality who voiced those words in measured, matter-of-fact tones. I realized that wherever I was in that nonphysical state, "I" was still very much alive. The impression I got was being part of a vast psychic network of similar creative energies, dancing, vibrating and interacting in natural, innate harmony, completely beyond words or emotions.

In all our past- and future-life sessions together, I had never felt so detached. Words are inadequate to express my experience of that inner persona. There was no value judgment, no superior feeling, attached to my statements. I didn't feel either happy or sad about my prospects. Everything was simply calm and collected, with a "that's the way it is" atmosphere to it. At that level of reality, whatever is, just "is," period.

Nevertheless, before leaving that state, which we'd discovered only at the end of a long session devoted to my trip to Canada in 2002 A.D. as discussed in Chapter 1, I got the distinct impression that I still had one additional lifetime to experience in the intervening century. I understood it as the completion of a promise made long ago in terms of historical, human time. Consequently, as we began our first attempt to pull this project together, Helen and I finally decided to look into that possibility. Although neither of us realized it consciously, it was to be our last "future progression" session together.

Any such awareness was far, far away, however, as I allowed my body and conscious mind to relax in Helen Wambach's Pinole, California, apartment on that cool December afternoon. The rhythm of her soothing voice lulled my outer senses and I focused inward at her suggestion. Soon I had left Chet Snow's physical body behind and my mind was at peace as I listened to her start to name years for my next potential rebirth: 2015 A.D., no, too early; was Chet even "dead" yet, I wondered; 2025 A.D., closer but still no signal that I was about to return to Earth; 2035 A.D., yes, that seemed more like it. I twitched on the bed and the word "yes" popped out of my mouth almost before her lips had finished pronouncing the year.

Smoothly, almost without transition, I felt my consciousness slip into a little baby's body. As I noted later, I experienced "a funny and strange feeling of being squashed into this tiny bit of protoplasm whose main concerns obviously centered around its stomach and the consequences thereof." I noticed a kind of white blankness to the "ceiling" of my surroundings; apparently I lay in a crib covered with some kind of gauzy white covering. At the same time I also felt warm and secure, such a difference from the cold and dampness I'd undergone previously as Chet Snow on the Arizona ranch at the end of 1998!

Not terribly interested in my placid recollections as a crib-bound infant, Helen took me rapidly forward until I'd reached about the age of four. I felt my body growing, stretching like a lithe young animal, proud of its healthy limbs and functions, its muscles and nerves tingling in its still-small skin. It felt sensual and good! Additionally, I already was aware of my distinct personality as well as a feeling of shared community with those around me.

"I'm standing in a shallow bathing pool in the complex where we live," I said in response to Helen's query as to my whereabouts. "There are half a dozen other children about my age here. Some are white, while others have brown, tanned skin. Two friendly, plump Slavic-type women are laughing and joking as we bathe. It's a kind of communal nursery, I think, for I know neither is my mother. I get the impression that we live together by family units within a larger, planned community with common facilities. It's pretty small, however; perhaps fifteen to twenty families."

Asked to look at my own reflection in the water, I remarked, "Oh, yes, I'm a little boy and I have light brown skin. I look a bit like someone from northern India or Pakistan, with fine features, a straight nose and dark hair. And I have the most unusual eyes, Helen; they're fairly wide and the irises appear deep violet. I've never seen anything like them! They're striking but beautiful. And my name is Mark."

Having thus ascertained my future identity, Helen Wambach propelled me forward along the stream of linear Time to my mid-teens. Somewhere around 2050 A.D. This time I found myself wearing a kind of soft, loose-fitting tunic and pants, which tied at the waist with a string. It reminded me of judo pajamas with Velcro-like fastenings that made it appear as one piece. The entire outfit was loose and comfortable. It seemed to come in various colors. I noticed that although mine was a pale violet, other teenagers in my group had on similar pink, green and blue suits.

"There are around twenty of us here outside on a recreation field in an area some distance from our residential compound. Most are kids about my age along with a few adults. There aren't many adults, though. I feel that I still live with my parents but spend most of the time with this group in school. Even though I'm not with them, I am aware of my parents' activities and feel their love; it's a warm reassurance just beneath my conscious level of awareness."

As I spoke those words vivid flashes of my future-life mother and father came unbidden into focus. She was small, dark and slender, a beautiful Indian woman, sometimes dressed in a bright-colored sari, sometimes wearing a long, ivory-colored robe belted at the waist. I noticed just a wisp of white in her otherwise jet-black hair as she darted about, reminding me of a lovely little bird whose many jeweled colors flash in the sun, constantly humming a bright, fast-moving tune as she went about her daily chores. So very light yet capable and responsible. Her dark eyes flashed with intelligence and affection. I loved her deeply.

My father was quite different. A large, fair-skinned blond, he looked Russian to me, combining the bulk and bearing of a Viking with a good sense of humor and a gentle shyness that set him apart when he was not discussing his work. I think he was an engineer or mathematician. His keen, inquiring mind and strong deft hands filled me with a kind of awe and loving respect. Whatever happened, I knew I could count on him. It was a reassuring thought.

After listening for a few moments to these family reminiscences, Helen then returned me to my immediate surroundings by asking me about the landscape. Were there any trees nearby?

"It's like a brisk spring morning although fairly dry," I replied. "Yes, there are trees, mostly eucalyptus and several varieties of junipers and pines. Funny, now that you mention them to me," I said, "they all seem to have been planted within the last twenty to twenty-five years. I just know that trees didn't used to grow here and I don't see any really tall or old ones. There are a few young oaks; we consider them especially precious, a community resource."

As I answered Helen's questions I realized that wherever this community was, great changes in climate and plant life had occurred there a couple of generations ago. Many people had suffered but the Earth had survived. I found my attitude toward the past was curiously neutral. Whatever had happened seemed ancient history without any direct impact on me. Apparently even my parents had been born shortly after the "shift." We accepted things as somehow part of a larger plan of human self-development and spiritual progress. Life demanded effort but we were strong and organized and it seemed a good time to be alive. I was especially aware of our deep sense of community, as if each one lived in constant empathy with everyone else.

"You mentioned that you were with some other teenagers during school recreation." Helen's warm insistent voice broke into these thoughts. "Now I want you to move forward until you're learning something important as Mark. What are you doing? Where are you?"

Her questions brought me back to my immediate surroundings.

"I can see several large adjoining pyramidlike structures nearby," I replied as the scene came into focus. "I think they are classrooms. I know they are. We're learning to improve our telepathic communication skills; not just being in contact with each other here, that seems natural, but sending and receiving specific messages at a distance to other groups with whom we maintain contact. Something about the shape of those buildings and their copper roofs helps focus our thoughts and makes it easier.

"Yes, I've got the thought now. I'm living in a kind of scientific center, selecting and training volunteers for a telepathic communications project. The best of us are still teenagers, although there are a few older men and women with exceptional skills. Because this ability is still selective, one part of the project is to see if it can be enhanced by prenatal stimuli and special birth techniques. I think my parents and I are participants along with the other people born here. It seems very important to us, as if we are part of some special project that has spiritual as well as scientific significance. We're both a scientific and spiritual community."

At this point Helen decided to move me into early adulthood for a look at how my work, apparently an extension of what I'd seen myself beginning in the late 1990s as Chet Snow, was progressing. As we had earlier discussed the prospects of my being reunited with my "twin soul"* in this future lifetime, she then asked me a question that nearly jolted me out of trance since I was so torn as to how to answer her.

The subconscious mind is very literal, and when no one single answer fits all the "facts" it is experiencing, it puts nearly unbearable stress on the subject. Thus anyone working in altered states such as hypnosis must

---

* For both Helen Wambach and myself the term "twin soul" referred to that unique entity with whom one has always been linked since the instant of Creation. This special psychic bond lasts forever, whether the two "twins" are spending a specific physical lifetime together or not. This concept is different from "soul mates," who are kindred souls that frequently reincarnate together, often in close emotional relationships such as husband and wife or parent and child. Therefore it was our understanding that each individual has only *one* twin soul. This limiting concept, although apparently accurate heretofore, now caused confusion.

be extremely careful about the exact words they use when in dialogue with someone in trance. The best trance mediums or channels know this and thus frequently "filter" audience questions through a trusted friend or associate who rephrase them correctly. Helen was usually very sensitive about such things, but this time there was no way she could have foretold my reaction as I also was surprised at what I felt.

Although I wanted to answer Helen's question, in the way she put it, it had no single, unique answer. She had asked:

"Become vividly aware of your twin soul. . . . Now, is that soul with you there physically and if so what is your relationship with that soul?"

As I listened to her words I knew she was referring to someone I'd last known as "Louise" during an earlier past life (c. 1900) who had promised to reincarnate with me in the future. My conscious mind readily accepted that this entity was my twin soul. I knew that it had reincarnated and was sharing this future lifetime as my beloved partner once again.

However, and here was the problem, my subconscious mind now told me that as Mark, I was "twined" to another soul in a bond as tight and meaningful as that linking me with "Louise" but also different. It was a bond transcending physical boundaries, which seemed to extend forever. Yet, at the same time, it also felt very real and present in a material sense and for a moment the joy of what I felt as a long-sought "soul reunion" overwhelmed me emotionally. Again, mere words are inadequate to express what I was experiencing.

Thus I felt a "twin oneness" with two souls simultaneously! The conflict between my feelings and my conscious beliefs boggled my mind and almost precipitated me back to the "here and now." What was going on?

Helen sensed my distress as a tear (of joy) rolled down one cheek. She suggested I remember *vividly* what had flashed into consciousness and that everything would be "crystal clear" in an instant.

It was at that moment that I understood: The "scientific and spiritual project" Mark and his community were engaged in was nothing less than the preparation for and receiving of the return of the Christ into this world. And it was a success! We lived daily "in His presence," sending those waves of love and light telepathically around the planet to all who could and would receive them. The Christ was my other "twin soul"!

I am sorry to say that both words and ordinary "left-brain" logic fail to express my experience of the future-life presence of that twin soul. As Mark, I never "saw" any one individual man or woman among us that I could point out as being "the Christ." Yet Christ was there *in person* and not a mere psychically shared "consciousness." And there was nothing exclusive about that personal presence either. We were not some special, singled-out group of "privileged" people. Christ was not a specifically Jewish or Christian Messiah, nor even male nor female. Christ was universal.

There was no doubt of this universality to my future-life persona. The Christ's presence came to each in his or her own unique way, although it was also everywhere the same. If I have occasionally used the masculine pronoun "His" in this chapter, it is because to me, as Mark, that presence was male and, although I have tried to use gender-free language wherever possible, the neuter pronoun "Its" robs the experience of its essential human character. Thus I am convinced that some will see Jesus, others the Buddha, some Krishna, others the Mahdi and still others the "Goddess," but they will *all* be in the presence of the Christ. The only limitation on this experience is that imposed by our own right to refuse to acknowledge that presence. Thus, even in 2050 A.D., the Christ could appear only to those prepared to receive Him in whatever form is appropriate for them.

It was as if the Christ were suddenly personally present for whomever would allow that miraculous "soul reunion," that at-one-ment (atonement), to occur. Each individual experienced that presence as real and as material as his or her chosen mate or incarnate twin soul. It was undoubtedly slightly different for each one, but it was also everywhere the same presence, the same person. Somehow the Christ had become the twin soul of planet Earth. If there was anything "special" about our group, it was only that we had prepared for this eventuality and were consciously broadcasting the experience of being "in His presence" through our bodies and our minds. It was a responsibility and a gift we had accepted . . . joyously.

I've already said that words and ordinary logic cannot adequately express the experience that swept over me when my dear friend and mentor, Dr. Helen Wambach, suggested my thoughts and feelings would become "crystal clear." Edgar Cayce often suggested that the only way to resolve Earth's problems was for everyone to adopt the same "Ideal." That Ideal is the Christ, regardless of how we represent Him. Cayce then went on to say that we will each continue to have our own "ideas," that is, our own individual opinions and experiences, but when we subscribe to a common Ideal we are manifesting God's oneness in the Earth. This Second Coming of the Christ is the embodiment of that unitary Ideal. As such it transcended religious, ethnic or historical distinctions.

After reassuring me that I would remember my feelings about the emotional incident in detail (I found myself unable to describe the Christ's presence in words at that moment), Helen continued to progress me forward through Mark's twenty-first century lifetime. She asked me to go to any experience of "a bright light in the sky" that appeared meaningful. Instantly I moved forward to what I identified as the year 2067 A.D., although, as always, the exact timing of events by the nonconscious mind is the least reliable aspect of altered-states work. It was definitely *after* the Christ's return to Earth.

"I'm standing in a large field with over a hundred other people; I feel it is the biggest crowd I've ever seen. It's exciting but everyone is calm and looks happy. There's a hushed expectancy, as if we're waiting for something to happen. Now there's a bright light in the sky. It's moving closer at a tremendous rate of speed but in complete silence. I think it's going to land here."

"Now the aircraft has landed and you can get a better look at it. What does it look like? What's happening?"

"It doesn't exactly touch the ground but sort of hovers a few inches above the flattened grass without any obvious power source. It's clearly a very advanced spaceship. Its shape resembles the form of a flattened figure eight or connected ellipses. It's not terribly big, perhaps forty yards long and half again as wide. . . . Now a hatch is opening and figures appear. They look just like we do and are dressed in what seem to be shiny silver jumpsuits. They're people!"

Helen cut in at this point to instruct me further:

"Now move forward until the people in the ship are communicating with your group. What is their message?"

I hesitated a second to receive the communication and then I laughed out loud.

"They're saying, 'Congratulations . . . Welcome to the human race!' "

After a moment I went on to describe the scene. "Apparently this is just a small scout ship, as there seem to be only half a dozen or so of their people aboard. They tell us that they come from a star system identified as 'D-629,' according to their charts. I don't know which one it is as seen from Earth. My feeling is that it's from another galaxy, perhaps Andromeda. They can manipulate electromagnetic vibrations in some way and 'skip' across Space-Time. They're appearing at several Earth locations at the same time right now to invite Earth's humanity into their fellowship and help us clean up some areas of the planet where dangerous radioactivity was liberated during the earlier 'shift.' Several of our scientists seem particularly interested in helping with that cleanup.

"Some of our people will also accompany them back to their home system to learn interdimensional navigation techniques. It's all coordinated through the Christ, who is apparently also present with them, and I think that only those who perceive His presence here can see them. It's fascinating, but I know I'm not going with them as my telepathic communication work is here on Earth. I get the feeling that this is an incredible moment, one both they and we have been working for on nonphysical levels through many aeons of human historical Time. It's a celebration of life!"

"All right, now I want you to let yourself move forward again in that lifetime as Mark. . . . Go to any other particularly important time, anything that seems meaningful to you as Mark." Helen's calm tones brought me out of that happy throng around the spaceship and I felt myself searching for another key moment.

Once again I had the video recorder "fast forward" sensation of seeing a kaleidoscope of images flash rapidly before my eyes. I caught a clear glimpse of my other twin soul, whom I continue to think of as Louise. In this future life she appeared as a comely Eurasian woman with high cheekbones, dark, sparkling eyes and long black hair. Helen didn't ask me her name but it didn't matter. Our union seemed complete in that greater oneness of His presence, which filled our lives. I knew we had three children—two girls and a boy. All looked healthy and bright. I saw one as a teenager, the other two slightly younger.

"Space is their destiny," I whispered to myself as the scene changed. Somehow at that instant I knew that I was not going to see them grown up. A regretful thought flashed across my mind, only to be instantly replaced by the knowledge that this was our mutual choice. We were all souls who had shared many other human lifetimes together, learning and growing. Our love and communion were far greater than a mere physical presence together. For now, each of us had other projects to complete, other dimensions of life to explore. Such "ties that bind" congenial souls together are solid far beyond ordinary human comprehension.

After a few more such scenes flashed quickly by, I realized that one of the lessons Mark had learned was that *each* of life's moments is, in fact, a pivotal one. Living every day "in His presence" meant surrendering regrets from the past and fears of the future, existing totally in the present, what philosophers call the "Now," in complete trust and love. Of course we made plans and had jobs; of course we fondly remembered special occasions and departed friends. Such things are part of the normal course of living within the linear "illusion" of a cause-and-effect universe. But we did them because they gave pleasure and meaning to our physical journey through Time and Space, not out of fear, necessity or a sense of duty. It was all part of a grand design, part of the evolution of a Greater Being in whom we shared our existence.

After seeing a few more work scenes testing new mechanical and biochemical inventions designed to enhance human telepathic functions and a few family highlights, such as the day when my youngest daughter correctly "bounced" a message off a satellite relay, thereby sending it halfway around the world to another research group, I realized that this future life as Mark would shortly end. I told Helen that there were no other critical events to examine right now.

"All right, now I want you to go to the day that you die in that lifetime. You will feel no pain and have no fear. Go there, now!" Helen's instructions were clear and easy to follow.

Still looking remarkably young, I found myself, as Mark, consciously preparing for "the transition," as death was named by our people. Everyone in that community knew that life continues after this human phase and that separation is just another mutually shared illusion, like Space-Time itself. Nothing could ever separate those who had chosen to be united in the Christ. My work in this body was completed; I knew that my beloved would remain awhile until the children all left home as that was her choice. His promise had been fulfilled and I was ready to depart.

"It's fascinating," I said as I described the experience to Helen Wambach. "We have a lovely glassed-in garden that we call 'the preparation field' and that's where transitions take place. It's all planned and considered as sort of a celebration. Usually just one individual leaves at a time, although sometimes couples or groups choose to go together. In any case, it is a purely personal decision.

"Now it is time. I'm dressed in a soft white robe and sitting on a carved stone bench. I've already said good-bye to everyone important to me earlier. Of course Christ is still there beside me and I look deeply into those clear blue eyes that project love across so many dimensions and contain so many memories. He smiles and nods, almost conspiratorially, as we share a last breath of air together. And that's it. My body simply disintegrates into a rather small heap and I am free. I feel an instant's amazement that my physical body reduces down to so small a dust pile and just a bit of curiosity about what my children will accomplish but that's all. Enfolded in a warm, bright light, I know that I remain 'in His presence' no matter where I am."

As soon as she felt that I had eased out of Mark's body, Helen posed the two questions she always asked her research subjects: "Look down at the Earth and let the name of the location where you lived that lifetime come into your mind" and "What was the year of your death?"

Instantly the numbers "2091" flashed across my mind and I knew that was the year Mark would make his transition. The geographical "fix" took a bit longer. I saw a big blue-green ball floating below me and knew it was the Earth. As I watched it turn, the "top" of the world, the Arctic Ocean surrounded by Canada and Siberia, appeared. At first it was mostly white, covered with an ice cap and clouds. Then slowly the ocean turned a deep blue and the Siberian land mass became a mottled green-brown as it moved about halfway "down" toward the equator. I realized I was watching the predicted "shifting of the poles." Islands appeared off the north Russian coast and I heard the words "Novaya Zemlya" pronounced distinctly in my ear in a strange accent. That was where Mark would live.

As soon as I pronounced those words, which had no meaning to my conscious mind, Helen began the process of returning my awareness totally to the "here and now" reality of Pinole, California, in December 1984. As with our earlier future-life progressions, she suggested my experience would resemble a "vivid dream" that would not unduly affect me emotionally. Of course, this life had been so much more fulfilling and pleasant than our earlier forays ahead in linear Time that I was almost euphoric when fully conscious once again.

Among my first thoughts, however, was to look up that strange name I had so clearly heard at the end of the session in a geographical dictionary. What I found nearly "blew me away," as they say. It seems that Novaya Zemlya (or Nova Zembla) is an archipelago of two large islands (35,000 square miles) in the Arctic Ocean off the north coast of the Soviet Union, to which they currently belong. Today largely frozen tundra, they are noted as being the site of the U.S.S.R.'s main underground nuclear test center!

"Omigod," I thought, "does that mean I'm slated to return on top of a former nuclear weapons test site? Could that explain the scientific character of our community, its survival of the 'shift' relatively intact and unusual mix of Eurasian races I noticed there? But a spiritual center in Siberia and the return of the Christ to a former nuclear weapons depot?" Again, conventional wisdom and ordinary logic seem inadequate to deal with the possibility. No wonder the scientists in "Mark's community" were so concerned with "cleaning up" the planet's nuclear waste problem, as proposed by the UFO's astronauts!

I remain puzzled by this aspect of the experience but can only report what I "saw" and "heard" during the session. I know that until that day at the end of 1984, "Novaya Zemlya" meant nothing to my conscious awareness. As for its ultimate meaning in my next Earth incarnation, that is up to the future to reveal.

✳   ✳   ✳

Despite my mixed feelings about foreseeing a future life set amid what was once a nuclear weapons underground test site, the experience proved quite thought-provoking. In looking back over those session notes, made several years ago, I understand that even that small detail reveals the primary theme of this entire look at our current "mass dreams of the future." That theme is "choice" or "decision."

As I have remarked earlier in this book, natural forces such as the splitting of the atom are morally neutral by themselves. They are simply aspects of the unified, creating force we know as the "Whole," "God," "Goddess" or "All That Is." It is our individual and collective human choices that determine whether atoms are split inside thermonuclear bombs, dangerously waste-producing nuclear power plants or radioactive isotopes that kill cancer cells. It is our human choices that create ethical distinctions among such activities, all of which depend on the same neutral factors. Similarly, it may be that at some future date the scientific knowledge and physical isolation that were combined to create the Novaya Zemlya test center will serve humanity instead of threatening it with mass destruction.

As human beings we live and move through a Space-Time universe whose primary function is providing opportunities for choice. The New Physics of quantum mechanics demonstrates that the aspect of the material world we choose to observe actually influences the basic nature of the reality we experience. Psychology teaches that choice, as opposed to instinct, is a uniquely human characteristic. It is a function of what we call "the Will," or "willpower." Philosophy and religion relate our choices to moral responsibilities, assigning them either "good" or "bad" consequences. If we live in a morally accountable world, it is our daily decisions of what we do and why we do it that determine how, where and when we must pay our mutual debts.

Learning to choose wisely between competing alternatives forms the basis for education in human systems as long as they exist within the bounds of linear Time. The age-old Law of Cause and Effect, also known as Karma, illustrates this educational function of Space-Time existence. Whether we choose to accept the concept of having many lifetimes to perfect our knowledge of "All That Is" or believe we must cram every-thing into one physical incarnation, we all must live with the consequences of our actions across linear Time while in human form. We *need Time's buffer* between what our ever-active minds conceive and experiencing the results of our mental decisions. Life would be chaos if our every thought produced an immediate response!

Let us look at a very basic example—learning to walk. For most healthy adults, walking is a "natural" function. Normally we pay little attention to how we do it. Our conscious minds assume we can walk, and when we so choose, we simply take a step and go. It has become a habit pattern. For most of us the conscious mind has turned over the choices involved in walking to the subconscious, which deals with repetitive ac-tivity, including breathing, digestion and circulation. Who thinks of such things very often? And yet physical health depends on their proper func-tioning!

However, for a baby the art of walking must be learned. Such learn-ing is always a time-consuming process, involving making choices and suffering their consequences. At first the little one must think consciously before choosing how to make every step. Each wrong decision has painful results, such as stubbed toes or a fall. In learning to walk, these conse-quences usually occur quickly and their relation to the "wrong" decision is obvious. This speeds the learning process. Therefore, after a few stubbed toes, etc., most babies learn to pick up and coordinate their feet while attempting to walk. Eventually, after surviving the painful results of many "bad" choices, making the correct ones that lead to walking becomes a habit. The child has used linear Time to learn.

The Ageless Wisdom philosophy, modern channels like Edgar Cayce and discarnate intelligences such as "Seth" and "Lazaris" all tell us that we incarnate on Earth because we need linear Time's educational qual-ities. We are here to learn from experiences that are designed to make us better co-creators of new and exciting realities within All That Is or God. Regardless of whether we believe in a prehistoric "fall from grace," or that this is a self-imposed experiment, it's clear that making choices and learning from their results is critical to our development in this Space-Time universe. As long as we exist here we cannot avoid making choices and reaping the consequences.

Furthermore, according to ancient teachings and traditions from around the world, we are now approaching a special time of critical choices whose consequences will have widespread and lasting influences on human his-tory. Conditions within our linear Time line must and will change soon.

The collective psychic energies pushing for change have already become irresistible. Like a fetus nearing its term, in our deepest selves we feel the approaching birth pangs even though we still cling to our warm, dark and familiar womb. Whether we ascribe the coming changes to ecological imbalances, socioeconomic inequities, astrological cycles, UFOs or the Will of God matters less than our recognition that the first contractions of a new birth have already begun.

What remains to be seen is how this dynamic for change will be channeled and what kinds of changes will occur. The future-life progressions begun by Dr. Helen Wambach and discussed in Chapters 5 to 8 provide a glimpse of some of the prevailing alternative archetypes of our future, at least for contemporary Americans. These stories, coming largely from the subconscious mind during dreamlike reveries, illustrate a framework of common expectations already deeply embedded in the collective subconscious of today's world. They confirm our inner conviction that significant changes are about to take place. In large measure they also reaffirm ancient and modern predictions of widespread natural and man-made catastrophes just around the corner.

However, these contemporary visions, including my own progressions, also assure us that there will be a future for the human race and that the much-touted nuclear threat is less likely to destroy civilization than continuing global ecological irresponsibility. Finally, these "mass dreams of the future" hold out the promise that, despite severe losses, humanity can and will replenish "Spaceship Earth" (albeit with some help!) and eventually claim our heritage among the stars.

The sources of such archetypical visions are many and varied. They have entered our subconscious through religious writings and prophetic traditions, from a common genetic inheritance as descendants of the survivors of some prehistoric cataclysm we call the Great Flood and via reincarnational memories of previous lifetimes. Many alive today carry the anguish of lost Atlantis's last hours deep in their subconscious minds. We have also been influenced by supernatural interventions such as the appearances of the Virgin Mary at Fatima and Medjugorje, by psychic predictors from Nostradamus to contemporary channels like Edgar Cayce and Jach Pursel ("Lazaris") and by phenomena like NDEs, UFOs and OBEs, which cannot be explained by ordinary physical causes. All these sources converge to form our current "mass dreams" of the road ahead.

Today we are faced with two distinct and fundamental models for the upcoming changes, which have been so widely foreseen that they already possess tremendous dynamic psychic energy. We have been warned by prophets and supernatural appearances of the Virgin Mary that what happens in the future is largely conditional on our current attitudes and actions. Thus our individual and collective choices over the next several years will, to a great extent, decide which of these two alternative models will most influence the coming birth of the New Age, astrologically known as the Age of Aquarius.

The first model is the one we commonly call the Apocalypse. It is humanity's traditional revolutionary archetype and has been widely predicted for the end of this twentieth century A.D. by many prophets across the ages. One distinctive feature of the Judeo-Christian-Moslem version is that our Apocalypse is considered to be a once-only "End" to linear Time and history. Non-Western Apocalypses, such as the Hindu Age of Kali, are based on cyclical Time and therefore are seen as necessary, periodic cleansings or renewals. They thus provoke a less despairing reaction than the Judeo-Christian-Moslem "one and only" catastrophic model.

The Apocalyptic archetype involves an interplay of force, resistance, conflict and destruction. If the force is particularly dynamic and the resistance especially widespread, then the conflict is correspondingly great and immense destruction results. As noted above, our Western model is particularly violent because it is a one-time purge of all human shortcomings provoked by the ultimate dynamic force known as God. The resulting consequences are also especially important, for nothing less than the ultimate triumph of Good over Evil is predicted. We expect Heaven on Earth to follow our passage through Hell.

Moreover, our Western Apocalyptic concept of a radical "all or nothing" change has gathered psychic force within the collective unconscious of humanity as its unfolding has been announced and then rescheduled by succeeding generations of prophets for several thousand years. Thus it is hardly surprising that it both fascinates and terrorizes us. This is particularly true today, when several natural and cultural Time cycles appear to be culminating together. The best known of these include the Christian millennium (2000 A.D.), the Age of Aquarius (2011 A.D.), geometric analysis of the Great Pyramid (2010 A.D.), the twilight of the Hindu *Kali Yuga* (1939 A.D., plus or minus fifty years), the Aztec and Mayan cycle (2012 A.D.), and the Hopi "Great Purification" (post-atom bomb, 1945 and after). To these should be added Nostradamus's prediction of a 1999 A.D. disaster and Edgar Cayce's mention of 1998–2000 A.D. as a potential pole shift, for both have had widespread impact.

Although we tend to be "culturally hypnotized" by powerful, global psychic archetypes such as the Apocalypse, with its tremendous dynamic of fear and attraction, it does not represent the only vision of our planetary future. The arrival of the alternative archetype has not been so explicitly prophesied across the ages but it is nonetheless growing as a model in human consciousness today. This alternative is humanity's ancient dream of mass cooperation, initiation and rebirth. It is the extension of the Christ spirit across the planet so that the Earth itself takes on a unified planetary identity (Gaia).

Spiritual sources throughout history have reminded us time and again that despite our seeming separateness, all beings, indeed all of creation, stem from a single, common Source. Our physical existence within the Space-Time universe has as its ultimate goal a complete and perfect self-reunion within that Source, enhanced and glorified by what we have experienced here. Ageless Wisdom's eternal promise is that this reunion must and will occur for, at some level beyond material Space-Time reality, it already is. The greater all-encompassing Whole is forever one and indivisible.

Nonetheless, as loved co-creators of All That Is, we retain the individual free will to advance or retard this reunion within our awareness. Thus, although Unity's ultimate realization is already set, the type and quality of process used to make it happen depends on our individual and collective choices. Somehow, for whatever reasons, it has been our choice to experience this temporary separation from Universal Consciousness, this cosmic amnesia. Enlightenment is recognizing our real self within everything and everybody else, at all levels of existence. How and when we finally remember our multidimensional nature is up to us. When we can be one with the Whole and yet retain self-awareness, then we add to Universal Mind and accomplish the purpose of being.

As discussed in Chapter 4, "Channeling the Future Today," achieving this complete self-reunion takes discipline or willpower. Like learning how to walk, before discipline can become a subconscious habit it must be learned by making repeated choices and suffering occasional "stubbed toes." Psychiatrist M. Scott Peck's best-seller *The Road Less Traveled* points out that it is, however, the only sure path to lasting spiritual growth, just as attaining planetary consciousness is the only sure way to avoid the Apocalypse. Divine grace, like "His presence," appears only after we have exerted our willpower and chosen to accept it into our lives.

Edgar Cayce's psychic readings, one of the purest spiritual channelings of recent times, insist that "consistency and persistency" are required for success at any endeavor. Cayce asserts that the most fundamental "sin" (a choice that separates us from God and from our true identity) is that of selfishness. It is choosing to follow the ego or lower self's limiting, Time-bound desires (including the desire to be right regardless of the consequences!) instead of extending our awareness beyond immediate self-gratification and seeing our true multidimensional role within the greater Whole of All That Is.

Attuning our Will to that Higher Power brings us the ability, and joy, of unconditional love. For, as Cayce often reminded those who sought his assistance, "like attracts like." Thus if you want to be loved, you must first act lovingly toward others and yourself. If we want world cooperation and peace instead of competition and violence, we likewise must internalize these virtues in ourselves and act accordingly in our current relationships, right where we are today. New Age author and "inner-space" explorer Catherine Ann Lake, whom I first met at Robert Monroe's Gateway Experience in 1986, has written a touching personal account of how getting in contact with her Higher Self and like-minded searchers transformed her life. Specific suggestions in her book *Linking Up: How the People in Your Life Are Roadsigns to Self-Discovery*, may help you get started on your own spiritual quest.[1]

When we move beyond egoistic pride and desire, we are ready and able to cooperate with others to find mutually acceptable solutions to current problems. As we set self aside more and more, seeking to serve a greater good, we naturally raise our spiritual energy level. Our very cells begin to vibrate more rapidly and we reestablish contact with the sense of wonder and love we hold inside our "child within." Paradoxically, only by dying to selfish desires do we attain the true spirit of eternal life, which is actually all around us right now if we would only realize it! It is this spirit, which we can manifest right here as bioelectrical energy within our physical bodies, to which New Age teacher Chris Griscom calls us in her recent pithy treatise *Ecstasy Is a New Frequency*. It is this spirit that acknowledges the Christ ("the Anointed One") within each human soul.[2]

This is why I personally feel that one of the most important groups in the world right now is the Planetary Commission, the ad hoc collection of millions of individuals around the world who have agreed to spend the hour of noon to 1:00 P.M., Greenwich mean time, each December 31, united in prayer and meditation around the theme of world peace and healing. Begun in December 1986, this movement has the potential to raise Earth's bioenergetic vibrational field if enough people from all races, creeds and nations can set aside their differences for that hour and concentrate on visualizing our Earth as a united, healthy and peaceful whole. Along with the Harmonic Convergence celebrations, the December 31 Annual World Healing Day represents a hope that we still have time to break free from our suspicious, limiting egocentric belief systems and avert an Apocalypse already looming on the horizon within the world's collective subconscious.*

Among the many recent psychic channelings inviting us to lower our ego barriers and assume our true loving human nature, those by former postal employee turned New Age farmer, Ken Carey, stand out for their poetic beauty and call to worldwide cooperative transformation. In his books *The Starseed Transmissions* and *Vision*, Carey presents a sweeping view of human evolution. We are told that the stage has now been set for the "emergence of the Planetary Being" here on Earth and that we are called to participate in its destiny.

Poetically evoking a process similar to "Lazaris's" theory that we are continually influenced by future choices (see Chapter 9), Carey asserts that "islands of love and harmony" from the future are already forming among today's human communities. These beacons of love and cooperation are helping overcome the majority's destructive anger and fear. A Divinely inspired transition period of the next thirty years, *culminating in 2011 A.D.*, is predicted.

During these critical decades most of humanity will recognize untapped levels of creative potential. We will recognize our status as living cells of the one Divine Body and understand that individual differences need to be understood in that light. Each cell contains the life essence of the Whole. They cooperate instead of competing. Liver cells do not fear or envy brain cells, for example. Further, even though individual cells die and are replaced, the identity and destiny of the overall Being remains stable.

Ken Carey foresees this panorama of human transformation unfolding in three phases. Currently we are living through what he calls the "Period of Individual Awakening," or changeover from competition and

---

*For further information about the Planetary Commission and how to participate in upcoming annual December 31 events, please contact the Quartus Foundation, P.O. Box 1768, Boerne, TX 78006-6768. Over a billion people were estimated to have participated on December 31, 1988. The 1989 celebration promises to be even larger as José Arguelles and other Harmonic Convergence activists have joined in a call to our "Space Brothers" to come down and help us clean up Earth's polluted environment. See chapter 10, note 5.

fear to cooperation and love. This is necessary for us to adjust to the Earth's changing energies. Only those who attune to these higher vibrations will be able to continue living here. This phase will be followed by a thousand-year "Period of Planetary Awakening" as all Earth's life forms cooperate in creating a planetary Christ consciousness. Finally, after the planet itself is transformed, we will participate in an "Age of Discovery," seeding ourselves among the stars.

Thus, according to both ancient prophetic traditions and contemporary channels like Cayce and Carey, a transformed world of tomorrow is rapidly heading our way. How we meet it, through Apocalypse or Awakening, depends on the choices we make today. What, then, can we do to foster the brighter alternative? Again, Ageless Wisdom as expressed through Edgar Cayce asserts that "Mind is the builder"—we become what we believe.

Beliefs are a product of the interplay of both subconscious habit patterns, developed from many life experiences, and the conscious decisions of the Will. Our culture's current beliefs are steering us toward an Apocalyptic solution to the world's grave problems. Therefore only a sustained effort of collective willpower and individual self-transformation is going to stem that tide and turn us toward the kind of Planetary Awakening described by Ken Carey and others.

But the conscious mind cannot bear the burden alone. It simply is not strong enough. We need to avoid the "New Age machismo" kind of pride which insists that one's conscious thoughts are responsible for every success and guilty of every failure or disease. We must also tap the limitless potential of the subconscious, acknowledging (to ourselves, at least) our negative hidden agendas stemming from fear and selfish desire. Get in touch with your inner past if you wish to change your outer future. This begins the cleansing process.

Many paths lead inward. The best known include introspective prayer and meditation, past-life therapy, yoga, dream interpretation, Dr. Stanislav Grof's "holotropic therapy," the Silva Method and Robert Monroe's Gateway Experience. Local study groups such as the A.R.E.'s "Search for God" groups, "A Course in Miracles" groups or even a weekly church prayer circle can provide a framework within which to start. Choose one that appeals to you *from your current perspective* and begin there. The exact nature of your initial exploration is far less important than your commitment to start *now*. I have tried all of the above-mentioned approaches and found each one helpful at different times. For those interested in my current method, I have prepared an experiential cassette tape, independent of this book, designed to help initiate an internal self-dialogue and attunement with one's inner creative forces.*

Further, once we begin to look within, we must then replace our outmoded negative programming with the most positive spiritual Ideal that we can currently conceive. Let that Ideal become a pattern on which to base daily decisions. Make it personal and real in your life. Meditate on it and pray for guidance. Opening the powers of our inner minds without a spiritual Ideal is foolhardy and, as in Jesus's parable of the man who was exorcised of one "unclean spirit" only to have seven more vile entities possess him, may leave us vulnerable to even worse influences than we knew heretofore (see Luke 11: 24–26).

As we begin to acknowledge who we really are and follow a spiritual growth pattern in our day-to-day activities, two things usually happen, often simultaneously or nearly so. The first is encountering an unimagined amount of resistance, both from within and from so-called unrelated exterior circumstances. It takes time to break established habit patterns, and our restless minds, like rivers, often seek their old, familiar channels. They test our willpower.

Beginning meditators, for example, are often frustrated as all kinds of forgotten conscious thoughts initially interfere with the process of "stilling" outer awareness so as to focus on what lies within. The practice of maintaining a routine of fifteen minutes of meditation at the same time daily often helps. Also, don't hesitate to seek assistance from like-minded friends or small spiritual groups. As for those "external hindrances," a new job to do, an unexpected visit or phone call, etc., these are also part of your own mental resistance! Your inventive inner mind calls them to you to test your resolve. There is no better test of one's new resolutions than to have to choose between them and old priorities!

The second result of beginning this "inner awakening" is more subtle at first. Ultimately, however, it is far more powerful than the resistances described above if we maintain our resolve to change. This is the slow but sure altering of reactions to problems, emotional attitudes and even physical cravings as our bodies and minds adjust to the spiritual growth we have set in motion. Moreover, even though specific results may take time to materialize, spiritual growth begins internally from the moment we set a better course of action and begin to follow it.

Although I am far from a paragon of spiritual development (believe

---

* Available c/o Dr. Chet B. Snow at P.O. Box 4452, Bluejay, CA 92317, U.S.A.

me!), I remember that when I began my own journey toward self-awareness, initially everything in my life became more difficult. Then, slowly,
almost imperceptibly, I began to "catch myself" in the process of reacting
when my old emotional "buttons" were pushed. And I am a rather emotional person! Often the old negative reaction would erupt before that
"still, small voice" reminded me of what was really going on. That still
happens sometimes! But more and more frequently I found myself stop-
ping in mid-reaction and realizing how I was replaying "old tapes" instead
of employing my new awareness. I was then faced with a conscious choice.
Would I apply my self-determined Ideal or remain stuck in my past?

I'd be dishonest if I said I've always made the right decision, even
today; some old patterns are very stubborn. I still need linear Time's
buffer between my first thought and what I ultimately choose to do. But
now it has become unusual for me to react blindly. The same kind of
change has taken place in other areas of my life, such as eating habits.
I love to eat flavorful foods; it is one of physical life's greater pleasures!
Raised in a traditional middle-class American home, meat was a staple
of my diet for decades. I've now become about 80 percent vegetarian,
however, entirely naturally, by my body's choice. Those are the foods
my body now tends to desire. Perhaps in the future meat won't appeal
to me anymore at all, but for today I still love an occasional leg of lamb
or roast turkey dinner, and that's fine too! My priority is to be aware of
what I need within (as opposed to what my ego desires) and then to act
on that knowledge.

Even though it may take months or even years to achieve an "inner
knowing" that real change has occurred, any effort made in this direction
helps provide a basis for future spiritual progress. Such progress is apparently carried within the soul from one physical lifetime to another,
although without activation of the conscious Will it can lie dormant for
years. Moreover, because our being is multidimensional, existing outside
Space-Time, what appears as our "past" from the current personality's
perspective may not yet have been added to our soul's repertory. Similarly, the "future" we now perceive may have already been lived before.
If Einstein is right, that's how it would appear to an Alpha Centaurian!
This is why all comparisons of the soul's spiritual "progress" along a
strictly linear Time line are merely superficial. The underlying All That
Is reality exists in a Timeless present, accessible only to the deepest
levels of our minds, but it is the natural home of our souls.

Nonetheless, difficult as this concept is for the conscious mind to
grasp, "consistency and persistency" in whatever spiritual practice best

meets one's individual needs always brings us closer to the ultimate self-reunion that is our birthright and life's final goal. It is only then that we can wake up from our ageless dream and claim past, present and future as one and the same experience. This knowledge, as old as Creation itself, has perhaps been put best by the ancient Oriental masters, one of whom expressed it in a venerable poem I have chosen as a fitting conclusion to this discussion of "mass dreams" about our planetary future, because for the wise man or woman, the future, like the past, is only accessible through the soul's infinite "Now," whose full emptiness calls us into quiet joy.[3]

EMPTY INFINITY

Without beginning, without end,
Without past, without future.
A halo of light surrounds the world of law.
We forget one another, quiet and pure,
altogether powerful and empty.

The emptiness is irradiated by the light
of the heart and of heaven.
The water of the sea is smooth
and mirrors the moon in its surface.
The clouds disappear in blue space;
the mountains shine clear.
Consciousness reverts to contemplation;
the moon disk rests alone.

NOTES

CHAPTER 2
Past-Life Regression to Future-Life Progression

1. Jeffrey Mishlove, *The Roots of Consciousness*, Bookworks, New York, and Random House, Berkeley, 1975, pp. 225–28, provides an excellent discussion of Kirlian photography and Dr. Moss's experiments. See also Stanley Krippner and Daniel Rubin, eds., *The Kirlian Aura*, Doubleday & Co., Garden City, N.Y., 1974.

2. William K. Stevens, "Life in the Stone Age: New Findings Point to Complex Societies," *The New York Times*, Dec. 20, 1988, p. C-1.

3. Viola Petitt Neal and Shafica Karagulla, *Through the Curtain*, DeVorss & Co., Marina Del Rey, Calif., 1983, pp. 275–76. Quoted material is reprinted by permission of the publisher.

4. See Chapters 4 and 11 for additional material on "Seth" and *The Starseed Transmissions*, respectively. Ken Carey, *The Starseed Transmissions*, Uni Sun (P.O. Box 25421, Kansas City, MO 64119), 1982.

CHAPTER 3
Hunting for the Future, An Ancient Tradition

1. David Wallechinsky, Ann Wallace and Irving Wallace, *The Book of Predictions*, William Morrow and Co., Inc., New York, 1980, pp. 381–82. Also, Renée Paule Guillot, "Les Oracles de l'Antiquité," pp. 28–33, *Historia*, No. 397, bis, Paris, 1979.

2. Michael Damien and Charles Hirsch, *La Crainte de l'An 2000*, Editions Seghers, Paris, 1979, p. 206.

3. John Mitchell, *The New View Over Atlantis*, Harper & Row, San Francisco, 1983, pp. 127–31 (first published, 1969).

4. Manly P. Hall, *The Secret Teachings of all Ages*, The Philosophical Research Society, Inc., Los Angeles, 1977, pp. 53–56 (reprint of the original 1928 edition).

5. André Barbault, *Petit Manuel d'Astrologie*, Editions du Seuil, Paris, 1972, pp. 8–14.

6. Dane Rudhyar, *Occult Preparations for a New Age*, The Theosophical Publishing House, Wheaton, Ill., 1975, pp. 131, 280–82. The sum of the diagonals of the base of the Great Pyramid equals 25,826.4 "pyramid inches"; the Pyramid's geometry correctly identifies many celestial and terrestrial cycles. See Peter Lemesurier, *The Great Pyramid Decoded*, Element Books, Longmead, U.K., 1977, Appendix B, p. 309.

7. Manly P. Hall, *op. cit.*, p. 54.

8. Norman Lockyear, *The Dawn of Astronomy*, Macmillan and Co., New York and London, 1894, p. 146; William R. Fix, *Star Maps*, London, Octopus Books, 1979, pp. 61–62.

9. Manly P. Hall, *op. cit.*, pp. 55–56.

10. Dane Rudhyar, *op. cit.*, p. 132; Hades, *L'Astrologie et le Destin de l'Occident*, Editions Robert Laffont, Paris, 1971; Daniel Ruzo, *Les Derniers Jours de l'Apocalypse*, Payot, Paris, 1973, p. 210; personal conversation with Pierre Lassalle, French astrologer and author (*L'Astrologie Holistique*, Paris, 1987), June 1988.

11. Peter Lemesurier, *op. cit.*, p. 138.

12. Greta Woodrew, *On a Slide of Light*, Macmillan Publishing Co., New York, 1981, pp. 87–88; also Charles Berlitz, *Doomsday: 1999 A.D.*, Doubleday & Co., Garden City, N.Y., 1981, pp. 168ff.

13. Frank Waters, *Book of the Hopi*, Ballantine Books, New York, 1963.

14. See Viola Petitt Neal and Shafica Karagulla, *Through the Curtain*, De Vorss and Co., Marina Del Rey, Calif., 1983, pp. 273–76 for a good discussion of the new energies said to be entering the Earth today.

15. Sun Bear, Wabun and the Bear Tribe, *The Bear Tribe's Self Reliance Book*, Bear Tribe Publishing, Spokane, Wash., 1977; see also, "Earth Changes Essential for Cleansing," by Sun Bear in *Venture Inward*, Vol. 4, No. 3, May/June 1988, pp. 12–17. (*Venture Inward* is published by the A.R.E.).

16. Frank Waters, *op. cit.*

17. The Bear Tribe, P.O. Box 9167, Spokane, WA 99209.

18. Sun Bear, Wabun and the Bear Tribe, *op. cit.*

19. Kristina Gale-Kumar, *The Phoenix Returns*, Cardinal Enterprises, Hilo, Hawaii, 1983, p. 203.

20. Page Bryant, *The Earth Changes Survival Handbook*, Sun Books, Santa Fe, N.M., 1983, pp. 226–36.

21. Frank Waters, *op. cit.*; Sun Bear, Wabun and the Bear Tribe, *op. cit.* Also, Maurice Chatelain, *La Fin du Monde*, Editions du Rocher, Monaco, 1961, p. 22. Chatelain was a former NASA engineer.

22. Henry H. Halley, *Halley's Bible Handbook*, Zondervan Publishing House, Grand Rapids, Mich., 24th edition, 1965; pp. 75–80 (first published 1927), discusses archaeology and the dating of the Deluge; see also, Zecharia Sitchin, *The Twelfth Planet*, Avon Books, New York, 1978, pp. 388, 409 (first published 1976 by Stein & Day Publishers).

23. Zecharia Sitchin, *The Twelfth Planet*, p. 401; also R. W. Fairbridge, "The Changing Level of the Sea," *Scientific American*, Vol. 202, No. 5, May 1960, discusses the rise of the oceans between 15,000 and 3000 B.C.

24. Sitchin, *The Twelfth Planet*, pp. 21ff.

25. *Ibid.*, pp. 188–90.

26. *Ibid.*, p. 197.

27. *Ibid.*, p. 400 (emphasis added).

28. *Ibid.*, pp. 390–97.

29. *Ibid.*, pp. 248–53 on Sumerian kings; Zechariah Sitchin, *The Wars of Gods and Men*, Avon Books, New York, 1985, pp. 33–35, on Egyptian god/kings; also Henry H. Halley, *op. cit.*, pp. 71–72.

30. All Biblical passages quoted in this book are from the Revised Standard Version Bible, copyright 1946, 1952, 1971 by the Division of Christian Education of the National Council of Churches of Christ in the U.S.A., and are used by permission.

31. Sitchin, *The Twelfth Planet*, pp. 395–96.

32. Henry Halley, *op. cit.*, p. 75, mentions various ancient flood legends; Charles Berlitz, *op. cit.*, pp. 146 ff., provides an extensive list.

33. Sitchin, *The Twelfth Planet*, p. 402.

34. *Ibid.*, p. 409. Evidence of past magnetic reversals is discussed in N. A. Morner, *et al.*, *the New Scientist*, Jan. 6, 1972, p. 7.

35. Sitchin, *The Twelfth Planet*, p. 409.

36. "Uranus Is Perturbed," *Discover*, Sept. 1987, p. 16.

37. David M. Raup, *The Nemesis Affair: A Story of the Death of Dinosaurs and the Ways of Science*, W.W. Norton & Co., New York, 1987.

38. John White, *Pole Shift*, A.R.E. Press, 1983, Virginia Beach, Va. (first published by Doubleday & Co., 1980).

39. Charles Berlitz, *op. cit.*, p. 169.

40. Roland Benevides, *Dramatic Prophecies of the Great Pyramid*, Editores Mexicanos Unidos, Mexico, 1969; David Wallechinsky, *et al.*, *op. cit.*, pp. 340–41.

41. Peter Lemesurier, *The Great Pyramid Decoded*, Element Books, Longmead, U.K., 1977.

42. *Ibid.*, pp. 135, 169–70, 178–81.

43. *Ibid.*, pp. 225ff.

44. *Ibid.*, pp. 279–80. The Swedish research by N.A. Morner, J.P. Laespers and J. Hospers appeared in *The New Scientist*, January 6, 1972, p. 7.

CHAPTER 4
"Channeling" the Future Today: The "Ageless Wisdom" and Edgar Cayce

1. Raymond Moody, M.D., *Life After Life*, Mockingbird Books, Atlanta, 1975.

2. Karliss Osis, M.D., and E. Haraldson, M.D., *At The Hour of Death*, Avon Books, New York, 1977; Kenneth Ring, Ph.D., *Heading Towards Omega*, Morrow & Co., New York, 1984.

3. Jon Klimo, *Channeling*, Jeremy P. Tarcher, Los Angeles, 1987, p. 3.

4. *Ibid.*

5. Alice A. Bailey, *Prophecies by D.K.*, compiled by Aart Jurriaanse, World Unity & Service, Inc., Craighall, South Africa, 1977.

6. Anon., *A Course in Miracles*, The Foundation for Inner Peace, Tiburon, Calif., 1975.

7. M. Scott Peck, M.D., *The Road Less Traveled*, Simon & Schuster, New York, 1978.

8. Thomas Sugrue, *There is a River*, Holt, Rinehart & Winston, New York, 1942; Dell paperback edition, New York, 1967; Jess Stearn, *Edgar Cayce, the Sleeping Prophet*, Bantam Books, New York, 1967.

9. Lytle W. Robinson, *Is It True What They Say About Edgar Cayce?*, Vulcan Books, Seattle, 1979.

10. Jeffrey Goodman, Ph.D., *We Are the Earthquake Generation*, Seaviewbooks, New York, 1978; Berkley Books, paperback edition, 1979.

11. Mark A. Thurston, *Visions and Prophecies for a New Age*, A.R.E. Press, Virginia Beach, Va., 1981, pp. 12–13.

12. *Ibid.*, p. 12.

CHAPTER 5
Mass Dreams of 2100–2200 A.D., Part I: Life in Space and a Budding New Age

1. *The Journal of Regression Therapy*, Vol. I, No. 1, Spring 1986, is available through the Association for Past Life Research and Therapy, P.O. Box 20151, Riverside, CA 92516.

2. World Resources Institute/International Institute for Environment and Development, *World Resources 1986*, Basic Books, New York, 1986.

CHAPTER 6
Mass Dreams of 2100–2200 A.D., Part II: Hi-Tech Cities and Primitive Survivors

1. George Gedda, "U.S. Space Station," Associated Press release, Washington, D.C., Sept. 30, 1988.

2. Information about Dr. Verna Yater's trance channeling and Blue Mountain is available through the Blue Mountain Center, 2250 Little Turkey Creek Road, Colorado Springs, CO 80919, and from the Spiritual Sciences Institute, P.O. Box 22714, Santa Barbara, CA 93121.

3. World Commission on Environment and Development, *Our Common Future*, Oxford University Press, Oxford, England, and New York, 1987.

4. Cited in "Greenhouse Peril in the 1990's," *The San Francisco Chronicle*, Oct. 18, 1983, p. 1; see also, "The Heat is on," *Time* magazine, Oct. 19, 1987; and Philip Shabecoff, "Major Greenhouse Impact Is Unavoidable, Experts say," *The New York Times*, July 19, 1988, p. C-1.

5. Janine Delaunay, *Halte à la Croissance?*, Editions Fayard, Paris, 1974.

CHAPTER 8
Mass Dreams of 2300 A.D. and Beyond, Part II: Operation Terra

1. Jeffrey Goodman, Ph.D., *We Are the Earthquake Generation*, Berkley Books, New York, 1979, p. 191.

2. From Stanley Krippner's anthology, *Galaxies of Life*, cited in Sheila Ostrander and Lynn Schroeder, *The E.S.P. Papers*, Bantam Books, New York, 1976, pp. 174–75.

3. Jeffrey Goodman, *op. cit.*, pp. 243–49.

4. Elaine and Arthur Aron, *The Maharishi Effect: A Revolution Through Meditation*, Stillpoint, Walpole, N.H., 1986.

5. *Ibid.*

CHAPTER 9
Is the Future Already Past? "New Age" Physics and the Holographic Universe

1. For thorough discussions of the background of the "New Physics" in laymen's terms, see Fred Alan Wolf, *Taking the Quantum Leap*, Harper & Row, New York, 1981; and Paul Davies, *Other Worlds*, Simon & Schuster, New York, 1980. I am indebted to their outstanding explanations of such challenging concepts to people like me whose mathematical abilities are limited!

2. Fred A. Wolf, *op. cit.*, pp. 45–46.

3. M. Jammer, *The Conceptual Development of Quantum Mechanics*, New York, McGraw Hill Book Co., 1966, p. 329, cited in F.A. Wolf, *Taking the Quantum Leap*, p. 111.

4. From a personal letter written in 1955, cited in Larry Dossey, M.D., *Space, Time, and Medicine*, Shambala, Boulder, Colo., London, 1982, p. 157.

5. Even though the details of this example are my own, the basic ideas come from the works of Drs. Fred Wolf and Paul Davies, previously cited, and that of Dr. Fritjof Capra, *The Turning Point: The New Physics*, Simon & Schuster, New York, 1982.

6. All quotations are reprinted from pp. 111–113 of *Consciousness and Survival: An Interdisciplinary Inquiry Into the Possibility of Life Beyond Biological Death*. Spong, John S., Editor, Institute of Noetic Sciences, 1987. By Permission of the Institute of Noetic Sciences, P.O. Box 97, Sausalito, CA 94965. All rights reserved.

7. *Ibid.*

8. *Ibid*, pp. 112–13 (emphasis in original).

9. See J.A. Wheeler in *Proceedings of the NATO Advanced Study Institute Workshop on Frontiers of Nonequilibrium Physics*, Plenum, 1984, cited in *Consciousness and Survival*, *op. cit.*, p. 112.

10. See John Boslough, *Stephen Hawking's Universe*, Quill Books, New York, 1986, for more on this remarkable scientist who has never allowed his near-total paralysis, from "Lou Gehrig's disease," to hinder the functioning of his remarkable mind.

11. Judith R. Skutch, "Interview with Russell Targ," *New Realities*, Vol. 5, No. 6, Dec. 1983, p. 85.

12. *Ibid.*, p. 85.

13. *Ibid.*, p. 87.

14. *Ibid.*

15. "Targ: Remote viewing of future may be easier," *Brain/Mind Bulletin*, March 3, 1986, p. 3.; the 1984 Soviet experiment was discussed in *Brain/Mind Bulletin*, Dec. 31, 1984.

16. See David Bohm, *Wholeness and the Implicate Order*, Routledge & Kegan Paul, Ltd., London, 1980, for a thorough discussion of Bohm's theories.

17. Larry Dossey, M.D., *Space, Time and Medicine*, Shambala, Boulder, Colo., and London, 1982, pp. 82–97. See also, "Prigogine's latest model: an evolving universe," *Brain/Mind Bulletin*, Vol. 11, No. 15, Sept. 8, 1986, p. 1.

18. Rupert Sheldrake, *A New Science of Life: The Hypothesis of Formative Causation*, Jeremy P. Tarcher, Los Angeles, 1982. Dan Drasin's, "Interview with Rupert Sheldrake, Ph.D.," *New Realities*, Vol. 5, No. 5, Dec. 1983, offers an excellent summary of Dr. Sheldrake's views.

19. Daniel Drasin, "Interview with Rupert Sheldrake, Ph.D.," *New Realities*, Vol. 5, No. 5, Dec. 1983, pp. 8–15.

20. *Ibid.*

21. "View from the top: Lazaris on Brain, Mind, Feelings," *Brain/Mind Bulletin*, Oct. 1987, p. 4, P.O. Box 42211, Los Angeles, Calif. 90042. Reprinted by permission of *Brain/Mind Bulletin*.

22. Cited in Jean Millay, Ph.D., "Chakra Associations: A guide for the guide," mimeographed, unpublished manuscript, dated 1986.

CHAPTER 10
Spaceship Earth: UFOs, "Star People," "Walk-ins" and the Future

1. *IEE Spectrum*, "Communication with Extraterrestrial Intelligence," March 1966, pp. 153–63, cited in Raymond E. Fowler, *UFOs, Extraplanetary Visitors*, Prentice Hall, Inc., Englewood Cliffs, N.J., 1979, pp. 267–75.

2 Raymond E. Fowler, *op. cit.*, p. 306; Don Elkins and Carla Rueckert, *Secrets of the UFO*, L. & L. Research, Louisville, Ky., 1977, p. 8.

3. Fowler, *op. cit.*, pp. 228–30.

4. Don Elkins and Carla Rueckert, *op. cit.*, p. 8; also J. Allen Hynek, "Twenty-one Years of UFO Reports," in *UFOs, A Scientific Debate*, eds. Carl Sagan and Thornton Page, W.W. Norton, New York, 1972.

5. José Arguelles, "Open Letter to the World Community regarding UFO Contact," dated July 31, 1988. For further information contact Bear & Co., P.O. Drawer 2860, Santa Fe, N.M. 87504-2860.

6. With thanks to the International Association for Near Death Studies (IANDS) journal, *Vital Signs*, Vol. 3, No. 2, Sept. 1983, p. 11, where this cartoon (but not the cartoonist) is mentioned.

7. Hundreds of UFO books exist. Among the most serious are Raymond E. Fowler's *UFOs: Interplanetary Visitors*, cited in note 1, and Dr. J. Allen Hynek, *The UFO Experience: A Scientific Inquiry*, Henry Regnery, Inc., Chicago, 1972. The late Dr. Hynek, formerly head of Northwestern University's Astronomy Department, advised the USAF *Project Blue Book* from 1947–69. His UFO typology led to the phrase "close encounters of the third kind." In addition to references cited in this chapter, Robert Anton Wilson's *Cosmic Trigger*, Falcon Press, Phoenix, Ariz., 1977, takes a solid metaphysical look at this phenomenon.

8. John A. Keel, *The Eighth Tower*, E.P. Dutton & Co., New York, Inc., 1975, p. 94; Raymond J. Fowler, *op. cit.*, pp. 225–26.

9. Ruth Montgomery, *Aliens Among Us*, Fawcett Crest Books, New York, 1985, pp. 214–15.

10. Dr. R. Leo Sprinkle, "The Possible Relationship Between Reincarnation and the UFO Experience," unpublished manuscript, presented at "Psi Expo: Advances in Psychical Research," Denver, Colo., September 29, 1984, pp.

26, 30. See also, Harvey D. Rutledge, *Project Identification: the first scientific field study of the UFO phenomena*, Prentice Hall, Inc., Englewood Cliffs, N.J., 1981.

11. Ida K.'s story is taken from an unpublished manuscript she wrote and entitled "The Night of the Flaming Moon"; undated. Sent to me December 30, 1984, and used by permission of the author.

12. "A Message from Hweig," unpublished paper from the Rocky Mountain Conference on UFO investigations, held in Laramie, Wyo., May 23–25, 1980.

13. Personal letter from Ida K., dated Nov. 16, 1984.

14. Originally self-published as a pamphlet in 1952; excerpts appeared in Winfield S. Brownell, *UFOs: Keys to Earth's Destiny*, Legion of Light Pubs., Lytle Creek, Calif., 1980.

15. Jon Klimo, *Channeling*, Jeremy P. Tarcher, Los Angeles, 1987, p. 56.

16. Tuella, *Project: World Evacuation*, Guardian Action Publications, Deming, N.M., 1982, p. 19. Current address: P.O. Box 27725, Salt Lake City, UT 84127-0725.

17. Tuella, *ibid.*,; also, Ruth Montgomery, *op. cit.*, pp. 43–45. Ruth's "Guides" have vouched for Tuella's "Ashtar Command" writings except for those messages purportedly received from Mary, Jesus and several saints. In these cases she is said only to be "feeling what they might have conveyed."

18. Tuella, *op. cit.*, p. 94.

19. Personal letter from Diane Tessman, November 13, 1984. Rev. Tessman also publishes a "Star Network Hotline." Contact her c/o P.O. Box 622, Poway, CA 92064.

20. Brad and Francie Seiger, *The Star People*, Berkley Publishing Co., New York, 1981, pp. 46–53.

21. Brad Steiger, *The Promise*, Timewalkers, Inc., 1987, p. 106.

22. *Ibid.*

23. Erich von Daniken, *Chariots of the Gods*, Souvenir Press, London, 1969, p. 80; George H. Williamson, *Secret Places of the Lion*, Destiny Books, Rochester, Vt., 1983 (original copyright, 1958), pp. 43–44.

24. See *Halley's Bible Handbook*, pp. 111–13. It is intriguing to note that, according to Zecharia Sitchin, the Sinai, where Moses met God both before and after the Exodus, had formerly been the site of the spaceport of the ancient astronaut "gods" who had civilized Sumer and Egypt. Although Sitchin argues that this site had been blasted into ruins long before Moses, the area obviously retained special energy connections between Earth and the heavens. See Zecharia Sitchin's *The Wars of Gods and Men* for further details on the purported Sinai spaceport.

25. Ruth Montgomery, *op. cit.*, pp. 128–9.

26. Jon Klimo, *op. cit.*, p. 72.

27. Page Bryant, *The Earth Changes Survival Handbook*, Sun Books, Sante Fe, N.M., 1983, pp. 94, 151–53.

28. Ruth Montgomery, *Aliens Among Us*, p. 80. For two different views about a possible "Earth-Sirian connection" see Robert Temple, *The Sirius Mystery*, Sidgwick and Jackson, Ltd., London, 1976, and Musaios, *The Lion Path*, Golden Sceptre Publishing, Berkeley, Calif., 1985.

29. Ruth Montgomery, *op. cit.*, p. 167.

30. William R. Fix, *Star Maps*, Jonathan James Books, Toronto, 1979, pp. 89ff.

31. Robert A. Monroe, *Journeys out of the Body*, Doubleday & Co., Garden City, N.Y., 1971, and *Far Journeys*, Doubleday & Co., Garden City, N.Y., 1985. Jeffrey Mishlove, *The Roots of Consciousness*, Random House, New York, 1975, pp. 195–96.

32. Robert Monroe, *Far Journeys*, pp. 231–32. Quotations are reprinted by permission.

33. *Ibid.*, p. 232.

CHAPTER 11
"In His Presence"

1. Catherine Ann Lake, *Linking Up: How the People in Your Life Are Roadsigns to Self-Discovery*, The Donning Company, Norfolk, Va., 1988.

2. Chris Griscom, *Ecstasy Is a New Frequency*, Bear and Company, P.O. Drawer 2860, Santa Fe, N.M. 87504, 1988.

3. "Empty Infinity" from *The Secret of the Golden Flower: A Chinese Book of Life*, trans. by Richard Wilhelm and C.G. Jung, A Harvest Book of Harcourt, Brace, Jovanovich, Inc., New York, 1962 edition, pp. 77–78 (first published in 1931). Reprinted by permission of Harcourt, Brace, Jovanovich, Inc.

BIBLIOGRAPHY

BOOKS

Anon. *A Course in Miracles*. The Foundation for Inner Peace, Tiburon, Calif., 1975.

Arguelles, José. *The Mayan Factor*. The Bear Company, P.O. Drawer 2860, Santa Fe, N.M. 87504.

Aron, Elaine, and Arthur Aaron. *The Maharishi Effect: A Revolution Through Meditation*. Stillpoint, Walpole, N.H., 1986.

Bailey, Alice A. *Prophecies by D.K.* Compiled by Aart Jurriaanse, World Unity & Service, Inc., Craighall, South Africa, 1977.

Benevides, Roland. *Dramatic Prophecies of the Great Pyramid*. Editores Mexicanos Unidos, Mexico, 1969.

Berlitz, Charles. *Doomsday: 1999 A.D.* Doubleday & Co., Garden City, N.Y., 1981.

Bohm, David. *Wholeness and the Implicate Order*. Routledge and Kegan Paul, Ltd., London, 1980.

Bryant, Page. *The Earth Changes Survival Handbook*. Sun Books, Santa Fe, N.M., 1983.

Capra, Fritjof. *The Turning Point: The New Physics*. Simon & Schuster, New York, 1982.

Carey, Ken. *The Starseed Transmissions*. Uni Sun, P.O. Box 25421, Kansas City, MO 64119, 1982.

319

Chaney, Earlyne. *Revelations of Things to Come.* Astara Press, P.O. Box 5003, Upland, CA 91786, 1982.

Cheetham, Erika. *The Prophecies of Nostradamus.* G.P. Putnam's Sons, New York, 1973.

von Daniken, Erich. *Chariots of the Gods.* Souvenir Press, London, 1969.

Davies, Paul. *Other Worlds.* Simon & Schuster, New York, 1980.

Dossey, Larry, M.D. *Space, Time, and Medicine*, Shambhala, Boulder, Colo., and London, 1982.

Elkins, Don, and Carla Rueckert. *Secrets of the UFO.* L.&L. Research, Louisville, Ky., 1977.

Fowler, Raymond E. *UFOs, Extraplanetary Visitors.* Prentice Hall, Inc., Englewood Cliffs, N.J., 1979.

Gale-Kumar, Kristina. *The Phoenix Returns.* Cardinal Enterprises, Hilo, Hawaii, 1983.

Goodman, Jeffrey, Ph.D. *We Are the Earthquake Generation.* Seaview Books, New York, 1978; Berkley Books, paperback edition, 1979.

Hall, Manly P. *The Secret Teachings of all Ages.* The Philosophical Research Society, Inc., Los Angeles, 1977. (Reprint of the original 1928 edition.)

Halley, Henry H. *Halley's Bible Handbook.* Zondervan Publishing House, Grand Rapids, Mich., 24th edition, 1965. (First published 1927.)

Hynek, J. Allen. "Twenty-one Years of UFO Reports," in *UFOs: A Scientific Debate*, ed. by Carl Sagan and Thornton Page. W.W. Norton, New York, 1972.

———. *The UFO Experience: A Scientific Inquiry.* Henry Regnery Inc., Chicago, 1972.

Klimo, Jon. *Channeling.* Jeremy P. Tarcher, Los Angeles, 1987.

Lemesurier, Peter. *The Great Pyramid Decoded.* Element Books, Longmead, U.K., 1977.

Mishlove, Jeffrey. *The Roots of Consciousness.* Bookworks, New York, and Random House, Berkeley, 1975.

Mitchell, John. *City of Revelation.* Ballantine Books, New York, 1972.

———. *The New View Over Atlantis.* Harper & Row, San Francisco, 1983.

Monroe, Robert A. *Journeys out of the Body.* Doubleday & Co., Garden City, N.Y., 1971.

———. *Far Journeys.* Doubleday & Co., Garden City, N.Y., 1985.

Montgomery, Ruth. *Aliens Among Us.* G.P. Putnam's Sons, New York, 1985; paperback edition by Fawcett Crest, 1985.

———, and Joanne Garland. *Ruth Montgomery: Herald of the New Age.* Doubleday & Co., Garden City, N.Y., 1986.

Montgomery, Ruth. *A World Before.* Fawcett Crest, New York, 1971.

Moody, Raymond, M.D. *Life After Life.* Mockingbird Books, Atlanta, 1975.

Musaios. *The Lion Path.* Golden Sceptre Publishing, 1442A Walnut St., Suite 61, Berkeley, CA 94701, 1985.

Neal, Viola Petitt, and Shafica Karagulla, M.D. *Through The Curtain.* DeVorss & Co., Marina Del Rey, Calif., 1983.

Neihardt, John G. *Black Elk Speaks.* University of Nebraska Press, Lincoln, Neb., 1979.

Osis, Karliss, M.D., and E. Haraldson, M.D. *At the Hour of Death.* Avon Books, New York, 1977.

Peck, M. Scott, M.D. *The Road Less Traveled.* Simon & Schuster, New York, 1978.

Ring, Kenneth. *Heading Towards Omega.* William Morrow & Co., New York, 1984.

Roberts, Jane. *The Coming of Seth.* A Seth Book, Pocket Books, New York, 1976.

———. *Seth Speaks.* A Seth Book, Prentice Hall, Inc., Englewood Cliffs, N.J., 1972.

———. *The Unknown Reality*, Vol. II, A Seth Book, Prentice Hall, Inc, Englewood Cliffs, N.J., 1979.

———. *The Seth Material*, A Seth Book, Prentice Hall, Inc., Englewood Cliffs, N.J., 1970.

Robinson, Lytle W. *Is It True What They Say about Edgar Cayce?* Vulcan Books, Seattle, 1979.

The Rosicrucian Ephemeris: 1900–2000 and *The Rosicrucian Ephemeris: 2000–2050*, Maison Rosicrucienne, Aubenas, France, 1984, 1987.

Rudhyar, Dane. *Occult Preparations for A New Age.* The Theosophical Publishing House, Wheaton, Ill., 1975.

Sheldrake, Rupert. *A New Science of Life: The Hypothesis of Formative Causation.* Jeremy P. Tarcher, Los Angeles, 1982.

Sitchin, Zecharia. *The Twelfth Planet.* Avon Books, New York, 1978. (First published 1976 by Stein & Day Publishers.)

———. *The Wars of Gods and Men.* Avon Books, New York, 1985.

———. *The Stairway to Heaven.* Avon Books, New York, 1980.

Sprong, John S., ed. *Consciousness and Survival: An Interdisciplinary Inquiry Into the Possibility of Life Beyond Biological Death.* Institute of Noetic Sciences, P.O. Box 97, Sausalito, CA 94965, 1987.

———. *Edgar Cayce, the Sleeping Prophet.* Bantam Books, New York, 1967.

Steiger, Brad, and Francie Steiger. *The Star People.* Berkley Publishing Co., New York, 1981.

Sugrue, Thomas. *There Is a River*. Holt, Rinehart & Winston, New York, 1942; Dell paperback edition, New York, 1967.

Sun Bear, Wabun and the Bear Tribe. *The Bear Tribe's Self-Reliance Book*. Bear Tribe Publishing, P.O. Box 9167, Spokane, WA 99209, 1977.

Temple, Robert. *The Sirius Mystery*. Sidgwick and Jackson, Ltd., London, 1976.

Thurston, Mark A. *Visions and Prophecies for a New Age*. A.R.E. Press, Virginia Beach, Va., 1981.

Tuella. *Project: World Evacuation*. Guardian Action Publications: Deming, N.M., 1982.

Vaughan, Alan. *Patterns of Prophecy*. Dell Books, New York, 1973.

Wambach, Helen. *Life Before Life*. Bantam Books, New York, 1979.

————. *Reliving Past Lives*. Harper & Row, New York, 1978.

Waters, Frank. *Book of the Hopi*. Ballantine Books, New York, 1963.

White, John. *Pole Shift*. A.R.E. Press, Virginia Beach, Va., 1983. (First published by Doubleday & Co., 1980.)

Wolf, Fred Alan. *Taking the Quantum Leap*. Harper & Row, New York, 1981.

————. *Star Wave*. Macmillan/Collier, New York, 1986.

World Commission on Environment and Development. *Our Common Future*. Oxford University Press, Oxford, England, and New York, 1987.

World Resources Institute/International Institute for Environment and Development. *World Resources 1986*. Basic Books, New York, 1986.

PERIODICALS

Brain-Mind Bulletin. P.O. Box 42211, Los Angeles, CA 90042.

The Journal of Regression Therapy. The Association for Past Life Research and Therapy, P.O. Box 20151, Riverside, CA 92516.

New Realities.

Venture Inward. Association for Research and Enlightenment, P.O. Box 595, Virginia Beach, VA 23451.

FRENCH SOURCES

Damien, Michel, and Charles Hirsch. *La Crainte de l'An 2000*. Editions Seghers, Paris, 1979.

Melot, Nicholas. *Qui A Peur des Années '80?* Edition du Rocher, Monaco, 1981.

de Sède, Gerard. *L'Étrange Univers des Prophètes*. Editions J'ai Lu, Paris, 1977.

Vallée, Jacques. *Le Collège invisible*. Editions Albin Michel, Paris, 1975.

INDEX